DLM70

THE PUBLIC CAREER
OF SIR JAMES GRAHAM

THE PUBLIC CAREER

of

SIR JAMES GRAHAM

by

ARVEL B. ERICKSON

Professor of History
Western Reserve University

OXFORD: BASIL BLACKWELL
CLEVELAND: THE PRESS OF WESTERN
RESERVE UNIVERSITY
1952

FIRST PUBLISHED 1952

PRINTED IN GREAT BRITAIN IN THE CITY OF OXFORD AT THE ALDEN PRESS
FOR BASIL BLACKWELL & MOTT LTD.

PREFACE

THE purpose of this study is to present a critical analysis of the role played by Sir James Graham in one of the most important epochs of reform in British history. In no sense have I intended to write a biography. Justification for a study of Graham's public career lies in the fact that from 1818, when he first entered Parliament, until 1861, the year of his death, Graham was one of the ablest members of three different ministries.

Two works on Graham are extant: William T. M. Torrens, *Life of Sir James Graham*, and Charles S. Parker, *Life and Letters of Sir James Graham*. Neither is a satisfactory study of Graham's career. The former, published in 1863, is an unreliable contemporary account. The work by Parker is primarily a source book containing many of Graham's letters linked together with brief and unimportant connecting paragraphs. While at Netherby, the Graham's ancestral home, in the summer of 1947, I discovered letters which Parker had not used and some which he had not copied correctly. Throughout this work I have cited Parker's volumes, because they would facilitate cross-checking and reviewing, in those cases where he has correctly reproduced the letters. Whenever Parker does not suffice, I have cited the letters, newspaper clippings, scrapbook, and other private papers at Netherby as the *Graham Papers*.

In addition to these Netherby sources, I have used the *Home Office Papers* and the *Admiralty Papers* at the Public Record Office, the manuscript materials at the British Museum, and the excellent periodical collection at the Library of the Royal College of Surgeons in London.

I wish to acknowledge with gratitude the graciousness of Sir Fergus Graham in permitting me to use all of the private papers at Netherby; the kindly helpfulness of the officials of the Royal College of Surgeons, the Public Record Office, and the British Museum; and the generosity of the Alumnae Historical Association of Flora Stone Mather College in giving me a research grant, and the Executive Council of the Graduate School of Western Reserve University for research and publication grants.

I have especially to thank Donald Grove Barnes, Professor of

v

History at Western Reserve University, whose scholarly criticism and constant encouragement have helped me bring this work to completion. Thanks are also due two other colleagues: Marion C. Siney, Professor of History, and Walter P. Bowman, Professor of English, for many valuable suggestions. For any errors of omission and commission which remain I alone am responsible. Finally, my wife and daughter are deserving of commendation for their affectionate understanding during many months of research and writing.

CONTENTS

CHAPTER I

ANTECEDENTS

SIR JAMES GRAHAM came from a family which for generations had dominated the Border region between England and Scotland. Unfortunately no exact date can be set for the time when this family became permanent residents in Cumberland county, England. Although some writers consider the 'Graems'[1] to be aboriginal inhabitants of Cumberland, it is relatively certain that at least the greater part of this clan came into England with the waves of Scottish invasion of the early sixteenth century. According to Lord Burghley, the first of the Grahams to settle in England was William Graham — 'Long Will' — who had been banished from Scotland in 1516.[2] Local tradition, however, relates how, in the anxious and troubled days of Henry IV, a gallant knight, 'John with the Bright Sword', son of Malise, Earl of Mentieth, irritated by the ingratitude of the Scottish king for whom he had risked his life on many a field of battle, withdrew from service to the Crown of Scotland and with some of his retainers took up his abode in the famous 'debatable land', the ownership of which was claimed by both England and Scotland. In this wild and barren region where force passed for law, John of the Bright Sword made himself popular as a protector of the weak and a scourge to the ruthless Border ruffians.

> His skill and prowess in defending the frontier land he had often harried became the favourite theme of fire-side tale; and long after he had passed away from scenes of feud and foray the child of the moss-trooper dreamed of his fleet horse and sable plume.[3]

Appropriating the land he desired, John of the Bright Sword constructed his dwelling-place on the summit of a hill overlooking the valley of the river Esk. A Roman military camp had once occupied this commanding site and John Graham, like many

[1] See THOMAS H. B. GRAHAM's interesting article on the genealogy of this family in the *Cumberland and Westmoreland Antiquarian and Archaeological Society Transactions*, New Ser., IX, 216. See also *Ibid.*, XIV, 143 et seq.; XVII, 1 et seq.

[2] BERNARD BURKE, *Burke's Genealogical and Heraldic History of the Peerage, Baronetage, Knightage, Privy Council, and Order of Precedence*, 1135.

[3] WILLIAM T. M. TORRENS, *Life of Sir James Graham*, I, 1-2.

1

other Englishmen, used some of the remains in erecting his home. Not many years had passed before the Grahams had seized the nearby forests and valleys and established complete control over the borderland. When the kings of both England and Scotland claimed the allegiance of this powerful clan they found that the independent Grahams would pay it to neither.

Early in the sixteenth century, Lord Dacre, then Warden of Cumberland, decided to root out the Grahams and to lay waste the 'debatable land'. The fire-brand and sword were not to rest, he declared, 'until it be clerely waiste, without one house or holde standing within it'.[4] This was a task, however, which the ambitious and militant warden could not accomplish. Finally, in 1552, the land was divided between England and Scotland and the former was given that part which lay between a line drawn from the Esk[5] to the Sark rivers and the sea.[6]

To the Grahams, and other border clans of their type, such a line meant absolutely nothing. Lawlessness was rampant, and border feuds and forays continued with unabated fury throughout Elizabeth's reign. Most of the land was too poor even for subsistence farming; cattle rustling, which supplied the clansmen with sport as well as with fresh meat, became an accepted occupation.

An even more exciting, if often less profitable, undertaking was the kidnapping of sons or daughters of neighbouring clansmen. There was so much of this kidnapping and blackmailing in the counties of Cumberland, Northumberland and Westmorland, and in the bishopric of Durham, that an Elizabethan Statute made it a capital felony to levy blackmail.[7] The death penalty, without benefit of clergy, was to be inflicted upon any who even so much as harboured an outlaw. But the authorities in far-away London found it impossible to put teeth into such a law and the independent border outlaws continued to ignore its existence.

In what practically amounted to a collectional stage of economy,

---

[4] Cotton MSS., cited in DANIEL LYSONS and SAMUEL LYSONS, *Magna Britannia*, IV, xxii *n*.

[5] 'The Esk . . . rises in the Cheviot hills. At Canonby, it becomes for a short distance the boundary between Kirkandrews, Netherby, by the edge of Solway Moss, and after being joined by the Leven, falls into the sea near Rockliffe Marsh; its course through Cumberland being about six miles.' LYSONS, *op. cit.*, cvi.

[6] WILLIAM HUTCHINSON, *History of Cumberland*, II, 531.

[7] *Statutes at Large*, 43 Elizabeth, c. 13.

the natural rivalry and the resulting jealousies and hatreds of the border marauders, was the cause of almost perpetual warfare.

> But war's the borderer's game —
> Their gain, their glory, their delight,
> To sleep the day, maraud the night
> O'er mountain, moss or moor.[8]

In other lands the Church had been able to maintain at least some semblance of peace and order even if the Government had been unable to do so. Not so in the 'debatable lands', however, for among the 'moss-troopers', the name applied to the border outlaws, the Church had no *locus standi* whatever. On those few occasions when the moss-troopers did attend Church, the attraction was the sacramental silver, not the confessional. Respecting neither God nor Royal power, Gordie Bourne, one of the most notorious of the moss-troopers, acknowledged

> that he had lived long enough to do so many villainies as he had done . . . that he had killed seven Englishmen with his own hands, cruelly murdering them; that he had spent his whole time in . . . drinking, stealing, and taking deep revenge for slight offences.[9]

But Gordie Bourne's reputation for lawlessness and independence could not match that of the Grahams, whose name became synonymous with tumult and anarchy.[10] The reports of their brigandage and depredations, their overt and contemptuous defiance of Royal authority, their scornful disregard for law, became so vexatious that James I decided to exterminate the entire clan. About 400 of them, in 1606-1607, were driven from the 'debatable land', some to Ireland, others to the Low Countries. Only a few of the most peaceable were allowed to remain in Cumberland, and of these the most important was Fergus Graham of Nunnery.[11]

Having cleared the land of its unruly and recalcitrant inhabitants, King James granted it to Francis, Earl of Cumberland, at a fee-farm rental of £150 per annum. 'In the letters patent', says

---

[8] SIR WALTER SCOTT, *Marmion*, Canto V, part IV.
[9] Cory's Memoirs, 123, cited in HUTCHINSON, *op. cit.*, II, 552.
[10] LONSDALE, *op. cit.*, II, 10 et seq.
[11] See T. H. B. GRAHAM's article, 'The Debatable Land,' in *Cumb. and West. Ant. and Arch. Soc. Trans.*, XIV, 152.

Torrens, 'it is described as lying between the rivers Sark [which is the boundary between Cumberland and Scotland for about five miles near Solway Moss], and Esk, the Scotch Dyke, and Solway Sands, and containing 2895 acres of meadow and arable, called "known grounds", 2635 of pasture, besides marsh lands and moss, in all 8400 acres.'[12]

Possession of this property did not, however, remain long in other hands for many of the Grahams began to filter back into Cumberland from Ireland. By means of his charm and pleasing manners, Richard, son of Fergus Graham, had, while at court, made himself a friend of Royalty and the special protégé of the Duke of Buckingham for whom he served as Master of Horse. Later he accompanied Prince Charles on his alluring and exciting, but fruitless, mission to Spain. On May 21st, 1628, Richard began the process of recovering the lands he considered Graham property by purchasing Netherby Hall, the manors of Arthuret, Rodillington, and Lydell, and also Nicoll forest, from George, second Earl of Cumberland. This territory included the parishes of Kirkandrews, Arthuret, and a part of Bewcastle.[13] Appendant to the manor of Arthuret was the advowson of the parish of the same name, which, in ancient times, had belonged to the Abbots of Jedburgh, in Dumfries. That of Kirkandrews and the chapelry of Nicoll forest likewise went with the estate.[14] At the conclusion of the Civil War, in which Sir Richard had been a partisan of the Royalists, he retired to Netherby to spend the remaining days of his life in seclusion. Of his two sons, Richard and George, the latter became the second baronet. Although an adherent of the House of Stuart, George had been discreet enough not to attack the Commonwealth. For this loyalty to the Stuarts Charles II transferred the baronetcy to his brother Richard, who then removed to North Conyers, Northumberland.

Sir George had married Mary, daughter of the Earl of Arrondale, by whom he had a son, Richard. The latter, educated at Westminster, and later married to Ann, daughter of Lord Carlisle, was intensely interested in politics. As M.P. for Cockermouth, he had spoken strongly against the Exclusion Bill, which would have set aside the lineal heir to the throne, James, Duke of York,

---

[12] TORRENS, op. cit., I, 6.   [13] LYSONS, op. cit., IV, 28.
                                       [14] Ibid., 10-12.

without naming a successor and would therefore have been likely to plunge the country into confusion and possible civil war.[15] Possessing a large estate and royal favour, Richard was created Viscount Preston of Haddington in 1681, and took his seat in the upper house of the Scottish Parliament. At the same time, however, he retained his rights as an English Commoner and as such was chosen one of the Knights of Cumberland. Politically, as one would naturally expect, he was an avowed Tory; religiously, a stout defender of the Anglican Church. In 1682 he was sent to Paris as the ambassador only to be recalled three years later to serve both as Commissioner of Excise and Chancellor to the Dowager Queen. In the religious quarrels which James II foolishly provoked, Preston counselled moderation. But James foolishly ignored this sound advice and thus hastened the coming of another tragic episode in the annals of the house of Stuart and a like one in that of the Grahams. When Sunderland was dismissed on October 27th, 1688, because of his secret intrigues with the Prince of Orange, Preston succeeded him as Secretary of State. He was one of the few who remained loyal to his Sovereign in that eventful year, and because he refused to surrender the seals of office and pay court to William, he was thrown into the Tower. This was but the beginning of his misfortunes. Lord Montague successfully sued him for the profits of the office of Master of the Wardrobe, claiming it under a life patent granted by Charles II, but which James II had given to Preston.[16] Since Preston had been created Baron of Esk by James II on January 21st, 1689, he had previously claimed the right to be tried as a peer. Unfortunately, however, this was three weeks after Parliament had proclaimed James's abdication. The judges therefore declared the patent void and Preston was given over to the custody of the Black Rod for having falsely claimed the privileges of a peer. When he petitioned for release, declaring that he had meant no disrespect, Preston was set at liberty.[17]

William of Orange had his troubles too. Increased taxation, the presence of his Dutch guards, and a marked preference for Dutch

[15] GRAHAM, 'The Debatable Land', loc. cit., 153.
[16] Narcissus Luttrell's Diary, June 28th, 1690, cited in TORRENS, op. cit., I, 12.
[17] Journals of the House of Lords (Nov. 9th, 11th, 12th, 27th, 1689), XIV, 336-338; 354-355.

B

officials and advisers, all combined to make him an unpopular king. Many began to contrast unfavourably kingship as exemplified by William with that of James. In December 1690 a small group of Protestant loyalists met to discuss plans for a possible restoration. They decided to send three of their number, Ashton, Elliot, and Preston,[18] to St. Germain to convince James that he should change his despotic and Catholic course. They were instructed to tell James that, in the event of his restoration, he must go no further than to grant legal liberty to Catholics, and that he must agree to a Protestant administration. 'He may reign a Catholic in devotion', they said, 'but he must reign Protestant in government'.[19] The unfortunate messengers were discovered, dragged from their place of concealment in the hold of a ship bound for France, and deprived of the incriminating papers discovered in their possession. On January 3rd, 1691, Preston was sent to the Tower and his estates and title reverted to the Crown.[20] On the sixteenth he was indicted for treason, the next day was declared guilty, and on the nineteenth was condemned to death.[21] His life was spared, however, when he revealed the names of his co-conspirators.[22] As soon as he was released he repaired to Netherby to spend the few remaining days of his life reading and meditating upon Boëthius's Consolations of Philosophy.

Edward, Preston's son, at the age of seventeen, succeeded to his father's inheritance. Edward's only son, Charles, third viscount, died at an early age without issue, leaving his estates to his father's two sisters — Catherine, wife of Lord Widdrington, and Mary. On the death of the latter, who had never married, the whole of the inheritance was vested in Lady Widdrington. In 1715, as the result of his activities in the Jacobite cause, Lord Widdrington was attainted for treason. Like Viscount Preston, his life was also spared, but he had to forfeit his honours and estates. But since

---

[18] The other conspirators were Clarendon, Dartmouth, Turner, and the Bishop of Ely.

[19] State Trials (T. B. Howells edition), XII, 711.

[20] Except, of course, the Scottish peerage.

[21] For a full account of the trial see State Trials, XII, 645-817.

[22] There is an account in Dalrymple, Book VI, of how Preston's daughter was once seen by Queen Mary gazing at a picture of James — Mary's father. Seeing the girl weeping, Mary asked the cause of her grief. 'I am thinking', said the child, 'how hard it is that my father should suffer death because he loved yours.' Mary, it is then stated, aided in securing Preston's pardon. Cited in TORRENS, op. cit., I, 18.

Netherby was the inheritance of his wife, it consequently escaped the attainder. On the death of Lady Widdrington, who outlived her husband by four years, the estates passed into the possession of the Reverend Robert Graham, the second son of William, Dean of Carlisle and Wells.

Upon receiving this property, Graham gave up his small living of Kirkandrews and instead of redeeming souls, devoted himself to the more lucrative task of redeeming the estate. It was completely run down; the tenants were lazy, indifferent, and negligent in their work. But the very demoralized condition of the estate and its inhabitants was a challenge which he cheerfully accepted. He enclosed and then drained a nearby waste of about a thousand acres, built some cottages upon it, and let them out for three years rent-free. Always interested in his tenants, he willingly helped those who were making some effort to help themselves. The lazy and indolent, on the other hand, were promptly evicted. Constantly at work liming the fields, mending the fences and gates, stooping to do the most menial of tasks, he set an excellent example for others.

The ex-parson's energies were also directed towards the improvement of his living quarters. While rebuilding the Netherby mansion, he unearthed a tablet bearing the inscription of the second legion of Hadrian as well as numerous Roman coins. The nearby gardens and pleasure-grounds were carefully landscaped by the well-known gardener, Howard of Corby.

Not far removed from Netherby was a bog known as Solway Moss. Due to excessive and prolonged rains, and to the fact that it had been cut loose from its surroundings by the peat-diggings on all its sides, the moss, on November 16th, 1771, began to move.

> The moss had burst, spewing out from its maw a putrid mass that spread relentlessly, engulfing house after house . . . For weeks the horrible eruption spread, and ere its advance was stayed thirty families were homeless, their houses, furniture, and livestock buried twenty feet deep under a black slime that stank like the pit of Tophet.[23]

The damage to the estate and the losses to the tenants were

---

[23] ANDREW and JOHN LANG, *Highways and Byways in the Border*, 408. It was in this same moss that the English, in November 1542, trapped and annihilated an entire army of invading Scots.

quickly repaired, however, and so great were the changes accomplished by Robert Graham that Netherby was soon a model for the entire north country and one of the Border bards could exult:

> How changed the scene! what glorious prospects rise;
> Where'er around I turn my wond'ring eyes!
> Here guardian Peace, here smiling Culture reigns,
> And endless Plenty clothes the fertile plains.[24]

Like most of his family predecessors and successors, the Reverend Robert Graham was courageous, independent, a kind father, and a devoted adherent to the Anglican Church. But he 'had sinned and fallen short' in one respect — he had become a Whig! The house of Lowther had exercised a preponderating influence in Cumberland politics,[25] and to keep them in check the parson joined the 'Blues' — the opposition party.

Robert Graham was succeeded by his son Charles, who died in 1782 leaving an only daughter. Since the estate had been settled in the male line, possession was left in abeyance until the autumn of that year. Then it devolved upon James, the next brother, who, being a devoted friend of the Duke of Portland, was honoured with the baronetcy.

Then only twenty-two years of age, possessing an excellent estate known throughout England for its beauty and for its unexcelled facilities for hunting and fishing, James proceeded to enjoy the good things of life. England's years of strife and turmoil were over; a spirit of hopefulness, confidence in the return of prosperity, and a wholesome respect for Pitt's ability to establish fiscal stability were everywhere manifest. The increased rents of the Netherby tenants, made necessary by James's extravagances, occasioned no serious complaints so long as the new markets in Ireland and in the manufacturing towns in Lancashire and

---

[24] Cited in HUTCHINSON, *op. cit.*, II, 558 *n.*

[25] See the excellent article in the *Dictionary of National Biography*, XXXIV, 217-220 (Hereinafter cited as *D.N.B.*). *The Rolliad* describes the power of James Lowther, Earl of Lonsdale, who stated that he owned all the land, fire and water in the town of Whitehaven, as follows:

> E'en by the elements his pow'r confessed
> Of mines and boroughs Lonsdale stands possess'd,
> And one sad servitude alike denotes
> The slave that labours and the slave that votes.
> *The Rolliad*, 164.

Cheshire increased the demands for grain and hence kept prices high. Concurrently, of course, land became more valuable, and James, following the example of those around him, began to enclose the surrounding waste and arable lands. Knowing little, if anything, about the fertilization of soil, James over-limed his fields. For a few years lime increased the productivity of the soil, but constant use was harmful. 'The wet clays were *mortarized*', says Dickinson, 'and the light soils worked and disintegrated till their texture was destroyed, and both were rendered almost sterile, until drained and re-cultivated with manure and no lime.'[26] While the natural beauty of Netherby remained unimpaired, the soil became less and less productive, and the tenants less and less interested in keeping up their holdings as the example of diligence set by their former lord faded from memory.

James Graham was a Tory and a devoted follower of Pitt. He believed that the war with France was necessary, but disgusting; that negro slavery was repulsive; and that in order to strengthen, not to weaken, the Established Church, religious disabilities ought to be removed. For the nine years (1798-1807) in which he represented Ripon in the House of Commons he adhered steadily to these principles. In the latter year he gave way to F. J. Robinson, later Lord Goderich and Earl of Ripon.

James had married Lady Catherine Stewart, daughter of John Stewart, seventh Earl of Galloway, and on June 1st, 1792, there was born to them a son — James Robert George — the future statesman. The latter had a good start in life. His mother was a very intelligent woman widely known for her beauty, her deep religious feeling, and her kindly interest in, and willingness to help, those whom life had seemingly passed by. Few mothers have surpassed her in the care which she constantly exercised to instil into the youthful minds about her those abiding virtues of honesty, diligence, loyalty to home, to Church, to State, and an undeviating fidelity to principle. She apparently knew what so many have failed to see, or seeing, have ignored — that when life is robbed of its cares, duties, and responsibilities, it is robbed of its pleasures too.

A happy, congenial family living in substantial Netherby Hall, set in the midst of a region famous for its natural beauty and its

[26] Dickinson's Report, cited in TORRENS, *op. cit.*, I, 38.

unexcelled facilities for hunting and fishing, inevitably had its full measure of visitors. Lady Graham, especially solicitous for the welfare of her eldest son, encouraged frequent and prolonged visits at Netherby by those friends and acquaintances whose influence would be most beneficial. The most important of these visitors were Archdeacon Paley, Dean Isaac Milner, and Bishop Vernon.

William Paley,[27] Archdeacon of Carlisle, divided his attention between the study of philosophy and fishing in the river Esk. At Cambridge, in 1765, he had won a prize with his essay comparing the Stoic and Epicurean systems of philosophy. In his *Reasons for Contentment*, published in 1792, he warned his fellow-countrymen against the 'revolutionary' ideas then spreading throughout England. Two years later he brought all his talents and energies into the defence of Church and State in his *Evidences of Christianity*. To Paley, an established religion was an absolute necessity. He had on one occasion declared that it was 'an indispensable saddle and bridle, without which society could not be made to subserve its highest uses'.[28] Paley's daughter had married Fergus Graham, a brother of James Graham, and family ties were added to those of friendship that already existed in and about Carlisle.

Another frequent visitor at Netherby was the gay, genial, and entertaining Dean Milner. He and Lady Graham became close friends. The dean imparted to her his strong evangelical opinion, which she in turn promptly passed on to her children. To Dean Milner, cards and dice were playthings of the Devil; theatres and 'the races' veritable sinks of iniquity. He sympathized with the Catholics because of the numerous disabilities to which they were subjected, but he dreaded the consequences of granting them concessions.

The third of this special group of influential friends was Dr. Vernon, who for many years held the See of Carlisle. Between the Grahams and this hospitable and virtuous man, there sprang up a lasting and sincere friendship.

The young James Robert George Graham was greatly influenced by his contacts with these family friends and relatives. The debt of gratitude he owed to them for their kindly interest in his welfare he frequently recognized. But to none of them, to no one on

---

[27] See *D.N.B.*, XV, 101 et seq.
[28] Cited in TORRENS, *op. cit.*, I, 42.

earth, did he ever accord a place even remotely commensurate with that of his mother. 'Tell her', he wrote to his father in 1814, 'that to please her — sometime to be worthy of her — is my greatest joy and pride. All that is good in me, all that others praise, I have derived from her. All that is bad I acquired away from her. She made me what I am.'[29] These were no idle words written on the spur of the moment. They revealed a sentiment he continued to feel and to express to the end of his life.

[29] CHARLES S. PARKER, *The Life and Letters of Sir James Graham*, I, 6 (Hereinafter cited as *Life of Graham*).

CHAPTER II

THE EDUCATIVE PROCESS

FIRMLY convinced of the necessity of placing his son's education in 'safe' hands, James Graham wrote to his friend Boucher, Rector of St. James's:

> Lady Catherine and I hope you will let us have the pleasure of seeing you at Netherby, and we should then trouble you with several questions relative to our boy, who is now about five years old, and upon whose education I must have good advice.
>
> Our wish is to give him as good an education as he can receive, and to make him a good man and useful member of society. And by the word 'good' I mean a religious man — a point I am convinced should be attended to in preference to all others.[1]

Whether as the result of Boucher's advice, or for other reasons, James was sent to the Reverend William Fletcher's school at Dalston, where the sons of the neighbourhood gentry were taught Greek and Latin. While it is doubtful whether the youthful Graham learned very much of either subject from Fletcher, the latter did exert a lasting and powerful influence on him. When Fletcher died, in 1846, Sir James Graham, then an elderly statesman, wrote to Mrs. Fletcher:

> With some knowledge of mankind, I can truthfully say that I regard him as one of the best and most blameless men I ever knew.
>
> I owe to him very great and eternal obligations. The principles which he inculcated were the purest, and his own never-failing example proved that a sincere Christian may so live on earth as to have God and his duty constantly in view.
>
> ... Once again I thank you for the care and the admirable instruction which I received in the happy parsonage at Dalston.[2]

Together with young William Blamire who was destined to be his life-long friend, James frequently visited in the Fletcher home. It was fortunate for him that he got along so well with his tutor because, being something of a dandy and always scrupulously careful in his dress, James did not have many friends among the students.

[1] Cited in PARKER, *Life of Graham*, I, 7.   [2] *Ibid.*, 8.

When he reached the age of fourteen, he was sent to Westminster school, where, in company with such classmates as Charles Lennox, later Duke of Richmond, John Russell, and Thomas Short, later Bishop of St. Asaph, he continued his study of Greek and Latin. Westminster was an excellent educational institution and to it were sent the sons of the aristocratic Whig families. Originally it was a royal foundation to which paying pupils had occasionally been admitted, but by 1806 the latter were in the majority. The younger boys — those in the lower forms — acted as the menial servants, under the 'fagging' system, to the older boys. Punishments were as a rule tempered neither with judgment nor mercy and the younger boys were driven to devious expedients to escape their tormentors. Graham 'showed border ingenuity', says Lonsdale, 'in outwitting proctors and beadles, the custodians of college morals and discipline'.[3] With very few exceptions, the parents of the pupils felt that this was the ideal type of training for their sons.[4]

The formal education in these citadels of aristocracy was almost exclusively classical,[5] and little did it profit the utilitarians to complain about the uselessness of this type of education in an increasingly dynamic and commercial age because the parents of the pupils attending these public schools did not wish their sons to be trained for participation in business or in trade. Not geometry, arithmetic, and accounting, but Greek and Latin comprised the desired Westminster diet. While some complained about this restricted education, Graham was not one of them. Having an excellent memory, he learned Latin verses readily, and, because of its musical quality, he also developed a fondness for Greek.[6] Homer and Horace were his favourites and he committed to memory many of the choicest verses of the latter.

Because of its proximity to Parliament, Westminster had

[3] Lonsdale, *Worthies of Cumberland*, II, 19. Sydney, in writing about his friend George Keppell, says that he went to Westminster 'for seven years of purgatory'. William C. Sydney, *Early Days of the Nineteenth Century*, II, 84.

[4] For a contemporary criticism of these public schools, see *Edinburgh Review or Critical Journal*, XVI, 326-334 (Hereinafter cited as *Edin. Rev.*).

[5] Elie Halévy, *A History of the English People in 1815*, p. 468.

[6] William Cunningham, while visiting at Netherby in 1809, wrote to his friend Lord Grenville that James Graham was 'a very fine young man indeed; finest disposition, and clever, and — what will be no blemish in your eyes — loves Greek'. Cited in Parker, *op. cit.*, I, 9.

decided advantages for those students who were interested in politics, oratory, and debate. Since Graham was one of these, he spent much time in Parliament listening to the debates and orations on Government policy. He probably had the good fortune to hear the speeches of both Pitt and Fox,[7] and was no doubt captivated by Romilly's attacks on the penal laws, Grattan's pleas for the liberation of Ireland, Wilberforce's appeals for the abolition of the slave trade, Curwen's denunciation of election jobbery, and Lord Archibald Hamilton's expressed fears that any tampering with the Constitution would be fatal to England. Thrilled by these brilliant oratorical efforts, Graham's desire for a parliamentary career increased in intensity. In later life he considered the chief advantage of the school at Westminster to be the opportunities it afforded students to attend Parliament and to hear statesmen discuss the problems of the day, and for this reason he later opposed an attempt to change the school's location.

Further preparatory work was necessary before entering the university and in 1809 Graham left Westminster for Bampton. Here he was placed under the charge of Richards, Vicar of Bampton, a man with a reputation for skill in composition, from whom Graham received valuable training in rhetoric and logic. At Bampton, he met Sir John Throckmorton, one of the leading agriculturalists of the day, and developed a lively interest in animal husbandry, estate-management, and the application of scientific methods to soil cultivation.[8] At the same time his interest in politics was growing stronger. 'The administration', he wrote to his father on March 20th, 1810, 'seems tottering to a fail. Lord Sidmouth is determined to keep himself out, whoever may come in, by dissenting frivolously from all.'[9]

Having completed the required preparatory work at Dalston, Westminster, and Bampton, James entered Christ Church, Oxford, in 1810. Despite the reforms made in 1800, when a new scheme of public examination was inaugurated, the intellectual

---

[7] Lonsdale does not think so. 'Nor can it be supposed,' he writes, 'that he took interest in the parliamentary debates of Pitt and Fox, both of whom passed away in 1806, when he was only twelve years of age.' LONSDALE, *op. cit.*, II, 18. Graham was, of course, not twelve but fourteen years of age in 1806.

[8] TORRENS, *Life of Graham*, I, 57.

[9] Graham to his father, in PARKER, *op. cit.*, I, 10.

training at this traditionally Tory university was woefully inadequate and defective.[10] As at Westminster, attention was directed almost exclusively to the classics, and the college exercises in Latin and Greek were trite, dull, and lifeless. 'The whole university', according to Sydney, 'partook of this somnolency.'[11] Edward Gibbon,[12] Adam Smith,[13] and Lord Eldon[14] have all testified to the same effect. New movements, new courses of study, new ideas could not penetrate the dead weight of inertia that had settled over this pillar of Anglicanism. New and exact sciences, economics, accounting, and like subjects would have been a concession to materialism and Oxford could not risk that.

The sons of the rich often came to Oxford with no other object than to escape from parental influence and control, to enjoy life gambling, drinking, smoking, and riding to hounds. It would have been shameful, they thought, to have permitted school work to interfere with one's 'education'. The real students at Oxford were those few talented young men, rich or poor, whose sole ambition was to acquire enough knowledge of history and government and to memorize enough quotable phrases to supply them with the rudiments necessary for their parliamentary careers. This ambition could be satisfied, of course, without its interfering too much with their social affairs.

James Graham was one of the latter group and since he was interested in mathematics as well as in the classics and history, the Reverend E. Goodenough[15] was selected as his tutor. Goodenough wrote to James's father that he was very happy to hear that his son was coming to him and that he would be greatly

[10] CHARLES E. MALLET, A History of Oxford, III, 167-169.
[11] SYDNEY, op. cit., II, 94.
[12] Gibbon denied owing any obligations whatever to Oxford. The fourteen months he spent there, were, he said, 'the most unprofitable of my whole life'. Autobiography of Edward Gibbon, John Murray edition, p. 67.
[13] Adam Smith said that the professors had given up 'even the pretence of teaching'. ADAM SMITH, An Inquiry into the Nature and Causes of the Wealth of Nations, II, 208 et seq.
[14] Lord Eldon tells how he was asked what the Hebrew word for 'place of the skull' was and that he answered, 'Golgotha'; and when asked who founded University College answered, 'King Alfred'. He was promptly granted his degree. Cited in HORACE TWISS, Public and Private Life of Lord Chancellor Eldon, I, 44-45. Twiss declared that 'Oxford saw at least as much of hard drinking as of hard study'. Ibid., 42.
[15] Through Graham's help, Goodenough later became Dean of Wells.

disappointed if James did not 'do both himself and us much credit in this place'.[16]

James, however, did no special credit to himself, to his tutor, or to Oxford. He did fairly well in history, was above the average in mathematics, and learned to quote the Latin classics exceedingly well, but otherwise he was a typical Oxonian. With a private servant, plenty of horses, and sufficient money and credit, James spent his numerous holidays and vacations at Netherby, or at the homes of his friends, hunting and fishing. Chief among these were the Starkeys and the Stourtons. At the latter's home, in Allerton Park, Graham spent many happy hours enjoying the company of Stourton's two sons. Charles, one of them, was desirous of travelling abroad and proceeded to urge upon James the advantages of a grand tour of Europe over further study at Oxford.

By the beginning of his last term, James was not in the right frame of mind to profit even from the meagre offerings of Oxford. Conservative in manner, intolerant of the weaknesses of others, quick to find fault, impervious to criticisms of his own conduct, he went the daily rounds of dull routine enlivened only by the pleasures of vacation periods. Those, like Lord Middleton and the Bishop of St. Asaph, who remembered him during his two years at Oxford, agreed that he was only an average student at a time when the average was very low, and that his forte was memorizing particularly apt quotations from history and the classics.[17] James himself testified in after years to the fact that he had not over-exerted himself at Oxford. When addressing the students of the University of Glasgow in 1839, just after his election as the Lord Rector, he declared that from his 'own experience' he could tell them that 'the waste of time in a college life is an irreparable loss, ever visited with the bitterest pang which memory inflicts'.[18]

Oxford was then not only intellectually weak but spiritually dead. While speaking on the Irish Colleges Bill in 1839, Graham criticized this lack of discipline and religious training in these words:

> I now solemnly state that during the two years of my residence at College, I was never — with the exception of the required atten-

[16] Cited in PARKER, op. cit., I, 11.   [17] See TORRENS, op. cit., I, 58 et seq.
[18] 'Address on Being Installed as Lord Rector of Glasgow University', in Graham Papers.

dance at chapel — once called upon to attend any lectures either upon theology or divinity. During the whole of that time, I never received any religious instruction whatever independently and apart from that which I derived from enforced attendance upon chapel. I never, during those two years, attended a university sermon; and I am ashamed to say, that whilst I was at Oxford, I never, during the whole period of my residence, heard one single sermon.[19]

In the spring of 1812, therefore, since Oxford had no irresistible appeal to him, since he was not in a frame of mind to profit by further attendance, and since he had become firmly convinced that the best preparation for his parliamentary career was a trip abroad to acquire first-hand knowledge of men and nations, James decided to leave Oxford. His father, on the other hand, wished him to remain at Oxford at least until the end of the term. But when his son got the Dean of Christ Church to agree that travel would contribute more to his education and advancement than a longer stay at college, the disappointed father reluctantly acquiesced. The spring of 1812 was therefore spent in London making the necessary preparations for his European tour.

And, fortunately for James, these were interesting and exciting days in London. Political feeling was at fever heat. The Prince Regent,[20] who had just broken with his party, was now the object of the biting sarcasm and wit of Tom Moore and Leigh Hunt. Grey, Greville, and other leading Whigs refused all of the Regent's efforts to get them into a combination with Perceval. Many Tories even refused to join the administration, which, except for Plunket and Castlereagh, was anything but a strong one. At the same time, Napoleon had not yet lost his winning ways, while Wellington had not yet really begun his. In this predicament, losses abroad and dissension at home, the administration managed to do nothing but vote new loans and taxes. It was both natural and logical that Graham, who was young, enthusiastic, and

[19] HANSARD, *Parliamentary Debates*, 3rd. Ser., LXXX, 1146 (Hereinafter cited as *Hansard*).

[20] The Prince of Wales had married Princess Caroline of Brunswick and by her had one daughter — Charlotte. When the couple separated, the Prince, who had sided with the Whig Opposition, was defended by them. But when he became Regent, he shifted to the Tory side and the Whigs, becoming his opponents, espoused the cause of the Princess.

ambitious for a parliamentary career, should join the ranks of the Opposition. That spring, his election into the exclusive Brooks's Club,[21] by now the recognized headquarters of the Whig party, marked his official affiliation with that group.

Preparations and plans having been completed, Graham left London for Lisbon on June 12th. A storm in the Bay of Biscay prevented the ship on which he was travelling from reaching its destination until the twenty-fourth, but except for the annoyance of having his riding equipment seized by the customs officials, the voyage was uneventful and Graham used his time to good advantage studying the construction and management of the ship.

While Lisbon was such a dirty place as to beggar description, Graham thoroughly enjoyed its excellent climate and its commanding view of the Tagus and the Atlantic. Entertained in the homes of the British Minister, Sir Charles Stuart,[22] and Admiral Berkeley, he was given a splendid opportunity to meet most of the English as well as the best of the Portuguese families in Lisbon. It was a stroke of good fortune for him to be thus able profitably to spend his time in Lisbon while waiting for the new saddles and riding equipment which he had ordered to replace those seized by the customs officials. Why didn't he purchase some saddles in Lisbon? Because he did not think it possible for anyone to travel through Spain on the 'Don Quixote' saddles they still used in that country. Such saddles, he declared, were 'more adapted for the sun-burnt skins of the natives than for the leather of Englishmen'.[23]

By the time Graham's new riding equipment had arrived, Wellington, after having taken Salamanca, had pushed towards Madrid, thus making possible Graham's trip inland. First he visited the sites of the battles of Vimiera and Frolica, then rode about the adjacent countryside and after a few days returned to Lisbon. When he got back to the city he found that Admiral Berkeley had left for England. The gap which his departure

[21] A list of the rules of this club is given in ARTHUR ASPINALL, *Lord Brougham and the Whig Party*, App. C, 272-273.

[22] Sir Charles Stuart, Baron Stuart de Rothsay, had been the Chargé d'Affaires in Austria from 1803-1806; Minister Plenipotentiary in Russia from 1806-1807; Special Minister in Spain and Austria in 1808-1809; and Envoy Extraordinary and Minister Plenipotentiary in Portugal from February 11th, 1810, to April 2nd, 1814. See S. T. BINDOFF, et al., eds.; *British Diplomatic Representatives 1789-1852*, Camden Third Ser., L, 91.

[23] Graham to his father, in PARKER, *op. cit.*, I, 15 et seq.

occasioned in Lisbon society could not be bridged by the 'operas and balls, at which they [the Portuguese] make all unhappy Englishmen dance without ceasing',[24] and Graham therefore determined to quit Lisbon and travel south to Cadiz.

On July 9th, just before leaving for Cadiz, he wrote to his father that though there were plenty of partridges in Portugal, it was too hot to go shooting, and even though his zeal for politics was abating somewhat, he asked about the possibilities of a speedy dissolution (he did not admire Liverpool's Government) and as to what course, in such an event, his father would take.

The ride to Cadiz was made in the remarkably short space of forty-eight hours. He carried from Charles Stuart to Henry Wellesley,[25] now Ambassador to Spain, the news of the Duke's victory at Salamanca, and readily accepted the ambassador's invitation to live with his family. Living at the embassy, however, meant active participation in the continuous round of social festivities and James soon tired of it. He would rather, he wrote to his father, be hunting and fishing with him at Netherby than be feasting with ministers and regents. In the same letter he explained his views on Spain and on the situation of the Government at home.

It is impossible for the French to carry this place with less than thirty thousand men, and at present there are not above six thousand in their lines. The battle of Salamanca has raised the drooping spirits of the Spaniards, increasing their confidence in the English, and added more vigour to their own paralyzed exertions. But we, on the other hand, should abandon our half-measures, strain every nerve to reinforce Lord Wellington, and put a happy end to the Spanish war before Bonaparte can conclude with the Russians. This, alas! is now out of the question, for promptitude and energy are requisite; and can we hope to find these necessary qualities in 'a household administration'?[26]

[24] *Ibid.*, 18.

[25] For Wellesley's diplomatic career, see BINDOFF, et al., *op. cit.*, L, 142-143.

[26] Graham to his father, August 12th, 1812, in *Graham Papers*. This criticism of the administration is too sweeping and much too unjust. Liverpool, who became Prime Minister in June 1812, while possessing only average ability, was a man of much experience having held at some time almost every cabinet post. His tactfulness gave to the cabinet its needed solidarity. Bathurst, the Secretary for War, was a good administrator. Castlereagh, the Secretary of State for Foreign Affairs, was a diligent though cautious worker. 'All three had held the offices both of Foreign Minister and of Secretary of State for War', says Webster, 'and the unity of political and

Graham's predictions proved well founded. The French did have to abandon the siege of Cadiz, which meant their withdrawal from Andalusia and, as a result, the British occupation of Seville. Graham had arrived at Cadiz in time to watch the French blow up their works and abandon the siege of the city. The unbounded joy of the Spaniards at this turn in the fortunes of the war was of short duration. All knew that a dreadful battle was impending and many feared that its result would not be favourable to the Allied cause. Graham, however, letting his patriotism and enthusiasm get the better of him, could not see how there could be room for despondency 'when British troops under Lord Wellington are opposed to a French force, however great'.[27]

Our future M.P. enjoyed every minute of the six weeks he was in Cadiz — 'the most beautiful and pleasant' city he had thus far seen. Henry Wellesley was especially kind to him and Graham came to admire the ambassador and to consider him one of his best friends. When not visiting with Wellesley, Graham was usually attending the sessions of the Spanish Cortes which was now meeting in Cadiz. He thoroughly enjoyed the debates and particularly admired the speeches of Argüelles,[28] the patriotic liberal.

With a friend whom he had met in Cadiz, Graham spent the first three weeks of October travelling about the interior of Spain. The joys of such a trip, the interesting scenery, the even more interesting people whom he met on the way, the striking absence of any 'deferred living' on the part of the Spaniards, led him to become indifferent to politics and to his own future.[29] But this indifference was only momentary. As soon as he reached Madrid he wrote to his father asking him what he proposed to do now that Parliament had been dissolved. More specifically he wished to know about the election in Cumberland, where, he supposed, the election would be directed by Lord Lonsdale 'with all his

military strategy obtained was doubtless due to this fact.' C. K. WEBSTER, 'The Pacification of Europe', in Cambridge History of British Foreign Policy, ed. by A. W. Ward and G. P. Cooch, I, 394 n. Nor was the rest of the cabinet especially weak since even in the minor offices there were such men as Palmerston and Huskisson.

[27] Graham to his father, August 19th, 1812, in PARKER, op. cit., I, 20.

[28] In 1812, Argüelles was a member of the committee which drew up the draft of the new constitution. An excellent speaker, this Liberal was hailed as the Cicero of Spain. See New International Encyclopedia, Second ed., II, 96-97.

[29] See Graham to his father, October 26th, 1812, in PARKER, op. cit., I, 22.

accustomed disregard for the wishes or interests of the county'.[30] Graham ardently desired the election of Lord Morpeth because otherwise the house of Lowther would return both members for the county of Cumberland, which, because of its size and importance, Graham believed should be independent. His father had evidently not sent him enough particulars on the political situation at home because, in this same letter, he requested that the Carlisle journals be sent to him.

Having taken care of the necessary correspondence, Graham left Madrid to return to Lisbon and from this gay Portuguese capital went to Seville; from Seville to Aranjuez, the headquarters of Sir N. Will's army; from there to Toledo; then back to Madrid. In the last city Graham enjoyed the society of 'the flower of the British army'. The customary and entertaining round of operas, balls, and teas, the main diversion of the officers and the socially prominent visitors such as Graham, was suddenly cut short by Wellington's order that the city be evacuated. Most of those who left Madrid stopped at the nearest convenient place but Graham with an acquaintance named Wynn, went on to Oporto, Portugal. From Oporto he travelled south to Lisbon where he spent a few more delightful days with his old friend Sir Charles Stuart. Then he continued his journey to Badajoz and Seville, and at last back to Cadiz. Arriving at that 'dear place' on Christmas Day, he immediately entered into the Christmas festivities. Grand balls, dinners, and dances were of almost daily occurrence. His constant companions during these gala days were Fitzroy Somerset, John Russell, and 'the very best of all', Sir Henry Wellesley.

And, to add spice to his pleasures, he heard from his father that in the Cumberland elections he had proposed Lord Morpeth, a Whig, and furthermore had given one of his freeman's votes to James Lowther in order to prevent Lord Lonsdale from returning both members for Carlisle. This independent action of his father, who was a member of the Tory party, called for commendation. James immediately wrote him a congratulatory letter in which he disclaimed any desire on his own part to sit in Parliament, but at the same time gave his father some advice as to future action. 'You and I', he wrote, 'can only succeed by standing aloof from all parties, and coming forward uninfluenced, unbiased, and

[30] *Ibid.*

c

uncorrupted, without previous concert, or the connivance of Lord Lowther or any other peer.'[31] He was most insistent that both he and his father remain absolutely independent and free to act in any situation as the exigencies of the moment dictated.

Having met many of the leading men in Spain and in Portugal — Englishmen, Portuguese, and Spaniards — and having seen much of those countries, Graham eagerly seized the first opportunity to go to Italy. Travelling by way of Gibraltar, Port Mahon, and Cagliari, he arrived in Palermo, Sicily, towards the latter part of May. Conditions in this country and in Naples were very critical, and fortunately for Graham an incident occurred which gave him a splendid opportunity to acquire some knowledge of the useful art of diplomacy.

On May 27th, 1813, Lord William Bentinck, commander of the British forces in Sicily and to all intents and purposes the governor of the island, left for Alicante, Spain, to take charge of the army. During his absence the embassy was left in the hands of Lord Montgomerie, who, in need of a private secretary, employed the young traveller. From the standpoint of enabling one to acquire first-hand information of the basic essentials of diplomacy, no better position existed than that of private secretary at an embassy. Furthermore, the position kept James occupied. Six or more hours each day were spent at the office, while an equal number were spent each evening at balls and operas. The extent to which he enjoyed his employment is revealed in the following letter to his father:

> I am as happy as it is possible to conceive me. I live with Lord Montgomerie at a very pretty villa about two miles from town. At ten in the morning I come into the office, and am generally busily employed until about five in the evening. This employment being all political, you may imagine how cheerfully and how warmly I enter into it. . . .
> I flatter myself that this summer will be of lasting use to me. For besides acquiring the forms and habits of business, I have the advantage of enlarging my present humble stock of political information, learning the hidden mysteries of diplomacy, and gratifying my curiosity as to several transactions of the last year.[32]

Due to the fact that Montgomerie was a very sick man with but a

---

[31] See Graham to his father, October 26th, 1812, in PARKER, *op. cit.* I, 24-25.
[32] *Ibid.*, 27-28.

short while to live, Graham did almost all the work at the Palermo embassy. It was intensely intriguing business and Graham liked it so well that he began to toy with the idea of a diplomatic career. Since his present employment would end with Lord Bentinck's return, he planned to join his old friend, Sir Charles Stuart, in Lisbon, and if possible find employment with him. He preferred, however, to remain in Palermo in his present position if Lord William Bentinck would keep him.[33] That is just what Bentinck did, and Graham, delighted with his good fortune, wrote to his father that Bentinck was 'a superior character', and that to gain his approbation and esteem 'would be the pride and honour' of his life.[34]

Lord William Bentinck entered the army in 1791. From 1803 to 1808 he served as the Governor of Madras. In 1813 he joined the staff of the army in Portugal, and later on in the same year was appointed minister at the Court of Sicily and commander-in-chief of all the forces in the island. This Sicilian post was an exceedingly important one to England for with the aid of a naval force Bentinck could strike at Naples or Spain almost at will. 'To a man of his unmeasured ambition, masterful character and ultra-whig views', writes Webster, 'the temptations were immense.'[35] He quarrelled with Queen Mary Caroline, drove her from the island, and then promulgated a new constitution for Sicily, modelled, of course, on the English Constitution, which Bentinck looked upon as well-nigh perfect. This done, he took his forces to Spain where he attempted to detain Suchet, the French marshal, in the province of Catalonia. This campaign was not successful, and so with the Duke of Wellington's sanction Bentinck went back to Sicily. It was now the last part of September and there existed some apprehension that Murat might invade Sicily. It was hoped that Bentinck would not only prevent this, but might actually succeed in getting Murat to agree to desert Napoleon.

In 1808 Napoleon had appointed Murat, 'the first cavalry officer of Europe', king of Naples. After the Emperor's disastrous defeat at Leipzig,[36] Murat, who had fought with him through this battle,

[33] *Ibid.*, 30.   [34] *Ibid.*   [35] WEBSTER, 'Pacification of Europe', *loc. cit.*, 455.
[36] See 'Observations par le Général Comte Nugent, sur la Pièce intitulée, Memoire Historique sur la conduite politique et militaire de Sa Majesté le Roi de Naples, depuis la Bataille de Leipsic d'Octobre, 1813, jusqu'à la Paix de Paris de Mai, 1814', in *British and Foreign State Papers* (1814-1815), 258-268 (Hereinafter cited as *State Papers*).

fled to Naples. On his arrival there, in November, he busied himself with various intrigues. First he obtained proposals from Count Mier, the Austrian Minister at Naples, for an Austro-Neapolitan alliance. At the same time, there had been growing in Italy an active, intelligent, though small, group of intense nationalists who hoped for a unification of the peninsula under an independent Italian government. Since this movement was stronger in Naples than elsewhere, Murat considered the possibility of placing himself at its head. Then he could move his troops to the Po, turn back the Austrians, create a united Italy, and proclaim himself king. He tried to convince Napoleon, during the fall of 1813, of the feasibility and wisdom of such a plan, suggesting that if Napoleon did not agree it might be necessary for Murat to come to terms with the Allies.[37] Since the English held Sicily, it was obviously necessary for Murat to come to terms with them. Bentinck refused Murat's proposed armistice, feeling, no doubt, that Murat's position in Naples was insecure at best, and knowing that he could not move his troops to the Po as long as an Anglo-Sicilian army remained at his rear. In addition, up to this point, 'la conduite de Murat', in the words of Comte Nugent, 'n'était pas faite pour inspirer de la confiance à Lord Bentinck'.[38]

While these machinations and negotiations were being bandied about, the British and Austrian cabinets were exchanging notes on the Neapolitan question. On October 28th, the Austrian Chargé d'Affaires at Naples told Bentinck that an Austro-Neapolitan alliance[39] was about to be concluded and that Aberdeen, the Ambassador to Vienna, had full power to sign such an alliance on behalf of England. Bentinck replied that he knew nothing about such a treaty and that he had received no instructions from Castlereagh, the Foreign Secretary. He entrusted this reply to Graham, whom he sent to the Neapolitan court with the object of trying to secure an alliance. At the same time, however, according to Johnson, Bentinck gave Graham secret instructions 'to get all the information he could at Naples, and, if possible, to find some

[37] See R. M. JOHNSON's article, 'Lord William Bentinck and Murat', in *English Historical Review*, XIX, 263-280.

[38] 'Observations par le comte Nugent', in *State Papers*, II, 265.

[39] This alliance was finally consummated on January 11th, 1814, and by its provisions Austria guaranteed the Crown of Naples to King Joachim Murat, who had married Caroline, Napoleon's sister. *Ibid.*

pretext for getting passports with which to proceed to the head-quarters of the Allies. There Bentinck hoped Graham would be able to get precise information or instructions from Aberdeen or Castlereagh'.[40]

Before sailing from Palermo on New Year's Day 1814 Graham, who had just been appointed Bentinck's aide-de-camp, wrote to Netherby telling his father about the confidential mission with which he was entrusted.

In the space of three days Graham arrived in Naples. He immediately opened negotiations with Count Neipperg, the Austrian Minister, for an armistice with Murat. During the discussions he became sceptical about Austrian promises, and in order to assure himself went to the headquarters of the Austrian field marshal, Bellegarde, at Vicenza. The marshal urged Graham to return to Bentinck at once and to press upon him the necessity of the proposed armistice. Graham hesitated for two days. Then, hearing from Robert Wilson, an accredited British agent, that England desired the armistice and that Bellegarde had in the meantime decided to attack Beauharnais on the Adige, armistice or not, he left at once for Naples[41] where he negotiated the armistice with Count Neipperg and Count Mier. The object of this armistice was to sever Murat from Napoleon and to affect the co-operation of the British and the Neapolitan forces. Unable to locate Bentinck, Graham signed the armistice himself. 'I signed it with peculiar satisfaction', he wrote to Aberdeen, 'because, while it gained my main object of empowering the Austrian minister to demand the immediate co-operation on the Po, of the Neapolitan army, it involves no recognition of title, no question of a political nature.'[42] Even though Bentinck did not favour co-operation with Murat, whom he did not trust, he agreed to the armistice because its terms were in line with the policy he had been steadily pursuing.[43]

[40] JOHNSON, 'Lord William Bentinck and Murat', loc. cit., 271. See also WEBSTER, 'Pacification of Europe', loc. cit., 454-456.

[41] See PARKER, op. cit., I, 34-35. See also WEBSTER, loc. cit., 456.

[42] Graham to Aberdeen, in PARKER, op. cit., I, 37. See also WEBSTER, loc. cit., 456. It was the policy of Bentinck and Graham not to give Murat any guarantee as to power in Italy and to keep England's hands free to assure the Neapolitan Crown to the reputedly liberal Ferdinand.

[43] Since the armistice made no political commitments it saved Castlereagh the necessity of recognizing Murat as King of Naples. See State Papers, II, 235-236. Castlereagh, on February 21st, 1814, wrote to Bentinck that Graham had just

Graham had, therefore, been singularly successful in carrying to a satisfactory conclusion his first diplomatic mission. From Châtillon-sur-Seine, on February 18th, Aberdeen replied to Graham's letter:

> I had the honour of receiving your letter from Lord Castlereagh on his arrival in this town. I understand that his lordship conveys through Lord William Bentinck the expression of his approbation of your conduct; and I take the liberty of adding (what you may think of much less consequence) my thanks for the very clear and satisfactory statement of your proceedings which you have had the goodness to send me; as well as my opinion of the judgment and discretion which you have shown when placed in a situation of considerable difficulty and embarrassment.[44]

The truce with Murat had set at liberty the Anglo-Sicilian army and Bentinck thereupon decided to take his 8000 troops to Italy, disembark at Leghorn, and then march against Genoa. It was necessary for him to apprise the British Government of his activities, and, confident of Graham's ability, Bentinck chose him as his emissary. Passing through the Neapolitan and the Austrian armies, Graham reached Châtillon, where he found Castlereagh busily engaged in negotiating a general peace; after spending two days with the Foreign Secretary informing him of Bentinck's movements and acquainting him with conditions in Italy and Sicily, he returned to Palermo. Finding that Bentinck had already arrived at Leghorn, Graham hastened to that city to join him.

Graham related all these activities in a long letter to his father in which he declared that despite his exciting diplomatic experience he was still interested in the political situation in England, and furthermore, that he had regained his interest in a parliamentary career. He advised his father not to interfere in the elections in Carlisle because that city was too close to Netherby, and then went on to declare that he would be proud some day to represent the County of Cumberland in Parliament. But, and this is the significant condition, it must be as an independent! 'That is,' he said, 'without any collusion of parties or coalition of interests, unpledged as to politics or factions.'[45]

informed him of what had been done and that the armistice was 'perfectly satisfactory'. See Castlereagh to Bentinck, in *State Papers*, II, 236-237.

[44] Aberdeen to Graham, in PARKER, *op. cit.*, I, 38.

[45] Graham to his father, in *Graham Papers*.

With the capitulation of Paris to the Allies in March and the subsequent abdication of Napoleon, military action was over for a time and Bentinck dispatched his aide-de-camp to the Congress at Vienna. He remained in this gay city for ten days and then returned to bid Bentinck farewell.

On his way home he stopped in Moravia to do some hunting, which, though it was great sport, could not of course be compared to that at Netherby. From Moravia he returned to Vienna in time to see most of the European potentates and to attend some of the grand fêtes and balls. But he was now thoroughly tired of all these social activities and yearned for the 'quiet and simple' life. Nevertheless, he was glad to have had the opportunity of being in Vienna while the Congress was in session because it gave him an opportunity of 'seeing all that the present age can boast in the shape of statesmen, conquerors, and heroes'.[46]

He had spent July and August in Baden and from there had written two very interesting letters to his father. Both of them reveal Graham as a shrewd political observer and tactician. In the first he declared that he was still a Whig, that his experiences and first-hand knowledge of Tory measures had only served to confirm his early judgment in joining the Whig party, but that he was despondent and pessimistic as to his own future:

> To be in the House of Commons I no longer desire. I can never sit there to support men I despise, and I never shall be able to support those whom I prefer. Moreover, I begin to know my own powers. The heaven-born gift of eloquence is denied me, and without it there the rest is nothing.[47]

A month later the sky was not quite so overcast and his desire for a parliamentary career was regaining some of its lost power. On the twenty-ninth he counselled his father to obtain, if possible, the Cumberland seat in case of Lord Carlisle's death, but to be very certain to do so as an independent and that only if unopposed.[48] Any other policy, he said, would lose for the family its vantage ground which consisted 'entirely in its independence'.[49] On November fifth he wrote that he would be home for Christmas and that in February he would return to the Continent to tour France.

[46] *Ibid.*   [47] *Ibid.*
[48] A contested election would be too costly.
[49] Graham to his father, in *Graham Papers.*

So far as his future career was concerned these two years in Spain, Portugal, Italy, Germany, and Austria were of tremendous value to Graham. Twenty years at Oxford would probably not have been as profitable to him. He learned to know Europe, its people and their habits and customs, at first hand. And, what is still more important from the standpoint of his future career, Graham returned to England firmly convinced that the English Constitution was well-nigh perfect and that no government on the Continent could even remotely compare to that in London. He had become the friend of kings, emperors, diplomats, generals, and officials of all kinds. He had acquired a knowledge of diplomatic techniques; was impressed with the necessity of keeping promises and commitments inviolate; and by his willingness to work and his mental alertness, had managed to make a favourable impression upon his associates.

While in Spain Graham's liberal tendencies had been strengthened by observing the tremendous efforts of the Spanish liberals, led by Argüelles, to liberalize their Government. In Italy he had served under that redoubtable Whig, William Bentinck, who not only had no confidence in Tories, but had laboured most assiduously to bless the Mediterranean area with English constitutionalism of the Whig variety.

Older and wiser, his liberal principles strengthened, with increased knowledge of men of all types and ranks, with experience in military, naval, and diplomatic affairs, he returned to the joys of a happy Christmas at 'dear old Netherby'.

CHAPTER III

EARLY POLITICAL CAREER

WHEN the holiday season with its parties and neighbourhood visits was over, Graham left Netherby for London. It was necessary, now that the lure of a diplomatic career had faded before anticipations of a parliamentary one, to make the necessary contacts. Consequently, most of the time in London was spent at Brooks's Club with his influential Whig friends, among them his cousin, Lord Archibald Hamilton, the advocate of electoral reform for Scotland. Although Hamilton acted with the Whigs he was known for his independent spirit. The measures that chiefly attracted his attention, the subjects which Romilly and Whitbread had discussed in such detail, were administrative reform, taxation, and trade. Among Graham's other associates were Lawson, his radical brother-in-law; Howard and Aglionby, the liberals; and Curwen, Morpeth, Russell, Brougham, and Stanley, all of whom were moderate Whig reformers. Most of these so-called 'impracticals' were firmly convinced that the social order could not be maintained unless the lot of the common man was improved.

But in 1815 the Tories were in office and Graham feared for the welfare of his country. While in Spain and Italy he had become firmly convinced that the leaders of the Tory party did not possess the necessary ability to cope effectively with State problems. The Tories, on the other hand, claimed the credit for having saved England from Napoleon, and had apparently decided to defend it against the changes advocated by the Whigs. To them the demands for reform should be either sternly repressed or else ignored and the constitution in Church and State be 'let alone'. They comforted themselves with the conviction, carefully nurtured in them from their youth, that they alone, by virtue of their birth and training, were capable of governing the country. They insisted that to prevent a repetition in England of what had happened in France in the years following 1789, it was necessary to rule the country with a firm hand.

There was no denying the fact that in 1815 England was in need of a firm hand; but it was equally in need of an intelligent one.

Waterloo had marked the end of many years of foreign strife and had freed England from the danger of immediate attack from abroad. Historically, it also marked the end of the eighteenth century, which had witnessed the assumption by England of the naval, colonial, and industrial supremacy of the world. Ending an era of imperialism, Waterloo marked the beginning of another era, one in which England was compelled to face the social, economic, and political effects of industrial changes that had been going on for generations. Unemployment, pauperism, regulation of agriculture and industry, and a host of other new and serious problems arose to plague the men who were administering the government in town, county, and nation.

The troops returning from the Napoleonic Wars found economic conditions deplorable. Trade languished due to the newly developed agricultural competition from the Continent and to war-surpluses at home; wages of agricultural labourers were so low that they had to be supplemented out of the rates; pauperism was growing at an alarming pace; and the price of bread was too high even though the Corn Law of 1815 did not succeed in keeping it as high as its framers had hoped it would. This high price of grain meant profits for the landlords and their tenant farmers, but it meant untold suffering and starvation for the masses. To make matters worse, 1816 was a year of widespread crop failures and general destitution.[1] In the counties of Norfolk, Suffolk, Huntingdon, and Cambridge discontent assumed menacing proportions. Nightly meetings were held at which the malcontents made plans to set fire to houses, barns, and rick-yards. In the northern manufacturing districts, long hours, low wages, and unemployment resulted in attacks on factory buildings and the breaking of machinery. In South Wales disturbances were so serious that the Government felt justified in resorting to military action to restore order. Numerous petitions were sent to Parliament complaining of governmental extravagance, denouncing the Corn Laws, and demanding parliamentary reform.

To complicate matters, an odious political situation existed. George III was now a hopeless lunatic unable to recognize even his closest friends. His disreputable and dissolute son, the future

---

[1] *The Annual Register or a View of the History, Politics, and Literature for the Year* (1816), 91 et seq. (Hereinafter cited as *Annual Register*).

George IV, was acting as Prince Regent. To both Government and country he was a decided liability.

Too obstinately behind the times, the Tory Government of Liverpool, Castlereagh, and Sidmouth proceeded to silence by a series of repressive acts the reasonable demands for socio-economic reforms. To Sidmouth, the Home Secretary, fell the task of stamping out all manifestations of public discontent. He sternly repressed the London Riot in 1816 and then proceeded to enforce with vigour the laws against the destruction of machinery in the mines and collieries.[2] When, in the following year, an attack was made on the Prince Regent, Sidmouth had an Act passed permitting the quartering and billeting of the Corps of Yeomanry in homes when assembled for the suppression of tumults and riots. In addition, he had the Habeas Corpus Act suspended[3] and the laws against seditious libel revived.[4] Finally, he issued a circular letter to the Lord Lieutenants of the counties ordering them to deal severely with all unlicensed vendors of pamphlets.

These measures of the Tories only served to quicken the desire of the young Graham to enter Parliament where, in conjunction with such Whigs as Grey, Holland, Brougham, and Althorp, he could actively oppose a Government which he considered inept, extravagant, and reactionary.

Most of the year 1815 Graham spent at Brooks's Club or on hunting trips with his friends. In May of the following year he wrote from Goldsborough, where he had been hunting with his friend Starkey, stating that he was going to France until August, at which time he would return to Netherby 'for grouse'. While in Paris, he met Henry Brougham, the Whig reformer, who, finding Graham young, good looking, and spirited, formed with him a lasting friendship. Brougham soon volunteered to ask Earl Grey to exert his influence to secure a seat in Parliament for Graham under the auspices of the Whig party. It was expected that one of the Cumberland seats would soon be available,[5] but while Graham earnestly wished to represent his county, he would not present himself for the seat if it fell vacant, because, he wrote to Brougham:

[2] *Statutes at Large*, 56 Geo. III, c. 125.
[3] *Ibid.*, 57 Geo. III, c. 3.
[4] *Ibid.*, 57 Geo. III, c. 6; 60 Geo. III-IV; Geo. IV, c. 8; c. 9.
[5] The death of Lord Carlisle, who then held the seat, was believed to be imminent.

Let us suppose a vacancy for the County of Cumberland; let us suppose even that I am the only candidate. I cannot, I would not, be returned without a frank exposition of my general politics, and these would be found opposite to those of my father. I should be supported by a party with which he does not act, be reprobated by a party to which in early life he unhappily attached himself.[6]

In the general election of 1818, a chance to present himself as a candidate for Hull was eagerly seized by Graham, since there would be no family loyalties or feelings to offend. Hull was represented by two Tories — Staniforth[7] and Mahon[8] — and since the latter was to retire from politics, the Whigs decided to contest the seat. Elections in this town had been bitterly contested and therefore very costly, and until Graham came forward as a young man of position and promise it had been difficult to find a good candidate to oppose the Tory choices. Dean Milner vouched for Graham's 'safety', i.e., that he was well qualified by birth, training, and conviction to support the established Constitution in Church and State. This assurance seemed doubly necessary to the aristocratic Whig leaders in view of the fact that the young liberal was accompanied to the first hustings by two liberal Roman Catholics, Langsdale and Haggerton. On June 10th, Graham delivered his first campaign speech. In it he enunciated his liberal Whig principles in the following words:

Ministerial extravagance and undue influence are objects of my unfeigned abhorrence, and all my efforts will be used in restraining them, whether in the shape of places, sinecures, or pensions.

I consider war as a curse to human nature, and peace as an inestimable blessing, which it will be my constant endeavour to preserve.

I am a friend to reform in Parliament — not that wild enthusiastic reform which, instead of improving the Constitution, would, by producing anarchy and confusion, undermine and destroy it, but a moderate reform, which would infuse new life into the Constitution, and restore it to its former health and vigour.[9]

[6] Graham to Brougham, June 30th, 1816, in PARKER, *Life of Graham*, I, 49.

[7] Staniforth had been a successful business man and was firmly devoted to the Liverpool Government. He had supported the suspension of the Habeas Corpus Act in 1817, and despite opposition in his district, had voted for the Corn Law of 1815. He was now thoroughly unpopular.

[8] Mahon was a wealthy West-India-man with similar principles.

[9] Cited in PARKER, *op. cit.*, I, 51.

To these principles of peace, retrenchment, and moderate reform Graham was to remain loyal — that is, to what *he* conceived each of them to mean and not to what the Whig party decided that they meant. In addition to enunciating the above principles, Graham also avowed his hostility to slavery, severely denounced the recent suspension of the Habeas Corpus Act, and affirmed his adherence to the principle of religious liberty. While he loved the Established Church from the bottom of his heart, as he himself put it, he nevertheless declared openly and clearly that 'pains and penalties or disabilities of any kind are in my opinion persecution, when suffered by men on account of their faith, whether they be Dissenters or Roman Catholics'.[10]

In this election Graham revealed one of his besetting weaknesses, a trait that was to remain characteristic of him throughout almost his entire public career. By nature he was intolerant of others' frailties, quick to find fault, unable gracefully to bear criticism, and often disdainful of the opinions of others. In the heat of debate, carried away by the spell of the occasion, or suspecting the motives of his opponents, he too frequently stooped to satirical remarks and cynical and offensive repartee, which, his friends frequently pointed out, achieved nothing but damage to his own case and even made enemies of would-be friends. These characteristics, plus his immaculate and fashionable dress, earned for him the sobriquets: 'Cock of the North' and 'Yorkshire Dandy'. When his opponents in the Hull election satirized him in these allusive terms, he countered by denouncing one of them as a slave-owner, and the other as a 'docile hack of Lords Liverpool and Castlereagh'.[11]

During the campaign his opponents pointed in derision to his youth, to his religious liberalism, and to his limited finances. In 1818, however, these were assets rather than liabilities, and Graham made the most of them. One of the handsomest men in all England, he presented a splendid appearance in public, and when he boldly admitted his youthfulness, his religious liberalism, and his financial embarrassments, he became for the time being the darling of the mob. One of the popular rhymes of the day illustrates the attitude of many towards both the candidates and the issues:

[10] *Ibid.*   [11] TORRENS, *Life of Graham*, I, 96.

Blue Mitchel spoke next, he was hardly a minute,
It was all very well, but there wasn't much in it;
I hope he will mind all he says to perform,
And vote for economy, peace, and reform.
Our Graham spoke next, and he spoke like a Briton;
When he spoke of taxation, the right nail he hit on;
By taxes, tea, sugar, and malt are made dear,
They lessen our bread-loaf, they spoil our strong beer;
And Graham has told us again and again,
That it is the duty of Parliament men
To see that the money is properly spent
Which up from the country in taxes is sent.[12]

In his last campaign speech, on June 17th, Graham attacked the recent increases in the Army declaring that it gave the Crown an unwarranted increase in power, and that if any branch of the service needed increased revenues it was the Navy.

The election resulted in a victory for Graham, but it was so close that his opponents decided to contest it; Graham won, but at the stiff cost of £6000. His mother, while no liberal, rejoiced in the success of her son; his father, a good Tory, felt that £6000, even though it was paid by a friend, was rather costly 'amusement'.[13]

It was a happy day for Graham when he took his seat in Parliament as the member for Hull and joined the Opposition benches with such men as Hume, Althorp, Burdett, and Wilson. When, on February 19th, 1819, Sir Robert Peel asked leave to bring in a Bill for the preservation of the health and morals of apprentices employed in the cotton mills and in other mills and factories, Graham, unlike other liberals, declared that he would give general support to the Bill, but that he would object at every point where the provisions of the Bill interfered with free labour.[14] On March 2nd he helped defeat the Election Laws Amendment Bill by objecting to the clause requiring each freeholder to furnish proof that his tenement was assessed to the land tax. He also objected to the proposal that the expenses of county hustings be paid out of the county rates, and to the power which the proposed Bill gave to the constables. 'The returning officers were not,

[12] 'Spirit of Party', cited in TORRENS, op. cit., I, 102.
[13] See Ibid., 106-109. See also the pamphlet, Records of the Hull Election.
[14] Hansard, 1st Ser., XXXVII, 566.

always of the highest description', in his estimation, and furthermore, they 'might make a job at the county expense'.[15] A few
weeks later Peel presented a petition from those labourers above
sixteen years of age who were working in the factories at Stockport,
requesting favourable action on the Cotton Factories Bill, which
was designed to reduce the hours of labour. Peel affirmed that
seven manufacturers, thirteen resident clergymen, eight medical
men, as well as a great number of labourers, had signed the
petition. Graham, not at all impressed, assured the House that
Peel had paid too much attention to this petition, especially since
the petitioners were nothing more than 'a set of idle, discontented,
discarded, and good-for-nothing workmen',[16] who thought they
did too much work for what they were paid. Idle, discontented,
and discarded many of them certainly were, but only an aristocratic snob like young Graham could have been so foolish as to
call them 'good-for-nothing'. He openly proclaimed his resolute
opposition to any reduction in the hours of labour on the principle
that if Parliament once began that policy it would never be able to
stop. This Bill of Peel's would be but an entering wedge to be
followed by an endless chain of successive demands for shorter
and shorter working days. When, on April 14th, Burrell moved for
the appointment of a select committee to inquire into the causes
of the dormant state of the wool trade and then claimed for the
agriculturalists the right to export their wool, Graham vigorously
opposed the motion. He declared that the price of wool during
the past few years had actually risen, that not a single petition on
the subject was now on the table of the House, that such an inquiry
would cause needless alarm, and that above all he could not consent to change a system that had existed for almost 200 years.[17]

On the last day of April Graham helped to defeat the Country
Bank Notes Bill. He had conversed with many intelligent people
on the subject, he said, and had come to the conclusion that the
Bill was injurious to credit, that it interfered with the regular
payment of taxes,[18] and that it would only serve to unsettle the
country. He had absolutely no faith whatever in Bank of England
notes. How could he have, he asked, when at least one-half of
those circulating in the three northern counties were forgeries.[19]

[15] *Ibid.*, 698.   [16] *Ibid.*, 1260.   [17] *Ibid.*, XXXVIII, 39.
[18] *Ibid.*, 411-412.   [19] *Ibid.*, 434.

Country bank notes, on the other hand, since they were easily identified, were scarcely ever forged, and for that reason were infinitely preferable to the Bank of England notes.

In the early part of May Graham revealed his independent spirit in his readiness to vote against his friends or party if the occasion arose. Brougham had attacked the sale of the Barony of Kendall to Lord Lonsdale for £14,000, declaring it to be worth at least four times that amount. The M.P. for Hull rose to the defence of Lord Lonsdale, a Tory, declaring that the latter had not received more than £1000 by means of enfranchisements, the real basis of Brougham's charge, and that Brougham's misrepresentations were groundless.[20]

By June it was apparent to all that the Tory Government would introduce no reform measures and would insist on maintaining the *status quo*. This occasioned a blast from the *Edinburgh Review*, which stigmatized the Tories as 'the enemies of every reform, and of none more than of retrenchment'.[21] The author of the article went on to declare that the Tories were favourable to large military establishments, were patrons of arbitrary foreign governments, were opposed to a revision of England's commercial system, and that they gave 'protection and palliation' to abuses of every description.[22] In December the *Review* demanded Catholic emancipation and justice for Ireland in order to achieve economy and to put an end to excessive military rule.[23]

Demand for retrenchment and economy was in the air and Ridley, a member of the Opposition, capitalized on it by asking, on March 18th, for a reduction in the number of junior lords of the Admiralty. It was utterly inexcusable, he said, to have the same number of junior lords for a navy of 137 ships and 20,000 men as there were in 1797 for a navy of 1000 ships and 120,000 men.[24] This was just the opportunity for which Graham had been waiting and he seized it with alacrity. While he had no desire to diminish the just patronage of the Crown, he contended that it had of late been unjustly extended, and ought therefore to be brought back

[20] *Hansard.* 1st. Ser., XXXVIII, 563-564.
[21] 'State of Parties', in *Edin. Rev.*, XXX, 204.
[22] *Ibid.*, 205.   [23] *Ibid.*, XXXI, 259.
[24] On behalf of the Government, Admiral Codrington defended the Admiralty Board on the puerile grounds that it had remained unchanged for over a hundred years and was incapable of improvement!

to normal. With respect to the junior lords of the Admiralty, all they had to do during time of war was to sign papers; and he, for one, could not see how they could have very much to do in time of peace. The number could easily be reduced without any detriment to the service. The reason the Government clung so tenaciously to such offices should be obvious to anyone, he declared, for,

> By the disposal of a multitude of such offices only could a majority of votes in that House be secured by an administration that had lost the confidence of the Country which wished to see these offices diminished. He wished an end put to this system — he wished to see a government which trusted rather to public opinion as its strength than to the power of giving away such offices.[25]

No administration should be permitted to use its power so as effectively to defy public opinion.

Lord John Russell, who followed Graham, charged the Admiralty Board with being both ignorant and incompetent, and maintained that the administration's tenure of office was entirely dependent upon its ability to retain numerous offices.

These criticisms of the Government by Graham and Russell earned for them the caustic remark of Wellington that they were 'sacrificing their public duty at the shrine of popularity',[26] a charge which Graham strenuously denied. The same conclusion, however, was reached by Torrens, one of Graham's biographers, who described Graham's first speech as savouring 'too much of anxiety for out-of-door applause'.[27] Others thought he had been over-confident, unduly sarcastic, and much too intolerant. Henry Lascelles, who sat near Graham when he made his maiden speech, is reported to have whispered to a friend: 'Well, there is an end of Graham; we shall hear no more of him.'[28] Tierney, with a mixed sense of humour and disgust, dubbed him 'the manly puppy'. The M.P. for Hull, however, treated these criticisms with a haughty disdain, for while he undoubtedly welcomed popular[29] approval and acclaim, he would not sacrifice his principles for the sake of it,

[25] *Hansard*, 1st Ser., XXXIX, 1064.   [26] *Ibid.*, 1067.
[27] TORRENS, *op. cit.*, I, 114.
[28] Cited in GEORGE H. JENNINGS, *An Anecdotal History of the British Parliament*, 1881 ed., 252.
[29] This meant, of course, popularity with the propertied classes, not with the masses, who, in the early nineteenth century, did not count for much.

D

nor would he waste much time or effort in pursuit of such a mundane and fickle thing. Not many years were to pass before praise or blame alike were to be matters of utter indifference to him.

In 1819 a bad harvest, aggravated by industrial distress, brought renewed demands for parliamentary reform. A mass meeting to discuss plans for political action was scheduled to take place in Manchester on August 16th. In attempting to arrest the speaker, the magistrates lost their heads and ordered the yeomanry to charge the crowd; half a dozen citizens were killed and fifty or more wounded. The terrified Tories, fearing the overthrow of Church and State and the destruction of property, hastily passed, under Sidmouth's leadership, the repressive 'Six Acts'.[30] During the debates on the first Act — to prevent military drill — Graham, who regarded this so-called 'Peterloo Massacre' with a feeling of horror and alarm, told the excited House that for many weeks the blacksmiths in the north of England had been making pikes and other weapons. The citizens of Carlisle and neighbouring towns were nervous and apprehensive of the future and looked to the Government for protection. Laws guaranteeing security of persons and property must be enforced and if the people did not immediately get this protection from the Government, they would, he warned, overthrow the Government and 'look up to the Opposition for it'.[31] 'Good God!' cried Brougham, 'if this had been going on for weeks, why look either to the ministers or to the Opposition. Where were the magistrates all the while?'[32] They were there all right, but it is extremely doubtful if all of them were on the side Graham and Brougham expected them to be, and while a majority willed to do their duty, many lacked the necessary courage.

In the debates on the fourth measure, the Seditious Meetings Bill, Graham pointed out that one of the clauses went so far as to

---

[30] 'An Act to prevent the Military training of persons', *Statutes at Large*, 60 Geo. III, c. 1; 'An Act to authorize Justices of the Peace to seize all Arms kept for purposes dangerous to the public peace', *Ibid.*, c. 2; 'An Act to prevent delay in the administration of justice in cases of misdemeanour', *Ibid.*, c. 4; 'An Act to prevent seditious meetings and assemblies of more than 50 people', *Ibid.*, c. 6; 'An Act to more effectively punish seditious libel', *Ibid.*, c. 8; and 'An Act subjecting certain publications to stamp duties', *Ibid.*, c. 9.

[31] *Hansard*, 1st Ser., XLI, 854.   [32] *Ibid.*

make it illegal for an M.P. not living in the borough he represented even to address his constituents for re-election without official permission.[33] Castlereagh saw Graham's point immediately and agreed to an amendment remedying the defect. But the Tory party did not understand that these disturbances were due more to their refusal to grant a few moderate and reasonable reforms, than to any popular desire for revolutionary change.[34]

When, early in 1820, George III died, Parliament was dissolved and a new election held. Graham, who would not again hazard the expense of another Hull election, was invited to become a candidate for Carlisle in the interest of the Anti-Lowther, or 'Blue' faction. Even though the thought of not being in Parliament mortified him, Graham refused to accept the invitation because an election so close to home would embarrass his father who was a Tory. Therefore when a friend undertook to secure him a seat for St. Ives, in Cornwall, he accepted with alacrity and won the seat in a closely contested election.

The Commons had decided, in 1818, to pay a salary of £24,000 to the junior members of the Royal family. All of them accepted this sum except the Duke of Clarence. When, in 1821, the latter asked that he be given his back pay, Graham proposed that the House agree on the grounds that the country had already saved that amount in interest.[35] He was thus able, he calculated, to maintain his loyalty to the Royal family and at the same time adhere to his principle of economy.

A large Civil List proposed by the Government led to a series of Opposition efforts to check Royal extravagance. On May 3rd Joseph Hume, the Westminster radical, proposed that the House be furnished with a detailed account of all expenditures since 1815, to enable it accurately to estimate what the actual needs were; Graham was one of the minority of sixty who voted for Hume's motion.[36] Two days later he voted for Brougham's motion that the House take into account the Droits of the Crown, Admiralty, and other funds which until now had been considered as under the immediate control of Parliament before it settled the question of the Civil List.[37] On the eighth, he voted for Russell's

[33] *Ibid.*, 840.   [34] See *Edin. Rev.*, XXXIII, 225.
[35] *Hansard*, New Ser., V, 1212.
[36] For the division see *Ibid.*, I, 83.   [37] *Ibid.*, 163.

motion that the vote on the Civil List be deferred until the year's estimates could be examined;[38] on the fifteenth, he supported Brougham's motion to reduce the number of Barons of the Exchequer in Scotland from five to four;[39] on June 1st, against renewing the Alien Bill;[40] and during the unsavoury Queen Caroline affair,[41] he voted with the Whig Opposition in support of the Queen.

Graham's first stint in Parliament, therefore, revealed him to be a real independent. As he had promised, he advocated economy, retrenchment, and reform and kept company with, or parted from, anyone or any party that did not agree with him on these issues. But since these were the chief principles of the Whigs he was, of course, counted a member of that party.

Early in 1821 some of the electors of St. Ives presented a petition against Graham's return, alleging that the election had been fraudulent. Unable to afford the costs of such a contest, knowing that the Netherby estate had been neglected, and feeling that his first years in Parliament had been anything but successful, he withdrew from political life to his new home at Croft Head near Netherby, a home which was now presided over by Fannie Callander, the unusually attractive daughter[42] of Colonel Callander of Craigforth, whom James had married in July 1819.

[38] For the division see *Hansard*, see New Ser., I, 226.
[39] *Ibid.*, 386-387.   [40] *Ibid.*, 798.
[41] In 1795 George IV had married Caroline of Brunswick and he now decided to divorce her in order to prevent her from sharing with him in the coronation ceremonies. They had been separated for some years during which the King had illegally married another woman and had carried on illicit relations with others. In seeking this divorce he alleged that Caroline, who had taken up her abode on the mainland of Europe and had not been discreet in her own affairs of the heart, was guilty of infidelity. Since the King had no unassailable evidence of the Queen's guilt and since his own conduct might come up for unsavoury discussion, the cabinet advised him not to proceed with the trial, but the stubborn King insisted. When she returned to England for the trial, the Queen became, for the time being, the darling of the London mobs. The Tory House of Lords decided in the King's favour, but the decision was so close that the cabinet decided that the bill of pains and penalties against the Queen could not possibly pass the Commons and therefore dropped it. A few months later the Queen died and the matter was dropped. The scandal, however, had weakened the position of the cabinet.
[42] See *Dyott's Diary*, ed. by REGINALD W. JEFFREY, II, 265-266.

CHAPTER IV

A GENTLEMAN FARMER

IT certainly should have been a pleasure for Sir James to retire to Netherby, for according to Lonsdale:

> Few sights in England can be more charming than Netherby, placed on a natural knoll that slopes gradually downwards to a richly-verdured park, studded with noble beeches and other forest trees, traversed by the Esk, whose waters, along with the gradually expanding meadows, become lost to view in the silvery sands of the Solway . . . The hall itself, its surrounding gardens, evergreens, and notably the rhododendrons and hawthorns, so beautiful in their season, are pleasant to look upon; whilst the landscape to the west beyond affords great wealth and variety of surface, and much that is grandly picturesque.[1]

But while this natural beauty of Netherby could scarcely be surpassed, the economic condition of the estate in 1821 was little short of hopeless. Due to the lethargy of James's father, it had fallen into a state of almost complete dilapidation. The young heir almost despairing of its repair, nevertheless put his talents to work in earnest to restore the property to some semblance of order and efficiency.

In the years following the Napoleonic Wars, English agriculture was at a low ebb. The Corn Law of 1815 had given it a maximum of protection by hermetically sealing the ports of England against foreign grain until the exorbitant price of eighty shillings a quarter for home-grown wheat had not only been reached but maintained for six weeks. The Law, however, did not prevent prices from fluctuating, and agriculture remained in an unsatisfactory condition.[2] Wheat, in 1816, stood at 76s. 2d. per quarter.[3] The next year, due to a crop deficiency at home and abroad,[4] the price rose

---

[1] LONSDALE, *Worthies of Cumberland*, II, 16.

[2] See WILLIAM R. CURTLER, *A Short History of English Agriculture*, 262 et seq.; LORD ERNLE, *English Farming Past and Present*, 322-323.

[3] GEORGE R. PORTER, *Progress of the Nation in its Various Social and Economic Relations from the Beginning of the Nineteenth Century to the Present Day*, I, 156 (Hereinafter cited as *Progress of Nation*).

[4] THOMAS TOOKE, *A History of Prices and the State of the Circulation from 1793-1837*, II, 16-19 (Hereinafter cited as *History of Prices*).

to the high annual average of 94s.[5] In the following years, good crops at home[6] and on the Continent caused prices to fall steadily until by 1821 the average price of wheat was 54s. 5d.[7] This fall in prices dealt a staggering blow to the agricultural population. The long years of war, plus the Law of 1815, had led in many cases to the enclosing of inferior soils upon which a slight profit could be realized only as long as the price of wheat was very high. But when prices fell to the 54s. 5d. level, many farmers were completely ruined. On the assumption that the price of wheat would always be at or near 80s., landlords had raised their rents, but they refused to lower them now that prices stood below that figure, though the tenants were now getting less for their wheat than formerly.[8] The fall in prices hurt the landlords also, many of whom were heavily in debt on war-time mortgages, by making it difficult, and often impossible, to pay the interest as it fell due. As a result many lost part, and frequently all, of their estates.[9]

Conditions in Cumberland were probably worse than in any other county in England.[10] As a rule the farms were small[11] and therefore agricultural improvements were, for the most part, out of the question. Almost all of the larger landlords were heavily mortgaged, their rents were in arrears, and, what was far worse, they had become the victims of an overpowering sense of futility and despair. In addition, rainfall was excessively heavy in Cumberland, averaging from forty to fifty inches per year, and farming was therefore largely unprofitable unless good drainage systems could be installed. But most of the farmers knew nothing

[5] PORTER, *op. cit.*, I, 156. In June, wheat had reached the unbelievable price of 117s. See TOOKE, *op. cit.*, II, 18.

[6] Spencer Walpole is no doubt right when he says that the Law of 1815 stimulated overproduction by leading the agriculturalists to believe that the Law would perpetually keep wheat at or near 80s. SPENCER WALPOLE, *A History of England from the Conclusion of the Great War in 1815*, II, 100-101 (Hereinafter cited as *Hist. of Eng.*).

[7] PORTER, *op. cit.*, I, 156.

[8] For the attitude of the tenants towards the Corn Law of 1815, see DONALD GROVE BARNES, *A History of the English Corn Laws, 1660-1846*, 145-146.

[9] See WILLIAM SMART, *Economic Annals of the Nineteenth Century*, II, 2 (Hereinafter cited as *Economic Annals*).

[10] In 1827, of the 670,000 acres in Cumberland, 125,920 were unfit for profitable cultivation. PORTER, *op. cit.*, I, 173.

[11] JOHN H. CLAPHAM, *An Economic History of Modern Britain*, I, 112 (Hereinafter cited as *Econ. Hist. of Britain*).

about drainage and the few who did were so deeply in debt that in any event they could not finance its installation.

Netherby, when James returned in 1821, was a good example of the extent to which some of the estates had been allowed to degenerate. The good lands, exhausted by repeated corn crops and lack of fertilization, were divided into small farms averaging from 40 to 100 acres. About three-fourths of the land was saturated with water, and much of the remainder was moss and uncultivable pasture. Many of the barns and sheds were so dilapidated as to be absolutely useless. The farm houses, with their small, dingy, poorly-ventilated rooms, were not much better. The fences were uneven and in many places had long since actually fallen down. The roads had become nothing but muddy cow trails.[12]

James's father, typical of so many other English landlords, had found business exceedingly irksome and unpleasant and had made no effort to extricate himself from the impending disaster. Brown and Yule, two stewards, reported that

> The management of the estate had been committed for some time, almost without control, to a Mr. Ellis, in whose hands the tenantry and work-people deposited their earnings, and by whom a running account was kept of these deposits as against rent. Sir James drew upon the steward as he wanted money, without regard to half-yearly or annual balances, interest was charged or allowed as the case might be on the various sums that passed through Mr. Ellis's hands; and the result was that while he became virtually master of all around him, neither laird nor tenants could tell, or wished perhaps to inquire, exactly how they stood with regard to each other.[13]

With the passing of each year this state of affairs assumed a more gloomy aspect, the arrears grew larger, and the interest and obligations pressed more heavily. A mere cursory examination of the estate convinced the youthful Graham that a radical change in management was imperative. He was unable, however, to convince his obdurate father that any change in methods was either desirable or possible. His mother, on the other hand, cheered by

---

[12] WILLIAM DICKINSON, 'On the Farming of Cumberland', in *Journal of the Royal Agricultural Society of England*, XIII, 222. Dickinson's information comes from the report of Brown and Yule, the stewards of the Netherby estate.

[13] TORRENS, *Life of Graham*, I, 152.

the hopes of better days to come, agreed with her son's plans, and together they prevailed upon the 'laird of the manor' to turn over its management to his son.

As soon as James began to disentangle the skein of twisted accounts, Ellis, the steward, who did not relish books, records, and accounts any better than James's father had, felt unwanted and resigned his position and moved to Liverpool. When James examined the rent-roll Ellis had kept, he found some 300 tenants so hopelessly far in arrears that he determined to wipe out completely their accounts. This was done, however, with a perfect understanding that there was to be no recurrence of rental delinquencies.[14] Some of the tenants, themselves little removed from farm-labourers, had been keeping servants. The most worthy of these were granted land as tenants, and to enable them to get a good start money was loaned them at a very low rate of interest. His study of the situation also convinced him that small-scale farming was uneconomical and inefficient and in the years from 1821 to 1850 he decreased the number of farms by more than fifty per cent and increased the size of those remaining. Many of the tenants who thus lost their farms became farm-labourers; others, through Sir James's kindness in giving them the necessary money, migrated to America.

By the beginning of the nineteenth century, Galloway cattle had made their appearance along the northern border of England.[15] This hardy breed of beef-cattle was well adapted to the neede of Cumberland, and Graham and other landlords began to build up herds of this type instead of long-horns. Each year Graham distributed among his tenants, as prizes for excellent work, three or four bull-calves of the Galloway breed from his own carefully selected stock.[16] Although other landlords followed Graham's example and thus made Galloway cattle popular in Cumberland, it was not many years before the short-horns[17] predominated, chiefly because the latter type of cattle was able to thrive under diverse conditions of soil and climate and because they matured earlier than the Galloway. James Graham and J. C. Curwen

---

[14] DICKINSON, 'Farming of Cumberland', *loc. cit.*, 221 et seq.

[15] ERNLE, *op. cit.*, 180.

[16] See DICKINSON, 'Farming of Cumberland', *loc. cit.*, 252.

[17] See the article by HALL W. KEARY, 'Management of Cattle', in *Jour. of the Royal Agric. Soc.*, IX, 424-452.

of Workington Hall were two of the most prominent leaders in
the introduction of this new breed.

At the Curwen estate, which was the model of the entire neighbourhood, frequent meetings were held at which the farmers of
the surrounding region gathered to discuss cattle-breeding, soil
culture, drainage, and kindred subjects. Among those usually
present, in addition to Curwen and Graham, were Blamire of
Thackwood, and Rigg of Abbey Holme. The latter was regarded
as one of the best stock-breeders in Cumberland and was probably
more influential than any other in introducing and improving the
Galloway breed.[18] From these meetings at Workington Hall,
Graham increased his own fund of agricultural knowledge, besides
gaining further insight into the needs and problems of landlords,
tenants, and farmers.

On the death of his father in 1824, James came into outright
possession of the estate. Since much of the land was wet, swampy,
and unfit for cultivation, he began to study the problem of
drainage. Crude surface drainage, in which stones and turf were
used, had long since proved practically useless, and in 1821,
therefore, James had employed a shrewd Scottish agriculturalist as
his steward to aid him in 'reclaiming' large sections of the land.
At the same time he employed an experienced tile-worker of
Staffordshire who helped him establish a tile manufactory on the
Netherby grounds.[19] He then induced his tenants, by making
them a free gift of the tile, to install pipe on their farms. Before
many years had elapsed there were over forty miles of tile drains
on the estate. Although this experiment was costly, it was entirely
successful, and the example was eagerly followed by neighbouring
landlords.[20] Nor did Graham ever cease to experiment with
types of drainage. In 1839 he wrote a letter to the editor of the
Journal of the Royal Agricultural Society, an organization of
which he was a life-governor, describing a drainage experiment in
which he had used the sub-soil plough very effectively. In it, he
declared that one of the reasons why drainage experiments were
so frequently unsuccessful was that the landlords did not take into

---

[18] DICKINSON, 'Farming of Cumberland', *loc. cit.*, 253.
[19] There was a great amount of wet clay land on the estate and therefore clay for
the tiles was easily obtained.
[20] *Ibid.*, 286.

consideration local conditions of soil and climate. 'It has always appeared to me', he wrote, 'that skill in agriculture does not so much consist in the discovery of principles of universal application, as in the adaptation of acknowledged principles to local circumstances.'[21]

While the improvements at Netherby had been successful they had been exceedingly expensive and the estate was soon burdened with an indebtedness of approximately £120,000. This excessive overhead, plus grief over the death of his father, and discouragement caused by the relentless opposition of his tenants to his insistence on efficient operations, served to intensify his natural inclination to despondency. So intense did this become that he actually entered into negotiations for the sale of the estate with the intention of becoming a partner in the banking house of Peter Pole and Company. Fortunately for him this firm failed before the negotiations had been completed, and Graham, with renewed vigour and interest, returned to his labours on the farm.

There was much to do, much that was interesting and stimulating, even if difficult. Daily he rode about the estate suggesting changes, encouraging the sluggish tenants, commending and rewarding the thrifty and industrious, and lending a helping hand where needed. Nor did he give less time to his experimental work in cattle-breeding, seed-selection, soil-drainage, and fertilization. Rainy days, and there were many of them in Cumberland, furnished him the leisure to check over the accounts of the estate and its tenants, and to consider carefully all possible means of retrenchment. As a result, the Netherby estate was soon regarded as one of the best managed and most efficiently operated in the entire country and was affectionately referred to as 'the pride of Cumberland'. Robert Brown, who had minutely examined the estate in 1821, revisited it in 1840 and was so impressed by the changes that had been made that he wrote to John Yule, the manager: 'Sir James Graham has raised an imperishable monument to his honour, in the highly improved condition to which he has brought his Estate — a monument that he will contemplate

---

[21] JAMES R. G. GRAHAM, 'On the Deanston Frequent Drain System, as Distinguished from and Compared with the Furrow-Draining and Deep-Ploughing of the Midland Counties of England', in *Jour. of the Royal Agric. Soc.*, I, 31.

with pleasure all his life, and his memory will be revered during ages when he is gone.'[22]

Besides the aforementioned activities, Graham found time to do considerable reading. His favourites were Dryden, Pope, Shakespeare, and Burke. The latter's orations, which he read and re-read, had a peculiar fascination for him; he felt as he read them that they were speaking down deep into life and bidding deep answer unto deep in echoes that would never die. There were frequent occasions when Graham, in the company of his family or with some of his genial friends, became happy and carefree. Too often, however, such occasions would be succeeded by prolonged periods of gloomy pessimism, and an overpowering sense of futility. Despite all his efforts, the estate would never be profitable; the Government was weak, inefficient, and corrupt; the landlords were attempting to fight a battle which they were bound to lose; and life, at its very best, always presented to him a vain choice, not between either of two things which he really wanted to do, but between two things neither of which were desirable. From these recurring periods of despondency, Graham was rescued by his deep religious convictions and by his intense spirit of loyalty. This loyalty to home, to church, to friends, and to principles, repeatedly dispelled the clouds of cynicism and mistrust and brightened the gloom of the darkest days. To the world without he maintained a steady calm, and to the casual observer there was nothing in any of his actions that betrayed the slightest anxiety, but rather an absorbing interest in the work at hand. The solemn sadness of Burke no doubt tended only to increase Graham's own predisposition to melancholy and this meeting of the minds really became a meeting of souls, for while Graham probably lacked Burke's originality and imagination he had a deep sympathy, says Torrens,

> with his [Burke's] unselfish hopes and fears, his scournful defiance of unpopularity, and his feminine sensitiveness to neglect or reproach, — his eager grasping at power, which he felt he would have used not unworthily, and the painful intensity of his consciousness that in his sunniest hours of triumph, disenchantment dogged his steps, and that his most loved illusions would forsake him ere he reached the grave.[23]

[22] Robert Brown to John Yule, July 25th, 1840, in *Graham Papers*.
[23] TORRENS, *op. cit.*, I, 168.

Naturally suspicious of people, aloof and independent, Graham did not have many close friends. People respected him as a man of ability, of decision, of unquestioned honesty; they did not look upon him as a 'good fellow', as one to whom they might go for sympathy and a heart-to-heart talk. In his home, on the other hand, it was different. Here he was the very embodiment of kindness and was all that a dutiful and loving father could be. Janus-like, therefore, he was one thing at home and among his few close friends, and another to the world at large.

But if Graham read Dryden, Pope, Shakespeare, and Burke for pleasure, he carefully studied Smith's *Wealth of Nations*, Hume's *Essay on Money*, and the various works of Ricardo in the hope that he might find an answer to some of his problems. In February 1821 Ricardo had advocated the repeal of the Corn Laws as the best remedy for agricultural distress.[24] He had admitted, however, that a moderate duty might be required to compensate the landlords for the special burdens they were compelled to bear. An independent politically, he had been a sponsor of parliamentary reform and the use of the ballot; he had opposed the passage of the Six Acts; and he had denounced all religious persecution. One of his best-known theories, that of the natural price of wages — the so-called 'Iron Law of Wages', hypothesized that the rate (price) of wages depended upon 'the price of the food, necessaries, and conveniences required for the support of the labourer and his family'.[25] In other words, wages tended to remain at the subsistence level. It was a pessimistic philosophy and one which deepened Graham's own tendency to melancholy. In 1816 Ricardo had advocated the resumption of cash payments, and Peel's Act of 1819[26] resulted from the efforts of a committee that had accepted Ricardo's reasoning. It provided for the resumption of cash payments by 1823.

But while Ricardo, Burke, Smith, and Hume exercised a great influence on Graham, some of his neighbours in Cumberland influenced him even more. Of these, one of the most important was the Reverend Richard Mathews, whose home, Wighton Hall,

---

[24] *Hansard*, New Ser., IV, 944-945.
[25] DAVID RICARDO, *Principles of Political Economy and Taxation*, ed. by E. C. K. Gonner, 70. See also W. J. ASHLEY, 'The Rehabilitation of Ricardo', in *Economic Journal*, I, 484-485; *D.N.B.*, XLVIII, 93-96.
[26] *Statutes at Large*, 59 Geo. III, c. 49.

was close to Netherby. Local jobbery and political dishonesty never failed to rouse this clergyman's anger. The cost of living, he said, needed to be lowered, and the rate of wages raised. At the same time trade should be freed of its multitudinous shackles and the excessive burden of taxes reduced. Mathews did not believe that the Constitution needed to be reformed so much as it needed to be honestly applied. With each one of these principles Graham was in substantial agreement.

At the agricultural shows at Workington, Graham had met Rooke, a member of the now disappearing middle-class yeomanry. If Torrens can be trusted, this industrious and independent class were 'the fairest dealers, the most independent jurors, the stoutest backers, the best neighbours, and the steadiest friends'.[27] But in 1820 the future looked rather hopeless to these men. For the most part they were unable to buy the new machinery that an improved husbandry had made necessary; they had lost faith in the power of Parliament to guarantee them a good price for their grain; and sinking deeper and deeper into debt, they became impatient and restless. Rooke was characteristic of this class. He had studied political economy and had become well versed in the views of Smith and others. With Graham he frequently discussed the question of prices, wages, profits, rents, poor laws, and population. Rooke had come to the same conclusion which Ricardo later reached, i.e., that free trade in grain was preferable to protection. To Graham, on the other hand, the question of the Corn Laws could not be separated from that of currency and both of these questions were intimately bound up with the problems of taxation, class, and party. It was chiefly on the question of currency that he was in disagreement with his own party — the Whigs.

In the fall of 1825 a serious business depression began and in a short while many financial institutions were forced to close their doors.[28] As unemployment became widespread the price of agricultural commodities began to decline, wheat dropping from an average of 66s. 6d. in 1825 to 56s. 11d. in 1826. Simultaneously the export trade slumped. The total declared value of woollen goods exported dropped from £6,185,648 in 1825 to £4,966,879 in

[27] TORRENS, op. cit., I, 170.
[28] The complete list of failures is given in Annual Register (1825), 123-124. See also WALPOLE, op. cit., II, 190-193.

1826;[29] that of cotton textiles from £18,359,526 to £14,093,369;[30] and that of British manufactured silk from £296,736, to £168,801.[31] The resulting stagnation in industry,[32] which forced many men out of work, was accompanied by extensive rioting.[33] The Government concluded that the chief cause of this economic depression was the rash speculation[34] brought about through the issuance of small notes by the country banks, and hence it decided to withdraw the one and two-pound notes from circulation. It is difficult to understand, however, why the Government should have held the small notes responsible because these rarely circulated in such populous centres as London and Manchester, the very centres of the speculative mania.[35]

Meanwhile, in the light of his discussions with Rooke and Mathews and his thorough study of Smith and Ricardo, Graham was carefully analysing the situation. The conclusions to which he came were embodied in a pamphlet, *Corn and Currency*, which he addressed to the landlords of England. The latter, he asserted in a typically pessimistic manner, would probably not pay any attention to his suggestions and would no doubt continue to dissipate their strength in petty party squabbles. As long as they continued so to act they formed but a mere rope of sand instead of the solid phalanx which their control of the Crown, Lords, and Commons could enable them to form. The power of a united aristocracy would, he thought, be almost invincible. In fact there could be but one check upon that potential power and that was the force of public opinion. And by 'the public' Graham, as well as the other liberals of the day, did not mean the great masses but those in 'the middle ranks of life', a numerous group, which, as he put it, were 'removed alike from the wants of labour and the cravings of ambition'.[36]

After asserting that the questions of the Corn Laws and the currency were indissolubly linked together and had to be treated

[29] PORTER, *op. cit.*, I, 192.   [30] *Ibid.*, 208.   [31] *Ibid.*, 260.
[32] See SMART, *op. cit.*, II, 329.
[33] Riots occurred in such places as Norwich, Paisley, Manchester, and Glasgow (chefly among the hand-loom weavers).
[34] For an interesting account of the rashness of much of this speculation see *Annual Register* (1824), 1-3.
[35] See SMART, *op. cit.*, II, 339.
[36] JAMES R. G. GRAHAM, *Corn and Currency in an Address to the Land Owners*, 10 (Hereinafter cited as *Corn and Currency*).

as one subject, he went on to deprecate the attempts that had been made since 1815 to raise the home price of grain above the continental level. The obvious result of such a policy was an increase in wages, but so long as the price of food was high an increase in wages could be of no particular value to the labourer. In other words, while nominal wages had increased, real wages had not. Moreover, high wages were economically undesirable because, declared Graham, wages could be increased only at the expense of profits. He was here, of course, resting his case on the false assumption that wages are paid exclusively out of profits. On the other hand, rents on the better soils increased when inferior soils were forced into cultivation. As Graham's views on wages were based partially on Ricardo, so his theory of rent was almost identical with that of John Stuart Mill, who wrote: 'The rent . . . which any land will yield is the excess of its produce, beyond what would be returned to the same capital if employed on the worst land in cultivation.'[37] It was certainly no pleasure to the landlords to be told by one of their own group that their best customer was the manufacturer and that the latter's prosperity was dependent upon high profits which the high price of agricultural products reduced by making high wages a necessary *quid pro quo*.

From the subject of wages, profits, and rent, Graham proceeded to a treatment of the much-debated Corn Laws. The Laws of 1815 and 1822, he declared, had not been successful because, in the first place, wheat, instead of remaining at the expected 80s., had been steadily dropping, and in the second place, rents, many of which had been based on the 80s. wheat price expectation, had also been steadily falling.[38] By 1826 Graham, and many other landlords, had therefore come to the conclusion that rents and prices could not be kept up by law even when a monopoly of the home market up to 80s. was given to wheat. In the light of these facts, he advocated a reduction of the Corn Laws to such a duty 'as may amply countervail the peculiar taxes to which the produce of the soil is subjected'.[39] Such 'peculiar' taxes were the land-tax, poor-rate,

---

[37] JOHN S. MILL, *Principles of Political Economy*, 235.

[38] The law of 1815 provided for a sliding scale of duties by which no corn was to be imported until the home price of 80s. was reached. Then the ports would be opened, only to close again when the home price dropped to 70s. Since the 80s. was not reached, this law never went into effect. *Statutes at Large*, 3 Geo. IV, c. 60.

[39] GRAHAM, *Corn and Currency*, 14.

county-rate, highway-rate, church-rate, and others. While the duty should be fixed at a point where it would just compensate the landlord for the taxation to which he was subjected, it was impossible, declared Graham, to fix the duty at all until the price of money was fixed. He knew at first hand that the subject of money was 'foreign to the tastes of the country gentlemen',[40] but unless they wished to be completely ruined they would simply have to study it and learn how it affected the price of grain. Before Pitt debased the currency in 1797, the price of wheat had for 150 years been less than 50s. per quarter, and since Peel's Act of 1819 had restored cash payments, approximately the same price had prevailed.[41] So it was not the price of wheat that had been changing, but the price (value) of money. For the benefit of his readers Graham prepared one chart showing the amount of Bank of England notes in circulation, and another showing the average price of wheat.[42] From a comparison of the two, he hoped that the landlords would see for themselves that increases in the issues of the Bank had in almost every case led to a rise in prices. With the return to cash payments and the gold standard in 1819, a fall in the price of wheat immediately followed the contraction of the currency. To Graham it was impossible to escape the conclusion that a contraction of the currency had been responsible for the financial difficulties of the landowners, and that an inflation of the currency had helped to cure them. The Corn Laws did not and could not, according to his line of reasoning, protect the landed interest against a fall in prices resulting from a deflation of the currency, while on the other hand, they did benefit the annuitant and the fund-holder. Furthermore, he seriously questioned the right of the Bank of England to increase or decrease the quantity of circulating medium at its own discretion.[43] This was a serious matter to the young lord of Netherby because the Bank, answerable neither to the public nor to the legislature, was an 'irresponsible' organization. In addition, this Bank had advocated the return to the gold standard in 1819, and had thereby, said Graham, sponsored a policy the result of which was to transfer 'the property of the debtor to the creditor — of the

---

[40] GRAHAM, *Corn and Currency*, 22.
[41] Actually the average for 1820-1829 was 58s. 5d. See PORTER, *op. cit.*, ed. by F. W. Hirst (New ed.), 181.
[42] GRAHAM, *Corn and Currency*, 30.
[43] *Ibid.*, 58.

Land Owner, to those who have charges on his estate'.[44] All this would not have been quite so serious had it been accompanied by a decrease in the costs of government, but such had not been the case.

Graham's study of Peel's Act had convinced him that it benefited the fund-holder at the expense of the landlord, because it conferred on the fund-holder 'a benefit, to the extent of the depreciation of the money which he advanced', which, in many cases, was equal to 35 per cent.[45] And Graham, characteristic of his class, resented the steady advance of the annuitants and fund-holders to a position of power and influence. If Parliament refused to redress these wrongs, he told the landlords, the ancient aristocracy of England would ultimately be sacrificed to creditors and annuitants — a totally undesirable class.

Since rents had decreased about thirty per cent after the passage of Peel's Act, and since 'the addition to the debts, the mortgages, the settled encumbrances' on the landlord's property was 'equal to the increased value of money' (which Graham estimated at 30 per cent),[46] he advocated, along with a freer trade in corn and the abolition of the monopoly of the Bank of England — so as to secure free trade in money as well [47] — the imposition of a new tax, a tax of thirty per cent on all annuitants.[48]

In short, therefore, Graham's advice to the discouraged and heavily-burdened landlords was to consent to a downward revision of the Corn Laws, retaining only a moderate fixed duty;[49] to insist on a complete revision of all other monopolies such as the Bank of England and the East and West Indies monopolies; and to demand a great reduction in taxes on land.[50] But could Parliament reduce taxes and hence reduce its revenue? Yes! by a reduction of salaries and pensions, the application of the £5,000,000 in the sinking fund to annual expenditures, and by the direct tax on annuitant.[51]

[44] *Ibid.*, 66.   [45] *Ibid.*, 68.   [46] *Ibid.*, 87.
[47] Western, speaking for the landed interests, had declared that Peel's Act was the sole cause of the agricultural depression: 'It is not a *ruinous* abundance of corn, but a destructive famine of money that is the bane of the country; let us have plenty of corn and plenty of money.' Squire Western, 'Second Address to the Landowners of the United Empire', cited in BARNES, *op. cit.*, 175.
[48] GRAHAM, *Corn and Currency*, 102-103.
[49] 15s. a quarter would be, he thought, a sufficient duty to countervail the special burdens of the landowners. *Ibid.*, 99.   [50] *Ibid.*, 101, 102.
[51] To add weight to this argument, Graham quoted from Hume's *Essay on Public Credit*: 'The revenue must be raised from a continued taxation of the annuitant.'

E

The weakest part of this programme was the suggested tax on annuitants, and it was immediately and properly denounced by them as class legislation (of the landowners against their creditors), and the imposition of a tax on annuities payable from the Exchequer was, as Parker has correctly observed, 'a departure by the State from its contract that such annuities should not be made to bear exceptional burdens'.[52] On the other hand, Graham's class, with less logic to be sure, favoured this part of his programme but firmly resisted the free trade in corn.

Earl Grey, the leader of the Whig party, could not agree that the protective laws were the cause of the agricultural distress, but he did agree that no corn duty could be accurately set until the value of money had also been fixed. The labouring classes, while they doubtless were favourable to Graham's point of view, had no effective means of making their opinion felt.

The Tory *Quarterly Review*, in answering *Corn and Currency*, declared that Graham had mistaken cause for effect, and that as long as paper was payable in cash on demand, an increased issue of Bank of England, as well as country bank notes, 'must always be the consequence, and never the cause, of a rise in the market price of wheat. Whenever wheat advances in price, the credit of the grower is extended, — bankers become more free and liberal in discounting his bills, — and by this means an increased quantity of bank paper is thrown into general circulation'.[53] On the first point, according to the quantity theory of money, Graham was right and the landlords wrong because an increased amount of circulating medium would naturally raise the price of wheat, and not the reverse as the *Quarterly Review* contended. Furthermore, while it was true that bankers would be more liberal in discounting the landlords' bills when the price of wheat was rising, it was also possible that they would be less liberal in discounting the bills of those who would be adversely affected by an increased price of wheat.

The *Westminster Review*, spokesman of the philosophical

GRAHAM, *Corn and Currency*, 115. He would exempt from such a tax, however, the merchants and manufacturers, because, like the landowners, they were producers. Annuitants, on the other hand, were nothing but drones and sluggards. *Ibid.*

[52] PARKER, *Life of Graham*, I, 66.

[53] *The Quarterly Review*, XXV, 467 (Hereinafter cited as *Quart. Rev.*).

radicals, declared that *Corn and Currency* was a pamphlet which held 'a conspicuous place among the endeavours which have been made to show the propriety of robbing the public creditor'.[54] It went on to criticize Graham for having attacked two classes of men, those who lent money to the State, and those who lent it to the landlords. On the question of Graham's proposed tax of thirty per cent on all annuitants, the *Westminster Review* asked why it was that the landlords and the Government should have the privilege of contracting debts without paying. 'For one reason,' it declared in answering its own question, 'and one reason only, that it is for the interest of the landlords.'[55]

William Cobbett's bitter attacks on Graham's pamphlet probably did more than anything else to popularize it and to bring publicity to its author. In 1826 Cobbett had begun his famous tours, traversing England on horseback and printing in his *Political Register* accounts of his travels. Because of its interesting style and news, as well as the fact that its price had been reduced to twopence, this journal now enjoyed great popularity. In 1830 his articles, written while on tour, were collected into one set called *Rural Rides*. On Saturday, September 23rd, 1826, he began his attacks on Graham by calling him a 'conceited and impudent plagiarist'.[56] On the twenty-ninth, after describing landlords collectively as mean and cowardly reptiles, he overdid himself in his castigation of Graham. He had been attacking the proposal to tax annuitants, many of whom, said Cobbett, were widows and orphans, while the Church still kept its income from its livings. 'Oh, no!' he said, 'thou stupid, thou empty-headed, thou insolent aristocratic pamphleteer, the widow and the orphan *shall not* be robbed of their bread, while this Parson of Droycot Foliot keeps the income of his living!'[57]

While *Corn and Currency* did not influence the policy of the Government in 1826, it did act as a potent factor in helping to popularize the cause of free trade, partly because it was no common thing for a young landlord, possessing one of the largest estates in the realm, to advocate a repeal of the Corn Laws, or even a reduc-

[54] *The Westminster Review*, VI, 272 (Hereinafter cited as *West. Rev.*).
[55] *Ibid.*
[56] WILLIAM COBBETT, *Rural Rides in the Southern, Western and Eastern Counties of England, Together with Tours in Scotland and in the Northern and Midland Counties of England*, ed. by George D. H. Cole and Margaret Cole, II, 427.
[57] *Ibid.*. 443.

tion of the duties. If, therefore, the pamphlet caused annuitants and landlords alike bitterly to assail its author, at the same time it served to bring Graham's name before the country. Part of the anger of the landlords was assuaged by Graham's attacks on the rentiers, a group which had for years been very unpopular with the landed class.

CHAPTER V

PEACE, ECONOMY, AND REFORM

In 1826 Graham accepted an invitation to stand for election in Carlisle, where he became the popular liberal champion against the powerful Tory house of Lowther. Typical of Carlisle elections, this was a bitterly fought campaign enlivened by a first-rate riot. The crowd, soon after the arrival of the election writ, met Sir Philip Musgrave, one of the candidates, complained about his having voted for the Corn Laws, and demanded that he promise to vote in favour of parliamentary reform.[1] Not satisfied with Musgrave's answer, the crowd, according to the *Annual Register's* chronicler, 'assailed [Sir Philip] with stones, brickbats, and other missils'.[2] In describing this scene about a year later, Graham admitted that this 'badgering' of the candidate had probably been 'carried somewhat to excess'.[3] Sir Philip thought so too, for he beat a hasty retreat to the house of a friend where he securely barred himself in. The crowd followed closely at his heels, and, surrounding the house, frightened Musgrave with their lusty hooting and jeering. The mayor and two constables, not a whit less unpopular than the candidate himself, were subjected to vocal and physical abuse when they attempted to rescue him. At this juncture one of the county magistrates swore in a special force of 300 constables; another sent to a nearby garrison for military aid. Both groups approached Carlisle, but when the constables saw the military coming to the city they withdrew, leaving the military to take charge of the situation. The crowd, thoroughly detesting the intervention of the troops, greeted them with a chorus of boos and a volley of stones and brickbats. The nervous magistrates answered by ordering the troops to fix bayonets. At this show of force, the crowd retreated, but the soldiers nevertheless charged into them, killing two and wounding many others.[4] In relating what had taken place Graham

---

[1] See *Annual Register* (1826), Chron., 94-95.　　　　[2] *Ibid.*, 94.

[3] *Hansard*, New Ser., XVII, 200.

[4] At the inquest which was subsequently held, the verdict of the jury was that Isabell Patterson and Mary Birrell were killed by shots fired by soldiers of the 55th regiment. It concluded, however, 'That in consequence of the Riot Act having been read, and the mob not dispersing, the soldiers were in the first instance justified in

declared that the use of the military had been unnecessary and that the civil authorities could satisfactorily have handled the difficulty. He told the House of Commons that this case was sufficient to prove to them that something ought to be done to prevent the interference of the military in elections. Musgrave, of course, said that the local constabulary had proved insufficient to preserve peace and order, and for that reason had closed the polling. Peel, while defending the use of the military, because Carlisle's whole civil force consisted of only two constables, congratulated Graham on his wisdom in bringing to the House the facts in the case because it would help to secure a more adequate civil force for that city. It was Graham's conviction that the rioting had broken loose when the crowd feared that the military force would interfere in the election on behalf of one of the candidates.[5]

During this exciting election Graham advocated a reduction in the Corn Laws on the grounds that they were harmful both to producers and to consumers; a reduction in Crown patronage; the sweeping away of rotten boroughs and transferring their representation to the larger cities; the removal of religious disabilities; and retrenchment in all branches of government. The popularity of these proposed reforms, and the unpopularity of his opponent, combined to win the election for Graham.

His first speech on returning to Parliament was one in which he opposed, on the grounds that it was contrary to the spirit of English law and custom, Horton's request that Parliament seriously consider a petition from a number of citizens of Glasgow in favour of emigration as a relief measure. But while he opposed emigration he told the House that some measure of relief for the destitute in Glasgow was imperative because conditions there were steadily getting worse. The hand-loom weavers were now receiving only five shillings a week for working fourteen hours a day. Many of them, far in arrears on their rent, were being ejected from their tenements. Oatmeal and potatoes were practically their sole food, and thousands, unable to secure enough, were on the verge of starvation. And what was the chief reason for this state of affairs?

firing their muskets; but the jurors cannot refrain from expressing, as their opinion, that they continued to fire in a very indiscreet and inconsiderate manner, and particularly at private houses, when the necessity for so doing seems to them to have ceased.' *Annual Register* (1826), 95.

[5] *Hansard*, New Ser., XVII, 207-208.

Simply, said Graham, that the hand-loom weavers were unable to compete with the power-looms, and furthermore were unable easily to convert themselves into power-loom weavers. In fact their condition was so bad that while Graham would not agree to granting them aid to emigrate, he was willing to agree to a grant of public money for their relief.[6]

While very little was accomplished in the short session of 1826, the following year was one of great political change. On February 18th, 1827, Liverpool, who had been Prime Minister since 1812, became paralysed and never regained the use of his faculties. His cabinet, long at odds on many issues, personal as well as political, began to split into factions. One section,[7] led by Canning, advocated Catholic Emancipation, free-trade doctrines, and the principle of national independence in South America, Greece, and Portugal. The other section, led by Peel and Wellington, was decidedly conservative on all these issues, although Peel was beginning to waver on the Catholic question. Because Canning would not accept a subordinate position in any ministry, and because Peel thought himself too young to be Prime Minister and considered an all-Protestant cabinet to be hopeless, and since Wellington declared that he was not quite 'mad enough' to accept the premiership, the King was at last forced to ask Canning to accept the seals of office. When this champion of Catholic Emancipation took office, on April 10th,[8] Bathurst, Eldon, Melville, Peel, Wellington, and Westmorland all resigned. Canning was thereupon forced to enlist the aid of the Whigs, a task made easier because the Whig party was now divided against itself. When he agreed that the Catholic question and parliamentary reform should be held in abeyance, a group of Whigs found it an easy matter to join him.[9] Sir John Copeley, now Lord Lyndhurst, was elevated to the Lord High Chancellorship, the post which Eldon had held for so many years; Bourne went to the Home Office,

[6] *Ibid.*, XVI, 299-300.
[7] GEORGE C. BRODERICK and J. K. FOTHERINGHAM, '*The History of England from 1801 to 1837*', in *Political History of England*, ed. by William Hunt and Reginald Poole, XI, 226 et seq.
[8] *Ibid.* See also, *Annual Register* (1827), 100 et seq.
[9] As a matter of fact, a body of Whigs had for some time considered Canning a member of their group. They agreed on both foreign and commercial policies, but were not of one mind on the question of reform.

Ward to the Foreign Office, Robinson, now Lord Goderich, to the Colonial Office, and C. Lamb to Ireland as Chief Secretary. Grey and Althorp, who were favourable to reform, would not join Canning at all.

This cabinet met its first Parliament in May, and due to Wellington's opposition in the Lords, was immediately beaten on its Corn Bill. Before the cabinet could accomplish anything at all, the session was over and five weeks later the Prime Minister was dead. When Goderich then failed to form a working government, the King summoned Wellington, who accepted office on the understanding that the Catholic question should be treated as an open question and that both the Lord Chancellor and the Lord Lieutenant of Ireland should be Protestants.[10] When Peel joined Wellington's cabinet as Home Secretary, Huskisson, Palmerston, and Grant also came in. Goulburn became Chancellor of the Exchequer and Ellenborough Lord Privy Seal. During this same year, Curwen, who represented the County of Cumberland, died and Graham succeeded to his seat.

The session of 1828 was a busy one for Graham. In Parliament he was active in the interest of economy and reform; out of Parliament he was busy concocting political schemes. His zeal for economy found an outlet on March 12th when Joseph Hume called the attention of the House to the 'novel, injudicious, and ruinous' manner in which army promotions were made.[11] On May 2nd, 1825, said Hume, officers were given permission to sell their half-pay commissions to officers of a lesser rank on the full pay. Hume calculated that this procedure had cost the country, in one year's sale of commissions, about £656,785. In all, he said, 765 officers had sold their commissions and there were instances of lieutenants and ensigns who had sold out to young men who had never seen a single day of service. This was just the type of speech that Graham liked to hear. It 'had disclosed to the House', he said, 'a source of profligate expenditure and of corrupt influence, which required to be checked without delay'.[12] Then he turned to Palmerston, the Secretary for War, for information relative to two cases. One was that of an army officer who had been serving in the

---

[10] Wellington to Peel, January 9th, 1825, cited in CHARLES STUART PARKER, *Sir Robert Peel*, II, 27 (Hereinafter cited as *Life of Peel*).

[11] *Hansard*, New Ser., XVIII, 1126 et seq.   [12] *Ibid.*, 1129.

civil office for fifteen years but who was so employed that after those years, during which he received no money in virtue of his military commissions, he was not allowed to dispose of his half-pay. 'By that arrangement, a charge which had no existence for the last fifteen years, had been thrown upon the public. Now, did, he wished to know, this gentleman still continue in his civil employment?'[13] The other case concerned a similar instance in Ireland. He hoped that Palmerston could prove that he, Graham, was misinformed; if not, a motion for a committee of inquiry was certainly in order. The Secretary for War answered that he had no objection to granting the desired returns; that he knew nothing about the case in Ireland; that the former case was an exception to the general practice; and that he had no way of knowing how all the officers were employed.[14]

But Graham had not finished questioning the Government. He was intensely interested in the currency question and relative to it he had three questions to ask. In the first place, did the Government intend to adhere to the policy of preventing, after April 5th, the issuing, re-issuing and negotiating in England of small notes (less than £5)? Secondly, would such notes be permitted to circulate in Ireland and Scotland? Finally, did the Government intend to alter the law of banking so as to permit joint-stock companies of more than six partners, within 65 miles of London, to issue bills of exchange for less than £50?[15]

The Chancellor of the Exchequer, Goulburn, answered that the Government could see no reason for departing from the policy of 1826 with respect to the small notes, that it would follow the same course in England as it had in Ireland and Scotland, and that the question of the joint-stock companies had to be taken up with the Bank of England.

But this knotty currency question once more came to the fore when, on June 3rd, Goulburn moved for leave to bring in a Bill to check the circulation in England of the popular £1 Scottish bank notes. In opposing this motion, Graham admitted that he had voted for Peel's Act of 1819, which provided for a resumption of cash payments by 1823 at the Bank of England, and which had declared trade in bullion free. He explained his vote by saying that he had then yielded to 'the most palpable folly that ever had been

[13] *Ibid.*   [14] *Ibid.*, 1133-1134.   [15] *Ibid.*, XIX, 190.

palmed upon that House as sound and wise policy', and that he had been misled by Ricardo, 'a very high authority', into believing that the whole difference of the standard of value would be the difference between the value estimated by the Mint and the price of the gold bullion, a difference of about five per cent.[16] He knew now that he had been mistaken in 1819 and that he could therefore now be charged with inconsistency. But in 1819 Graham and many others had felt, as Redford puts it, that 'the degree of inflation was measured by the premium on gold, which was merely about five per cent, and that prices would only fall to that extent'.[17] As a matter of fact, the Bank began to cash the small notes (under £5) in May 1821 and prices promptly dropped from 30 to 40 per cent. The Act of 1819, while it gave a limited trial to Ricardo's plans, had contemplated the prohibition of any additional issues of small notes, and gold had been accumulated for the purpose of withdrawing them. The break in prices in 1821 led Parliament to change its mind, and the following year it sanctioned the use of small notes until the year 1833. Four years later (1826) Parliament changed its mind again and decided that no more notes of less than £5 denomination were to be stamped for duty and that none already stamped were to be re-issued after April 5th, 1829. It did so because it rightly understood that where coin and paper currency of the same denomination circulated concurrently, the latter would drive the former out of circulation. At the same time Parliament authorized the formation of joint-stock banks with power to issue notes, provided that such banks were not less than 65 miles from London.[18]

But Graham was definitely opposed to any attempt to suppress the Scottish notes. And now he had better authority than Ricardo — the report of the committee of 1828 — which had stated that during the years in which Scotland had had a paper currency for paying all sums above 20 shillings, England had had a currency consisting exclusively of metal to the legal exclusion of all notes

---

[16] *Hansard*, New Ser., XIX, 993.

[17] ARTHUR REDFORD, *The Economic History of England (1760-1860)*, 156. Ricardo advocated the return to the gold standard but not to gold coin. He desired the small £1 and £2 notes based on gold.

[18] Huskisson looked upon this surrender by the Bank of England as entitling the Bank to insist on the suppression of the small notes. See CHARLES R. FAY, *Great Britain from Adam Smith to the Present Day, An Economic and Social Survey*, 96.

under £5, and that both systems had worked satisfactorily. It appeared to him, therefore, that the suppression of the Scottish £1 notes was unnecessary. In the county of Cumberland, said Graham, these Scottish notes were used almost to the complete exclusion of English coins. If the people in that section of the country agreed on nothing else, he continued, they were agreed that the Scottish notes were preferable to English coins. At least seven-eighths of the rents in his county were paid in Scottish notes. To substantiate his statement that these notes were 'safe' and not a cause of financial instability, Graham quoted from Liverpool and Goderich, both of whom had declared that since failures in England had not been accompanied by failures in Scotland, there was an unsound currency in one country and a sound one in the other.[19] Furthermore, the thirty or more Scottish banks had stood firmly, while in England, according to Clapham, 'failures were astonishingly frequent, even apart from times of special crisis'.[20] To Graham this was beginning to assume the aspects of a banking instead of a currency problem. What had been England's experience, he asked the House, in the suppression of small notes? It had been decided in 1815, he said, to suppress these notes, and both the Bank of England and the country banks had contracted their issues in preparation for the change. What had happened? The price of wheat had dropped from the 107 shillings per quarter of 1813 to 64 shillings, and the number of bankruptcies had increased from 1000 for 1814 to 2300 for 1816. Then, said Graham, the Government 'postponed the payment of the one-pound notes to a more distant period; and the effect was, that prices got up again, and a season of prosperity ensued'.[21] And that was the record of the first period of speculation. A second occurred in 1825 when the banks, hearing that one-pound notes were to be suppressed, acted as before and contracted their discounts. Once again the result was general distress. When the price of wheat went down to 43 shillings in 1822, the Marquis of Londonderry declared that the currency of England was too contracted, and there was forced into circulation an additional £4,000,000 and the operation of the Small-Note Repeal Bill was postponed till 1833. Wheat immedi-

---

[19] *Hansard*, New Ser., XIX, 996.
[20] CLAPHAM, *Econ. Hist. of Britain*, I, 266.
[21] *Hansard*, New Ser., XIX, 997.

ately went up to 68 shillings and prosperity returned. These experiences had convinced Graham of one indisputable fact:

> ... the value of money in any country must always rise or fall in an inverse ratio to the quantity of it. The quantity of commodities remaining the same, if there was an increase in the quantity of money prices must rise, and the quantity decreased, a fall would as certainly be the consequence. Whether the quantity of money was decreased, or the supply of commodities increased in the country, the effect upon prices was the same. Therefore the House would perceive that it was just the same thing to the landed interest, whether the quantity of money in the country was contracted, or the ports thrown open to foreign importation.[22]

Did the House require proof that the price of wheat was regulated by the amount of money in circulation? He could supply that proof. From 1810 to 1818 there had been about £21,000,000 of currency in circulation and the average price of wheat was 92s. 4d. per quarter, and this despite the fact that during those years the ports had been open to foreign importation. From 1819 to 1827[23] the note currency was diminished to about £10,000,000 and while 'the ports had been hermetically sealed, the average maintained was only 57s. 10d'.[24]

Tampering with the currency in 1822 had caused the price of wheat to go down to 43 shillings per quarter. The landowners had thereupon experienced great losses because the value of money increased while at the same time contracts remained fixed at their nominal amounts. The landowner got less for his products while his fixed charges were actually increased. He paid in a currency thirty per cent higher in value than that which he had borrowed and was compelled to retrench, to live niggardly and to squeeze his tenants, 'or', prophesied Graham, 'the monied man, in five years, walked in and took possession of his estate'.[25]

To Graham the only real value of a currency was its convenience for circulation. For that reason the £5 notes and those of larger denominations were not of much value. If £1 notes produced panics, as had been alleged, why was it, he asked, that Scotland

---

[22] *Hansard*, New Ser., XIX, 999.

[23] The official statement of the circulation of bank-notes and bank-note bills on April 6th, 1821, showed a total of £22,976,425 of which amount £6,481,233 was in £1 and £2 notes. See *Annual Register* (1821), Chron., 69.

[24] *Hansard*, New Ser., XIX, 1000.   [25] *Ibid.*, 1001.

had had no panics?[26] Had not Pitt resorted to £1 notes in 1793 to check the panic of that year? The same thing had been done in 1825 too, and Graham could see no reason for abolishing the paper system simply because it might be in need of some regulation. To abolish the £1 notes because there had been abuses in the issuance of these notes was equivalent, he said, 'to the stopping of the supply of water to the Metropolis without providing another because the present supply was not so pure as it ought to be.'[27] It was his firm conviction that

> The paper currency was one of the great wheels of our system, . . . it was cheaper and better, and more easily managed. Paper, convertible into gold on demand, was, beyond a doubt, preferable to any other. It was more plastic, and could be more easily applied to all our purposes of commerce . . . They had commenced, and had gone on with the paper system too far to recede. The debt had been, for the greater part, contracted in paper, and must be paid in paper.[28]

He then concluded this needlessly long address, in which he repeated much of the material from *Corn and Currency*, by moving for the appointment of a select committee to inquire into the currency problem to determine whether or not it was expedient to alter the currency laws. Liddell 'cheerfully' supported this motion, as did Howick, Ridley, Hume, Burdett, and many others who had taken a lively interest in this question. Denison, on the other hand, opposed it on the grounds that cheap paper caused prices to rise and hence drove gold out of circulation. Peel objected to the motion because he was opposed to 'unsettling' things. The motion was defeated by the huge majority of 154 to 45.[29]

But it was Graham's efforts on behalf of economy, a subject which very few knew or cared much about, that gained for him popularity both in and out of Parliament, rather than these strictures on the currency question. Furthermore, economy was a subject more strictly in the Whig line, and the party decided to attack the Wellington administration by making motions for retrenchment and economy. 'Their foremost speaker in debates

[26] *Ibid.*, 1006.
[27] Quoted in the *London Morning Chronicle*, June 4th, 1828 (Hereinafter cited as *Chronicle*).
[28] *Hansard*, New Ser., XIX, 1010.
[29] *Ibid.*, 1099.

of this nature', says Butler, 'was young Sir James Graham.'[30] The leaders of the Whig party were overjoyed that Graham was willing to assume the leadership in a task which to many of them was highly onerous, and Graham, himself believing implicitly in retrenchment, careless alike of praise or blame and independent of party ties, was glad to bear the brunt of such an attack. He therefore found himself working in company with the Whigs because their principles now conformed with his.

The campaign for economy was officially begun on February 12th, 1830. Since the depression of that year was chiefly in agriculture, it was a good time for a landlord to demand economy in government. In Ireland, the potato crop failed; in England, rents went unpaid, for although the price of grain was rather high, it was better quality foreign grain that commanded the highest prices.[31] Rick-burnings began in Kent in August and soon spread to Surrey, Sussex, and other nearby counties. The grievances which led to this lawlessness were the game laws, the obnoxious Poor Law, the equally obnoxious tithe, enclosures, low wages, the increased use of machinery, and the high cost of living.[32] The Hammonds[33] have painted a moving picture of the plight of the agricultural labourers living on small portions of bread and potatoes in a state of desperation. In the extreme north conditions were not so bad, but in parts of southern England many expected a widespread insurrection to break out, and the frequent burning of haystacks, barns, and machines struck terror into the hearts of the landlords.

Neither Whigs nor Tories could be expected to attack the Corn Laws, the root of much of this trouble, and so the former fastened upon demands for governmental economy instead. When the Chancellor of the Exchequer, on February 12th, brought in the annual Supply Bill, Graham immediately moved for a reduction in the salaries of all officials.[34] It was an unsavoury task which Graham now undertook, for although the M.P.s were in favour

[30] JAMES R. M. BUTLER, *The Passing of the Great Reform Bill*, 69 (Hereinafter cited as *Great Reform Bill*).

[31] SMART, *Economic Annals*, II, 513.

[32] See CLAPHAM, *op. cit.*, I, 139.

[33] JOHN L. HAMMOND and BARBARA HAMMOND, *The Village Labourer, 1760-1832*, 217 et seq. (Hereinafter cited as *Village Labourer*).

[34] *Annual Register* (1830), 32; *Hansard*, New Ser., XXII, 435 et seq.

of economy in the abstract, they seldom liked it when it affected them personally. He did not shrink from the task, however, for his sympathies went out to those who paid the taxes rather than to those who lived from the public purse. When the Government increased the value of money without reducing taxes, it encroached, declared the member for Cumberland, upon the comforts of the labouring classes. He had heard some talk of 'luxuries', but where were they? Kings, Ministers, East India-men, Jew Loan Contractors, India Nabobs might have splendid palaces, but

> where was the furniture that adorned the poor man's cottage? All was gone — pinching hunger and despair now held their place in the labourer's habitation. The weaver in the county which he represented earned but 4s. 2d. a week, out of which he had to supply his family. Oatmeal, water, and peas were his sole food, and for these he had to work fourteen or fifteen hours a day.[35]

An ameliorative measure of some kind was imperative but there was a huge obstacle to overcome. The Government was inexorable, as Graham sarcastically explained it: 'The Duke of Wellington had said, "You shall not inquire." If you argue the question keenly in print, the Attorney-General is ready to pounce upon you.'[36] These remarks drew from the House some lusty cheering, but it is difficult to see how either a reduction in salaries or a reduction in the number of government employees could have helped very much. In the first place, the masses would not benefit to any noticeable extent because neither of these proposals would materially reduce the high cost of living.[37] And as for the hand-loom weavers in Cumberland, it was hopeless for them to continue the competition with the power-loom.[38] On the other hand, a reduction in the costs of government would result in a slight decrease in taxation, which, so far as the landed interest was concerned, was an improvement devoutly to be wished. The basis of Graham's motion for a reduction in official salaries was that the Bank Restriction Act of 1797 had caused a depreciation in the

---

[35] *Ibid.*, 444.   [36] *Ibid.*

[27] Using 1790 as the base year, the cost of living index number for 1830 stood at 108. This was five points below the average of 113 for the ten preceding years. It rose the next year, in spite of government economies, to 111. See NORMAN SILBERLING, 'British Prices and Business Cycles, 1779-1850', in *Review of Economic Statistics*, supplement (1923), 234-235. Cited in CLAPHAM, *op. cit.*, I, App., 602.

[38] See SMART, *op. cit.*, II, 511.

currency, a rise in prices, and an increase in salaries. But the Act of 1819 had restored the value of money by about 25 per cent and had reduced both wages and prices, and therefore, since high prices had brought high salaries, low prices ought now to bring low salaries. He agreed, however, to exempt from prospective salary reductions the Privy Purse and the Royal establishment because these rested on agreements made at the beginning of the reign and as such were sacred and inviolable obligations. The members of the Army and Navy should also be exempt; the former because their salaries were based on a contractual agreement to serve a stated number of years at a specified salary; the latter because their pay had been fixed in 1798 when prices were comparable to what they were in 1830.[39] But because their salaries had been raised without a sufficiently good reason Graham included in his motion all the military officers who held civil posts. Perhaps the House would like to hear some figures that were not only interesting but also convincing! In 1797 the annual salary of the Governor of New Brunswick was £1000, it was now £1500; that of the Governor of Prince Edward Island had been £800 and was now £1000; that of the Governor of Nova Scotia had been £500 and was now £1000; that of the Governor of Port Jackson had been £1000 and was now £2000. The same situation, he told the House, existed in the military service. In 1793 the cost of the Army, including half-pay, was only £2,005,000; it was now £8,000,000. In the same years the cost of the Navy had risen from £2,450,000 to £6,000,000; that of the Ordnance had advanced from £459,000 to £1,400,000. The entire expenditure in 1793 was only £5,300,000, while in 1829 it had been £15,500,000. In the Civil Service the average annual salary had risen from £84 to £121. The real significance of these salary increases, said Graham, was that they had been doubled while the price of food had been halved. It was therefore absolutely necessary that the balance be readjusted.[40]

This would have been the ideal place for Graham to have concluded his address, but the temptation to make some cutting remarks about his opponents was more than he could resist. He declared that he had opposed Wellington's elevation to power in

---

[39] According to Silberling, the index for 1798 was 121 against 108 for 1830. SILBERLING, 'British Prices and Business Cycles 1779-1850', *loc. cit.*, 602.
[40] *Hansard*, New Ser., XXII, 445 et seq.

1828 because he did not think that 'a military was the best preparation for a statesman seeking to administer the affairs of a free people'.[41] Not only that, but hadn't the Duke just recently appointed 'a tame elephant' to the Board of Control?

It was, apart from the offensive personal remarks, a very powerful address, and Robert Peel, though defending the Government on the grounds that it had effected all the economies which circumstances permitted, was greatly impressed by the statistics which Graham had produced as well as by his obvious industriousness, and paid Graham the compliment of saying that he trusted that the House would 'ever remember the eloquent and impressive sentiments in which his warning was conveyed'.[42] To meet these stinging charges of extravagance, the Government brought in a motion of its own by which a saving of about £1,000,000 was effected. Graham then withdrew his motion.

Increasingly conscious of his own powers, encouraged by the Whigs, and carried on by the momentum of his first successful drive for economy, Graham again advanced to the attack on March 12th by proposing a resolution calling for the abolition of the office of Treasurer of the Navy.[43] It was an office the duties of which were so small that they could easily be performed by the Paymaster and a saving of £3000 would be effected. Huskisson, Hume, and others supported this motion while Peel led the opposition. The latter was no doubt partly right when he said the object of this motion was merely 'to visit those who made this appointment with condemnation and censure',[44] because while Graham was chiefly interested in the saving that would result from the abolition of the office, the Whig party was naturally attempting to censure the Government. Peel and his colleagues declared that the office was a necessary one and succeeded in defeating Graham's motion by a vote of 188 to 90.[45]

Two weeks later the young economizer launched his third attack. He was somewhat reluctant to bring up the subject of economy again because he might gain notoriety as an economical reformer and if this was joined to his other character, that of a

[41] *Ibid.*, 449.
[42] *Ibid.*, 471. The *Chronicle* (February 13th, 1830, p. 4), described the speech as one which rose 'to a very high pitch of eloquence'.
[43] *Hansard*, New Ser., XXIII, 256.   [44] *Ibid.*, 286.
[45] The division is to be found in *Ibid.*, 295.

F

parliamentary reformer, it 'might make him as obnoxious a person as any in that House'.[46] But was there really any need to retain the office of Lieutenant-General of Ordnance? The duties of that office could easily be performed by the Master-General and the salary of £1200 could be saved. It was not a great amount, to be sure, but the principle for which he was contending was a great one. Maybe the Government did not realize it, but the time was speedily approaching when the force of public demands 'would teach Ministers to think less of their own patronage and private ends, and somewhat more of the wishes and the necessities of the people'.[47] Sir Henry Hardinge resented Graham's 'slur upon the Duke', while Colonel Ward reminded him that the price of corn on Market Lane had risen, and that conditions in England were improving.[48] That was just exactly the point, answered Graham; an increased price of food and low wages was the very cause of the distress now prevalent among the poor. Then, in answering the charge that he had cast a slur upon the Duke of Wellington, Graham struck the note of a clear but cautious reformer, and enunciated a policy that eventually carried the day in England and which helped to save that country from a repetition of the excesses of the French Revolution. He emphatically declared that the only good government was a strong one, a government possessing the courage to remedy obvious abuses. If these abuses were not remedied the time was not distant when 'the people would see abuses, and would see nothing else; those abuses they would correct, and it was notorious that their correction was not always of the sort which prudent men would most desire'.[49]

By May 14th 'the indefatigable member for Cumberland', as the *Annual Register* described him,[50] was ready once more to take up the cudgels on behalf of economy. This time he asked for a return of all the fees, salaries, and emoluments paid to the Privy Councillors. After stating that it was the highly paid officials whose salaries should be cut, he declared that he had three objects in

[46] The division is to be found in *Hansard*, New Ser., XXIII, 1008.
[47] *Ibid.*, 1021.
[48] Colonel Ward was right. By March conditions had taken a turn for the better. See SMART, *op. cit.*, II, 511 et seq. For tables indicating the amount of exports from England and Ireland in 1829 and 1830, see PORTER, *Progress of the Nation*, II, 104-105. The totals given are £35,842,623 for 1829 and £38,271,597 for 1830.
[49] *Hansard*, New Ser., XXIII, 1044.   [50] *Annual Register* (1830), 60.

view: first, to see if the services rendered were commensurate with the salary received; second, to see if the rule that military half-pay ceased on taking a civil post should not apply to those on full pay; third, whether retired allowances and pensions of ministers should stop when they came back into office. When Portman, an interested M.P., said that he intended to ask for a ten per cent reduction in all salaries above £200 Graham retorted that he 'was as little disposed as himself [Portman] to stoop to ignoble game, while flights of voracious birds of prey were gloating in the upper regions of the air'.[51] Then, to the dismay of friend and foe alike, he proceeded to name the 'birds of prey'.

The Chancellor of the Exchequer, 'stung by the insinuations of Sir James Graham', as the *London Morning Chronicle* put it,[52] attempted to take the wind out of Graham's sails by moving an amendment to the motion requiring a return of the fees and salaries of all public officials. Admiral Cockburn, one of Graham's 'birds of prey', childishly offered to resign his office if the House decided that the labourer was not worthy of his hire. Evidently amused by the success of his thrust, Graham insisted that he had received too much. He had requested a list of 175 names and was given from 1500 to 2000! 'He asked, as it were, for a glass of wine, and they gave him a glass of wine, certainly, but diluted with a bottle of water.' The gallant Admiral, however, 'had taken the glass of wine without having diluted it with the bottle of water'.[53]

It was a powerful and highly effective speech which was supported on the division by 147 members. It had dismayed not only the Tories, but many of Graham's Whig colleagues. Mallet, Secretary of the Board of Audit, adequately described it in his diary in the following words:

> Those are fearful words to promulgate from the house-tops, and the Opposition gave a cheer at every pause, as if they never meant to take their share of the loaves and fishes . . . We shall never hear the last of the £650,000 distributed among 113 people, and of the £375,000 distributed among forty seven peers. . . .
> Whatever Sir James Graham undertakes he does extremely well. Nothing could exceed the spirit, the talent, and the propriety of his speech . . . The carelessness of consequences, and whether his

---

[51] *Hansard*, New Ser., XXIV, 519.　　　[52] *Chronicle*, May 18th, 1830.
[53] *Hansard*, New Ser., XXIV, 756-757.

arrows might hit the present Ministers, or ex-Ministers, or Ministers 'in petto', whether on this side or that side of the House, and all,
as he well knew, arrayed against him in their hearts, was that of a
tribune of the people.
His success was immense and the cheers unbounded. . . .
What with his industry and talents, his fine manner and person,
his aristocratical bearing and connections, and his factious independence, Sir James Graham may go a great way.[54]

Brougham, a good judge of ability, came to the same conclusion.
'You may well believe', he wrote to Graham, 'the great pleasure
your *perfect success* gave me.'[55] Bentham acknowledged Graham's
services in the cause of government economy and efficiency by
sending him a copy of his *Official Aptitude Maximized and
Expense Minimized*,[56] while the *London Globe*, a Whig paper,
declared that Graham's efforts had produced 'a considerable
impression on the public'.[57]

A few weeks later Graham reviewed for the edification of the
House the inordinate expenses of the South American diplomatic
missions. For eight months of service in Mexico Morier had
received £8987; Ward's mission to the same country had cost
£19,862 for two years; Cockburn had been paid £15,975 for
thirteen weeks in Columbia; Lord Strangford had received £6786
for the Bengal mission. In 1828 Chad had been appointed and
ordered to proceed to Bogota and had received £1666 for his
outfit; his departure was delayed and he was paid £1334 more.
In 1829 he had been paid £2062. During these years he had never
gone to Bogota; in fact, he had not left London, and yet he had
received £5100 of public money. So convincing was this speech
that Graham's motion that the cost of these missions be reduced
from £28,000 to £18,809 came within nineteen votes of upsetting
the ministry.[58]

On June 11th, Dawson, on behalf of the Government, proposed
a grant of £87,970 to defray the expenses of the consuls-general
and superannuations. He began by telling the House of the nature
of the economies that had already been made in the consular

[54] MS Diary of J. L. Mallet. Cited in PARKER, *Life of Graham*, I, 78-79.
[55] Brougham to Graham, in *Ibid.*, I, 79.
[56] JOHN BOWRING, *The Works of Jeremy Bentham*, XI, 51.
[57] *London Globe*, May 17th, 1830, p. 2 (Hereinafter cited as *Globe*).
[58] *Hansard*, New Ser., XXV, 32.

service, and said that these changes would be pleasing to the House and that as a result, 'the Honourable Baronet would henceforth spare his sarcasms on the present Ministers'.[59] Dawson explained that the Foreign Office had decided that consuls who were absent from their posts would receive only a moiety of their allowances and that allowances for house rent should henceforth not begin until the occupant arrived at his post. Graham was quick to congratulate the Government on the 'afterthought of his Majesty's Ministers respecting these estimates'.[60] But the reductions were not sufficient to satisfy him. In the first place, he thought that consuls should be paid fees instead of salaries because if this was done the consuls would take a greater interest in remaining at their posts of duty. He did not like to allude to the United States, he said, because such allusions were very unpalatable to Englishmen, but the House should know that the entire cost of the civil, military, and diplomatic service of that country was about £52,420, a sum not even half as great as the cost of England's consular service alone! He was not praising the United States; it was a republic, and he did not like republics, because, he said, he had too deep a stake in society to make him a friend of republican institutions, but England might profit occasionally by the American example. He concluded what the *London Morning Chronicle* called a 'very skilful speech',[61] by moving an £8000 reduction in the grant of supply.

While Hume, Mabberly, Wood, and others gladly supported Graham's motion, Peel certainly would not. 'It was too much', he declared, 'for the hon. Baronet to argue, that his Majesty's government disregarded public opinion because they disregarded his [Graham's] opinions',[62] and he resented the charge that the Government was both profligate and corrupt. This motion of Graham was also beaten, but by the narrow margin of twenty-three votes.

The squire of Netherby, however, was equally interested in other types of reform. On June 30th, 1828, he opposed a Bill for the construction of some additional churches. No one in that House, he assured them, had greater respect for the Church than he had, but he could not support any measure which 'unwise friends of

[59] *Ibid.*, 256.
[60] *Ibid.*, 257.
[61] *Chronicle*, June 12th, 1830.
[62] *Hansard*, New Ser., XXV, 278.

that Church might bring forward, to enable it to grasp more power and greater revenues than it already enjoyed'.[63] On March 4th of the following year he congratulated Peel for his efforts on behalf of Catholic Emancipation, and the Duke of Wellington for supporting the Bill for the repeal of the Test and Corporation Acts.[64] Furthermore, he had voted for both of these measures.

On the subject of parliamentary reform Graham had always taken an active interest, and had spoken and voted for it on every possible occasion. On the death of George IV in 1830, Parliament was dissolved and in the ensuing election Graham was returned for East Cumberland unopposed. At a banquet at Dalston given him by some of his Carlisle friends, he pledged himself to the Whig party, not because he was a party man, but because party action was necessary in order to accomplish the reforms he desired.[65] Despite his independence Graham was a thoroughgoing Whig in one sense — his philosophy of government was Lockian to the core. Speaking at a banquet in Whitehaven, held just after the French Revolution of 1830, occasioned by the action of Charles X and Prince Polignac, Graham stated in the best Lockian tradition:

> The rights of free men are not to be held at the will of despots, and this lesson cannot be too strongly impressed on all men, that the people have an indefeasible right of resistance to kings and to kingly power, wherever that power is exercised against their liberties. Constitutional kings reign only in virtue of their compact with the people.[66]

It must not be imagined that the so-called 'radical baronet' was radical in the modern sense of the word. It was only a very moderate reform that he wished — a sweeping away of the worst abuses — with the object of 'saving' the Constitution. There

[63] *Hansard*, New Ser., XIX, 1560.

[64] The Test Act of 1673 required all office holders to take the oaths of allegiance and supremacy; to take the sacrament according to the rites of the Anglican Church; and agree to the declaration against transubstantiation. The Corporation Act of 1671 provided that all corporation officials must take the sacraments according to the rites of the Anglican Church within twelve months after their election to office. They must also take the oaths of allegiance, supremacy, and non-resistance, and abjure the Solemn League and Covenant.

[65] A copy of his speech is preserved in his scrap book which is kept with his other papers at Netherby. He concluded the speech in these words: 'I became a Blue; Blue I am; Blue I have always been; and Blue I trust I shall always continue to be.'

[66] PARKER, *Life of Graham*, I, 82.

would be neither universal suffrage nor vote by ballot in his scheme of reform.

The year 1828 was one of political flux in which there appeared to be sufficient materials available for the formation of a new party. Five of Canning's friends (Huskisson, Dudley, Palmerston, Grant, and Lamb),[67] had left the cabinet of Wellington and it was beginning to look as if some of the moderate Tories, such as Peel and Lyndhurst, were beginning to change their minds on the religious questions of the day. With these facts in mind, Graham wrote to his friend Stanley:

> I hope you will take the field [next year] in force, and I think you will find a strong and respectable body willing to act under you. . . . The aspect of affairs is so clouded with difficulties that the chances are some capital blunder will be committed; and then will arrive the golden opportunity of forming a party in the House of Commons, on some broad and intelligible principles. . . .
> You are the person on whom I rest my hopes. You contain all the great requisites; you may reunite a scattered force which it is the interest of the country to see consolidated, and by concert and judicious management I really am disposed to believe the road to power is open.[68]

Since Stanley's answer, if he wrote one at all, is not extant, we do not know whether he took the matter seriously, but it is more than likely that he did.[69] Once again, on February 12th, 1830, in a speech in Parliament, Graham suggested the formation of a new party: 'If the fund-holder, the political economist, the lawyer, the Whig and Tory, are to rally under the banners of the Wellington Government', he said, 'the time is come when, on the part of the tax-payer, it is necessary to form another party to reduce the burdens of the country.'[70] Peel immediately rose to defend the Government but in doing so went on to state that no matter what political combinations arose in that House, there was 'a sufficient fund of good sense prevailing in the country, without reference to ultra-Whig or ultra-Tory, which will ultimately sanction and confirm the course that has been pursued'.[71] It appears from this

---

[67] *Annual Register* (1828), 21.

[68] Graham to Stanley, July 15th, 1828, in PARKER, *op. cit.*, I, 71.

[69] Stanley had accepted a place under Canning on the understanding that parliamentary reform was to be held in abeyance.

[70] *Hansard*, New Ser., XXII, 450.   [71] *Ibid.*, 475.

statement that Peel was referring to the same group that Graham hoped would form the nucleus of his new party, the group that desired a strong government and who hoped to make that government stronger by reforming it. Peace, economy, and moderate reform were to them methods of defending their class. These were the principles of Graham, and those who subscribed to these views were to be members of the new party which Graham hoped Stanley would lead. It appears, therefore, that the first suggestion that a new party, a conservative one, be formed came from Graham as early as July 1828.[72]

On November 1st, 1830, according to Ramsay,[73] Graham and Stanley secretly approached the Government through Arbuthnot, Wellington's 'tame cat', offering their alliance if they were assured that the Government would support a moderate reform bill. Their demands were very modest: representation for Leeds, Manchester, and Birmingham, and the transfer to large towns of the representation of those boroughs which had lost their seats because of corruption.[74] They accompanied this demand with the threat that if the concession were not granted they would oppose the Government.[75] It is quite likely that Peel was ready to consider accepting the offer, but events were soon to make it difficult if not impossible for him to do anything about it.

The July Revolution in France, instead of convincing the Duke of Wellington that reform was urgently needed, had the opposite effect upon him. He became more than ever committed to the maintenance of the *status quo*; some even accused him of being an ally of the reactionary Polignac.[76] It was an unjust charge and he vigorously denied it.[77] The general elections which were held

---

[72] Broderick and Fotheringham state that the term 'conservative' 'first came into use in 1831'. BRODERICK and FOTHERINGHAM, '*Political History of England*', *loc. cit.*, 319. Their source of information was *The Croker Papers*, II, 198, edited by L. J. Jennings. The latter states that Croker first used the term in 1831 in an article which he wrote for the *Quart. Rev.* K. B. Smellie writes that 'the Conservative Party was new born in 1833'. K. B. SMELLIE, *A Hundred Years of English Government*, 53. His source of information is George Peel, 'A Summary of the Life of Sir Robert Peel', cited in PARKER, *Life of Peel*, III, 617-618.

[73] See ANNA A. W. RAMSAY, *Sir Robert Peel*, 135-136.

[74] This was also the substance of Lord John Russell's motion of February 23rd, 1830. See *Annual Register* (1830), 100.

[75] See PARKER, *Life of Peel*, II, 163 et seq.

[76] *Annual Register* (1830), 145.

[77] *Hansard*, 3rd Ser., III, 1071.

in the same month, though they did not drive the party from power, resulted in Tory losses. Added to this defeat was the disaffection of the ultra-Tories who were not able to stomach the bitter pill of the Catholic Emancipation Act by which Catholics were given practically the same rights as members of the Church of England, and had not forgiven Peel and Wellington whom they held responsible for it.[78] Revolution abroad, disaffection within the ranks of the Government and widespread economic distress at home, were stimulating increased activity on behalf of reform. But the Prime Minister was resolute against change, and on November 2nd, announced that the English Constitution was incapable of improvement. Peel, though he did not agree with the Duke, felt bound to support him. The Duke's unfortunate remark was the spark which set off a widespread criticism and hatred of the Hero of Waterloo. Graham was of the opinion that his declaration against reform had made the Duke 'the most unpopular Minister that was ever known in England',[79] and Brougham attributed at least nine-tenths of the Duke's unpopularity to that unfortunate statement.[80] More to the point, it was the real reason for the fall of the Government, for on November 15th it was beaten on the Civil List, and the next day Wellington and Peel announced their resignations to the Lords and the Commons.[81] Tory government of the old type was dead, completely dead, and largely because 'no public men', as the *Edinburgh Review* put it, 'ever yet exhibited such a strange defiance of common sense and public opinion'.[82]

[78] Brougham says that such Tories as Richmond, Newcastle, Knatchbull, Wetherell, and Vyvyan were as anxious to see the Ministry ousted as were the Whigs. See HENRY BROUGHAM, *The Life and Times of Henry Lord Brougham*, III, 39 (Hereinafter cited as *Life of Brougham*). See also SPENCER WALPOLE, *Hist. of Eng.*, III, 176-177.

[79] *Hansard*, 3rd Ser., I, 292.   [80] *Annual Register* (1830), 161.
[81] *Ibid.*, 163.   [82] *Edin. Rev.*, LII, 531.

CHAPTER VI

FIRST LORD OF THE ADMIRALTY

WHEN Wellington resigned in November 1830, the King sent for Earl Grey, who, because of his constant advocacy of reform and his recognized leadership of the Whigs, was the one generally expected to take the position which the Duke had just vacated. Grey accepted office with the understanding that reform of Parliament was to be a cabinet measure. Except for the annoyance encountered in the case of Brougham,[1] Grey had little difficulty in constructing his cabinet. Althorp became Chancellor of the Exchequer, Lord Lansdowne President of the Council, Palmerston Foreign Secretary, Melbourne Home Secretary, Lord Holland Chancellor of the Duchy of Lancaster, and Lord Durham Lord Privy Seal. The Duke of Richmond was given the Post Office for having deserted the Tories; Grant, a Canningite,[2] was made President of the Board of Trade; and Sir James became First Lord of the Admiralty.

The latter appointment did not escape criticism. Brougham protested that Graham's selection was 'prematurely high' and complained of the appointment on the grounds that he was just 'a kind of pocket-vote of Lambton's'.[3] The Tory *Quarterly Review* was very caustic: 'The parts . . . seem to have been oddly cast . . . Sir James Graham, because he had made the subject of finance his particular study, was made First Lord of the Admiralty; Lord Althorp, who . . . would have been a fit and acceptable person at the Admiralty, was selected for Chancellor of the Exchequer; . . .

---

[1] Henry Brougham, easily the first orator of the day, the real leader of the Whigs in the House, and a staunch advocate of reform held in his hands the fate of the new Government. Grey first offered him the Attorney-Generalship, but Brougham refused it. The King refused to give Brougham the Mastership of the Rolls, but suggested the Lord Chancellorship instead. Brougham, says Molesworth, would probably have refused this post too had not Althorp begged him to accept it. See WILLIAM MOLESWORTH, *History of England from the Year 1830-1874*, new ed., I, 48 (Hereinafter cited as *Hist. of Eng.*). Brougham himself says that Althorp, Sefton, and Duncannon 'overpersuaded him', and that they had done so at the behest of Grey. See BROUGHAM, *Life of Brougham*, III, 61. Walpole concludes that Brougham 'gladly accepted the splendid post'. WALPOLE, *Hist. of Eng.*, III, 194.

[2] Palmerston and Goderich were also Canningites.

[3] BROUGHAM, *op. cit.*, III, 58.

Lord Palmerston, because he had committed himself more than any other person upon the affairs of Portugal, must be at the head of the foreign department.'[4] In a later issue the same journal characterized Durham, Grey, Richmond, Althorp, and Graham as the 'less intellectual members of the Cabinet', and declared that they were 'all irrevocably mortgaged beyond the extent of their capacities . . . to the Reform Bill'.[5] On hearing of the cabinet selections, Greville grumbled that the appointments of Auckland, Melbourne, and Graham were 'all bad' — that of Graham being 'too inconsiderable'.[6] Three weeks later, describing Graham's selection as 'the most monstrous of all', Greville wrote a biographical sketch of Graham as he then appeared to most of the Tories and to many Whigs:

> He came into Parliament ten years ago, spoke and failed. He had been a provincial hero, the Cicero and Romeo of Yorkshire and Cumberland . . . He . . . married and retired . . . to become a country gentleman, patriot, reformer, financier, and what not, always good-looking . . . pleasing, intelligent, cultivated, agreeable as a man can be who is not witty and who is rather pompous and slow, after many years of retirement, in the course of which he gave to the world his lucubrations on corn and currency. Armed with the importance of representing a great constituency, he started again in the House of Commons; took up Joseph Hume's line, but ornamented it with graces and flourishes which had not usually decorated such dry topics. He succeeded, and in that line is now the best speaker in the House . . . Years and years ago I remember his delight on Hume's comparison between Demosthenes and Cicero, and how he knew the passage by heart; but it is one thing to attack strong abuses and fire off well-rounded set phrases, another to administer the naval affairs of the country and be ready to tilt against all comers, as he must do for the future.[7]

---

[4] *Quart. Rev.*, XLIV, 316.

[5] *Ibid.*, XLV, 541.

[6] CHARLES C. GREVILLE, *The Greville Memoirs, A Journal of the Reigns of King George IV and King William IV*, ed. by Henry Reeve, II, 66 (Hereinafter cited as *Jour. of Reigns of Geo. IV and Will. IV*).

[7] *Ibid.*, 91. Greville was then piqued at Graham. 'He was once my friend,' wrote Greville, 'a college intimacy revived in the world, and which lasted six months, when, thinking he could do better, he cut me, as he had done others before. I am not a fair judge of him . . . but I take vanity and self-sufficiency to be the prominent features of his character, though of the extent of his capacity I will give no opinion. Let time show; I think he will fail.' *Ibid.*, 90.

In a short time Graham was to prove to Greville and to the country that he could not only 'fire off well-rounded phrases', but could also successfully administer the naval affairs of England and tilt against any one in the House.

Why did Earl Grey appoint this 'radical baronet' to the important Admiralty post in view of the fact that he was not only young and relatively inexperienced in administrative affairs, but was also known to be politically independent?[8] In the first place, Grey knew that Graham's radicalism was of the very moderate type. In the second place, Graham, like most of the members of the cabinet, was a baronet of great territorial influence. In the third place, the Whigs owed Graham a signal reward for his effective attacks on the late Government. Finally, Earl Grey had a healthy respect for Graham's ability, for the thoroughness with which he performed his allotted tasks, for his effective efforts on behalf of reform, and for his honesty, integrity, and steadfastness of purpose. And this confidence in Graham was richly rewarded, for he turned out to be a superb administrator, an able parliamentary tactician, and a hard-working First Lord of the Admiralty.

Oddly enough, the ministry, whose first commitment was to accomplish a reform of Parliament, was one of the most aristocratic Governments that England has ever had.[9] It was believed that only a very moderate reform would be likely to come from a ministry composed of men pledged to renovate, repair, and prop up the existing Constitution, and who would not, as the Whig

[8] According to Butler, Lord Lansdowne suggested Graham for the high post of Home Secretary, but that he was placed in the Admiralty 'where his dangerous inclinations to economy would not have too abundant scope'. BUTLER, *Great Reform Bill*, 146. When one recalls Graham's economies at Netherby; his outspoken demand for retrenchment in *Corn and Currency*; his economy record in the Sessions of 1828-1830; and that in no department of government was there as much room for economy as at the Admiralty, it is impossible to agree with Butler's statement. Roebuck concludes that 'Sir James early in life was intimate with Mr. Lambton, afterwards Lord Durham; and through the friendly influence of Lord Grey's son-in-law, was offered a high office in the Whig Government of 1830'. JOHN A. ROEBUCK, *History of the Whig Ministry of 1830 to the Passing of the Reform Bill*, I, 149 (Hereinafter cited as *Whig Ministry of 1830*). On the other hand, Stuart Reid declares that Durham did not like Graham at all. See STUART REID, *Life and Letters of Durham*, I, 236 (Hereinafter cited as *Life of Durham*). Graham's letters reveal that this feeling was mutual.

[9] Having appointed six of his relatives to the ministry, Grey was certainly guilty of nepotism. For a criticism of these appointments see *Manchester Guardian*, December 4th, 1830, p. 2.

Edinburgh Review put it, 'undermine its foundation, and . . . pull its bulwarks to the ground'.[10]

In the election of 1830 Graham had been returned for Cumberland unopposed. At a dinner given in his honour he demanded that election expenses be reduced, censured Wellington's opposition to retrenchment,[11] and declared for only a moderate reform of Parliament by transferring the franchise of rotten boroughs to large towns, and giving the franchise to £10 and £20 householders in cities and boroughs. On his return to London he immediately held conversations on the subject with Althorp, Brougham, Stanley, and Palmerston. The last wrote to Brougham on November 1st, saying that he had met Althorp, Stanley, and Denman to discuss the subject and that they had agreed to meet again on the following Sunday. They wanted Graham to join them and suggested that in the interval he should see Palmerston to find out just how far Palmerston would be willing to go.[12] The next day Graham answered that he would try to ascertain Palmerston's views, and that he thought their object should be 'to reform to the extent necessary for preserving our institutions, not to change for the purpose of subverting'.[13] He then suggested that Brougham merely give notice in his speech to the House the next day of his intention to bring up the subject, instead of making a formal motion. Brougham acted on this suggestion and announced to the House that his object was 'to repair, not to pull down', and that he would bring in his motion on the subject at a later date.[14] On the sixteenth he unwillingly postponed his motion until the twenty-fifth, but declared that he would bring it in on that date regardless of conditions, or of which ministers happened to be in office.[15] But six days later he went to the Woolsack and never spoke in the Commons again. At the same time Grey explained to the Lords the policy of the Government[16] and then Parliament was prorogued until the next February.

The task of drawing up the Government plan of reform was assigned to Lord Duncannon, Lord Durham, Lord John Russell, and Sir James Graham. According to Stuart Reid's account,

[10] *Edin. Rev.*, LII, 536.   [11] *Chronicle*, August 17th, 1830, p. 2.
[12] Brougham to Graham, November 1st, 1830, in PARKER, *Life of Graham*, I, 96.
[13] Graham to Brougham, November 2nd, 1830, *Ibid.*, 96-97.
[14] *Hansard*, 3rd Ser., I, 54-55.
[15] *Ibid.*, 563.   [16] *Ibid.*, 605-612.

Grey asked Durham if he would work with Russell in framing the Reform Bill. Durham agreed and he and Russell decided to summon Graham and Duncannon.[17] Reid further states that Durham did not like Graham but agreed to work with him out of deference to Grey, and that Graham, 'the least progressive member of the quartette', was 'certainly flattered by his inclusion in the committee'.[18] He further asserts that Brougham never forgot his having been passed over in favour of Graham.[19]

The reform plan was thrashed out in meetings of this committee held at Lord Durham's home during the fall and winter of 1830-1831. There was not much disagreement among the members of the committee on the provisions of Schedules A and B which provided for the total disfranchisement of boroughs of less than 2000 population, and for the loss of one seat for those having fewer than 4000. All agreed that towns exceeding 10,000 should be allowed representation. Graham was the author of the stipulation that no one could vote who had not registered in his constituency in the autumn preceding the election. At his suggestion the committee also drew up the necessary machinery for the compilation of electoral lists, the primary purposes of which were to reduce election costs, prevent fraud, and systematize election procedures.[20]

The main problem of the ministers, according to Seymour, was 'to fix upon a qualification that would enfranchise sufficient numbers without creating a thoroughly popular or radically inclined constituency'.[21] Closely connected with this problem was the question of the secret ballot. The first qualification considered by the committee was that of the £20 requirement, a rate

[17] REID, *op. cit.*, I, 235. See also JOHN E. RUSSELL, *Recollections and Suggestions 1813-1873*, 69.

[18] REID, *op. cit.*, 235-236.

[19] *Ibid.*, 352. Aspinal states that: 'The aristocratic Whigs who had tried to keep him [Brougham] out of the cabinet, were careful to exclude him from the Cabinet Committee of four. . . . To his [Brougham's] intense annoyance he found that Graham's claims to a seat on the committee were preferred to his own.' ARTHUR ASPINAL, *Lord Brougham and the Whig Party*, 189. Brougham, however, states that all agreed to submit the question to the committee consisting of Durham, Graham, Russell, and Duncannon. BROUGHAM, *op. cit.*, III, 68. Butler is of the opinion that had Brougham felt peeved at being passed over he would have said so. BUTLER, *op. cit.*, 172.

[20] See REID, *op. cit.*, I, 237.

[21] CHARLES SEYMOUR, *Electoral Reform in England and Wales*, 36.

which Russell, Grey, and the King thought low enough. Althorp,[22] however, thought that a £20 requirement was too high and so did Brougham. Seymour is convinced that Althorp induced Graham to work for a lower rate, and that Graham, with Brougham's assistance, advocated the ballot, 'not in the hope of obtaining it, but in order to secure the lower rate of franchise by way of compromise'.[23] It is very doubtful that Graham 'worked for' or 'advocated' the ballot, or that he ever did more than acquiesce in it with the hope and expectation that the cabinet would not agree to it. Apparently Lord Durham earnestly desired that it be adopted and succeeded in getting Duncannon and Graham to vote for it, while Russell steadfastly refused to agree.[24] When the final draft of the Bill was presented to Grey it included provision for the ballot, and for a £20 qualification for voting. The cabinet, including such opponents of reform as Grant, Melbourne, Palmerston, and Lansdowne immediately struck out the ballot. Grey and the King were also opposed to it. Brougham, however, succeeded, in the opinion of Ramsay, 'in reducing the town voter's qualification to £10, and would have introduced household suffrage if he could'.[25]

On the last day of January 1831 the King approved of the report as amended by the cabinet; on February 2nd Grey wrote to Graham praising the King for his 'noble conduct'.[26] In his answer to this letter Graham declared that the King's 'wise and generous conduct' had 'saved his throne and averted civil war'.[27] In many respects this was a 'milk and water' Bill but at that time it was regarded as an extremely liberal one by the members of the committee which drew it up and also by most of the cabinet members. In fact, Palmerston voiced the real sentiments of many

[22] Broderick and Fotheringham are in error in stating that Althorp was a member of the committee. To be sure, Althorp exercised some influence on the committee through his friend Graham, but he was not a member of it. BRODERICK and FOTHERINGHAM, *Hist. of Eng.*, 287. See also, RUSSELL, *op. cit.*, 69.

[23] SEYMOUR, *op. cit.*, 36-37.

[24] BUTLER, *op. cit.*, 180-181; WALPOLE, *Life of Russell*, I, 165; REID, *op. cit.*, I, 238. Disraeli says that Duncannon was the one who voted against the ballot and not Russell. 'Lord Lyndhurst's Recollections', in WILLIAM F. MONEYPENNY, *The Life of Benjamin Disraeli Earl of Beaconsfield*, I, append., B, 389 (Hereinafter cited as *Life of Disraeli*).

[25] RAMSAY, *Life of Peel*, 151.

[26] Grey to Graham, February 2nd, 1831, in PARKER, *op. cit.*, I, 102.

[27] Graham to Grey, February 3rd (?), *Ibid.*

of the cabinet when he stated that the party was most certainly identifying itself with the Radicals and helping in 'breaking down all our established institutions'.[28]

The provisions of the Bill had been kept secret and when Russell, on March 1st, introduced it in the Commons its extreme provisions were a complete surprise to many. The ultra-Conservatives, of course, hated it as much as the Radicals liked it. On the sixth day of the debate, Graham rose to answer Peel's attack on the Bill. All were agreed, he said, that some reform was necessary and the main question at hand was whether or not this Bill would accomplish a desirable reform or whether its provisions were too radical. Graham did not think it was. Furthermore the value of early concessions had been shown in the Catholic Emancipation Act. When a Government was too dilatory in granting needed reforms it laid itself open to demands for more extensive changes 'and ultimately to the necessity of making large and unwise concessions'.[29] He was convinced that 'moderate' men would all agree that 'enough was done, and not too much'.[30] The Bill was designed to strengthen, not to weaken, the established institutions of the land. He asserted that under the existing system there were 115 boroughs that returned members to the House 'although the number of voters in no instance was above 200'.[31] Listening to the arguments that had thus far been advanced against reform one must come to the conclusion, said Graham, 'that every rich Peer was almost entitled, as a matter of right, to have a Representative in that House', a condition 'which might be very congenial to their feelings', but which was not so congenial to the people.[32] His examination of the situation had revealed that 142 peers returned 173 members on their own nominations, and that 16 peers returned 26 members to the House. The question before them now was whether or not the members should represent the people, or property and patrons. To Graham, the great weakness of the existing system was that it did not matter whether property was held by a good or a bad man, or by the best or worst landlords: the influence was the same in either case. After defending the £10 franchise on grounds of justice and necessity, Graham

[28] Stanley to Graham, February 27th, 1831, in PARKER, op. cit., I, 104.
[29] Hansard, 3rd Ser., III, 218.
[30] Ibid., 219.   [31] Ibid., 224.   [32] Ibid.

told the House that there were only two methods of dealing with public opinion: concession or suppression. 'Concession, if it were possible, he would always counsel', while 'force . . . was inconsistent with the real interests of the nation and incompatible with the safety of the Crown'.[33] He knew that the Bill was not perfect, but the principle, 'to secure the safety of the Monarch, and to prevent the people from taking up dangerous doctrines', was a sound one and deserved the support of the House.[34] Leave to bring in the Bill was given by general consent and there was little opposition to the first reading largely because the Opposition was divided and lacking in leadership, and because several members, as the *Annual Register* put it, 'expressed their wish that it should be allowed to be brought in, so that a division would not have enabled its opponents to have the advantage of their whole strength'.[35]

The two weeks preceding the second reading of the Bill were weeks of intense agitation and excitement. Reformers of all types united in defence of the measure, not always because they approved of its provisions, but because it was the maximum that they could get at the time. Opponents argued that it would destroy the Monarchy and other time-sanctioned institutions of the land. The core of the arguments against the measure is to be found in Sir R. Vyvyan's statement: 'This reform is revolution.'[36] After two days of debate, during which some stated publicly their intention of voting for the Bill while privately hoping that it would be ruined in committee, the House voted on the second reading. There were 608 members present, which, says the *Annual Register*, was 'the largest number that had ever divided on any question in the House of Commons', and the Bill passed by a vote of 302 to 301.[37] In April the Tories defeated the Government in committee and the cabinet decided to press for a dissolution. In

[33] *Ibid.*, 231.
[34] *Ibid.* The *Chronicle* (March 9th, 1831, p. 4), thought this was 'an able speech', but the *Post* (March 9th, 1831, p. 2), described it as 'a poor display'.
[35] *Annual Register* (1831), 76.　　　　　　　[36] *Ibid.*, 83.
[37] *Ibid.*, 94. The one vote which carried the measure was that given by John Calcraft, Wellington's Paymaster of the Forces, who had shifted from his former opposition to it. He was subsequently elected to Parliament for the county of Dorset. But he had lost his former friends, failed to gain the confidence of the Whigs, and sinking into profound melancholy, committed suicide. See MOLESWORTH, *op. cit.*, I, 110 *n.*

G

the election which followed, the Government made excellent use of Brougham's slogan: 'the Bill, the whole Bill, and nothing but the Bill'.[38] Although it was feared that the condemned boroughs would not sanction their own extinction and would consequently vote against the Bill, the forty-shilling freeholders voted in favour of it and the popularity of the measure carried all before it. Graham was returned for Cumberland for a fourth time, and Grey, in great good spirits over the success of the election, wrote to him: 'I wish you joy, with all my heart, of your victory in Cumberland. It is one of the most important that we have gained.'[39]

Public approval of the Bill, as expressed in the election, convinced the ministry of the desirability of bringing in a second Bill similar to the first. On April 12th Russell explained to the House the few changes that had been made and the Bill was read a first time. On July 7th it passed the second reading by a majority of 136. In the committee it was met by dilatory tactics, such as motions for postponement, the object of which was to encourage the Lords to greater resistance, and to embarrass the Whigs by manœuvring them into the commission of tactical blunders. Strong opposition was expected from the Lords and as early as July 13th Graham was planning effectual means of circumventing defeat in the Upper House. 'We shall win the day', he wrote to Anglesey, 'perhaps, however, by making Peers.'[40] The *Edinburgh Review* advised the Lords not to defeat 'so safe, so moderate, and so constitutional a plan',[41] because reform was inevitable anyway, and because defeat of the Bill would most certainly be followed by the creation of a large body of peers to insure the success of the measure. But, disregarding threats, pleas, and advice, the Lords threw out the Bill by a majority of 41.[42]

As soon as the Lords had thus sealed their fate, Graham urged the creation of enough peers to ensure the passage of the measure he had helped to frame. Should the King refuse to appoint the

[38] RUSSELL, *op. cit.*, 74.

[39] Grey to Graham, May 10th, 1831, in PARKER, *op. cit.*, I, 112. The Tory *Fraser's Magazine for Town and Country* (III, 639), was critical of the election in Cumberland declaring that 'it would have been death for an unprotected anti-reformer to appear in the streets' (Hereinafter cited as *Fraser's*).

[40] Graham to Anglesey, July 13th, 1831, in PARKER, *op. cit.*, I, 113.

[41] *Edin. Rev.*, LIV, 269.   [42] *Annual Register* (1831), 275.

requisite number, the cabinet, he thought, ought immediately to resign.[43] Durham and Brougham agreed with Graham,[44] but others did not, and when Althorp, one of those who opposed the scheme, told Graham that the cabinet would not ask the King to appoint additional peers, Graham decided to resign.[45] This decision annoyed Althorp, who wrote to Grey:

> If he perseveres in bringing the matter forward, and with the intention of resigning in case of failure, our days are numbered. For any one Minister going out on this ground, in the present state of feeling of the country, must be fatal to us; and the only way this could be avoided would be, that the Cabinet should be unanimous in giving this advice to the King, and that the King should accept it.[46]

Grey succeeded in persuading Graham to remain in office, but the latter, says Butler, 'contented himself by drawing up a confidential paper in which he reserved the right to propose a creation of peers to the cabinet at any future date'.[47]

The cabinet was just about equally divided on this question, and since the idea was extremely repugnant to Grey, Graham wrote him a long letter on March 9th urging him to more vigorous action, saying:

> It is clear that the House of Lords now stands before the public pledged by a large majority to resist even the first principle of reform; that in ordinary cases the proof of the necessity rests with the government which has recourse to so strong a measure as the large creation of Peers, but that here the necessity has been demonstrated to the entire satisfaction of the great body of the nation; that with the full tide of public opinion in our favour we are at present able to make Peers to secure the principle of reform itself; that in no subsequent stage shall we possess the same advantage, since the principle will have been conceded. . . .
>
> I am also persuaded that immediate failure, after a bold and strenuous attempt to carry the measure, would be less disastrous to the country than partial success ending ultimately in defeat. . . .
>
> My fears, therefore, are almost equally great, whether we succeed or fail in the second reading, unless Peers be now made.[48]

[43] Althorp to Grey, November 23rd, 1831, in PARKER, *op. cit.*, I, 129.
[44] Durham to Graham, October 19th, 1831, in *Ibid.*, 128.
[45] Althorp to Grey, November 23rd, 1831, in *Ibid.*, 129.
[46] Id. to Id., in *Ibid.* [47] BUTLER, *op. cit.*, 323.
[48] Graham to Grey, March 9th, 1832, in PARKER, *op. cit.*, I, 138-140.

The cabinet, however, decided not to propose to the King the creation of new peers until after the second reading. When this was accomplished by a majority of nine, the Bill was sent to committee where Graham feared it would be mutilated beyond all recognition. However, when Lyndhurst succeeded in getting a postponement of Schedule A (disfranchising the smallest boroughs), and then proposed adding to the representation of the great towns and counties by another large enfranchisement, the cabinet decided to advise the King to create additional peers to secure the passage of the Bill.[49] It was agreed that if he refused, they would all resign. This was the very policy that Graham had been advocating for months, which even Palmerston considered 'infinitely wise',[50] and which was now adopted. The inability of Wellington, the new Prime Minister, to carry a reform bill forced the King to recall Grey and to give him and the Chancellor the right to appoint the required number of peers.[51] Sir Herbert Taylor informed some of the most active opponents of the Bill of the King's decision[52] and the result was that rather than permit a great addition to their ranks, the Lords gave up their opposition and permitted the Bill to pass.[53] Three days later (July 7th, 1832), it was given the Royal assent and became the law of the land.

It is difficult to ascertain the exact amount of influence exerted by Graham in the campaign for this reform. But we do know that as a member of Parliament he had steadily advocated reform in the House and at the hustings. As a member of the committee of four he helped to frame the provisions of the Bill and was personally responsible for the stipulation that no one could vote who had not registered in the autumn preceding the election, and that electoral lists should be compiled. In addition, he was one of the first to advocate the creation of additional peers as a means of securing the approval of the Lords to the measure.

Political reform having been effected, Graham turned his

[49] Cabinet Minute, May 16th, 1832, cited in *The Reform Act, 1832, the Correspondence of the late Earl Grey with His Majesty King William IV, and with Sir Herbert Taylor*, ed. by Henry Grey, II, 419.
[50] Palmerston to Graham, May 14th, 1832, in PARKER, *op. cit.*, I, 143. See also ROEBUCK, *op. cit.*, II, 324.
[51] MOLESWORTH, *op. cit.*, I, 222; RUSSELL, *op. cit.*, 108.
[52] *Annual Register* (1832), 187; RUSSELL, *op. cit.*, 107.
[53] *Annual Register* (1832), 194.

attention to the problems that beset agriculture. From 1828 to 1832 the price of wheat had remained high due to inadequate harvests at home.[54] In 1832, however, excellent weather from the last of July to the end of August resulted in abundant harvests. Imports thereupon dropped from the 1,491,631 quarters of 1831 to only 325,435.[55] The immediate effect of this abundant harvest was a decline in prices. According to figures cited in the *Annual Register*, the price of British wheat fell from 61s. 10d. in December 1831[56] to 53s. 7d. in December 1832,[57] and to 50s. 2d. in December 1833.[58] Unusually excellent weather in 1834 produced a bumper crop and wheat promptly dropped to the low average of 39s. 6d. for the year.[59]

Declining prices of wheat and other commodities were a decided boon to the masses but gave rise, as usual, to complaints of distress from the agriculturalists. Because the Government felt that the demands of the landed interests for relief were just, or because it felt constrained to heed the demands of those whose power had just been diminished by the Reform Bill, the problem was attended to at once. While no reference to agricultural distress was made in the Speech from the Throne,[60] a committee was appointed early in the session of 1833 to inquire into the cause of agricultural distress. Consisting of such leading landlords as the Marquis of Chandos, Peel, Russell, Althorp, and Graham, the committee summoned for examination a large number of occupiers, landowners, and surveyors in the hope that their testimony would reveal a solution to the problem at hand.

The first question with which the committee concerned itself was the relationship between the supply and the demand for home-grown grain. The agricultural committee of 1831 had reported that the annual production of grain was about equal to the annual consumption. The present committee, on the other hand, dissented from this opinion and declared that

[54] In 1829, 1,364,220 quarters of wheat had to be imported; in 1830, 1,701,885; in 1831, 1,491,631. PORTER, *Progress of the Nation*, I, 146.

[55] *Ibid.*

[56] *Annual Register* (1831), app., to chron., 292.

[57] *Ibid.* (1832), 258.   [58] *Ibid.* (1833), 288.

[59] TOOKE, *History of Prices*, II, 390.

[60] See *Annual Register* (1833), 8-10. Cf. TOOKE, *op. cit.*, II, 226; BARNES, *History of the Corn Laws*, 224.

the Stocks of Home-grown Wheat in the hands of the Farmer and of the Dealer at the time of Harvest have gradually diminished; that the Produce of Great Britain is in the average of years unequal to the Consumption; that the increased Supply from Ireland does not cover the deficiency; and that in the present state of Agriculture, the United Kingdom is in years of ordinary production partially dependent on the supply of Wheat from Foreign countries.[61]

The committee also reported that prices were inadequate and that government regulation of rents and wages would not relieve the situation. On the other hand, it said, burdens on agriculture could be materially lightened by a revision of the Poor Law and by a commutation of the tithe.[62]

Despite the evidence furnished by the agricultural revolt of 1830-1831,[63] many landowners still believed that agricultural labourers were better off when wheat prices were high than when they were low, because low prices caused unemployment. But, after a careful examination of the subject, the committee of 1833 came to the significant conclusion that 'the general condition of the Agricultural Labourer in full Employment is better now than at any former period, the Money Wages giving him a greater command over the necessaries and conveniences of life'.[64] There were, however, parts of England in which the supply of farm labour exceeded the demand and where it was necessary to resort to granting land attached to cottages to the labourers, and also to moving them about the parish in a more judicious manner than formerly.

The committee was glad to find that improved farming methods had done much to counterbalance the fall in prices, and listed the spread of the drill system of planting, more efficient fertilization of the soil, better drainage, crop rotation, and improvement in sheep and cattle breeding as evidence of this improvement.

[61] *Parliament Papers*, 'Report from the Select Committee on Agriculture with the Minutes of Evidence taken before them', v.

[62] *Ibid.*, vi.

[63] See ERNLE, *English Farming, Past and Present*, 324-325; WALPOLE, *Hist. of Eng.*, III, 436-437. The *Edin. Rev.* declared that the agricultural distress could never be cured without 'a decided modification of the Corn Laws'. It also advocated a more stringent Poor Law and the abolition of the game laws. *Edin. Rev.*, LIII, 46.

[64] *Parliament Papers*, 'Report from the Sel. Comm. on Agric.', vii.

On the subject of 'corn and currency' the committee came to the same conclusion that Graham had reached in his celebrated pamphlet of 1826. 'It cannot be denied', the report ran, 'that the restoration of that Standard [gold] has . . . been disadvantageous to . . . the productive classes of the community.'[65] Nevertheless, the committee opposed changing the coinage system because 'fresh experiments in the value of Money . . . might shake public confidence and . . . lead to the derangement of all settled Contracts'.[66] Furthermore rents were now approximating prices.

The committee could not agree with the conclusion of the *Edinburgh Review* that the Corn Laws needed to be modified, and declared that since prices under the Law of 1828 had been steady in spite of several deficient crops, there was no need of tampering with the Law. Any improvement in the condition of the landed interests, concluded the committee, 'rests rather on the cautious forebearance than on the active interposition of parliament'.[67]

Only one part of this report could have been of much consolation to the landlords and that was the recommendation that a reduction be made in the taxes and burdens that they claimed bore so heavily upon them.

In January 1834 the *Edinburgh Review* once more launched an attack on the Corn Laws. It declared that free trade was probably not necessary, but that a fixed duty of six or seven shillings was high enough to enable the landlords to pay their tithes and poor rates. 'When the tithes, poor rates, and other local burdens, that now press with peculiar severity on the agriculturalists, have been equalized, and made to press equally on the monied and mercantile classes', it declared, 'the right of the agriculturalists to a protecting duty will cease'.[68] The Marquis of Chandos, impatient at having to wait any longer for the dawn of that happy day which would witness a reduction of the burdens on the landlords, made a motion in the House, on February 21st, 1834, to that effect,[69] and so general was the sentiment in favour of this form of relief for landlords that Chandos failed by only four votes to carry his motion.

On March 6th Hume, in presenting to the House a petition against the Corn Laws, described them as 'a gratuitous blasting

---

[65] *Ibid.*, x.   [66] *Ibid.*, xi.   [67] *Ibid.*, xiii.
[68] *Edin. Rev.*, LVIII, 275.   [69] *Hansard*, 3rd Ser., XXI, 659.

of the blessings which nature had put within our reach',[70] and concluded his speech with a motion calling for the repeal of the Law of 1828, and for the substitution of a fixed, moderate duty on the importation of foreign corn. After Colonel Torrens had seconded this motion, Graham opposed it in one of his most effective speeches. First he analysed once again the burdens peculiar to land: 'there was Tithe to pay — there was the Land-tax — simply two millions — the Malt-duty, no very trifling impost — county rates which, in fact, put the landed proprietors in the place of the public prosecutor, these were the burthens resting solely on the land'.[71] Then he analysed the evils which he was certain would follow on the heels of Hume's proposed change. In the first place, it would throw land out of cultivation and consequently diminish the demand for agricultural labour. These unemployed labourers would then naturally consume less agricultural produce, to be sure, but they would buy less manufactured goods as well. A decrease in the demand for the latter would cause reduced wages and a resulting decrease in the purchases of agricultural products. Once that vicious circle was set in motion the manufacturing interests (in whose interest Hume was speaking) would regret free trade in corn. He desired foreign trade as much as did Hume, 'but the zeal to extend it should not lead to the destruction of the home market, which would be fatal to the prosperity of all'.[72]

To Hume's argument that high wheat prices hurt the manufacturing interests, Graham answered that exorbitant prices were impossible because past history showed that 'a scarcity, indeed, might arise from the vicissitudes of seasons, under the existing law, and the price might be raised at home; yet, in that case, importation was not only not prohibited, but it was even favoured'.[73] He desired a stabilization of prices at about fifty shillings per quarter, and the present law, he thought, would accomplish this object.

In the third place, Graham declared that the question of the Corn Laws was not solely a landlord's problem. It was a labourer's problem as well. Statistics were not always interesting to the House, he knew, but they certainly were convincing, and in the hands of one who knew how to handle them effectively, proved

[70] *Hansard*, 3rd Ser., XXI, 1212.   [71] *Ibid.*, 1233.
[72] *Ibid.*, 1235.   [73] *Ibid.*, 1237.

to many that labour was more concerned about this problem than the landlords were.

If 3,000,000 quarters of corn were imported into the country, the number of labourers who would be thrown out of employment must, of course, depend upon the number of acres of land necessary to produce so much marketable corn, and the inutility of the land so thrown out of culture. In a former part of his evidence he stated, that twelve bushels for each acre producing corn were required for seed and feeding farm horses, and consequently, the marketable corn was the excess of the gross produce over twelve bushels per acre. If, then, it were supposed, that land producing eighteen bushels per acre would be thrown out of cultivation, it followed that the excess would be one acre for each six bushels of the quantity assumed to be imported, which would give, in round numbers, 4,000,000 of acres. Assuming, then, that the land to be thrown out of cultivation in the case put, would be equal to the production of 24 bushels per acre, the extent thrown out would be 2,000,000 of acres; and, if the gross consumption of the empire, or the gross produce, at the usual Estimate of 50,000,000 were divided by 36 (the estimated average number of bushels produced per acre) it would give 18,000,000 of acres as the land annually producing corn. The quantity of land which would thus be rendered unsusceptible of cultivation by the annual importation of 3,000,000 quarters, would be 2,000,000 or about one-ninth part of the land now under corn crops, and, according to the proportion of the population dependent on agriculture, as ascertained by the last census, it followed, that between 900,000 and 1,000,000 of individuals would be deprived of their present means of subsistence, of whom about one-fourth, or say from 200,000 to 250,000 might be considered labourers.[74]

Did they still think this was solely a landlord's problem? Those who spoke for the manufacturing and commercial interests, on the other hand, argued that many of the labourers who lost their jobs on the farms would find employment in the new factories in the rising towns. This, thought the hon. Baronet, was very amusing. Did the members of that House not realize that labour was immobile? Could a ploughman be made to spin?

Let them conceive his iron hands manipulating cotton — his ponderous strength stooping to manufacture bobbin-net, and his

[74] *Ibid.*, 1239-1240.

hardened constitution ... transplanted to the atmosphere of a
workshop — and they would feel that such speculations were
impracticable; that they might, indeed, serve well enough for day
dreams to the political economists, but that nature herself would
rebel against the attempt to carry them into execution.[75]

Finally, Graham told the House that it was impossible because
of political considerations to separate this proposed alteration in
the Corn Laws from the problem of labour displacement. To him,
the 'relations between tenant and landlord, and between farmer
and labourer, which still existed in the rural districts of the country,
were ties of great importance, ties which existed with comparative
laxity in the manufacturing districts, and which were essentially
interwoven with the greatness, the security and the prosperity of
the country'.[76] He, for one, would not willingly consent to having
these ties broken.

After declaring that alterations in the standard of value in 1819
and 1826 had hurt the landlords and that it was unjust to expect
them to go through another change now, and after opposing a
reduction in the Corn Laws on the ground that it would result in
a reduction in rents, Graham wavered a little and stated that if the
change to a low fixed duty were made *gradually*, 'it might be safe',
but a sudden and great change would result in the destruction of
the landed interests, tantamount, in his estimation, to the 'destruction of the State itself'.[77]

This very able speech, coming from the 'radical baronet' who
had written that offensive *Corn and Currency*, was delightful music
to the ears of the landlords. The Tory *Quarterly Review* was un-
stinting in its praise, declaring that Graham's address

was one of the ablest ever delivered on such a subject — clear in
its arrangement, strong in its facts, irresistible in its arguments —
and pronounced with such appropriate eloquence and such evident
sincerity, as to obtain and deserve the applause and confidence of
an immense majority of the House. . . .
Sir James Graham's speech has already done much good in the
country, and will do more as it is more maturely considered.[78]

In a letter to his mother, William E. Gladstone reported that this
speech by a man 'who knew more of economics and trade matters

[75] *Hansard*, 3rd Ser., XXI, 1240-1241.   [76] *Ibid.*, 1243.
[77] *Ibid.*, 1246.   [78] *Quart. Rev.*, LI, 282.

... than the rest of the cabinet of 1841 all put together' was so convincing that it led him to vote with the Government against Hume's motion.[79]

Despite the excellent work which he had done on behalf of parliamentary reform, his labours on the agriculture committee of 1833, and his yeoman service in defence of a let-alone Corn Law policy, it was in his cabinet post as First Lord of the Admiralty that Graham was to make himself justly famous. From September 1830 to the following February he busied himself with a painstaking study of naval affairs, corresponded voluminously with admirals, Lords of the Admiralty, and others,[80] carefully studied the Naval estimates and the reports of each of the Naval branches, and on February 25th, 1831, brought before the House a statement of some of his findings. He had no desire, he said, to exculpate his predecessors, but they had been acting most unconstitutionally! Government works had been started, finished, and paid for in the Naval Department without the knowledge or sanction of the House. For instance, a work at Weavel had been completed and paid for by the Victualling Board without a vote of Parliament. And the cost? — £155,534. At Woolwich a sum of £184,465 had been voted by Parliament but £325,908 had been expended. What was still worse, 'the difference was made good without a vote or the sanction of parliament'.[81]

Another defect in the system was that of employing more men in the service than the votes of the House provided for. In one year, for instance, 3100 more men had been employed in the Naval Department than had been stipulated in the estimates. Since 1820 the cost of this practice had amounted to a sum of £1,243,100 in wages alone. Would the House like to know where the money came from? He could tell them that

> his predecessors in office had reduced, practically, the estimates for timber, and the materials for building ships, and for keeping our arsenals in such a state as that war should not take us at a dis-

[79] JOHN MORLEY, *The Life of William E. Gladstone*, I, 114 (Hereinafter cited as *Life of Gladstone*).

[80] I found many of these letters among the Graham papers at Netherby. Others can be found in the *Admiralty Papers* at the Public Record Office in the Admiralty Secretary In-Letters (Hereinafter cited as (Adm. Sec. In-Letters)). In one of Graham's letters to his friend Ellice, he stated that he was 'working like a dog'.

[81] *Hansard*, 3rd Ser., II, 950.

advantageous surprise; that is, the estimates voted for these specific purposes by that House were not entirely expended under these heads, and the difference between the sum actually expended and that voted, was appropriated to other items . . . the actual expenditure under which exceeded the sums specified in the voted estimate.[82]

In the case of timber the sums voted in four years amounted to £3,705,000 while the actual expenditure was only £2,675,000 thus leaving a surplus of estimate over expenditure of £1,030,000. In the case of army provisions the surplus of estimate over expenditure was £805,000.[83] The Deputy Chairman of the Victualling Board had told him that the Naval service was of such a nature, dependent as it was on contingencies, that it was difficult if not impossible to designate beforehand the actual outlay under each head.[84] Graham could never agree to that principle, and to remedy this unconstitutional and injudicious procedure he proposed to lay before the House annually a regular balance-sheet in which would be placed the specific expenditures in the Navy and in the Victualling Board. To simplify and clarify matters still more, he had decided to separate the estimates for the Navy from those of the Victualling Board. In addition, the expenditures of the sub-branches of each of these departments were to be classified under separate headings. He wished he could announce reductions for the current year, he said, but in order to finish projects already begun in consequence of 'the misappropriations in the four years [1828-1831]'[85] and because of 'circumstances',[86] he could not do so. He then asked the House to authorize an increase in the personnel of the service — 2000 more seamen and 1000 more marines — 'for the express purpose of not keeping a greater number of men than parliament by its express vote had authorized'.[87]

[82] *Hansard*, 3rd Ser., II, 952.   [83] *Ibid.*

[84] Graham had directed the Victualling Board to submit a balance sheet showing the sums of money voted for victualling the Navy between January 1830 and January 1831 and the amount actually spent under each head; the number of persons employed in each class, their salaries, fees, etc.; the amount of stores on hand. See *Admiralty Papers* (Adm. Sec. In-Letters), 1/3794; 3/223; 1/4306.

[85] *Hansard*, 3rd Ser., II, 954.

[86] The warlike preparations of France, the disturbed state of Italy, and the threatened march of Austria into the Papal States, required a large fleet in the Mediterranean. See secret letter of Graham in *Admiralty Papers* (Adm. Sec. In-Letters), 1/4365.

[87] *Hansard*, 3rd Ser., II, 955.

He also asked the House for increased funds to enable him to complete the unfinished projects which had been started in the dockyards and arsenals.

Graham did not like to ask for these increased sums, but he said they were necessary in order to straighten out the accounts and he promised that the estimates for the next year would show considerable reductions. In fact, some reductions had already been made: two commissionerships in the Navy Board, two in the Victualling Board, a Naval draughtsman, and two clerks. He was also going to abolish the office of Paymaster of the Marines and transfer his duties to the Victualling Board. In addition, he intended to reduce by 56 the number of civil officers in the dockyards, as well as eighteen other offices. In all, a saving of £27,238 was to be effected.

With respect to superannuations 'his rule was to allow just claims and length of service when the office was necessary; and in cases in which the offices were superfluous, his rule was, to abolish the office, but to allow a fair superannuation allowance'.[88]

When Graham concluded this long and able speech by moving for a grant of £1,081,600 for the service for the current year, Sir George Clerk immediately rose to defend the Victualling Board, of which he was a member, against 'the sneers of the right hon. Baronet'.[89] When the balance of £280,000 in the Naval service was added to the £280,000 additional for which Graham had asked, it would, said Clerk, be using £560,000 more than the previous Board had used. Did that look like retrenchment to the House? In case of an emergency, such as war, what would the First Lord do, if his expense accounts were to be so strictly balanced? Graham replied that he could not help 'admiring the playfullness and good humour' of Clerk. In case of war, he answered, he would simply come to the House, explain the situation, and ask for a special grant; if the House was not sitting, he would incur the expense and rely on the House to approve it later on. Parliament, he was certain, would approve the action if he had acted rightly, and if not, would drive the ministry out of office. If the House would

> insist upon this estimate being drawn in the same way for the
> future, and then, in every subsequent year, compare the items, and

88 *Ibid.*, 957.　　　　　　　　　89 *Ibid.*, 962.

demand how each individual sum had been expended, every hon. Gentleman would be able henceforward to understand the Navy Estimates, which was more, he believed, than any hon. Gentleman could say he had been able to do in former years.[90]

It was Graham's ambition and intention to establish a book-keeping system at the Admiralty and to bring some semblance of order out of its inextricably confused accounts. This effort naturally met with the hearty approval of Hume, to whom statistics and balanced accounts were almost as important as food itself, and to whom Graham's revelations of past corruption and inefficiency at the Admiralty were such an insult to the House that it 'called for an investigation'.

During the debates on the various items in the estimates, Sir Bryan Martin declared that Graham's assertion that the Admiralty Board, of which he (Martin) was a member, had made improper use of public money, was a 'slanderous falsehood'. Would Graham accuse any member of that Board of having used one shilling or one farthing except for the public service? 'Positively not', answered Graham, not one of them could he accuse of malversations, but only of 'misappropriation of these monies, proceeding from an error of judgment'.[91] This was the type of repartee in which Graham loved to indulge but which cost him dearly in friendship and popularity.

While the House was discussing the proposed vote of £810,000 to his Majesty for the purchase of timber and naval stores, Hume asked Graham what he could say in defence of the extravagance of keeping five Royal yachts afloat as well as one for the com-missioners of the Navy and one for the Lord Lieutenant of Ireland.[92] The expense of the yachts was small, answered Graham, and furthermore it was the only mode remaining to the Admiralty to keep veteran officers on full pay. Army men were put in charge of old forts and garrisons, and these five yachts were all the patronage the Admiralty had. As for the Lord Lieutenant of Ireland, he represented the Crown, and when he put out to sea, should not have to appear 'without the paraphernalia of Royalty'.[93]

When the vote of £63,363 for the expense of the victualling yards was proposed, Clerk asked Graham if the rumour that he intended

<hr />

[90] *Hansard*, 3rd Ser., II, 975.   [91] *Ibid.*, III, 952.
[92] *Ibid.*, 1113-1114.   [93] *Ibid.*

to discontinue supplying beer for the Navy at home was true. 'Yes', said Graham, this was one of the means by which he had been able to reduce the expense of each man from 32 to 29 shillings per day.[94]

As soon as Graham had become First Lord, he wrote to each of the branches of the Admiralty demanding that they send him 'correct' estimates of the amount of money voted and the amount actually spent and to send in the reports in such a form that they could be understood. In each case he demanded the strictest economy. The Navy Board was directed to reduce the salary of the Comptroller from £1200 to £1000; orders were issued directing the payment of clerks in the Vice-Admiralty Courts by salary instead of fees (accomplishing both economy and easier accounting); the submission of annual *and* quarterly reports was required of all officials; the staff of each department was ordered to be reduced to as small a scale 'as can be done consistent with the nature and quantity of business to be performed in each'.[95]

The bureaucrats in the various branches of the service, feeling as if a bomb had been dropped in their midst, were completely dismayed at Graham's demands for accuracy, economy, and efficiency. Sir John Barrow, at the Naval Board, protested against any diminution either in the number of clerks or in the amount of their salaries,[96] while the head of the Victualling Board, as already pointed out, complained of 'the difficulties we experience in a strict compliance with the directions they [Admiralty] have been pleased to give'.[97]

But, with the exception of such Tory magazines as *Fraser's*,[98] the economizing zeal of Graham met with universal approval. The *Morning Chronicle* thanked him for exposing 'the system of deception and mystification' practised at the Admiralty;[99] the *Morning Herald* declared that Graham was entitled to the thanks of the entire country;[100] the *Manchester Guardian* was happy that

---

[94] *Admiralty Papers* (Adm. Sec. In-Letters), 1/3796. The order was issued a few weeks later and those working in the Naval brewing establishments were discharged.

[95] *Ibtd.*, 1/3473. Additional information in numbers 1/4306 and 3/223.

[96] *Ibid.*, 1/3473. [97] *Ibid.*, 1/3794.

[98] 'As fuss'd Lawd of the Hammyrallyty, a most miserable figure maketh he.' *Fraser's*, III, 609.

[99] *Chronicle*, February 26th, 1831, p. 2.

[100] *Herald*, February 28th, 1831, p. 2.

he had exposed the gross jobbery which had been going on and asked whether those who had practised it were to escape prosecution.[101] *The Times* went still further and after praising Graham very highly, declared that high crimes and misdemeanours had been committed and that those guilty ought to be impeached.[102]

Those who thought that Graham would now rest on his laurels were mistaken, for, as the Admiralty bureaucrats were soon to discover, he had just begun his labours. With a clear resolve that the next Naval estimates to be presented to the House should show a substantial reduction, he set his face resolutely towards that goal. He began by writing to the Navy Board telling them of the great expense of maintaining the Naval force on the Great Lakes in Canada and asking whether or not it wasn't high time to show 'to the Americans the sincerity of the pacific policy of our Government',[103] and to save a goodly sum as well, by withdrawing it altogether. Then he demanded a report from the Victualling Board which must have reduced its officials to a state of nervous prostration. He wanted to know the names of all officials, their duties and salaries; how the duties of the Board were arranged; the number of clerks as well as their duties and salaries; how much was spent on advertisements in newspapers; how much on ink; how the accounts were audited; how many houses and apartments were occupied by the administrative personnel 'specifying by whom they are occupied, the number of rooms contained therein, the amount of expenses incurred ... during each of the last seven years ... in the way of buildings, repairs, furniture, or of any allowances of any description or kind';[104] and how many letters were written to each of the Naval branches. Next he sent Sir Pultney Malcolm to Falmouth to institute 'a rigid inquiry into the whole system of the Packet Service' to find out whether or not 'a smaller number of vessels might be employed' and still not hurt the service.[105] In October he sent out a circular to all department heads stating that in the future 'one clerk in each branch be at his desk by 10 o'clock and the remainder by half past 10 at the latest',[106]

[101] *Manchester Guardian*, March 5th, 1831, p. 2.
[102] *The Times*, February 28th, 1831, p. 4.
[103] *Admiralty Papers* (Adm. Sec. In-Letters), 1/3473.
[104] *Ibid.*, 1/3794 and 3796.
[105] *Ibid.*, 1/3475.
[106] *Admiralty Papers* (Adm. Minutes), 3/224.

and when the Store Department did not get its reports in on time this rule was suspended 'until the arrears are completely brought up, which their Lordships expect will be done by the first of January next'.[107]

When the reports of the Victualling Board came in, it was Graham's turn to be dismayed. Not only were they disorderly and confusing, but they revealed the existence of frightful extravagance. There was a quantity of duck trousers in store at Deptford for use in the convict service 'equal to 30 years consumption'.[108] In Bermuda, the expense of the Commissioner's house amounted to £26,113 — 'ten times greater than it would have been in this country', and the workmen who should have been labouring on the breakwater were actually working on his house.[109]

Reform and economy were obviously needed and Graham began to achieve this by reducing the meat ration on all guardships;[110] ordering a general reduction in salaries and wages of all personnel;[111] and reducing the total numbers employed. Then he obtained the approval of the Treasury Department to a plan for transferring the appointing power of personnel in the Coast Guard from that department to the Board of Admiralty.[112] In addition, he transferred the appointment of all surgeons and assistant surgeons in the Navy from the Victualling Board to the Admiralty Board, and consolidated the duties of the Paymaster of Marines with those of the Treasurer of the Navy and so eliminated the paymaster's office 'whereby a very considerable saving will be effected'.[113] Furthermore, he secured the hearty approval of the Treasury to his plan to discontinue the practice of issuing Sixty-Day bills in payment of stores in favour of making prompt payments as in other branches of the public service.[114] Finally, he prescribed a new and efficient system of keeping accounts for both the Navy and the

[107] *Ibid.*
[108] *Admiralty Papers* (Adm. Vict. Board In-Letters), 109/46.
[109] *Admiralty Papers* (Adm. Navy Board Out-Letters), 106/2505.
[110] 'Crews of Guardships shall receive only one day in each week [it had been two days] Salt Meat, Beef, and Pork alternately.' *Admiralty Papers* (Adm. Vict. Board), 109/45.
[111] *Admiralty Papers* (Adm. Sec. In-Letters), 1/3473.
[112] *Ibid.*, 1/4306; 1/3474.
[113] *Ibid.*, 1/5242.
[114] They recommended, however, that the new system be not brought into operation until 1832. *Ibid.*, 1/4306.

H

Victualling Boards, outlining the precise form in which all reports were henceforth to be made.[115]

The records and reports of the various boards had been so bad that Graham finally decided on a sweeping reform in all branches of the Admiralty. On February 14th, 1832, he laid these new plans before the House. Up to this time the Naval service had been conducted by three boards, the Admiralty, Navy, and Victualling Boards. There had been much overlapping of duties, much needless officialdom, and a woeful lack of reliable records because of the 'cabalistic' system of figures used. Therefore he proposed the total abolition of the Navy and Victualling Boards and the centralization of all naval affairs in the hands of one board which would be responsible to Parliament. In addition, he wanted the naval service divided into five great departments with a responsible officer at the head of each. There should be a Surveyor General to supervise the construction and repair of ships; an Accountant General to superintend the accounts of the Naval and Victualling Departments; a Storekeeper General to have charge of supplies; a Superintendent of the Victualling Department with the same duties as at present performed by the Victualling Board; and a Superintendent of the Medical Department and hospitals. These five officers should hold their positions by warrant from the Admiralty during good behaviour. Instead of four commissioners with the First Lord there would now be five commissioners, each responsible for the board over which he presided. This system

> gave the regular cognizance of each department to its own proper head, while the whole would be brought under the consideration of the general board, and everything that demanded an investigation would be decided before that board, and the proceedings would be regularly noted by the secretary. There would thus be a just division of labour, an undivided control, and a due responsibility, on the one hand, and, on the other, that unity and simplicity which he held to be the very essence and life of public business.[116]

[115] *Admiralty Papers* (Adm. Sec. In-Letters) 1/3475. In addition, he complained that the Stationery Office made excessive charges for binding, printing, etc.; that it was too slow; and that it used poor grades of paper, made mistakes, and was careless. He wanted the Admiralty to do its own printing and publishing. But the Comptroller of the Treasury refused to permit this on the grounds that if the Admiralty was given this privilege all other departments would wish to do the same and soon the office of Public Stationer would have no excuse for existence. *Ibid.*, 1/4307.

[116] *Hansard*, 3rd Ser., X, 358. See also *Annual Register* (1834), 287.

During a previous debate someone had jocularly referred to the 'gleanings' of the Government. He would now give them, he said, some examples of such gleanings and he sincerely hoped that they would not 'impede the labours of the gleaners'.[117] By reducing the number of commissioners he had saved £10,000; secretaries, £2600; superior officers, £19,750; inferior officers, £2725; clerks, £13,920; making a total saving of £49,059.

Next he proposed that on the thirtieth of November each year the Admiralty should transmit to the Board of Audit the Treasurer's accounts and these, together with all vouchers, should be subjected to a thorough audit. In addition, on the thirty-first of each January the auditors should lay on the table of the House a report which would embrace a balance-sheet comparing the expenditures with the estimates.[118]

Graham concluded his convincing address by stating that the proposed measures would make for an efficient service and a scrupulous attention to rules of Parliament and would redeem all his pledges of economy. He then asked leave to bring in a Bill 'to amend the laws relating to the business of the Civil Departments of the Navy, and to make other regulations for the more effectual carrying on of the duties of the same'.[119]

The debates on the measure were very interesting. John Bowring thought that it would be a good thing for the Army to put into effect 'the same system of consolidation which has enabled Sir James Graham to effect so large a saving in the administration of Naval Affairs'.[120] Sir Thomas Trowbridge and Sir Robert Peel, although of the opposition party, thought very highly of Graham's Bill, while Hume, who was hard to please in matters of economy, declared that Graham was deserving of the praise of the House and of the entire country. But Croker, the predecessor of Graham at the Admiralty, had serious objections to overthrowing a system 'which had stood the test of a century and a half'.[121] More than that, he objected to a scheme which increased the power of the Admiralty beyond that of the Monarchy itself! He would, he

---

[117] *Hansard*, 3rd Ser., X, 358.

[118] *Ibid.*, 360.

[119] *Ibid.*

[120] See *West. Rev.*, XVIII-XIX, 146. The *Manchester Guardian* (February 18th, 1834, p. 2) praised Graham very highly for the economies he had effected.

[121] *Hansard*, 3rd Ser., X, 765-766.

declared, have nothing to do 'with the pretty gew-gaws with which he [Graham] was seeking to dazzle his own eyes'.[122]

Opposition to Graham's proposed changes was weak and ineffective, as is indicated by Croker's simple arguments, and the Bill which reformed the naval service 'on a model remaining in force with very little alteration to the end of the century'[123] was easily carried through Parliament.[124] Few changes of any consequence were made in the service for many years, so thoroughly and effectively was the work done by Graham.[125]

With the administrative machinery changed to suit his desires, the First Lord applied his tremendous energy to the work of effecting every possible type of economy. He urged Lord Palmerston, the Foreign Secretary, to use his utmost endeavours to bring the Belgian trouble (to be discussed later), to a peaceful end. 'The expense', he wrote to Grey, of keeping 3000 more seamen this year than last, 'begins to be serious, and the consequent embarrassment will become formidable.'[126] On March 25th, 1833, the First Lord, in proposing the estimates to the reformed House,[127] stated that the committee of 1828 had divided the annual expenditure, which had for five years averaged £55,744,863, into two branches, the first being that in which no reductions could with safety be made. Comparing the gross expenditure of 1832 with that of 1827, he found that the Government had made a reduction of nearly £5,000,000 within the £20,000,000 in which it had the power to economize. He brought with him three charts which graphically portrayed the economies that had been achieved in the naval estimates,[128] the civil establishments,[129] and the half-pay.[130] When Hume declared that he was still not convinced that all possible savings had been made, Graham answered that England's national existence depended on her naval power. 'Let but her naval superiority be once lost . . . [and] she must necessarily fall into the

[122] *Hansard*, 3rd Ser., X, 801.

[123] GEORGE M. YOUNG, *Early Victorian England*, I, 322.

[124] *Statutes at Large*, 2 Will. IV, c. 40. The Order-in-Council was issued on June 27th, 1832. *Admiralty Papers* (Adm. Sec. In-Letters), 1/5243.

[125] WILLIAM L. CLOWES, *The Royal Navy, A History from the Earliest Times to the Present*, VI, 189 (Hereinafter cited as *Royal Navy*).

[126] Graham to Grey, December 23rd, 1832, in PARKER, *op. cit.*, I, 159.

[127] *Hansard*, 3rd Ser., XVI, 1020 et seq.

[128] See App. A.   [129] See App. B.

[130] See App. C.

place of a second-rate power.'[131]   Admiral Codrington, on the
other hand, protested that the Navy had been scandalously dealt
with. Seamen, ship-workers, marines, and many others, he declared,
were now out of work.[132] 'The fact was,' he said, 'there appeared
to be a systematic attempt to put down the Navy'[133] by making
unnecessary economies. Between this charge of undue economy
on the one hand and Hume's charge of undue extravagance on the
other, Graham found it difficult to draw a completely satisfactory
line, but the principle on which he acted was very succinctly stated
to the House on February 17th, 1834. After announcing that since
he had been in office annual naval expenditures had been reduced
from £15,000,000 to £12,000,000[134] and that taxes had been
repealed to the extent of £3,300,000, he declared that

> this great advantage had been the result of gradual and temperate
> reform. They could only be temperate by being gradual — only
> effective by being systematic; and, unless they were systematic,
> they could not be permanent; if not permanent, they could not
> possess that principle which was of vital importance — progressive
> decrease, while the efficiency of the public service was maintained;
> and without that, economic reform would be a curse rather than a
> blessing.[135]

In very few branches of the public service were there as many
opportunities for an extensive use of patronage as in the Naval
Department. Here, too, however, Graham's conduct set a new
example in honesty, purity of motive, and disregard for purely
partisan considerations. One of his first opportunities to make an
important appointment came in 1831. The Mediterranean command had been held by Admiral Codrington, the hero of Navarino,
who had by this victory over the Turks won the Grand Cross of
the Bath — even though the Tories had described the battle as 'an
untoward event'. Not long after, Codrington had been superseded

---

[131] *Hansard*, 3rd Ser., XVI, 1040.
[132] Petitions were sent to the Admiralty by clerks, coopers, brewers, and brick-
layers protesting against the loss of their jobs, and the inhabitants of the dockyards
complained of the loss of trade resulting from these economies. See *Admiralty
Papers* (Adm. Sec. In-Letters), 1/5135.
[133] *Hansard*, 3rd Ser., XVII, 130.
[134] Cobbett figured that of the savings made, at least £40,000 was due to the cheap-
ness of corn. He did not think it just to credit the First Lord with what God had
done!
[135] *Hansard*, 3rd Ser., XXI, 426.

because he had failed to prevent the Turks from carrying off thousands of Greeks from Navarino to Alexandria where they were sold into a horrible slavery. Since this command was again vacant, the Whigs, who felt that Codrington had been unfairly treated by the Tories,[136] urged his appointment and Graham promptly placed him in command.

Shortly thereafter he appointed Sir James Cockburn, a Tory of the old school, to the post of Inspector General of the Marines. Hume objected to this appointment on the grounds that Cockburn had never been in the Marines. Although agreeing with Hume, Graham said that Cockburn had been appointed to the post because he was an efficient administrator. Graham's colleague, Althorp, wrote to him that the appointment of Cockburn was creditable to him (Graham) and advantageous to the service. 'It would be dishonest', he continued, 'to allow politics to interfere with the naval service of the country.'[137] When someone protested that promotions in the dockyards were not being reserved for Whigs exclusively, Graham answered that promotions were all given 'as the reward of merit',[138] and not as a reward for party loyalty.

Some of the Whigs interpreted this political impartiality of Graham as a desire on his part to cultivate the 'Conservative Party'.[139] The party patronage chief wrote to Graham begging him in the case of future vacancies to 'endeavour to discover meritorious individuals of our own caste to fill them'.[140] Graham's answer to this letter is one of which any official could be justly proud, and one which very few could honestly have written:

> I have endeavoured to serve the public faithfully, and I have never prostituted the patronage of my office to any base purpose. The officers have generally been selected by me for their efficiency, and not for their politics; and if professional merits be regarded by my successor he will have no reason to complain of my appointments.[141]

---

[136] 'In my opinion Codrington ought to have the command,' wrote Althorp to Graham, 'he was shamefully used by the last administration.' In PARKER, op. cit., I, 161.   [137] Althorp to Graham, in Ibid., 164.

[138] Graham to —— M.P., in PARKER, op. cit., 163.

[139] The conservative Whigs and liberal Tories were now following Peel's leadership along lines almost identical with those Graham had advocated since 1828.

[140] See PARKER, op. cit., I, 164.

[141] Graham was to be 'highly commended', wrote Brougham, 'for his staunch virtue in refusing all jobbery. Nothing of Nepotism [so rife elsewhere] could be charged upon him'. BROUGHAM, op. cit., III, 255.

At this time all merchant seamen were paying sixpence a month to the Greenwich Hospital Fund. On May 16th, 1834, Lyall proposed that this payment be transferred to the Merchant Seamen's Institution on the grounds that there was distress among the seamen and because they did not get value received from the other. Graham objected to this proposal on the principle that such a loss of funds would cripple the hospital, and because the proposal would not aid the seamen. His reason for the latter view was that as soon as the sixpence were transferred, 'a corresponding reduction would be made in the wages of the men'.[142]

Early in 1834 Graham revealed his attitude towards trade unions. As First Lord of the Admiralty he had interfered on behalf of the master-coopers in their quarrel with the journeymen. The latter had struck for higher wages and for the dismissal of apprentices who they claimed had been hired for the sole purpose of reducing the wages of the journeymen. The purpose of Graham's interference was to teach the journeymen a lesson. If, because of government interference, the strike was unsuccessful, workmen would learn not to strike. He argued that if the Government did not stop these strikes in small industries, the day would not be far distant when a union in a vital industry might strike and so strangle the economic life of the State.

While his reorganization of the naval service, his successful efforts on behalf of economy, and his impartiality between Whig and Tory in the distribution of the patronage were the things for which Graham was praised by officials and M.P.s of all shades of opinion, his practical reforms which affected immediately the lives of the seamen were of equal importance. In fact, to the men who lived on the sea, the latter were more important than the former.

In the first place, he persuaded the cabinet to cease using convicts in the dockyards and to send them instead to Van Diemen's Land where there was a great demand for labour. Then, early in 1834, he opposed a motion of Yorke to the effect that convicted smugglers be used as seamen in the Navy. 'Was it likely that independent and honourable men would be anxious to enter

---

[142] *Hansard*, 3rd Ser., XXIII, 1149. *The Times* (May 23rd, 1834, p. 5), supported Lyall's motion on the grounds that merchant seamen could not get into the hospital unless they had first been in the Royal Navy.

the service', he asked, 'if the first object they saw on entering a ship was men in irons?'[143] In addition, Graham raised the allowance of each seaman from £5 to £15 upon the capture of prizes of £10,000 value; he increased the seamen's pensions;[144] raised their wages; issued regulations that guaranteed them prompt payment of their wages while in foreign ports; and issued orders forbidding the infliction of punishment until 24 hours after an offence had been committed.[145]

Another subject upon which the First Lord was compelled to exercise his talents was that knotty problem of impressment. On August 15th, 1833, impressment was attacked in the House as cruel, unjust, and unnecessary and as a relic of the Middle Ages. Graham unequivocally stated that he did not like impressment either but that it was a practice of long standing, recognized by Common Law and sustained by Statute Law; a 'right' which should exist but which should be used in cases of emergency only. There was a much better way to handle the question, he thought, than by legally abolishing impressment, and that was so to improve conditions in the naval service that young men would prefer it to the merchant marine: 'Let adequate wages and limited service, free agency and honourable treatment be tried; and there would be no more difficulty in getting men for the Navy than for any other service.'[146] This policy, it is obvious, was entirely in keeping with Graham's principle that all reforms must be slow and gradual. When Brougham showed an inclination to compromise on the subject, Graham wrote to the Prime Minister asking him to stand firmly for the right of impressment.[147] 'I entirely agree with you,' answered Grey, 'that we cannot assent to any proposition for

[143] Hansard, 3rd Ser., XXI, 828-829.

[144] The Order-in-Council was issued on August 24th, 1831. See Admiralty Papers (Adm. Sec. In-Letters), 1/5242.

[145] He estimated that this regulation resulted in a 30 per cent reduction in punishments. Graham's policy in this matter was carefully explained in a letter to all commanders-in-chief on January 10th, 1831: 'by a timely and assiduous attention on the part of officers to the prevention of crime among the men, punishment might be as much diminished as discipline would be improved'. Ibid., 1/3473. See also (Adm. Minutes), 3/223.

[146] Hansard, 3rd Ser., XXI, 1075. The Chronicle (March 5th, 1834), praised Graham for refusing to abolish impressment and for preferring to hold out inducements to men to join the Navy. The Times (February 27th, 1834, p. 2), took the opposite view. See also Peel Papers, CXXXVIII, 18-19 (Br. Mus. Add. MSS. 40318).

[147] Graham to Grey, October 18th, 1833, in PARKER, op. cit., I, 160.

taking away the power of pressing for the Navy.'[148] The surrender
of that prerogative, Graham wrote in an Admiralty Minute, 'will
in my judgement be the death blow of the Naval Supremacy of
this country'.[149] Roake and Varty, writing in the *Westminster
Review*, took the same view, asserting that it was no punishment
to a man to compel him to work on a clean Government ship after
he had served for years on the 'dirty, filthy, smoky, greasy, disorderly, sheep-smeared, goat-dirtied, pitch-plastered, tar-smothered
decks and gallies . . . of a heavy-going slug of a merchantman'.[150]

Very few First Lords have equalled and none has excelled Sir
James Graham in the management of that office. In the first place,
he presented to the House in a simple and intelligible form the
annual estimates for the Navy. Secondly, he introduced the
system by which the Government had to present to the House each
year an account of the naval expenditures audited by an independent Board of Audit. According to Anderson,

> These regulations have now been thirty years in operation; the
> improvements of which he laid the foundation have stood the test
> of war; and although the service has more than doubled, the
> system has continued to work admirably, and few departments of
> the State can account with equal clearness and accuracy for the
> expenditure of the public money entrusted to their charge.[151]

Perhaps the greatest achievement of Graham as First Lord was
his reform of the civil departments of the Navy, each of which was
placed under the individual responsibility of five officers under the
supervision of the Admiralty Board. 'This division of duty', says
Sir John Briggs who served at the Admiralty for 44 years, 'was
established on so sound a basis that after sixty years it still remains
in full force.'[152]

[148] Grey to Graham, October 21st, 1833, in *Ibid.*
[149] *Admiralty Papers* (Adm. Minutes), January to June, 1834.
[150] *West. Rev.*, XX, 253.
[151] 'Sir William Anderson's Memorandum', cited in PARKER, *op. cit.*, I, 168.
Anderson had aided Graham in drawing up these accounts while working with him
at the Admiralty. Writing of Graham's Naval estimates for 1833, *The Times*
(February 23rd, 1833, p. 5), declared that they were 'the best classified and the most
intelligible that we have seen'. The *Chronicle* (February 18th, 1834), and the *Globe*
(July 14th, 1834, p. 2) held the same opinion, while even the anti-Whig *Post* (March
9th, 1834, p. 2), admitted that his work was 'above all praise' and lamented that he
was a member of such a bad cabinet.
[152] Sir John Briggs, 'Record of Naval Administration', cited in PARKER, *op. cit.*, I,
152-153. Sir John Barrow is equally loud in his praise of Graham's work. See JOHN

When Graham went into office with the Whigs he told the House that the policies the Government intended to pursue were reform of the House of Commons, reduction in taxation, retrenchment, and 'a zealous endeavour to maintain peace in its foreign relations'.[153] And to no cause was the First Lord more firmly committed than the last.

The closing months of the Wellington administration had found the country disturbed by the progress of two revolutions, one in France and one in Belgium. The union of Holland and Belgium had been decided upon by the Powers at Paris in 1814, and had proved to be of advantage to the Dutch, who had secured not only the best government positions but also the chief benefits of the financial system. This state of affairs led to bitter discontent among the Belgians and eventually to a revolution which ended in a Belgian declaration of independence. Once independent, the Belgians chose the Duc de Nemours as their King. To this selection, said Graham, the English Government was opposed because the Duke was the second son of Louis Phillipe, the King of France, and French power would thereby be increased to a dangerous extent. War might even result from this situation and since the Government of Grey was opposed to war, it was opposed to the selection of Nemours. The Belgians therefore decided, on the suggestion of Palmerston, to elect Prince Leopold of Saxe-Coburg as King, and France reluctantly approved the choice. Holland, however, refused to accept Prince Leopold and in the war which again broke out the Dutch were easily victorious over the Belgians. At this point France, on the invitation of Leopold, intervened while England dispatched a fleet to the Downs. The French intervention in Belgium had created as much excitement in England as the Dutch invasion of Belgium had excited in France, and Palmerston insisted on the withdrawal of French troops from Belgium as soon as the Dutch troops had left. It was suggested that England send troops to Ostend, but Graham implored Palmerston not to do so because 'the presence of our troops at Ostend would be a signal for war'.[154] He also wrote to the Prime Minister

---

BARROW, 'Autobiographical Memoirs', cited in CLOWES, *op. cit.*, VI, 189-190. See also *The Times*, March 6th, 1834, p. 4.
[153] *Hansard*, 3rd Ser., I, 1375.
[154] Graham to Grey, in PARKER, *op. cit.*, I, 156.

that if England occupied Ostend, 'France . . . will not delay to occupy the whole line of fortresses, and to cover Belgium with her troops'.[155] When the Dutch refused to agree to the Protocol of June 25th, 1831,[156] drawn up by England and France, these countries agreed to coerce Holland by an embargo and by dispatching a fleet to the Dutch coast.[157] As soon as this decision was reached, Graham directed Commander Malcolm to bottle up the Dutch fleet and prevent it from leaving port.[158] A combined French and English fleet blockaded the Scheldt on November 4th, 1832, and two days later the embargo was proclaimed.[159] At the same time a French army had taken Antwerp and the hopelessly discomfited Dutch ceased fighting and agreed to a convention which ended the embargo and provided for the free navigation of the Scheldt and the Maas.[160]

'Having settled Belgium', Graham wrote gleefully to Earl Grey, 'we shall, I hope, arrange Portugal, and then we shall be in a position to talk boldly to Russia'.[161] Fortunately for the peace-loving Graham the Portuguese civil war was settled without recourse to actual fighting, although he had directed the Navy to be there to 'give all possible protection to the trade of this country'.[162] 'Talking boldly to Russia' was not necessary.[163]

On the other hand, it had by 1833 become necessary not only

---

[155] Id. to Id. in *Ibid.*, 157.

[156] This protocol left the Luxembourg question open for future negotiation; reduced Belgium's debt; and allotted to each country its share of the debts contracted since 1814. See G. W. T. Omond, 'Belgium, 1830-1839', in WARD and GOOCH, *Camb. Hist. of Br. For. Pol.*, II, 140.

[157] 'Convention between Great Britain and France, relative to the Netherlands', in *State Papers* (1831-1832), XIX, 258.

[158] Graham to Grey, November 15th, 1832, in PARKER, *op. cit.*, I, 159.

[159] *Admiralty Papers* (Adm. Sec. In-Letters), 1/5243.

[160] 'Convention between His Majesty and the King of the French, on the one part, and the King of the Netherlands on the other', in *State Papers*, XX, 282. Other parts of the settlement were not reached until 1839.

[161] Graham to Grey, August 2nd, 1833, in PARKER, *op. cit.*, I, 160. On August 31st, 1832, Graham wrote to Admiral Parker: 'I consider it an object of national importance, that we should not be dragged as Principals into this contest at its close, and that the use of Force to cover the retreat of Don Pedro, should, if possible, be avoided, since I fear such a measure would cast a shade of doubt over our strict neutrality and involve us in future difficulties.' *Graham Papers*.

[162] *Hansard*, 3rd Ser., X, 970.

[163] Graham felt that Russia was working for a Dutch victory in the war against Belgium in order to cause the overthrow of the English Government. See Graham to Stanley, November 5th, 1832, in PARKER, *op. cit.*, I, 158.

to talk boldly, but also to act boldly towards Ireland. Here was the perennial problem, the one that had ended the career of many statesmen, disrupted numerous ministries and overthrown many governments. When the Grey ministry came into office in 1830, only the persistent and more immediate problem of parliamentary reform prevented the Government from immediately grappling with this Irish problem.

The English attempts to collect the arrears of tithes in Ireland, even with force, had failed; many refused to pay their rents; and numerous bodies were formed whose object was organized defiance of the law.[164] A repeal of the Union, by force if necessary, became the objective of O'Connell and other Irish leaders. In defending the Government's 'strong' Irish policy, Graham declared in 1831 that the supremacy of the law had been vindicated, and though he felt that civil war was the greatest of all evils, yet he for one 'would fight for Ireland as he would fight for Kent'. If he had stopped there all would have been well, for very few could have expected that any member of the English Government would acquiesce in a repeal of the Union. But not being able to restrain himself, or else being indifferent to the effect of what he said, Graham went on to announce that he was certain that 'the whole people of England . . . would not allow themselves to be overthrown by the people of Ireland'. No sooner were those words out of his mouth than he realized that he had committed a serious *faux pas* and hastily corrected himself: 'it was not the people of Ireland who threatened it [the Union], it was only some demagogues'.[165] It was a leap from the frying pan into the fire. Since the only M.P. from Ireland present in the House was O'Gorman Mahon, the latter immediately demanded that Graham have the manliness to tell the House whether he was referring to him (Mahon) and if not that Graham immediately stand up and disclaim the imputation. The First Lord immediately apologized for having used the word 'demagogue' when 'agitator' would have been preferable![166]

The situation in Ireland during the summer of 1831 was very

---

[164] The more notorious of these organizations were the Whitefeet, Blackfeet, Lady Clares, and Molly Maguires. See LOCKER-LAMPSON, *A Consideration of the State of Ireland in the Nineteenth Century*, 154.

[165] *Hansard*, 3rd Ser., II, 715.

[166] Both the *Post* (February 23rd, 1831, p. 2), and *The Times* (February 22nd, 1831, p. 4), took Graham to task for this indiscretion.

bad. The Lord Lieutenant had written to Graham in July urging him and the cabinet to legislate for Ireland and to do so 'with the rapidity of lightning'. Nothing was done, however, because legislating with the rapidity of lightning, as Graham wrote to Anglesey, 'was not one of the characteristics of the government'.[167]

Disturbances in Ireland subsided somewhat during the investigations of the Select Committee that had been appointed in 1831, but, nothing having been done by the Government to ameliorate conditions there, rioting broke out afresh in 1832 on such a scale that stern measures were felt to be necessary. In view of Lord Anglesey's apprehensions that O'Connell's repeal agitation might occasion a resort to armed conflict, Graham sent Commander Pultney Campbell to Cork with seven or eight naval vessels and some marines in the hope 'that the moral effect' would be salutary.[168] By August conditions were so bad that Graham concluded that there was no alternative but to govern the land by force. He heartily desired that a middle-of-the-road policy could be found, but, this apparently out of the question, it appeared to him that England must choose between Protestant ascendancy or the mandate of Catholic agitators.[169] Early in October Anglesey wrote to Graham that unless the Church of Ireland were reformed it would not be long before there would be no church to reform. He not only advised reform, however, but also insisted that it be granted with good grace so that the Government would get credit for it. But while the liberal Anglesey advised reform, Stanley, the Chief Secretary for Ireland, did not agree that reform was the best solution. He introduced a Coercion Bill instead which would enable the Lord Lieutenant to suppress any meeting, to proclaim any district in Ireland so disturbed as to require the application of the law, to establish a curfew in tumultuous districts, and to place offenders under the jurisdiction of courts-martial.[170] A majority of the House was probably opposed to this extremely coercive measure, but Stanley's brilliant speech, which Russell characterized as 'one of the greatest triumphs ever won in a popular assembly by the powers of oratory',[171] enabled him to

---

[167] Graham to Anglesey, July 9th, 1832, in PARKER, *op. cit.*, I, 172.
[168] *Ibid.*   [169] *Ibid.*, 173.
[170] *Statutes at Large*, 3 and 4 Will. IV, c. 73.
[171] RUSSELL, *op. cit.*, 113.

carry his measure through the House, and it ultimately became law.

The Government at the same time pressed forward Althorp's Irish Church Temporalities Bill as something of a counterpoise to this coercive measure. It provided for the consolidation of many dioceses, the abolition of clerical sinecures, and the imposition of a graduated tax on all clerical incomes in excess of £200 a year and placed the proceeds (£60,000 to £70,000) in the hands of commissioners who would use it for repairing churches, building glebe houses, and sundry other purposes.[172] This would relieve the Irish rate-payers of the obnoxious 'vestry 'cess'.[173] Because of opposition in the cabinet as well as in the House, a clause appropriating part of the revenues of the Established Church to secular uses, i.e., Roman Catholic uses, was withdrawn and the Bill, stripped of this clause, became law on August 14th.

This Irish business had caused a split in the cabinet. Lord Anglesey, the Lord Lieutenant, was a liberal; Stanley, the Chief Secretary, was an uncompromising advocate of the hated Coercion Bill. In addition, Stanley, who had been angered by a coarse attack which O'Connell, leader of the Irish brigade, had made on him, decided to resign. Earl Grey felt that the resignation of Stanley in the midst of the Irish difficulty would be fatal to the Government and solicited Graham's aid in trying to keep him in the cabinet.[174] Graham promptly wrote to Stanley that it would be right for him to resign had the cabinet refused his Coercion Bill, but that he should not do so now that the Government had passed his measure. Then Graham added the significant statement that if Stanley had actually quit the Government on the subject of Church reform, he 'would not have resigned alone',[175] meaning that he (Graham) would have resigned with him. He concluded the letter by pointing out how Grey had stood by Stanley on many important occasions and by urging him to remain as the Irish Secretary in order to 'save the Church of Ireland'.[176] Although both Graham

---

[172] *Statutes at Large*, 3 and 4 Will. IV, c. 37.

[173] The vestry 'cess was a tax imposed for maintaining churches and meeting the expense of religious service. It was paid by a Catholic population, but administered by a Protestant vestry. Furthermore, it was uncertain as to amount and could be raised or lowered as occasion demanded.

[174] Grey to Graham, November 3rd, 1832, in PARKER, *op. cit.*, I, 175 et seq.

[175] Graham to Stanley, November 3rd, 1832, in *Ibid.*, 177.   [176] *Ibid.*

and Richmond then offered to resign in order to make room in the cabinet for Stanley, neither Grey nor Stanley would consent to it. Durham, whom Graham and many others disliked on account of his ungovernable temper and because he had caused trouble in the cabinet by his disagreements with Grey, his father-in-law, came to the rescue in November by resigning the Privy Seal. Goderich succeeded him and thus created a vacancy at the Colonial Office for Stanley. Lyttleton replaced Stanley in Ireland, and when Anglesey retired because of poor health, the Marquis of Wellesley became the new Viceroy.

With the opening of the session of 1834 Graham found himself at variance with his colleagues in the case of an Irish judge, Baron Smith. O'Connell had accused Smith of gross neglect of duty and of trying to compensate for his inefficiency and deficiency as a judge by turning into a violent partisan. He declared that Smith never got to court before 12.30, his state of health being such as to enable him to 'sit out the night; but did not allow him to rise by day'.[177] He accused Smith of having pronounced anti-Catholic sentiments from the bench, and demanded an official inquiry into the judge's conduct. Lyttleton, the Secretary, supported O'Connell's charge as did Stanley. The latter even went so far as to state openly that Smith's court, the first two days, had sat from 11.30 a.m. to 7.00 p.m.; the next day from 11.30 to 10.45; and on the fourth day from 6 p.m. until the next morning.[178] Peel, on the other hand, supported Smith on the grounds that he had never been accused of committing an act of injustice and that his remarks on the Roman Catholics were aimed only at agitators. Graham took the same line, stating that in this matter he would have to vote against his colleagues. To Graham, Smith's only offence was that he had delivered himself of an indiscreet charge against agitators and had denounced resistance to tithe and to Repeal. 'For this', he wrote to Grey, 'he is to be handed over by the Government to his enemies. Mr. O'Connell is to triumph, and the law in Ireland in the person of a judge is to be trodden down.'[179] He then declared that nothing could be done anyway, and that his colleagues had acted foolishly because the House of Lords would not agree to remove Smith and their concurrence was necessary

---

[177] *Hansard*, 3rd Ser., XXI, 274. [178] *Ibid.*, 301.
[179] Graham to Grey, February 13th, 1834, in PARKER, *op. cit.*, I, 185.

before that could be done. Independent as ever, Graham told
Grey that he was going to resign, but the latter succeeded in convincing Graham that such action would be unjustifiable. Graham
did not press the matter further and the House reversed the
favourable vote of 174 to 167 in favour of O'Connell's motion to
one of 165 to 159 against it.[180] The *Quarterly Review* praised 'the
high honour and consistency'[181] of Graham's conduct in this
affair, while the *Chronicle*, a paper usually hostile to Graham,
declared that Graham's conduct was 'impudent'.[182] Greville,
taking the same ground, maintained that it was 'a maudlin, stupid
sort of speech' that Graham had made.[183]

On May 6th, 1834, the breach in the cabinet, which had been
getting wider and wider, became unbridgeable. On that day Stanley introduced his Tithe Bill and in doing so quoted O'Connell and
Sheil as having declared that it was not the amount of the tithe
but the use to which it was put that was the real cause of complaint. Russell was willing to see justice done to Ireland regardless
of the sacrifice he had to make, even if it meant he had to agree to
appropriation. 'My speech made a great impression,' wrote
Russell, 'the cheering was loud and general.'[184] But while the
cheering was going on Stanley wrote a note to Graham saying,
'Johnny has upset the coach'.[185] And that is precisely what had
happened. At a cabinet meeting the next day some of the members
asked Russell to retract his statement on appropriation, but he
refused to do so. The split in the cabinet between what might be
called the liberals and the conservatives, could now no longer be
disguised. Palmerston blamed Graham for 'driving in the wedge'
that had now split the party wide open. According to the Foreign
Secretary, 'Durham and Co.'[186] got Ward to bring in a motion on
May 27th depriving the Irish Church of part of its temporalities.
This put the cabinet in a quandary because 'they would not',
as the hostile *Annual Register* saw it, 'meet it with a direct negative,
partly because they dreaded becoming unpopular . . .; partly
because they had no dislike to it in itself . . . To accede to the

---

[180] *Annual Register* (1834), 17-18.   [181] *Quart. Rev.*, LI, 282.
[182] *Chronicle*, February 22nd, 1834.
[183] *The Greville Memoirs, 1841-1860*, ed. by Lytton Strachey and Roger Fulford,
III, 14. (Hereinafter cited as *Memoirs*).
[184] RUSSELL, *op. cit.*, 120.   [185] *Ibid.*, 120-121.
[186] Palmerston to his brother, in PARKER, *op. cit.*, I, 188.

motion, on the other hand, was to cut off from the cabinet a very important section of its respectability, and of its oratorical and business talent'.[187] This meant Stanley and Graham, the very ones whom Durham liked the least. Efforts were then made by members of the party to get Stanley and Graham to resign,[188] because to vote against Ward's motion would drive out Althorp and Russell; to support it, Stanley and Graham would have to go, and possibly Grey as well. As a last expedient it was suggested that a committee of inquiry be appointed, but Graham objected to this on the very logical grounds that in consenting to a commission of inquiry the Government would be bound by its findings and advice and there was little doubt as to what such a commission would find. The Whig *Edinburgh Review* affirmed that the legislature had the right to appropriate some of the revenues of the Irish Church 'to such purposes as the Legislature may direct'.[189] It even went so far as to suggest that some of these funds might be used to pay the Roman Catholic clergy in Ireland. A majority of the party, as well as a majority of the cabinet, were of the same opinion. In other words, Whig principles were changing, and since Graham would not change his, they parted company. The majority of the party was in favour of appropriation; Graham was adamantly opposed to it. He was a devoted son of the Established Church; he 'loved it from the bottom of his heart'; and he would never consent to a measure that would deprive it of any of its property or power. When, despite his objections, a commission was appointed to inquire into the state of the Irish Church, Graham, along with Stanley, Richmond, and Ripon, promptly resigned.

As early as May 25th, 1834, Brougham had written to Grey that Stanley and Graham were going to resign. Their places would not, he said, be easily filled, but from Stanley who is 'quite honest and open', the Government would continue to get aid.[190] The implication was perfectly apparent — Graham was not open

---

[187] *Annual Register* (1834), 42.

[188] 'Graham's Papers', in PARKER, *op. cit.*, I, 190-192. See also BROUGHAM, *op. cit.*, III, 248. Lansdowne and Palmerston opposed the resignation while Ellice and Holland favoured it. Greville thought Stanley would have given in 'if Graham had not been very fierce and urged him on to resistance'. GREVILLE, *Jour. of Reigns of Geo. IV and Will. IV*, III, 38-39. *The Times* (May 29th, 1834, p. 2), took the opposite view saying that it 'could scarcely think [Graham] will take a direction opposite to that of Mr. Stanley'.

[189] *Edin. Rev.*, LX, 494.   [190] BROUGHAM, *op. cit.*, III, 248.

I

and honest.[191] Brougham also added that Graham had determined to leave in any event and that this appropriation fuss
simply furnished him a good pretext. Greville was surprised that
'after swallowing the camel of the Reform Bill, they [Graham
and Stanley] should strain at the gnats which were perched upon
the camel's back'.[192] O'Connell, who thought Graham 'a
political goose of the most foolish class', was glad that 'the worst
part of the government' had quit.[193]

But Brougham, Greville, and O'Connell were all mistaken.
Graham had been carefully nurtured in the doctrines of the
Established Church and he was a Tory in his insistence that that
Church be the exclusive one. In fact, one of the reasons for his
having joined the Whig party was that it was committed 'to a firm
maintenance of the Established Protestant religion . . . which
the revolution of 1688 bore triumphant over Popery and regal
tyranny'.[194] Now that the Whigs had deserted one of the planks in
their platform Graham could not continue in office with them
because to do so would be 'inconsistent with genuine Whig
principles'. From his point of view, he had not deserted the
party; it had deserted him by abandoning its principles. 'Appropriation' was not a 'pretext' but a genuine reason for leaving the
cabinet. Religion was a more important thing to Graham than it
was to Brougham. He had supported Catholic Emancipation
and the repeal of the Test and Corporation Acts; he favoured
reform of the Church in Ireland, i.e., enforcement of residence,
abolition of large pluralities, and augmentation of smaller
livings; and as a member of the Grey ministry he had advised a
fifty per cent reduction in the number of Irish bishops. But he
could never consent to appropriation. Reform was one thing,
confiscation of vested rights and interests quite another. On this
principle he was independent enough to leave his colleagues and
his friends, and to do as he thought proper whether his constituents

---

[191] Ramsay is also of that opinion: 'Graham was a politician with a reputation for
shiftiness.' RAMSAY, *op. cit.*, 225.

[192] GREVILLE, *Jour. of Reigns of Geo. IV and Will. IV*, III, 89.

[193] *Correspondence of Daniel O'Connell*, ed. by W. J. Fitzpatrick, I, 439. Creevey
was all wrought up over the resignation and described 'Canting Graham' and
'Pighead Richmond' as Stanley's 'bottle holders'. THOMAS CREEVEY, *The Creevey
Papers, a Selection from the Correspondence and Diaries of the Late Thomas Creevey*,
ed. by Herbert Maxwell, 616 (Hereinafter cited as *Creevey Papers*).

[194] Graham to Stanley, June 4th, 1834, in PARKER, *op. cit.*, I, 195-196.

approved his conduct or not.[195] That the appropriation matter
was not a mere pretext for leaving the cabinet is evident from a
letter which he wrote to Lyttleton:

> It is too painful — the wound is yet green — to enter on the causes
> which have led to a separation from the friends I loved the best
> and trusted most. But they are about to enter on a path where
> conscience, duty and all the obligations I value most forbid me to
> follow them; and though the wrench has been severe, yet I rejoice
> that I have ceased to be a party to measures which I cannot
> approve.[196]

Greville was as wrong as Brougham. The Church question was
no 'gnat perched on the camel's back' to Graham, for he considered saving the Church a more important task than reforming
Parliament.

O'Connell, of course, was completely wrong. Not only were the
seceders, especially Graham and Stanley, not the worst part of the
Government, but in many respects the best. They were by far the
most capable men in the ministry,[197] and Graham was incom-
parably the best administrator. No member of the Government
exceeded, and few, if any, equalled the efficiency and business-like
manner in which he had reformed and administered his department of the Government. This was almost uniformly the attitude
of the press. The *Morning Post* described Graham as Grey's
'ablest man of business';[198] the *Globe* took the same view, stating
that Graham would be hard to replace;[199] the *Manchester
Guardian* praised Graham for the magnificent job he had done at

---

[195] Graham to Aglionby, in *Ibid.*, 197-198. The *Standard* (May 28th, 1834)
declared that Graham had quit for genuine 'British and Christian principles', and
that no resignation from office had been so 'universally acquitted of any alloy of
selfish or sordid motive'.

[196] Graham to Lyttleton, June 3rd, 1834, in PARKER, *op. cit.*, I, 200. In an election
speech at Carlisle on January 12th, 1835, Graham stated his view in these words:
'In accordance with my principles I must and do look upon the State as the Trustee of
the property of the Church; and I consider the State, as such Trustee, bound to apply
it to such uses as were intended by its original donors.' Pamphlet in *Graham Papers*,
entitled 'Speech of the Right Honourable Sir J. R. G. Graham, on being nominated
as one of the candidates for the representation of the Eastern Division of Cumberland'.

[197] Saintsbury has come to the same conclusion. See GEORGE SAINTSBURY, *The
Earl of Derby*, 39. The *Annual Register* (1835, pp. 1-2), declared that the seceders were
the best members of the Government and those in whom most of the people placed
their confidence.

[198] *Post*, May 31st, 1834, p. 2.   [199] *Globe*, May 31st, 1834, p. 2.

the Admiralty.[200] Of the cabinet, Palmerston and Grey especially hated to see Graham leave,[201] while the King told Greville that the four 'seceders' were those whom he 'liked best of . . . all'.[202]

Perhaps, now that the great reforms of 1831-1834 had been accomplished and the ministry split wide open on the Irish problem, it was better for England, Ireland, and the Whigs that Stanley and Graham, Richmond and Ripon should go.[203] They merely complicated the Irish problem by standing squarely in the road of reform. Furthermore, by 1834, both Stanley and Graham were more at one with Peel than they were with the Whigs. Peel had accepted the reforms of 1831-1834, and practically all of his principles and those of Stanley and Graham were now identical. In addition, Peel wanted both of them. He was a conservative and so were they.

When Althorp announced, early in June 1834 the appointment of a commission to study the Irish Church question, Ward again brought in a motion on the subject of appropriation. The Government retaliated by moving the previous question and carried it by a large majority in which Graham voted with the Government. According to Russell,[204] Lord Lyttleton, on the authority of Althorp, informed O'Connell that the cabinet would probably not renew the Coercion Bill in its full vigour. Therefore, when Grey proposed the renewal of the Coercion Bill in its original severe form, O'Connell reminded Althorp of the promise he had made, with the result that, in July 1834, Althorp and his associates in the cabinet (Grant, Rice, and Abercrombie) all resigned.[205] Since the loss of Althorp deprived Grey of his leader in the House of Commons, he resigned as Prime Minister and the King promptly called upon Lord Melbourne to assume the seals of office. The King had never liked the Whigs very much for he assumed that the latter would form a coalition with Peel, Wellington, and

---

[200] *Manchester Guardian*, May 31st, 1834, p. 2.

[201] According to Mme d'Lieven, Graham was the only friend Palmerston had in the entire diplomatic corps but she thought Graham had 'no weight'. See PHILIP W. WILSON, *The Greville Diary*, I, 547.

[202] GREVILLE, *Memoirs*, III, 42. See also *The Times*, May 28th, 1834, p. 4.

[203] See GEORGE K. CLARK, *Peel and the Conservative Party*, 173.

[204] RUSSELL, *op. cit.*, 126-127. See also PARKER, *op. cit.*, I, 208.

[205] It was not hard for Althorp to resign since he did not relish holding office in any event. Russell says that each morning when Althorp arose, so long as he was in office, he wished he was dead. RUSSELL, *op. cit.*, 129.

Stanley so as to check effectively the 'radical' Whigs.[206] Although both Peel and Wellington refused to join such a coalition, Melbourne was able to form a ministry of his own, due in large part to the fact that Althorp was prevailed upon to withdraw his resignation.[207] In November, however, on the death of his father, Lord Spencer, Althorp went to the House of Lords. Melbourne then told the King that Russell was to be the new House Leader. The King did not approve of his choice,[208] nor would he approve of Rice or Abercrombie, and he had consequently to tell Melbourne that his services were no longer required.[209] The Duke of Wellington was called in and immediately recommended to the King that Peel should be summoned from Rome and entrusted with the task of forming a Government.[210] In twelve days Peel was back in England. In the meantime the Duke had sent him a list of suggested ministerial appointees which included both Stanley and Graham. Both were acceptable and on his first day in England Peel wrote asking them to join his Government.[211] Stanley answered by letter. Graham, at Peel's request, went to see him personally on December 14th and although he refused to take office[212] was perfectly delighted with Peel's cordiality and obliging ways.[213] Graham wanted Stanley and his friends to come out in the open, declare their views, and in that manner force Peel to join their 'third party', of which they themselves would form the centre.[214] In addition, having just left the Whig party, Graham felt that it was too early to join Peel's group. Graham and Stanley had publicly declared that they had left Grey's cabinet for reasons of conscience, and if they should so soon join with Peel people

[206] See BRODERICK and FOTHERINGHAM, *Pol. Hist. of Eng.*, 347.

[207] Walpole says that Althorp acceded to the petition of 206 liberals of all shades that he remain in office because they believed that if he ceased to lead the party in the House the Government could not stand. See WALPOLE, *Hist. of Eng.*, III, 468.

[208] See RUSSELL, *op. cit.*, 130; ROBERT PEEL, *Memoirs*, II, 31.

[209] See *Ibid.*, 22.

[210] Peel accepted office in order to save the King the humiliation of having to ask 'his dismissed servants to resume their appointments'. *Ibid.*, 32.

[211] Peel's letter to Graham, dated December 9th, 1834, reads as follows: 'One of my first acts is to make this earnest appeal to you for your co-operation as a Minister of the Crown.' See *Peel Papers*, CXXXVIII, 7-8 (Br. Mus. Add. MSS. 40318).

[212] *Ibid.*, 9. See also GREVILLE, *Memoirs*, III, 192-193.

[213] Graham to Stanley, November 21st, 1834, in PARKER, *op. cit.*, I, 214. See also the *Standard*, December 18th, 1834, p. 2.

[214] PARKER, *op. cit.*, I, 214.

would question their honesty. Then, too, Graham believed that they could help Peel more out of office than in — that is, if his measures were good.[215] Stanley was of the same opinion. Both of them were convinced that such action would strengthen their *own* Conservative party.

The election which was held on the dissolution of Peel's Government returned a House in which the Liberals had a majority.[216] As soon as Parliament met, the Opposition elected Abercrombie Speaker of the House, and followed up this success with carrying an amendment to the Address advising a reform of the municipal corporations. While Graham was not opposed to a moderate reform of these corporations, he nevertheless voted against the amendment because it would put Peel in a minority a second time.[217] Since it was apparent that Peel did not have the confidence of the House he resigned and the King summoned Melbourne once more to take over the seals of office as Prime Minister.

The first measure to confront the new House was a proposal to repeal the malt tax. Graham opposed this on the grounds that repeal would result in an increase in the price of barley grown on light clay lands, but would help the heavy clay land farmers, who, according to the findings of the agricultural committee of 1833, were the most depressed. Furthermore, repeal of the malt tax would lead to a repeal of the Corn Laws, he argued, and even worse than that, the loss of revenue would have to be made up somehow and the Government would in all likelihood resort to the hateful property tax.[218]

At the time of his resignation from the ministry Graham had had two reform Bills relating to the merchant service ready to introduce to the House. Since he knew more about these measures than anyone else in the House, Althorp asked him to take charge and to carry them through[219] — a task which Graham consented

---

[215] Greville says the Whigs were sorry that Graham did not join Peel, 'for they hate him and want to be rid of him'. GREVILLE, *Jour. of Reigns of Geo. IV and Will IV*, III, 176.

[216] Graham was returned for Cumberland having promised to vote for 'all reforms which I consider necessary and safe, and resent all changes which are urged in a restless spirit of innovation'. See Graham's letter to Howard of Greystoke, December 13th, 1834, in PARKER, *op. cit.*, I, 221.

[217] *Hansard*, 3rd Ser., XXVI, 390-394.

[218] *Ibid.*, 812-814.   [219] Althorp to Graham, in PARKER, *op. cit.*, I, 201.

to do. One of these Bills called for a registry of all seamen; the other for the voluntary enlistment of seamen. The first provided for a written agreement between the individual seaman and the ship-owners or masters, to protect the merchant seamen's rights, i.e., that no seaman could be taken to sea without a written agreement to which he was one of the signatories. All masters were compelled to furnish a half-yearly return of the muster-roll required by the Seaman's Act of 1834; and when his ship arrived from a foreign port, the master should immediately deliver his returns to the visiting customs officer. The result would be an exact registry of all merchant seamen.[220] The other Bill reaffirmed the right of the Crown to the service of merchant seamen in the event of war but limited the duration of such service to five years, which service, once performed, would for ever free a seaman from liability to impressment. It also provided that prior to the Royal proclamation of impressment a period of grace should be allowed the seamen, during which time all who *volunteered* would be given a bounty of £10, and such volunteers

> should be entitled to count every year served in war as two years of compulsory service with respect to their claims for pensions, so that for five years of voluntary service during war they should count ten years of service towards becoming entitled to their pensions which now could only be obtained after a full service of twenty years in peace or in war.[221]

These desirable reforms met with widespread approval, Buckingham going so far as to declare that the seamen should 'hold a jubilee in celebration of these announced measures of emancipation'.[222] And they were just the type of reform Graham liked, removing well-known abuses, introducing more efficient methods and systems, but not destroying any tradition vital to the safety of the State.

Peel had recently remarked that the country needed 'men and not measures', but Graham took the opposite view and told Stanley that what was urgently needed were good measures.[223] Further-

---

[220] This Bill easily passed the House and became law on July 30th, 1835. *Statutes at Large*, 5 and 6 Will. IV, c. 19.

[221] *Hansard*, 3rd Ser., XXVI, 1124.

[222] *Ibid.*, 1128. This Bill was also speedily passed and became law on August 21st, 1835. *Statutes at Large*, 5 and 6 Will. IV, c. 24.

[223] Graham to Stanley, in PARKER, *op. cit.*, I, 224.

more, he did not like some of Peel's men. But it was surely
unfair of Graham to accuse Peel of not having selected good
colleagues when both he and Stanley, able and influential,
refused to give him the benefit of their services and consequently
forced him to choose other men. So, from the time of the resignation of Stanley, Graham, Richmond, and Ripon, until the last of
March 1835, there were in reality three parties — the Whigs and
Tories, plus Graham's 'middle party' which consisted of about
thirty or forty members[224] dedicated to a policy of moderate
reform. Most of this group were Tories who, like Peel, had
accepted the Reform Bill, Whigs who resented that party's alliance
with O'Connell, or 'Radicals' who opposed any appropriation
of the revenues of the Irish Church to secular uses. It was this
group to which Stanley referred when, during the debate on the
Address, he said that he was speaking for a considerable body of
men.[225]

Because of Graham's effective work at the Admiralty, he was
'sounded out' in 1834 on the possibility of his accepting the office
of Governor General of India. But he did not 'communicate by
soundings',[226] and refused to accept the post. In 1835 the offer
was renewed, this time being made by Melbourne, but Graham
again rejected the post. His reasons for doing so are admirably
stated in a letter which he wrote to Stanley:

> It has thus happened that I have virtually twice refused the
> Government of India in four months, under two different Adminis-
> trations. I refused it from Sir Robert Peel, because having declined
> the offer of a seat in his Cabinet on the grounds of imperfect
> confidence and of the evils of premature coalitions, I thought that
> the acceptance of a lucrative appointment, which would remove
> me from the scene of a great impending struggle, would cast a
> shade over the motives of my past conduct and prove injurious to
> my reputation both of personal honour and political integrity.
> I refused it from Lord Melbourne, because I am opposed to the
> principles on which his government is formed, to the composition
> of his Cabinet, to the support of the Radicals and Repealers on

---

[224] GREVILLE, *Jour. of Reigns of Geo. IV and Will. IV*, III, 220. To this party,
O'Connell applied the epithet: 'the Derby Dilly'. *Ibid.*, 237 n.

[225] *Hansard*, 3rd Ser., XXVI, 257.

[226] Graham to Stanley, October 21st, 1834, in PARKER, *op. cit.*, I, 210. See also
GREVILLE, *Memoirs*, III, 133.

which it rests, and to the destructive changes which avowedly it contemplates.[227]

Early in 1835 the fateful alliance, under Russell's leadership, of the Whigs, Radicals, and O'Connell's Irish brigade was consummated.[228] The adhesive in the case of the Radicals was fear of Peel's hostility to reform; in the case of the Irish it was appropriation. The combination of Whigs, Radicals, and O'Connell was too much for Graham and Stanley and they therefore joined forces with Peel.[229] Together this group now laid plans of battle for the debate on Ireland which was to come on the last of March. It was agreed that Graham would speak early in the day, Stanley at night, and Peel was to 'wind up the whole'.[230]

To an excited House Russell declared that civil war raged in Ireland because of the Coercion Acts, the forcible collection of tithes, and the tyrannical character of the English Government. It was high time, he asserted, that the House consider the question of the Temporalities of the Church of Ireland. If the House agreed, and he was sure it would, he would like to propose a resolution calling for the application of the surplus revenues of the Church to 'the general education of all classes of Christians' in Ireland.[231] Graham now delivered one of his very best speeches. 'The present is but the commencement of a series of attacks', he began by saying, 'first on Corporation-property, then on private property, and as a conscientious man, I cannot support it.'[232] He then referred to his past record on the Church question and enumerated all the reforms to which he had agreed. Laughter greeted his statement that in voting for these reforms to keep the Government united, he had had to 'strain his conscience' to the uttermost. The object of Russell's resolutions, it seemed to him, was to despoil the Church just because it was rich. The Act of Union had declared that the Church of England and of Ireland should be for ever one and indivisible. It was a solemn contract between the Protestant minority in Ireland in Parliament assembled and the Government of England to assure the protection of Protestant property and religion in the midst of a population

[227] Graham to Stanley, March 1st, 1835, in *Graham Papers*.
[228] Stanley to Peel, March 29th, 1835, in PARKER, *Life of Peel*, II, 298.
[229] 'It places matters on a new footing', said Stanley. *Ibid.*
[230] *Ibid.*   [231] *Hansard*, 3rd Ser., XXVII, 374.   [232] *Ibid.*, 421.

almost entirely Catholic. Graham could not possibly agree to the violation of such a contract. It was clear to him that this was but the first of a series of attacks on the Church, which, he said, 'will lead to the establishment of Catholicism as the religion of Ireland and to the separation of the two united Protestant Churches of Ireland and England'.[233] He was firmly committed to the principle of an Established Church, and if an Established Church was necessary, the State must decide upon the *truth* of the favoured religion. That agreed upon, then it became necessary to pay the clergy a salary sufficiently high to enable them to maintain themselves and their families, for Anglican clergymen were permitted to marry. And he was glad they did marry, too, for 'the dark annals of the Church have taught us, that an unmarried is an unholy priesthood'.[234] From this Graham went on to tell the House what he considered to be the genuine Whig principles on this question:

I should say that they consisted in the assertion of the utmost liberty of thought and action in all matters, whether of politics or of religion consistent with law, order, and constituted authority. No death's head and cross bone denunciations against the free exercise of the elective franchise. No prayer of mercy, limited to heaven, but denied on earth, to the unhappy Catholic, who shall dare to vote for a Conservative candidate. No, Sir, they consist no less in love of freedom, than in jealousy of Popery as an instrument of dominant political power, and in ardent, uncompromising attachment to the Protestant religion as by law established in these realms . . . I told you that I had, upon this subject religious feelings; that the property, the disposition of which is the subject of our discussion, was set apart by the piety of our forefathers . . . to maintain and to propagate the Protestant religion — and I tell you that it is sacred, and must be applied to that purpose. Those who minister at the altar, shall live by the altar: this decree is high as heaven; you cannot take it away: it is strong as the Almighty, you cannot overthrow it: it is lasting as the Eternal; it can never cease to bind you. It is binding on you as Christian Legislators and as Christian men; and for one, there is no consideration on this earth, which shall induce me to compromise or to violate it.[235]

This speech, which Ripon described as 'An admirable compound of sound reasoning, high principles . . . and remarkable elo-

---

[233] *Hansard*, 3rd Ser., XXVII, 429.   [234] *Ibid.*, 438.   [235] *Ibid.*, 439-440.

quence',[236] and which Gladstone described in his diary as 'noble-minded',[237] left no doubt in anyone's mind where Graham stood on the question. It was clear, concise, and very much to the point.

Stanley and Peel also opposed Russell's resolution with excellent addresses,[238] but the resolution was carried by a majority of 25. On the morning of April 9th, Greville discussed the political situation at length with Graham and found that he now favoured an open junction of the Conservatives with Peel's liberal Tories.[239]

In June the question of the Municipal Corporations came up for debate. When the proposed Reform Bill was read, Graham strenuously objected to Clause Nine, the object or purpose of which was to give the franchise to those freemen who had domiciles, because it extended the franchise beyond the limits prescribed by the Reform Bill of 1832, a Bill which Graham regarded as a solemn engagement that must be rigidly adhered to. If they wished to amend the Reform Bill, he told the House, they should do so 'openly' and 'manfully' and not by 'indirection'.[240] Russell took Graham to task for his attitude in opposing a much-needed reform and for having changed his opinions since 1832. This piqued Graham so much that it led him into expressing an opinion which it would have been better to have left unsaid. Why did he support the Reform Bill of 1832? Because 'it provided a resting-place whereon he might resist steadfastly, manfully, and constantly, all further change'.[241] To be sure, he did not consider this binding on Parliament, but it was binding on him. He felt that when the Act of 1832 was passed it would and should lead to other necessary reforms such as Church reform (but no appropriation or separation of Church and State), and municipal reform, too, but not to any tampering with the elective franchise.

[236] Ripon to Graham, April 1st, 1835, in PARKER, *op. cit.*, I, 235.

[237] MORLEY, *op. cit.*, I, 126. The *Post* (March 31st, 1835, p. 4), described the speech as a masterful one, 'potent in argument, rich and copious in illustration, and eloquent both in style and diction . . . It produced a great effect upon the House'.

[238] Stanley's speech, however, cost the 'third party' some members because of his flippant attitude, and because of his attack on the Duke of Wellington. See GREVILLE, *Jour. of Reigns of Geo. IV and Will. IV*, III, 250.

[239] *Ibid.*

[240] *Hansard*, 3rd Ser., XXVIII, 1091-1092.

[241] *Ibid.*, 1099.

In accordance with his interpretation of the Great Reform Bill, he held the franchise to be fixed and immutable.[242]

By the end of the debates on the Municipal Reform Act of 1835, Graham and Stanley had openly allied themselves with Peel. On July 1st Graham was returning to his seat from a division when someone yelled out, 'Why don't you stay where you are?' and Graham, as Greville tells the story, bowed gracefully to the side from which the voice had come and went over to the other side of the House.[243]

[242] His attitude towards this question was clearly put in his Cumberland election campaign pamphlet circulated throughout the country: 'Gentlemen, the Reform Bill is a lever by which all obstacles to good government may be removed; but it is also a fulcrum by means of which the best institutions of the country may be overthrown. It is like fire: in the hands of the honest artisan, a purifying element; in the torch of the incendiary, a consuming flame.' This pamphlet was found in *Graham's Scrap Book* among his papers at Netherby.

[243] GREVILLE, *Jour. of Reigns of Geo. IV and Will. IV*, III, 273.

CHAPTER VII

'A SHABBY GOVERNMENT'

IT was much more enjoyable to be in the ranks of open opposition than to sit with colleagues with whom he could not agree, and hence the Netherby baronet lost no time in denouncing the measures proposed by the Melbourne Government. The first object of his denunciation was the Government's Irish Tithe Bill,[1] whose object was to transfer the burden of the tithe from the occupier to the owner of land, and, it was fondly hoped, bring peace to Ireland. Peace to Ireland? Graham could not possibly see how this measure could bring anything but the sword to that unhappy land. Ultimately, he said, it was a question of what the favoured religion of Ireland should be. It had already been decided that Anglicanism should be, and it was therefore clear that the Government's measure was an attack on the great principle of an Established Church.

Furthermore Graham was opposed to the principle of numerical proportions[2] since it would be equally fatal to the existing Church Establishment. If this principle were adopted, it might be a success, and in that case 'five years would not roll over their heads', he prophesied, 'before its extension to England would be pressed on them with irresistible force'.[3] If compelled to yield to the principle of numerical proportions, he would rather sacrifice it to the Protestant Dissenters at home than to the Roman Catholics in Ireland.

With respect to the tithe, Graham denied that it was paid 'by

---

[1] Every £100 of tithe was to be commuted for £70 rent-charge. The cost of collection was to be borne by the tithe-owner and would amount to about 6d. per pound. The Government Bill provided that no presentation to a benefice would be made if it had less than fifty Anglicans. In those parishes where there was no church, glebe house, or churchman, the minister of an adjoining parish was to receive an additional £5 per year for serving both. In parishes of more than fifty church people, and where the endowment was more than £300, the Lord Lieutenant was empowered to make reductions from the value of the Cure, but in no case should the income be less than £300. See *Hansard*, 3rd Ser., XXVIII, 1319-1334.

[2] Whether ministers should be withdrawn from parishes of less than a given number of members.

[3] *Ibid.*, XXIX, 913.

the husbandman, by the labourer, by the occupier; he contended, on the contrary, that it was a tax on property and was paid by the owners of it'.[4] Tithes were the property of the tithe-owner as much as rent was the property of the landowner. The abolition of tithes was therefore confiscation of property just as much as a confiscation of rent would be. To Graham, the Government's Tithe Bill was a concession to Catholic menaces and Catholic demands, and he refused to be driven to any such concessions. He had, he declared, much respect for conscience, but 'to the conscience of passive resistance — to the conscience of agitation — to the conscience of repeal — to the conscience of the "annual tribute"'[5] — and, least of all, to the conscience of Death's head and cross-bone menaces, he, for one, was not prepared to make the smallest concessions'.[6] However, the Tithe Bill, from which the Lords had stricken the sections relating to the sequestration of Church revenues, was passed over the opposition of Peel, Stanley, Graham, and others and became the law of the land.

In March 1836 Graham also opposed the Irish Municipal Reform Bill, which called for a lowering of the elective qualification both for voting and for holding office, on the principle that elective bodies in Ireland could not be trusted with the same degree of safety as those in England. This proposed measure was another entering wedge and experience had shown him, he told the House, that once they began to descend they must continue to do so until universal suffrage was reached, and that would be a fatal day for England.[7] He also opposed that part of the Bill which took from magistrates the power of appointing the constabulary and vested it in the Crown. In view of the diseased

[4] *Hansard*, 3rd Ser., XXIX, 915. In the election of 1835, Graham prepared a pamphlet for electioneering purposes. In it he declared that the Church was supported by the rich for the poor. On his own estates, he, rather than the parishioners, paid the parson. The *Chronicle* (June 4th, 1836, p. 4), declared that according to this reasoning, 'In determining what Church ought to be established in any country, the only question ought to be, What is the religion of the owners of the soil?'

[5] Referring to the O'Connell tribute.

[6] *Hansard*, 3rd Ser., XXIX, 926. In a letter to Hardinge, on January 22nd, 1836, Graham wrote: 'A Tithe Bill without the Appropriation clause, introduced *by the present government*, would be a monster of political deformity revolting even to the lax morals of the days of political expediency in which we live.' See *Peel Papers*, CXXXIV, 139-141 (Br. Mus. Add. MSS. 40314).

[7] *Hansard*, 3rd Ser., XXXII, 48.

state of society in Ireland, it was dangerous, he contended, to permit any extension of democratic tendencies. Evils would not, and could not, be cured by further concessions, especially concessions which were wrung from the Government by Catholic intimidation and threats. He would never consent to giving up the Protestants of Ireland 'an easy prey to the fury of the demagogue,[8] the vengeance of the priest, or the madness of the people'.[9]

The following month the Irish Municipal Reform Bill came up for reconsideration and Graham again opposed it with all the force at his command. He had been taunted by various members of the Government with having deserted the Whig party and its principles, and he answered these taunts by affirming that he was a real Whig and that his principles consisted 'no less in jealousy of popery and Catholic domination, than in love of liberty and hatred of oppression'.[10] He concluded by saying that he would stake his opposition to this Bill on the grounds that once Ireland received this concession it would go on to demand a complete abolition of tithes and then a repeal of the Union.

Meanwhile Graham was a very busy member of the committee which was then engaged in an inquiry into the state of agriculture. Because of the good crops of 1833, 1834, and 1835,[11] prices had steadily fallen from the 64s. 10d. of December 1830 to 35s. 4d. of December 1835.[12] The agricultural interests, alarmed by these skidding prices, came to the conclusion that the Government must do something about it. When Russell proposed a Select Committee of Investigation, he reminded the House that no changes in the monetary standard looking towards a lowering of its value were to be countenanced.[13] Since Graham and some other members of the committee felt that lowering the standard of

[8] This was a thrust at O'Connell who immediately thanked Graham for furnishing him with 'an additional number of powerful arguments for the Repeal of the Union'.
[9] Ibid.
[10] Ibid., XXXVI, 363. Graham wrote to Lord Granville Somerset on December 17th, 1836: 'It is needless to advert to my secession from the Whigs. They retain the name, but . . . have changed their principles. I adhere to my principles, and am indifferent to the name.' PARKER, Life of Graham, I, 249. The Chronicle (March 9th, 1836, p. 4), was disgusted with Graham and declared that he was now out-doing 'the most furious Tories in his Toryism'.
[11] The crop of 1834 was one of the finest on record.
[12] TOOKE, History of Prices, II, 390.
[13] The House had passed a resolution to that effect on April 24th, 1833.

value of the currency would be a desirable means of raising agricultural prices, while others did not, it was not to be expected that the committee would accomplish much. As a matter of fact, after questioning about seventy witnesses and taking hundreds of pages of evidence, the committee, unable to reach a satisfactory agreement, made no report at all. Only the evidence was reported,[14] and Graham reproached the Government for having appointed the committee and then not having carried the matter to a conclusion. 'They had gone on with imperfect and undecided views', he said scornfully, 'and were found, at the conclusion of the inquiry, totally unprepared with any plan or recommendation.'[15] Under these circumstances, it was probably to the advantage of the landed interests that the committee had made no report. Furthermore, the evidence taken revealed that prosperity was reviving, due to the increased consumption of wheat,[16] to the unfavourable appearance of the crops, and to the fact that less wheat had been sown. Prices reacted immediately and by the end of 1836 they had advanced from 35s. 4d. (Winchester quarter), to 57s. 9d.[17]

What had really been of greatest help to the agriculturalists was that by means of the Poor Law of 1834, the abolition of statute labour for maintaining roads, and the Tithe Act of 1836, the burden of taxation had been reduced and the decline in prices had not therefore been as great a hardship to them as would ordinarily have been the case. The Poor Law, administered so efficiently by Nassau Senior and Edwin Chadwick, was designed to abolish outdoor relief for the able-bodied and had imposed a workhouse test. In the cabinet of 1834 the Duke of Richmond and Graham, according to Aspinal,[18] had opposed the establishment of workhouses on the grounds that once a man entered a workhouse he was literally imprisoned for life, and that any effort to enforce the law would surely lead to trouble. Both were right. The working classes were loud in their complaints against the workhouses,

---

[14] *Parliament Papers, First Report from the Select Committee Appointed to Inquire into the State of Agriculture*, . . . March 4th, 1836.

[15] *Annual Register* (1836), 223.

[16] A large part of this increased consumption was due to the use of wheat in malting and distilling, and to its use as stockfeed. See TOOKE. *op. cit.*, I, 257-264.

[17] *Ibid.*, 390.

[18] ASPINAL, *Lord Brougham and the Whig Party*, 241

which they appropriately dubbed the 'bastilles'. The object of the Law, of course, was to make relief so distasteful that only those in the direst want would apply. In actual practice this Poor Law was therefore not so much a 'poor' relief measure as it was a landlord's relief act. To be sure, it enabled men to live where they might otherwise have starved, but its effect was to keep wages at a mere subsistence level. 'In face of the competition of pauper labour hired out by the parish', writes G. D. H. Cole, 'it was impossible for wages to rise.'[19] Furthermore, since rents were usually adjusted to the prevailing wage scale, the farmers did not profit either. Therefore, the ones who really benefited from the Poor Law were the landowners, and that is exactly what they had intended. In fact, the reduction in the poor rates was very considerable, dropping from a total (for England) of £6,509,466 in 1831 to £3,803,309 in 1836.[20]

Another facet to this problem was that of building and maintaining roads with the use of statute labour, i.e., the inhabitants of the towns. When this labour was in short supply, the justices of the peace, at quarter sessions, levied a labour rate based on the principle of the poor rate;[21] in 1835 highway rates were substituted for statute labour for the maintenance of the shorter roads.[22]

The Tithe Commutation Act of 1836, which commuted payments in kind into money payments, was a further boon to the agriculturalists. The tithe, a compulsory payment of one-tenth of the annual produce of land and stock, had previously impeded agricultural progress, and, because of the difficulty of collection, had led to endless bickering and disputes. Whigs and Tories alike, writes Lord Ernle, had therefore combined

> to commute tithe of produce in kind for a variable money payment charged on the land, to make the commuted sum fluctuate with the purchasing power of money, to preserve the existing relations between the values of titheable produce and the cost of living . . . It converted tithes into a corn-rent, fluctuating in value according to the septennial average of the prices of wheat, barley, and oats.[23]

[19] GEORGE D. H. COLE, *A Short History of the British Working Class Movement*, I, 133-134.
[20] PORTER, *Progress of the Nation*, II, 363.
[21] See ERNLE, *English Farming Past and Present*, 288.
[22] *Statutes at Large*, 5 and 6 Will. IV, c. 50.   [23] ERNLE, *op. cit.*, 344.

K

But the landed interests were still not satisfied with the reductions in taxes that had been achieved. On April 27th, 1836, the Marquis of Chandos requested the House of Commons to consider means of further lightening the burdens of agriculture.[24] Graham carefully listened to Hume's speech that the landed interests clamoured for relief more than any other class and needed it less, that they were the least taxed and most favoured class in England, and that this motion ought to be defeated. Then, though disagreeing with Hume's argument, he requested the Marquis of Chandos to withdraw his motion, stating that if he did not, he (Graham) would vote against it, because it was unwise to discuss this question while the committee on agriculture was still sitting. Prices were rising, he declared, and many farmers had begun a more diversified type of farming, growing beans, barley, and oats instead of wheat exclusively. The best thing to do, since the Government would not devalue the pound, was to leave well enough alone. He was absolutely opposed to any further reduction in the burdens on land, not because he was opposed to a further reduction in taxes, but because 'If they got rid of those burdens, they [the landlords] would be depriving themselves of the main argument in support of the policy of protective laws'.[25] When the Government proposed to repeal the malt tax, Graham opposed this too on the grounds that if it was repealed the Government would resort to a worse form of taxation — the property tax. Then Graham gave the landlords some very sound advice: They should not talk so much because all that was accomplished by their discussions on the burdens of agriculture was to place the landed proprietors 'in an invidious light' and lead other classes of people to criticize them.[26] On the division, Chandos's motion was defeated by a vote of 208 to 178.

During this session of Parliament Graham also opposed the Government Bill to abolish Church rates. He quoted a score of high law-officers to prove that Church rates were a legal burden on parishioners, and 'if they ... decline to impose a rate upon themselves for the repair of the body of the Church and the proper performance of Divine service, the church wardens had the power to make such an assessment as should be necessary for those

[24] *Hansard*, 3rd Ser., XXXIII, 333-340.
[25] *Ibid.*, 390.   [26] *Ibid.*, 392.

purposes'.[27] He looked upon the Bill as a Dissenter-Roman Catholic scheme to accomplish a separation of Church and State and to destroy the Church hierarchy. If this were to be accomplished, he prophesied that 'not five years would elapse before they [the Bishops] would be expelled from their places in the House of Lords, and five years more would not elapse before episcopacy would be wholly abolished in England'.[28]

Ever since Graham and his friends had left the Grey ministry in 1834, the Whig party had been just dawdling along. It had been pestered to death by the Irish and the Radicals and blocked by the peers at almost every step of the way. To be sure, it had kept Ireland quiet, but only by means of help from the O'Connell Compact, and that, as Young correctly puts it, 'seemed to English opinion a disgraceful subservience to a rebel'.[29] The Government were divided amongst themselves too, and the *Westminster Review* advised them to get together on a vigorous programme of reform or the Conservative party would gain additional adherents from their ranks.[30] Things looked very bad for the Whigs: the Lords were hostile; the Churchmen were angered and fearful; Conservatives who did not like Whig radicalism, and Radicals who did not like Whig conservatism, were in active opposition; and after 1835 the King became hostile to them.

This Royal obstacle was removed, however, when William IV died on June 20th, 1837. Two days later the new ruler, Queen Victoria, sent a message to Parliament asking it to wind up the business of the session as soon as possible so that a new election could be held.[31] When Russell appeared at the door with this message, everyone, except Graham, took off their hats. The *True Sun* newspaper, in reporting this scene, said that all had removed their hats but Graham who had only 'reluctantly' complied with this decent show of respect for the Crown. The next day, irked by the comment this had occasioned, Graham asked the Speaker if he had not been in the right in not removing his hat until the word Rex or Regina was heard from the chair. The Speaker assured him that he was.[32]

[27] *Annual Register* (1837), 102.
[28] *Hansard*, 3rd Ser., XXXVIII, 1031.
[29] YOUNG, *Victorian England*, II, 437.
[30] *West. Rev.*, XXV, 271-278.
[31] WALPOLE, *Hist. of Eng.*, IV, 99.
[32] *Hansard*, 3rd Ser., XXXVIII, 1581-1582. See also JENNINGS, *Anecdotal History of the British Parliament*, 252-253.

After the passage of the Reform Bill of 1832 there were really three parties in England: the Conservatives who were pledged to the 'finality' of the Act, the Radicals who looked upon it as but the entering wedge for further reform, and the Whigs who stood midway between. But the milk-and-water character of the Melbourne Government caused many Whigs to move to the 'right' to join the Conservative party, or to the 'left' to join the Radicals, or more accurately the Liberals,[33] so that by the election of 1837 the contest was one between the Conservatives and the Liberals. The difference between these two parties was brought out clearly by Peel early in 1837 when he declared his party's determination to uphold the Protestant religion, the Established Church in Ireland and England, and the independence of the House of Lords.[34]

Having deserted his party (at least that was the construction placed on his conduct by many of the electors of Cumberland who had five times returned him as a Liberal, or Whig), and having supported the despised Poor Law in the face of tremendous local opposition,[35] Graham knew he was going to have to face some very real opposition in the July election. As early as December 11th, 1836, he wrote to Peel that Granville Somerset had told him he would probably be defeated and that he (Somerset) might be able to find him a safe refuge in Middlesex. 'It is true', Graham wrote, 'that a violent attack on me here is inevitable, and that the result is doubtful; but my honour is at stake . . . I cannot desert my friends now and give an easy triumph to my enemies; and if I am to be turned out, defeat is more honourable than a surrender; and nothing can befall me which I did not anticipate, when I was driven by sense of duty to leave my party.'[36]

In April 203 electors of East Cumberland, resident in the

[33] See the public address of Fox Maule, of July 7th, 1837, in *Edin. Rev.*, LXV, 265-282.

[34] Possibly part of this determination is to be traced to his reception in Glasgow where, having spoken for two hours to 3500 people, he concluded that they were of one heart and mind persuaded 'to defend to the last extremity the Monarchy, the Peerage, and the Church'. Graham to Stanley, January 15th, 1837, in Parker, *Life of Graham*, I, 251. See also PARKER, *Life of Peel*, II, 336-347, and CLARK, *Peel and the Conservative Party*, 343 et seq.

[35] On July 9th, 1837, Graham wrote to Stanley that his brother-in-law had voted against him; the Howard influence was against him; the Government and the treasury 'in full operation' against him. PARKER, *Life of Graham*, I, 252. See also *Hansard*, 3rd Ser., XLIII, 175-198.

[36] *Peel Papers*, CXXXVIII, 52 (Br. Mus. Add. MSS. 40318).

vicinity of Brampton, signed and circulated a petition which they sent to Graham charging him with having deserted his party and with having abandoned his principles, and asked him to have the manliness to resign his seat. If he did not, they said, they would do everything in their power to defeat him at the next election. Graham replied that he *had* turned against the Government of Melbourne because he did not have confidence in its men or its measures, but, he said, 'I am bound very respectfully but firmly to remind you that I am not your delegate, and that you form only a small portion of that great constituency which it is my pride and good fortune to represent'.[37]

The Whig *Morning Chronicle*, regarding Graham rather than Peel or Stanley as the real leader of the Conservative party, bitterly assailed him for having left the Whig party and for having voted against his former colleagues. It called upon the East Cumberland electors to oust him from his seat. 'Away with him, . . . electors of Cumberland', it urged, 'and leave him to the house of refuge of the Lowthers. A penitentiary would not reclaim such a big offender.'[38] The *Manchester Guardian*, a liberal paper, gloated over the prospective defeat of the 'Netherby turn-coat', who, formerly almost ultra-radical, 'has now not only turned his back upon his old friends and colleagues, but completely gone over to the Tories'.[39]

As early as July 7th, Graham recognized the possibility of his defeat and informed Stanley of it.[40] Three weeks later he wrote the following letter to Peel:

I have sustained here all the annoyance of a bitter contest and extensive canvas: all the influence of Greenwich hospital and of the Government, subscriptions in London and in the country, the malignant hostility of the Press, the united forces of the Cavendishes and the Howards, outraged friends, who are the most implacable of enemies, Whigs and Radicals, Dissenters and Unbelievers, are banded against me in support of two candidates who avow extreme and destructive opinions: and though the tide

[37] The request to resign, as well as Graham's reply, were both published in *The Times* (April 20th, 1836, p. 5).
[38] *Chronicle* (July 3rd, 1837, p. 2). See also the same paper for August 5th, 1837, p. 2, and June 30th, 1837, p. 2.
[39] *Manchester Guardian* (July 15th, 1837, p. 2).
[40] 'You know . . . that I am never sanguine', he wrote. *Graham Papers*.

has rather turned in my favour, yet I cannot speak confidently of success.[41]

The vigorous campaign which Graham conducted was of no avail, and he was defeated by a considerable majority.[42] The Government of Melbourne, quite naturally, considered this defeat a real triumph and derived extreme satisfaction from it, because, as Greville put it, 'they hate him rancorously'.[43]

It had been an unusually turbulent election. Graham's own son had been knocked down in the street, and the extreme violence reminded Graham of the 'fiendish temper of the French Revolution'.[44] His opponents, accusing him of unfriendliness to the Queen, as well as of having double-crossed his own party, asked the support of the electors on the grounds of their greater loyalty to the young ruler. The Conservatives naturally objected to this 'unconstitutional' use of the Queen's name in an election, and one of the current bits of election doggerel ran as follows:

> 'The Queen is with us,' whigs insulting say,
> 'For when she found us in, she let us stay.'
> It may be so; but give me leave to doubt
> How long she'l keep you, when she finds you out.[45]

Neither Peel nor Graham was impressed by Queen Victoria's Address from the Throne, which said Peel, 'abused the privilege of saying nothing', and was 'barren and meagre, beyond the usual standard of such addresses'.[46] Peel was irked by its conservative tone, and by the obvious intention of the Government to stay in office and do nothing at all. Graham not only agreed with Peel's opinion, but wondered whether the Queen either read the debates or was capable of forming an opinion of her own.[47]

On January 4th, 1838, the East Cumberland Conservatives gave a dinner to Graham. In his address, at the conclusion of the dinner, he bitterly complained of the violence of the last election,

---

[41] *Peel Papers*, CXXXVIII, 98-99 (Br. Mus. Add. MSS. 40318).

[42] *Ibid.*, 100. As early as June 28th, O'Connell had predicted Graham's defeat. See *Correspondence of O'Connell*, W. J. Fitzpatrick, ed., II, 103.

[43] GREVILLE, *The Greville Memoirs, A Journal of the Reign of Queen Victoria from 1837 to 1852*, I, 9; *Annual Register* (1837), 240.

[44] Graham to Peel, in PARKER, *Life of Peel*, II, 349.

[45] *Annual Register* (1837), 239.

[46] Peel to Graham, in PARKER, *Life of Graham*, I, 254.

[47] Graham to Stanley, *Ibid.*, 256.

in which he had been called 'turncoat, bigot, apostate, renegade'.[48] Then launching an attack against Melbourne's assertion that the Tithe Bill containing the Appropriation clause had been 'forced' upon him, Graham insisted that it was the compact formed at Lichfield House that compelled the Government to stand pledged to Appropriation. He capped his very acrimonious address, which evidenced the fact that he was still smarting under the humiliation of his defeat, with these words, words that were to be quoted again and again:

> There may have been more wicked Governments, there may have been more powerful and dangerous Governments, but I defy any one to produce from the annals of our country a more shabby Government than the present.[49]

So it was a 'shabby' government! It was a good word, and an appropriate one too. Stanley picked it up and loved to repeat it.[50] Lord Ripon was delighted with Graham's attack on their former colleagues and wrote to Graham that what pleased him most of all was that neat word 'shabby'.[51] Lord George Bentinck wrote to Graham that he was amused by Graham's 'complete exposure of the shuffling, shabbiness, and the imbecility of the present Ministers'. He wanted Graham to have his address published in cheap pamphlet form 'so that it may be read and well digested in every £10 house in the country'.[52]

Despite his defeat in Cumberland Graham was soon back in the House. He was absolutely necessary to the Conservative party and they found a seat for him at Pembroke.[53] In Parliament he continued his attacks on his former colleagues and most of his

---

[48] *Ibid.*   [49] *Ibid.*, 258.

[50] CLARK, *Peel and the Conservative Party*, 378.

[51] Ripon to Graham, in PARKER, *Life of Graham*, I, 259.

[52] Lord George Bentinck to Graham, January 12th, 1838, in *Graham Papers*.

[53] According to the *Standard* (February 23rd, 1838, p. 2), some influential electors at Pembroke, highly pleased with Graham's speech to the Carlisle electors, went to Col. Owen who then held the seat as a 'duty' and persuaded him to accept the Chiltern Hundreds. This opened the way for Graham who was elected 'without a dissentient voice' to represent Pembroke. As soon as he was elected, Graham wrote to Peel: 'You see I have departed from my good intention of allowing no vacancy to be made by private arrangement for my admission: but in this as in most other cases, when I am highly tempted, I have yielded to the hope, that no peculiar circumstances may justify the violation of the rule: and my wish to sit beside you in the House of Commons has been stronger perhaps than my strict sense of right.' *Peel Papers*, CXXXVIII, 108-109 (Br. Mus. Add. MSS. 40318).

speeches were very partisan. Up to this stage in his career Graham
had been an independent. Now, with Peel, Wellington, Stanley,
Aberdeen and others united in one body, holding organization
meetings, accepting Peel's leadership, and developing a permanent organization and a definite programme, real political
party activity was being achieved by the Conservative party. To
his natural and caustic spirit, his chagrin over his election defeat,
his contempt for the Whigs, was now added political party
bitterness. 'I entirely subscribe to your doctrine respecting private
communications with political opponents', he wrote to Peel,
'and I have endeavoured to act on it ever since I took any part in
public affairs: unreserved confidence in political associates and
uncompromising open war with political adversaries is the course
which the British Public approves, and they are right, since it is
the broad high-way of strict integrity which leads to no mistakes.'[54]

On March 12th Joseph Hume moved a vote of censure on the
Government for an alleged Whig job — the appointment of
Primrose to the Post Office at Edinburgh.[55] Graham opposed
Hume's motion because the appointment of Primrose was not
contrary to the Post Office rules, but he nevertheless used the
opportunity once more to censure the Melbourne Government.
'There never was a government in England', he said, 'which
exercised the patronage of the Crown with a more direct and
exclusive view to the augmentation of their political power than
the right hon. Gentlemen opposite.'[56]

Shortly after this question had been dispensed with, the 'shabby'
Government brought in the Irish Corporation Bill for the third
time. This time Graham sought to effect a compromise. About
thirty Conservatives met at Peel's house where they agreed to
allow the Corporation Bill to pass, and also the Irish Tithe Bill,
provided Appropriation was dropped.[57] Russell and Melbourne
agreed to this plan and both Bills were subsequently passed into
law.

The other subject of special interest in 1838 was the ballot. The
Radicals and Chartists, the *Westminster Review* and other
journals and magazines, had been steadily and loudly advocating

[54] *Peel Papers*, CXXXVIII, 89 (Br. Mus. Add. MSS. 40318).
[55] *Hansard*, 3rd Ser., XLI, 767-769.　　　　　[56] *Ibid.*, 777-778.
[57] Graham to Stanley, May 20th, 1838, in PARKER, *Life of Graham*, I, 263-264.

its adoption. In 1832 Graham had acquiesced in the ballot as a possible means of securing a lower franchise rate, and since that had been accomplished, it had become, to his mind, a closed question. He looked upon the ballot as a radical nostrum and a dangerous democratic measure. In August 1838 he wrote to Tavistock that Russell was being pushed to the ballot by the Radicals and that the only security against it was to adhere to 'fixed principles'.[58] By this Graham meant a fixed opposition to the ballot. Tavistock agreed with Graham but asserted that Russell might find it impossible to maintain his ground against the ballot, i.e., that he would not be able to exclude from office those who favoured it.[59] In that event, the ballot would become an open question, as, in fact, it did early in 1839. In his answer to this letter Graham once more enunciated his ideas on reform:

> My part was taken at the passing of the Reform Act. I pledged myself to resist the Ballot, short Parliaments, and further extention of the Suffrage . . . The resistance may be hopeless, but I am bound to make it; and it would not be so desperate, if all who promised to resist were united.[60]

Graham resented Russell's truckling to the Radicals and was convinced that Russell had broken a pledge made in 1832 to resist further change. He held it to be incumbent upon Russell to resist the new measure. Graham's incessant attacks on his former colleagues on this question and on numerous others had caused many of them to detest him, and he put his finger on his own problem and on one of his most besetting weaknesses when he wrote: 'What I feel warmly I state explicitly, and I fear it is a course which I cannot alter.'[61]

In 1839 Graham was selected to succeed Peel as Lord Rector of Glasgow University. He was delighted because, despite his opposition to the 'voluntary principle' which the General Assembly of the Kirk had adopted, he felt that the election was

> proof that the rising youth entertains sound and decided principles; and when they prefer a country gentleman to the Queen's favoured uncle [the Duke of Essex] they rescue their countrymen from the charge of time-serving sycophancy and of interested calculation.[62]

[58] Ibid., 267.　　　　　[59] Ibid.　　　[60] Ibid., 268.　　　[61] Ibid., 269.
[62] Graham to Colquhoun, November 18th, 1838, Ibid., 274.

In his acceptance address, on being presented with the freedom of the city, Graham declared that the Reform Bill was a 'final' step: 'By that Act I will stand, with the feeling of solemn obligation to resist further democratic encroachment.'[63]

Lord Durham, who had been to Canada to attempt to compose the differences that had led to the rebellion of 1837, was now on his way home and Graham looked forward to his coming in the expectation and hope that an explosion would follow and that the Whigs and Radicals would split completely asunder. In this situation, he told Stanley, the best policy for the Conservatives was to sit still and do nothing,

> to avoid every ground of needless offence to the adversary, to keep our ranks open to receive every new recruit without examining his pass-ticket too closely, and until the meeting of Parliament to keep ourselves unpledged as far as possible, ready to avail ourselves of any accession of strength, and to pour our united force on the weakest point in the line of the enemy.[64]

This was sound political advice, the language of a shrewd political observer. He followed up this letter with one to Peel in which he elucidated the policy which he thought their party should pursue:

> Without any regard to possible consequences, we must resist every proposal which in our conscience we consider to be dangerous; we ought to be most careful in originating any motions intended to displace Ministers; we should steadily avoid all concert and private communication with the Radicals. But, let the motion come from what quarter it may, we must avoid a single vote which implies the least confidence in . . . the Government.
>
> With a dissolution in view, the grand object is to keep the Conservative party united and in good heart. Any marked fear of undertaking the Government, or any wish evinced to shelter the present Administration, would therefore be fatal. But on the other hand any eagerness to seize power would be a most dangerous indiscretion.[65]

Under Peel's leadership, Graham was certain that the Conservatives could follow this proposed middle course.

[63] *Speech of the Right Honourable Sir James Graham at Glasgow*, a pamphlet in the Graham Papers at Netherby, p. 16. The chairman described Peel, Graham, and Stanley as England's 'Committee of Public Safety'. See *Standard* (January 19th, 1839, p. 1).

[64] PARKER, *Life of Graham*, I, 275.

[65] Graham to Peel, January 30th, 1839, *Ibid.*, 278.

The year 1839 had been ushered in by a first-class assassination in Ireland, the murder, on his own estate, of Lord Norbury.[66] An 'Orange' leader, Lord Roden, consequently proposed the appointment of a committee of inquiry into the state of affairs in Ireland since 1835. The Government looked upon this as a resolution of censure and opposed it, but the Lords appointed a committee regardless. This put Russell in a critical position, because if the Irish policy of the Government was condemned in the Commons as a result of the inquiry, Russell and his colleagues would be expected to resign. The Radicals continued to support the Government, however, thus enabling Melbourne to continue in office at the head of a precarious and 'shabby' Government. In April Russell described the situation in Ireland to the House and announced that reform, i.e., concession, was necessary. Peel, on the other hand, countered with a resolution that in view of the disregard for law in Ireland, as revealed by the Committee of the House of Lords, it was wise 'to persevere in those principles which have guided the executive government of Ireland of late years'.[67] On the fourth night of debate on this question Graham stated that he could see no reason why the Government had forced this subject to a vote unless it was to pick a quarrel with the Lords and in that manner to bolster up a 'weak and tottering administration'.[68] Could, he asked them, a better committee be found than the Lords' Committee, consisting of the landed proprietors of Ireland — Lord Plunket, the Duke of Leinster, Lord Brougham, and others? He would like to know why there was so much murder, crime, and outrage in Ireland among such a kind, generous, warm-hearted, charitable people, 'willing . . . to share the humble meal, the scanty pittance, the broken potatoe, with any beggar that came to the cabin-door'.[69] Did not such a situation call for an inquiry by the House? The House did not think so.

In February 1839, as a sign of respect to the Church and to the

---

[66] Norbury was the son of the judge who presided at Robert Emmet's trial. He was known for his fairness and kindness and the Tories attributed his murder to the leniency of Normanby, the Lord Lieutenant.

[67] *Hansard*, 3rd Ser., XLVII, 76.   [68] *Ibid.*, 293.

[69] *Ibid.*, 299. The conservative *Standard* (April 19th, 1839, p. 4), advised all Protestants in Ireland to read 'the beautiful and impressive speech' of Sir James Graham.

Bishop of London, Graham opposed the opening of theatres in Westminster on Wednesday and Friday during Lent.[70] The following month he urged the adoption of a definite policy of ship construction. Each year, he said, a definite number of ships should be added to the Navy. A continuous building programme of this kind would mean a large and efficient fleet. Furthermore, Graham protested against the policy of keeping so large a part of the fleet in the Mediterranean. He thought that England's interests should be directed more to America whose trade was more valuable to England,[71] and that the fleet should not be in the Mediterranean but in the Caribbean.

But there were more important matters at hand. The wheat crop for 1837, because of the bad weather, had been the most deficient since 1816.[72] Heavy frosts, frequent rains, changes in climate, made the next year equally bad.[73] A rise in prices naturally followed, the average for 1838 being 64s. 4d. and for 1839 70s. 6d.[74] This increase in prices led to renewed activity on the part of the Anti-Corn Law Association for the repeal of the Corn Laws, and a meeting of the delegates from the chief manufacturing towns was held in London on February 4th to consider plans of attack. Among other things it was decided to send a deputation to see Melbourne and another to see Peel and Graham. Neither was successful. Graham talked a good deal about the vast amount of land that would be thrown out of cultivation were the Corn Laws repealed, and of how foreign nations were taking undue advantage of England at every possible opportunity.[75]

The Queen's Address, on the opening of Parliament, mentioned the Corn Laws, as did the speech of Buller moving the adoption of the Address, but Wood, president of the Manchester Chamber of Commerce, who seconded the motion, made the simple mistake of describing the prosperous state of the country and hence cut the ground from under the advocates of repeal.[76] Peel, the skilful parliamentarian, immediately thanked Wood for proving the inexpediency of altering a law that brought so much prosperity to England. But this thorny question would not stay down and on

[70] *Hansard*, 3rd Ser., XLV, 1033.
[71] *Ibid.*, 1352-1363 and XLVI, 292.
[72] TOOKE, *op. cit.*, III, 11.   [73] *Ibid.*, 14-15.   [74] *Ibid.*, App., 295.
[75] See ARCHIBALD PRENTICE, *History of the Anti-Corn Law League*, I, 153.
[76] *Ibid.*, 108.

March 12th Villiers returned to the attack on the Corn Laws with a motion to reconsider the Law of 1828.[77] On the third night of debate on this motion, Graham entered the verbal battle that was raging in the House. Admitting that prices were high, he alleged that if the free traders, instead of attempting to frighten the landlords (who refused to be frightened, and who, he reminded them, had possession of the soil of England), produced facts to prove that England would be benefited by free trade, the landlords 'would be willing to consider a re-adjustment of the duties on corn'.[78] Everyone ought to know, said Graham, that prices were regulated by the balance between consumption and production. If you destroyed this balance and by force of law provided that for a decreased consumption there should be no compensation in the form of an increased price, you 'laid the axe to the root of production itself'.[79] Any law which did not guarantee to agriculture a price above the cost of production was a law that struck at the very roots of English greatness. He then quoted Melbourne's speech of 1828 in which the latter opposed altering the Corn Laws, as well as Russell's declaration that it was dangerous business to meddle with those laws. Why had this change now come over the Government? Why did the Government continue to loosen and disturb everything and settle nothing? What was the object of this 'shabby' Government? If they desired a low price on corn, that would mean low wages. Low prices always resulted in low wages and low wages degraded character. For that reason nothing could be more dangerous to labourers than a repeal of the Corn Laws. Not only that, but repeal meant the end of England's agricultural self-sufficiency and made her dependent on foreign countries for the necessities of life. This was tantamount to reducing the country to a state of perpetual siege. In concluding this speech, Graham made an eloquent and convincing appeal to the House not to accede to Villiers's motion because of the disastrous effect it would have on labour. It would, he said, force agricultural workers to leave the farms for the city because with reduced prices the landlords could not afford to employ them. Untold misery, starvation and death would be the inevitable effect were the Corn Laws repealed. 'Little could they estimate', he went on,

[77] *Hansard*, 3rd Ser., XLVI, 334 et seq.
[78] *Ibid.*, 671.   [79] *Ibid.*, 672.

the wretchedness which sprang from change of habit, of house, of manners, of the mode of life itself. What change more cruel could despotism itself inflict than a change from 'the breezy call of the incense breathing morn', to a painful and grievous obedience to the sad sound of the factory bell — the relinquishment of the thatched cottage, the blooming garden, and the village green, for the foul garret, or the dark cellar of the crowded city — the enjoyment of the rural walk of the innocent rustic Sabbath, for the debauchery, the temptations, the pestilence, the sorrows, and the sins of the congregated multitude? . . . Talk to him of sending the Poles to Siberia, or the Hill Coolies from the Coromandel to Mauritius; the authors of the intended change contemplated the perpetration within . . . their native land of a cruelty far more atrocious.[80]

But all of this fine, foaming eloquence of Graham and other landlords could not stay the march of the inevitable. From the thatched cottage to the foul garret agricultural labour did go. The change was, for the time being, a change for the worse. And while their plight excited the sympathy of many landlords, it is equally true that many were thinking in terms of the increased wages that would eventually have to be paid to those labourers who remained on their farms. Graham and his fellows landlords were seeing England transformed from a predominantly agricultural to a predominantly industrial country, and, with that change, the inevitable diminution in the power of their class. The whole train of attendant economic, social, and religious changes that this industrial revolution had called into being were now disturbing the minds of the landed classes. Few there were who contemplated these changes with anything but misgiving and fear. While some landlords got in step by intermarrying with the sons and daughters of the *nouveaux riches*, or by purchasing stock in the new industrial enterprises, and ceased to attack the new order in direct proportion as they were able regularly to clip their coupons, others, spurning to contaminate themselves with either the money or the people who made up the new order, set themselves resolutely against all further change. To them, unless they were able to hold the fort against further innovations, the future was dark indeed. To keep things as they were was manifestly impossible; to change a whole nation's

[80] *Hansard*, 3rd Ser., XLVI, 694-695.

mode of life without conjuring up a mess of knotty problems was equally impossible. And so the lines were drawn and the duel between landlord and capitalist was begun in earnest. The gulf which for generations had separated the landlord from the annuitant and fund-holder was becoming wider and more impassable. England had once been a fair country to look upon, said the landlords — splendid estates, neat cottages, quiet, peaceful little hamlets, and wide open spaces of beautiful woodland where a man could enjoy life with a rod and gun. Now all was changed. The estates were going to ruin, they said; tumble-down shacks instead of neat cottages were everywhere in evidence; large, sprawling, filthy cities with their miserable tenements and dark, dangerous, and dirty streets had displaced the clean and quiet little hamlets; noisy, dangerous railroads had pierced the fairest hunting grounds and ruined the countryside. They did not want England to become the workshop of the world, dependent for its food upon foreign powers, and Graham voiced their sentiments precisely when he said that England would be 'the last country which he should wish to inhabit',[81] once that evil day arrived.

Villiers's motion was defeated by a vote of 342 to 195 and the advocates of free trade joined the Anti-Corn Law League and turned from Parliament to the more congenial atmosphere of the large towns to wage their campaign against the Corn Laws.

Most of the landlords had united to defeat Villiers's motion, but there were some amongst them who felt that a change in these laws might be a good thing. In fact, in January 1839, Graham himself had written to Peel that the sliding scale was preferable to the fixed duty because the duties on corn fell as the price of corn increased, while the fixed duty would be of no value when scarcity caused prices to rise. But at the same time he felt that concessions ought to be made to trade and industry; for instance, the tax on raw cotton should be repealed and land should be made to bear its fair share of the burden resulting from repeal.[82]

Intimately connected with these problems was that of the Poor Law. As a member of the Poor Law Commission[83] Graham had

[81] *Ibid.*
[82] Peel to Graham, in *Peel Papers*, CXXXVIII, 134 (Br. Mus. Add. MSS. 40318). The *Chronicle* (April 6th, 1840, p. 2), concluded that Graham, for political reasons, had to support the Corn Laws whereas he was actually opposed to them in principle.
[83] CROKER, *Correspondence and Diaries*, II, 337.

been a staunch advocate of this measure and had continued to support it after leaving the Government. He contended that the Law had worked well, that it had encouraged the industrious, and that it had kept alive the really destitute. At the same time, however, he admitted that there were extraordinary cases in which outdoor relief should be given. Widows who had suddenly been deprived of their husbands, for instance, should not be compelled immediately to move to the workhouse. Furthermore, his experience as a member of a board of guardians had proved to him that there were times when the Law could not be administered in exact accordance with the letter. [84]

In April 1839 the Government measure to suspend the Jamaica constitution for five years (because the liberal assembly had been checkmating the governor), was opposed by ten Radicals who normally had been voting with the Government. This defection in the party ranks placed the Government of Melbourne in a minority of five. [85] Melbourne promptly resigned and the Queen summoned the Duke of Wellington, who recommended that she call in Peel to form a government. [86] This being done, Stanley, Graham, Wellington, Lyndhurst, Aberdeen, Goulburn, Hardinge, and Ellenborough all consented to join Peel's ministry. [87] Four of these Conservatives — Hardinge, Peel, Stanley, and Graham — were thoroughly disliked by the Queen, but Graham, who was to have been the Home Secretary, was the special object of her dislike. [88] Therefore, when she wrote to Peel that she would not consent 'to adopt a course [with respect to the selection of the ladies of her bed-chamber] which she conceives to be contrary to usage, and which is repugnant to her feelings', [89] the new Prime Minister promptly resigned. The Queen was happy at this turn of events, for now she could have Melbourne back again, no matter how 'shabby' his Government might be. But by now Melbourne's Government was impotent as well as shabby and

---

[84] *Hansard*, 3rd Ser., XLIX, 579. In Graham's district in northern England, the opposition of the hand-loom weavers to the workhouses was very great. These men were unemployed, but were a very industrious group who objected to being treated as idlers. See the HAMMONDS, *Age of the Chartists*, 63.

[85] *Hansard*, 3rd Ser., XLVII, 967.

[86] PARKER, *Life of Peel*, II, 390.   [87] *Ibid.*, 391-393.

[88] *The Girlhood of Queen Victoria, A Selection from her Majesty's Diaries Between the Years 1832 and 1840*, Viscount Esher, ed., II, 162, 205.

[89] *Annual Register* (1839), 121,

could accomplish nothing. Divided amongst themselves, Peel cleverly nailing Russell and Melbourne to conservatism and thereby widening the breach between them and their Radical cohorts, the Government just barely managed to carry a grant of £30,000 for national education. And even to this meagre grant there was bitter opposition especially from Graham who declared that

> if they applied aid from the public purse to the education of the youth of the country in Dissenting principles, how could they refuse similar aid to the instruction of the adult population? If aid was to be granted to Dissenting teachers, how could it be denied Dissenting chapels, and how could endowments be refused to Socinian chapels?[90]

The Established Church was again in danger, thought Graham, and he was quick to come to its defence. Others might desert it in its hour of need, but not he. The exclusive right to have charge of the education of the people rested with the clergy. There could be no sound education without religion, of that he was certain, and there should be no education at the public expense except that conducted by the Established Church, which was the chief pillar of the State. 'If it were shaken, the government of the country would be shaken along with it; and if it were overthrown, then would the State be overthrown also.'[91] There is no denying that Graham was to a great extent correct. The Church was still a part of the State, and that which affected the one immediately affected the other. And as to the education question, he was certain that the day on which control of the education of the youth was taken away from the Church, the beginning of the end was reached so far as a State church was concerned.

Peel, Graham, and their colleagues now had the Government at their mercy. It could not balance its budget, pass its Bills, or present a united front on any issue. The Conservatives, on the other hand, were in great good spirits during the summer and autumn of 1839.[92] In December, Peel wrote to his chief colleagues

---

[90] *Hansard*, 3rd Ser., XLVIII, 649. [91] *Ibid.*, 655.

[92] Graham to Arbuthnot, August 7th, 1839, in PARKER, *Life of Graham*, I, 285. Greville had seen Graham in April and had told him that in the event of Peel taking office there was a disposition on the part of many of the leading Whigs, such as the Dukes of Bedford, Sutherland, and Devonshire, to support him. They disliked the Radicals and were moving towards a conservative point of view. Graham was much

L

asking them what policy the party ought to pursue when the next session commenced.[93] Goulburn did not answer; Wellington did not want to force the Government to resign; Stanley agreed with the Duke; but the independent Graham, who had no love for the Whigs, favoured hostile action. 'The constant legitimate object of an Opposition', he wrote to Peel, 'is the overthrow of an Administration which they consider bad, and hope to replace by a better.'[94] He was convinced that in the event of a dissolution the Conservatives would be returned to power and he therefore wanted them to press for a vote of lack of confidence as soon as Parliament met. He did not believe that the party could be kept together solely by remaining in opposition. 'The scheme of governing in opposition cannot be durable: the power lasts as long as the hope of succeeding to office endures; but extinguish this hope and the power vanishes: the leaders do not fly; but the troops are disbanded, the camp is broken up, and the nation is disheartened.'[95] The object of a party was political power and Graham was convinced that it was impossible to keep a party together for long unless it was able to get into office and enjoy the fruits of power.

On January 26th, 1840, the Opposition opened fire on the proposed grant of £50,000 to Prince Albert. In place of £50,000 they proposed £30,000.[96] Their case, put by Graham, was that since the Royal family of direct descent (the Prince of Wales and the Duke of Cambridge) received only £21,000, Prince Albert should not have more than £30,000.[97] Graham hoped that by so reducing the grant (and he was fairly certain that the House would approve the reduction), a wedge would be driven between the Queen and the Government.[98] The House passed Graham's proposal by a majority of 104. Under ordinary circumstances the

by this news and relayed it to Peel, but the latter did not put much stock in it. CHARLES F. GREVILLE, *The Greville Memoirs, A Journal of the Reign of Queen Victoria from 1837 to 1852*, I, 161-162.

[93] *Graham Papers*, December 14th, 1839.

[94] Graham to Peel, December 18th, 1839, in PARKER, *Life of Peel*, II, 421.

[95] *Peel Papers*, CXXXVIII, 171 (Br. Mus. Add. MSS. 40318).

[96] Graham to Arbuthnot, January 26th, 1840, in PARKER, *Life of Graham*, I, 291-292.

[97] *Hansard*, 3rd Ser., LI, 621.

[98] This speech of Graham angered Russell who took the occasion to deliver a rather bitter tirade against his former colleague. Peel immediately came to Graham's defence describing him as one of the ablest members of Earl Grey's ministry.

Government should have resigned, but Melbourne and his colleagues regarded this vote as a sympton not so much of the increased power of the Opposition as evidence of their own weakness. They did not regard it as a party defeat. The next day, however, Sir Y. Buller moved a direct vote of lack of confidence. Graham supported Buller's motion and in doing so asked Russell, in view of the fact that the Government had made the ballot, suffrage extension, and shorter Parliaments their programme, what the difference was between her Majesty's ministers and the Chartists. Then he charged Normanby, the Lord Lieutenant of Ireland, with misfeasance in office for countenancing huge mass meetings of Repealers; accused the Government of being free traders; with having abused the patronage; with having bungled the Jamaica question; and finally with having lost the support of the nation.[99] It was an adroit speech, revealing the contradictory opinions of the members of the Government, and parading before the House the absolute impotence of the ministry.[100] The Government was able to weather this storm but its majority was cut to a mere twenty-one votes.

Due to Palmerston's dislike of the rule that England communicate with the Chinese Government through the Hong merchants and to the fact that the British representatives had to kotow to the Emperor, and to the over-zealousness of Captain Elliott, the British Superintendent at Canton, war between England and China broke out in 1839.[101] Graham hated this war. China was a great country, with a great past, great wealth, and a great future, and he thought it would be much better to trade with her than to fight against her. He had read the State Papers on this problem and he declared that they were a perfect 'labyrinth of inextricable confusion, without a clue. There was not an index, there was no chronological arrangement; it was, in short, hardly possible to unravel the web of inextricable confusion of these papers'.[102] Robinson, who preceded Elliott as Chief Superintendent at Canton, had advised Palmerston to 'let well enough alone', i.e., to observe the Chinese rules of conduct. For this gratuitous

[99] *Ibid.*, 787-815.
[100] *Annual Register* (1840), 64-65.
[101] See G. P. MORIARTY, 'India and the Far East', in *Camb. Hist. of Brit. For. Pol.*, II, 215-219.
[102] *Hansard*, 3rd Ser., LIII, 682.

advice Palmerston promptly replaced Robinson with Elliott, and
the result, said Graham, was agitation, discord, violence, and finally
war. The whole sorry mess was due, he concluded, to the lack of
foresight and precaution on the part of the Government, for which
it certainly merited the condemnation of the House. The vote of
censure which he then proposed[103] came within nine votes of
succeeding.

Despite this failure of the Conservatives to oust the Government,
they knew that its days in office were numbered. In the summer of
1840 Graham and Stanley both joined the Conservative club, the
Carlton, and then, together with Peel and Wellington they composed their difference on the question of the Union of the Canadas[104]
and laid careful plans for overthrowing the Government of Melbourne early the following year. They expected to be aided in this
by the Radicals, who were disgusted with the impotence of the
Government and who had made the mistake of expecting too much
in the line of liberal reform from the Whigs. The Radical point
of view was well stated by their organ, the *Westminster Review*:

> To govern in the usual way;
> Do only what we must to-day;
> Put off all business that we may;
> And trust in all things to delay.[105]

---

[103] *Hansard*, 3rd Ser., LIII, 704; *Annual Register* (1840), 93. The *Edin. Rev.* (LXXI,
494), criticized Graham's demands that the Government resign. It declared that it was
inevitable that occasions would arise in which ministers would disagree, and that when
that happened the ministers could either quit the cabinet, break up the party, or continue
to work together. Graham, it said, would sanction the first course since 'he sees no
difficulty in abandoning former friends'. Greville thought Graham's speech was a
strong one but that its effectiveness was destroyed by Wellington's refusal to censure
the China policy of the Government. See GREVILLE, *Memoirs*, IV, 271. The usually
hostile *Chronicle* (July 13th, 1840, p. 2), described Graham's speech as 'a tissue of
absurdities'. See also *Fraser's*, XXII, 375.

[104] Wellington had been opposed to the Union while Peel had favoured it, but the
former, in order to keep the party together, agreed to follow Peel's leadership in the
matter. PARKER, *Life of Graham*, I, 295-298. Arbuthnot had been doing his best to
get Graham, Peel, and Wellington together. 'I have known upon many occasions',
he wrote to Graham, 'that Lord Stanley and you were the persons chiefly consulted
by Peel; and upon all occasions I have seen that the Duke had the same feelings.'
Arbuthnot to Graham, July 12th, 1840, in *Graham Papers*. Stanley also wrote to
Graham saying that he was anxious that he and Peel should cultivate the Duke of
Wellington and that the latter was easy to get along with if he was treated 'with frank
and cordial confidence'. Stanley to Graham, February 3rd, 1840, in *Ibid.*

[105] *West. Rev.*, XXXIV, 263. See also *Peel Papers*, CXXXVIII, 192 (Br. Mus.
Add. MSS. 40318).

A question on Ireland, as usual, opened the last session of the Melbourne Government. Morpeth moved for the second reading of the Registration of Voters Bill and Stanley countered by proposing that it be postponed for six months. Graham followed Stanley with another assault against his former colleagues, an assault which he concluded by quoting the following poem:

> When ancient fabrics nod and threat to fall,
> To patch their flaws and buttress up the wall,
> Thus far is duty: but here fix the mark;
> For all beyond it is to touch the ark.
> To change foundations, cast the frame anew,
> Is work for rebels who base ends pursue.[106]

It would be difficult, if not impossible, to find words that could more accurately describe Graham's philosophy of government: a slight concession here and there, reform of the worst abuses, increased efficiency in the existing branches of government, but no fundamental change in the Constitution of Church or State. All that was required was to 'patch the flaws and buttress up the walls'.

The Government was not only beaten on this Bill, but the Chancellor of the Exchequer was forced to announce a huge financial deficit. Peel, therefore, deciding that the time had come for the Conservatives to unite their forces and throw the Government out of office, proposed a vote of lack of confidence.[107] In supporting this resolution Graham reviewed at length the record of the Government. Power, he said, had long since passed from its hands. The policy which it intended to pursue in Jamaica in 1838 was defeated by the Opposition and replaced by one drawn up by Peel. Success had not attended the Chinese fracas either, unless they assumed that 'the unbridled licence of our troops in the attack on the undefended city of Chusan, which has exalted the British name, already immortalized in those seas by our smuggling of opium', was a great triumph.[108] The Government had been unable to carry its measures and despite one defeat after another had still

---

[106] *Hansard*, 3rd Ser., LVI, 1008; *Annual Register* (1841), 47-48. The *Quart. Rev.* (LXVII, 154), blamed all of Ireland's agrarian crimes on the Catholic priests and the Jesuits. It advocated the banishment of all Jesuits and a strict enforcement of all laws.

[107] *Hansard*, 3rd Ser., LVIII, 807.   [108] *Ibid.*, 943.

refused to resign. 'Never', he said, 'was a country cursed with a worse, a more reckless, or a more dangerous government . . . But, thank God, we have at last pinned you to something out of which you cannot wriggle — and as we have the melancholy satisfaction to know that there is an end to all things, so now I can say . . . Thank God, we have at last got rid of such a government as this.'[109] And Graham was right. Actual power had long since passed from Melbourne's hands. In fact, from 1837 to 1840 all his Government had been able to do was to remain in office. But it was just as well that it had not been able to do much. The Reform Act of 1832, the Poor Law of 1834, the Municipal Corporations Act of 1835, and the Tithe Act of 1836 had accomplished the needed reforms in Church and State and the country needed a few years in which to settle down to the new order of things and to consolidate its gains. By nature and temperament Melbourne and·his colleagues were well fitted to let things alone. In doing so, however, they naturally found themselves on the receiving end of criticism from the Radicals who desired more reform, and from the Conservatives who felt that the Government was an incapable and inefficient one, and who pointed with disdain at the mounting government deficit. But Graham's criticism of the Government as a 'reckless' and 'dangerous' one was sheer nonsense, for he had himself just told the House that it was so weak that it had been unable to exercise power for a period of three or four years.

At the conclusion of Graham's speech, the tottering Whig Government asked the Conservatives how they proposed to act when they got into power. Graham replied that he 'did not much value the skill with which the Ministers played their game, though he admired the sleight of hand with which they shuffled their cards; but at all events they had no right to look into their adversary's hands'.[110] On the division the vote of censure was carried by a majority of one, but even then the Government, instead of resigning, announced its intention to bring in a free trade Bill and ordered a dissolution of Parliament. It was a futile thing to do. By now almost all sections of the country were tired of the Whigs, who had really outlived their usefulness, and whose chief failing was their belief that the Government could cure only those evils which were due to the defects of the constitution or to poorly

---

[109] *Hansard*, 3rd Ser., LVIII, 963.   [110] *Annual Register* (1841), 125.

framed laws.[111] As soon as the new Parliament met, the ministry was beaten on a confidence vote by a majority of 91 and promptly resigned. The Whig Government was dead, hopelessly dead, and the newly published comic magazine, *Punch*, wrote the funeral dirge:

> The Whigs, who long
> Were bold and strong,
> On Monday night went dead.
> The jury found
> This verdict sound —
> *Destroyed by low priced bread.*[112]

[111] The *Quart. Rev.* (LXVIII, 496), said that the Whigs had sunk 'under the insuperable weight of an *empty budget*'. The Whig *Edin. Rev.* (LXXIV, 36), attributed the Government's defeat to a combination of Chartists who attacked the Poor Law and Tories who hated the Free Trade Bill.

[112] *Punch*, I, 87.

CHAPTER VIII

THE HOME OFFICE (1841-1846)

ENGLAND was ready for a change. Almost everyone was tired of the 'shabby' Government which for five years had pursued a policy of 'letting things alone'; tired of an inept and inefficient administration which had clung to office for dear life unwilling to let go and unable to tighten its grip. Great reforms had been accomplished from 1832 to 1836 and the Whigs, content with their work, had decided to let the country settle down to the new order of things. There were, nevertheless, two things which remained to be done: first, reform had to be carried into those areas, such as education, law, and medicine, which the early reform movement had neglected, and secondly, weaknesses in the administration of government had to be remedied.

To these tasks Peel and his colleagues devoted themselves with tireless energy and skill. Rarely has a Prime Minister surrounded himself with a corps of abler lieutenants. The chief posts were given to men each of whom was well qualified to administer the office assigned to him. 'Three of Peel's most intimate friends — the gentle Aberdeen, the practical Graham, the gallant Hardinge — became Foreign, Home and War Secretary respectively.'[1] Stanley became Secretary for the Colonies, Goulburn Chancellor of the Exchequer, Lyndhurst Lord Chancellor, Wellington, without office, assumed the leadership in the House of Lords, and four young men of great though untried talents received minor posts. These were Lord Canning, Lord Dalhousie, Sidney Herbert, and William E. Gladstone. Of this group Goulburn was not unusually strong, but since Peel did most of the work at the Exchequer that did not matter much. Ellenborough at the Board of Control was mediocre, while Knatchbull as Paymaster of the Forces and Ripon at the Board of Trade were inadequate. These latter appointments, as well as those of Wharncliffe as Lord President of the Council, and Haddington at the Admiralty, were obviously made to reward old friends and to satisfy the ultra-Conservatives. Lord Ashley deserved better of Peel and Graham. The insignificant post in the

---

[1] TRESHAM LEVER, *The Life and Times of Sir Robert Peel*, 191.

Royal Household which was allotted to him was justly regarded by Ashley as 'a plain, cruel, and unnecessary insult'.[2] In addition, there was one notable omission, that of Benjamin Disraeli, who was so hurt by his being left out that he wrote to Peel protesting the 'intolerable humiliation' and literally begging for a post.[3] The cold, but polite, refusal cut deep and Disraeli never forgot it.

Peel, the party chief, was one of the ablest premiers who have ever held that post. In the prime of life, possessed of tremendous business ability, an expert parliamentary tactician, a prodigious worker, he was ready and able to grapple with the problems of the day.

Next to Peel the ablest man in the cabinet was Graham. Now 49 years of age and in good health, he made an ideal chief lieutenant. He was what Peel admired, i.e., essentially a man of business, a tireless worker, a superb administrator, a facile debater and a man whose views on the problems of the day were precisely those of his chief. Ramsay is quite right in describing Graham as 'Peel's second self',[4] and there is as much truth as humour in the facetious comment of *Punch* that they were 'two persons with only one intellect'.[5] The Webbs conclude that Graham was 'perhaps the ablest of all the successors of Peel at the Home Office',[6] and Gladstone, the Vice-President of the Board of Trade in this ministry, later described him as knowing more about business 'than all the rest of the Government put together'.[7] His speeches, according to the Duke of Argyll, while often inanimate and lacking in variety, were distinguished for their 'general dexterity of . . . argument', and 'pithy, somewhat epigrammatic sayings', and always had 'a marked effect upon the House'.[8]

Reactions to Graham's appointment to the Home Office were varied, running all the way from high praise to bitter criticism.

---

[2] SIR EDWIN HODDER, *The Life and Work of the Seventh Earl of Shaftesbury*, I, 357 (Hereinafter cited as *Life of Shaftesbury*).

[3] The correspondence, including a letter from Mrs. Disraeli to Peel, is given in PARKER, *Life of Peel*, II, 486-489. See also *Peel Papers*, CCLXIX, 277 (Br. Mus. Add. MSS. 40449).

[4] RAMSAY, *Life of Peel*, 225.　　　　　[5] *Punch*, I, 54.

[6] SYDNEY WEBB and BEATRICE WEBB, *English Local Government*, VI, 134 (Hereinafter cited as the WEBBS, *Eng. Local Gov't.*).

[7] MORLEY, *Life of Gladstone*, I, 248.

[8] GEORGE DOUGLAS, EIGHTH DUKE OF ARGYLL, *Autobiography and Memoirs*, ed. by Duchess of Argyll, I, 157 (Hereinafter cited as *Auto. and Mem.*).

Most of those who approved of the appointment did so because they knew Graham was a capable administrator. The *Post* predicted that the Whigs would avail themselves of every occasion to oppose Graham, whom they hated, but that 'the excellence of his Administration' would overcome that opposition.[9] Incensed by Graham's attacks on the late Government, the *Morning Chronicle* predicted that Peel would soon find him 'too much of a busybody' and have to dismiss him.[10] The hostile *Globe* admitted that Graham's talents were 'by no means contemptible', but, with distress prevailing throughout the country, it would have preferred 'a cooler and less timid head at the Home Office'. It did not like his political inconsistency, his passage from Radicalism to Whiggism to Toryism, and described him as the 'Cumbrian Cassandra' and a 'Recreant Whig'.[11] *Punch*, characterizing Graham as the 'Ministerial Top', said he was suffering from severe fits of vertigo induced by 'his extraordinary propensity for turning around'.[12]

The Queen did not like either Peel or Graham for they were cold, stern, businesslike, so different from that 'frank, open, natural and most kind, warm manner of Lord Melbourne'.[13] Greville asserted that the Queen's 'childish and capricious fancy' was best exhibited in 'her hatred of Graham'.[14] But it was not long before Peel and Graham discovered how to manage her and she soon liked them as well as she had liked the members of Melbourne's Government (except for Melbourne whom she liked best of all). Graham told Greville that he 'made it a rule to address her as he would a sensible *man*, laying all matters before her, with the reasons for the advice he tendered, and he thought this was the most legitimate as well as judicious flattery that could be offered to her, . . . and the more because there was no appearance of flattery in it'.[15] The strategy worked perfectly, if we can believe Greville, for on August 6th, 1843 he wrote: 'The court is entirely on their side.'[16]

[9] *Post*, September 1st, 1841, p. 2.
[10] *Chronicle*, June 1st, 1841, p. 4; June 4th, p. 5; October 7th, p. 3.
[11] *Globe*, June 22nd, 1841, p. 2; January 7th, 1841, p. 2.
[12] *Punch*, I, 123.
[13] Queen Victoria to Lord Melbourne, May 8th, 1839, in *Letters of Queen Victoria*, I, 200.
[14] *Greville's Diary*, II, 140.
[15] *Ibid.*, 146.   [16] *Ibid.*

When Parliament met on September 16th, 1841,[17] Peel announced that the Government intended to adopt without change the last estimates of the Melbourne Government and to defer until the next session the explanation of the financial measures he was preparing by means of which he hoped to balance the budget. This announcement was approved, as was Graham's request that the Poor Law be renewed for six months, during which time he would prepare the necessary changes in it,[18] and on October 7th Parliament was prorogued.

The interval from October 7th, 1841, to February 3rd, 1842, when Parliament reassembled, gave Peel's ministry an opportunity to prepare the numerous measures of reform which the existing state of affairs urgently required. These measures touched almost every phase of life and affected vitally almost every human being in the British Isles. One may for convenience and clarity classify these measures as belonging to the following categories: political reform, legal reform, Poor Law reform, ecclesiastical reform, educational reform, social reform, economic and fiscal reform, changes in foreign policy, and lastly reforms needed for Ireland.[19]

Political Reform

It was fortunate for England that Peel's Government was such an able one for during the autumn of 1841 and the winter of 1842 the skies were very dark. Foreign countries, unable to stomach Palmerston's constant intervention, had become hostile. France was sulking; the United States was provoked about the Canadian boundary question; in China a disgraceful war was not yet over; in Ireland O'Connell was on the war-path; in Scotland a religious crisis was convulsing the land and threatening a disruption of the Church. And in England itself conditions were alarming.

In many respects the winter of 1841-1842 was one of the worst

[17] In the midsummer elections Graham had been defeated in Cumberland, but a seat was found for him in 'the snug pocket borough of Dorchester, under the patronage of Lord Shaftesbury'. See the *Globe*, June 22nd, 1841, p. 2; the *Post*, September 10th, 1841, p. 2.

[18] *Hansard*, 3rd Ser., LIX, 881 et seq.

[19] It is obvious that these categories and the order in which they are discussed is a purely arbitrary arrangement. I am aware of the great amount of overlapping that exists as well as the fact that measures herein discussed as 'social' may be regarded by others as 'economic' and that still others might prefer to call them 'socio-economic'.

through which the country has ever had to pass. A series of bad harvests, whose effects were aggravated by the Corn Laws, resulted in an increase in the price of bread while at the same time unemployment and low wages begat distress and starvation. Conditions in the industrial towns were frightful. In October 1841 Graham wrote to Peel: 'I am afraid we must expect a winter of great excitement and considerable tumult.'[20] That is precisely what occurred. At Bolton there was practically no employment and, it was reported, people had actually died from lack of food.[21] In Leeds 19,000 out of a population of 150,000 were subsisting on less than one shilling a week.[22] In such places as Manchester, Birmingham, Carlisle, Glasgow, and Rochdale the distress was so great that rioting occurred and troops were required to maintain some semblance of order and to protect property.[23] The towns of Manchester and Salford sent a petition signed by 60-70,000 persons asking for relief,[24] while at Paisley conditions were even more critical. Private charitable relief funds were completely exhausted, no jobs of any kind were available, and by October 1842 Graham predicted: 'without assistance I am afraid that a multitude will want bread, and that a serious outbreak will ensue.'[25] In December the Paisley Relief Committee sent out the following notice: 'On the expiry of this week . . . the persons now on the Relief List need not rely on obtaining from this Committee the present rate of allowances, nor even One Half of that rate.' At the same time, the Town Council informed Graham that there were 10,000 destitute in the city and that after December 15th they would all go begging and therefore would probably start to *take* food wherever they could find it.[26] Similar conditions existed at Stockport, Renfrew-

[20] *Peel Papers*, CCLVI, 60-61 (Br. Mus. Add. MSS. 40446).
[21] *Ibid.*, CCCIX, 39-41 (Br. Mus. Add. MSS. 40489).
[22] *Home Office Papers* (Domestic), 44/52.
[23] *Ibid.* (Disturbances Book), 41/16, p. 217 et seq.
[24] *Chronicle*, July 27th, 1842, p. 3. A delegation from the manufacturing interests of these towns had been sent to see Graham who said that the persons who had signed the petition did not understand the problem and that he would do only what he considered expedient. The delegation replied that they needed justice, not expediency.
[25] *Peel Papers*, CCLXVII, 275-276 (Br. Mus. Add. MSS. 40447).
[26] *Home Office Papers* (Disturbances at Paisley), 45/O.S. $\frac{345}{58}$.

On February 18th Wallace told the House that there were 17,000 on relief in Paisley, while Yorke said that 14,000 were actually starving. See *Hansard*, 3rd Ser., LX, 181-182.

shire, Stirling, Aberdeen, and other places. For England as a whole
almost one-tenth of the population was reduced to pauperism,
with the result that crime, rick-burning, and rioting grew apace.[27]
Political agitation was the inevitable consequence. The poor, who
had joined in the clamour for the Reform Bill in 1832, now realized
that only the middle class had gained by it. They concluded,
therefore, that their only salvation and hope lay in political
action,[28] and thousands consequently joined the Chartists[29] in
demanding votes for all adult males, secret ballot, equal electoral
districts, annual parliaments, payment of members of Parliament
and the abolition of property qualifications for holding office.
Characteristic of this action was the petition sent to the Queen by
the inhabitants of Newcastle upon Tyne: 'The sole cause of all
this accumulated mass of National Misery, Degradation and Woe,
lies in the Unjust, Partial and defective state of the Representation.'
It declared that there could be no lasting peace in England until
the *people* chose their representatives in the House of Commons.[30]

This was all very alarming to Graham, who distrusted this type
of democratic action and believed that organizations such as the
Chartist and Anti-Corn Law League were dangerous to the State.
Three things, he decided, needed to be done at once. First, relief
to the really destitute must be provided; secondly, order in all of
the disaffected areas must be restored; thirdly, concessions in the
shape of moderate political reform must be made.

Graham's policy with respect to relief is clearly demonstrated
in his handling of the serious situation in Paisley. In April 1842
he agreed to send a small sum of money to Paisley because local
funds were exhausted, but at the same time he informed the Provost
that the Government relied on local efforts to solve the problem.
Relief should be so administered that any 'habitual dependence

---

[27] For a description of disturbances in mid-August, 1842, see Graham's letters to
Queen Victoria in *Letters of Queen Victoria*, I, 530-535.

[28] 'The Character of these riots has assumed more decidedly a political aspect. It
is no longer a strike for higher wages, but the Delegates, who direct the movement,
avow that labour shall not be resumed until the people's Charter be granted.' Graham to Queen Victoria, in *Ibid.*, 530-531. Cf., *West. Rev.*, XXXVIII, 393. See also
Peel Papers, CCLXVII, 68-71 (Br. Mus. Add. MSS. 40447).

[29] This grew out of the Workingman's Association which had been founded in
1836 and whose object was 'creating and educating public opinion for the improvement of the working classes'. RAMSAY, *Life of Peel*, 220.

[30] *Home Office Papers* (Domestic), 44/52, October 5th, 1841.

on charity can be checked and able-bodied men brought to make exertions for finding the means of subsistence for themselves'.[31] By May 10th local funds were exhausted and Graham, in sending aid again to Paisley, demanded that 'a taste of work should be exacted in every case where it is possible in return for alms which are received'.[32] In December he wrote to the Paisley Relief Committee that he could 'hold out no hopes' that this aid would be continued and that 'distress can alone be relieved by increased exertions on the part of those resident in that town'.[33] His policy in dealing with distress in Paisley and in other places was based on a firm conviction that the Government had no power 'to permanently alter the condition of the working classes'.[34] Self-help was the only solution.

In addition, no matter how bad conditions became, peace and order had to be preserved. 'The supremacy of the law will be promptly vindicated', wrote Graham to the Queen, 'and [I] confidently hope that order will soon be restored.'[35] A careful reading of the Home Office papers reveals that Graham had worked out a procedural pattern for handling cases of this type. On first hearing of the possibility of trouble, he would address a communication to the local magistrates advising them to be on their guard and to do their duty according to the law.[36] If the disturbances were too great for them to cope with, they should swear in special

[31] *Home Office Papers* (Distress in Paisley), 45/O.S. $\frac{345}{42}$. To the Town Council of Greenock, which had petitioned for aid, Graham replied: 'Any aid from the public purse must not be expected The necessary funds must be supplied by local charity and local assessment.'

[32] *Ibid.*, May 16th, 1842. See also, *Peel Papers*, CCLXVI, 403-406 (Br. Mus. Add. MSS. 40446). Mr. Twisleton, Graham's representative in Paisley, was accused of having told the Relief Committee that 'it was necessary to render the condition of the operatives as disagreeable as possible, in order to compel them to locate themselves in other parts of the country' and that, as a result, they 'were treated worse than felons'. *Home Office Papers* (Distress in Paisley), 45/O.S. $\frac{345}{32}$. Twisleton's denial was certainly unconvincing.

[33] *Ibid.* (Scotch), 103/10, p. 14.

[34] *Ibid.* (Domestic Book), 43/63, p. 14.

[35] Graham to Queen Victoria, in *Letters of Queen Victoria*, I, 534. 'The Law must be upheld and property must be defended', and all must learn that the law would be enforced 'with temper but with determination', Graham wrote to the Marquis of Bute, the Lord-Lieutenant of Glamorganshire. *Home Office Papers* (Disturbances Book), 41/18, p. 52.

[36] *Ibid.*, 41/16, p. 470-472.

constables to help.[37] Occasionally, too, he offered to send, on the request of local authorities, some of the London police to augment local forces.[38] In some instances he also approved of the enrolment of the Yeomanry Corps, as well as the use of spies and informers.[39] Finally, in cases of extreme urgency, troops would be sent to the disturbed districts. But resort to the use of the military could be justified only where it appeared that a 'lawless multitude' would overthrow the local magistrates because for 'the general defence of property and for the preservation of the peace of the district, the Civil Authorities, not the Military Force, are responsible'.[40] The military force should be used only to support and to protect the civil force, not to replace it.

One result of Graham's prodigious exertions to secure the supremacy and full enforcement of the law was, according to Beer, that arrests were made 'of every leader or speaker among the Chartists or trade unionists, and of every working man suspected of complicity in the strike movement'.[41] Harsh punishment was meted out to offenders and injustice was too often done. On the other hand, Graham was equally insistent that the authorities should not exceed their legal powers. On September 16th, 1842, a group of London tradesmen sent a letter to the Duke of Wellington suggesting the enrolment of a body of 'respectable tradesmen' to put down 'Democratic meetings' and permitting them a stand of arms to enable them to act together in defence of their property. Wellington sent it to Graham asking him what answer he should give and Graham replied: 'acknowledge it in civil terms expressive of approbation of their loyalty and zeal'.[42] Two weeks later the Mayor of Newcastle requested permission to form a Rifle Corps armed with cutlasses and pistols, and Graham directed his chief secretary Manners Sutton, to 'decline civilly'.[43] Furthermore, he carefully restricted the use of troops. Lieutenant-General Arbuthnot, in command of forces at Manchester, was ordered to prevent

[37] *Ibid.*, O.S., 260.   [38] *Ibid.* (Domestic Book), 43/68, pp. 7-8.
[39] *Ibid.*, 9.   [40] *Ibid.*, 41/18, pp. 71-72.
[41] MAX BEER, *A History of British Socialism*, 151. Beer estimates the total at about 1500 of whom 800 were ultimately released and 710 of whom were tried at various assizes. Sentences ranged from two months in jail to transportation for life. See also SIMON MACCOBY, *English Radicalism 1832-1852*, p. 237 et seq.
[42] *Home Office Papers* (Disturbances, London), O.S. 252.
[43] *Ibid.* (Disturbances), O.S. 260.

any impression being spread 'that the Government or the Military are prepared to force the workers to resume labour at what they may consider inadequate wages'.[44] On the same day, August 24th, 1842, he wrote to the Earl of Talbot in Staffordshire: 'I am by no means prepared to use Military force to compel a reduction of wages or to uphold a grinding system of Truck: to preserve Peace, to put down Plunder, and to prevent the forced cessation of labour by intimidation, these are the sole objects of the Government: It is no part of our duty . . . to back the Master against the Workman in any harsh or unjust demand.'[45] In fact, he told his friend Croker that the labouring classes very often 'had just cause of complaint against their masters'.[46]

While this 'mad insurrection of the working classes', as he described these strikes, annoyed Graham tremendously, he was even more annoyed and angered by the actions of the magistrates and the 'men of substance'. On frequent occasions they not only did not do their duty, but even joined with the strikers. At Rochdale, in the riots which occurred in the summer, the magistrates had done nothing at all.[47] At Stockport, the magistrates, known to be Anti-Corn Law Leaguers, joined the Chartists in demanding universal suffrage and failed to preserve any semblance of order. Graham would have liked to have removed them from office, but the law-officers of the Crown said that it could not be done.[48] At Manchester, a justice of the peace told the rioters that he agreed to three-fourths of their demands,[49] while John Howard, a magistrate in Cheshire, told the crowd that as long as they were unemployed they could live in his house rent-free.[50] In some places, such as Huddersfield, the magistrates were manufacturers and mill-owners who, instead of going to the expense of keeping an adequate civil force, relied on the use of the military. 'It may be very convenient and economical for Magistrates who are manufacturers', wrote Graham to the Mayor, 'thus to protect their

---

[44] *Home Office Papers* (Post Office), 79/4, August 25th, 1842.   [45] *Ibid.*

[46] Graham to Croker, in CROKER, *Corr. and Diaries*, II, 389. In the troubles in the potteries, Graham blamed the masters more than the men and described their conduct as 'unreasonable'. See *Peel Papers*, CCLXVII, 56-57 (Br. Mus. Add. MSS. 40447).

[47] *Home Office Papers* (Censures on Magistrates for Truckling with the Rioters), O.S., 249, September 10th, 1842.

[48] *Ibid.* (Law Officer's Reports), 48/34, p. 19.   [49] *Ibid.*, n.p.

[50] *Ibid.* (Disturbances Book), 41/16, p. 368.

property by the sole employment of the military ... but I cannot but consider this to be ... a misapplication of Her Majesty's forces.'[51]

As to the landed proprietors and 'men-of-substance' in the towns, it was their duty, Graham told them, 'in the first instance to defend their own property by their own exertions, aided by their servants and dependants ...'.[52] However, many not only made no attempts in this direction but even housed and fed the rioters. The Anti-Corn Law mill-owners were at first inclined to smile at a disturbance of this kind, but, said Graham, 'when it reached their own doors were the first to cry aloud for soldiers'.[53] To Graham, if these people made no effort to defend themselves and their property, it did not matter whether the Government sent troops to every town in the manufacturing districts, 'outrage, lawless violence and plunder must necessarily prevail'.[54] But while he felt that these disturbances should be dealt with at the local level, he was slowly but surely becoming convinced that the problems rising from the rapid industrialization of the country were a type that could not be effectively handled by local authorities but required action by the national government. And when he ordered troops to disturbed areas he hoped that the mere presence of the soldiers would be sufficient to restore order and that resort to extreme measures would not be necessary.[55]

Graham knew very well, however, that force could only restore order temporarily and that the Government would have to introduce some moderate measures of political reform. He would, of course, have nothing whatever to do with what he called the 'wild schemes' of the Chartists, for, he told the House of Commons, it would mean the adoption of the principle of representation based on numbers instead of on property, and would end in the abolition of the Monarchy and in the 'subversion of all our great institu-

---

[51] *Ibid.* (Censures on Magistrates), O.S., 264 B, October 1st, 1842.
[52] *Ibid.* (Disturbances Book), 41/18, p. 90.
[53] Graham to H. T. Parker, in PARKER, *Life of Graham*, I, 324.
[54] *Ibid.*
[55] Graham to Queen Victoria, in *Letters of Queen Victoria*, I, 530. Brougham praised Graham for postponing the use of troops 'until it was no longer possible to do without them'. Brougham to Graham, in PARKER, *Life of Graham*, I, 323. But the free trade *Chronicle* (August 2nd, 1842, p. 4), denounced Graham for pursuing a policy of repression and told Peel that the sooner he could put 'this very indiscreet minister in some other office, the better it will be for both the government and the country'.

M

tions'.[56] The House agreed with Graham and by a vote of 226 to 67 defeated a motion, introduced by Crawford, that the representation be reformed along lines advocated in the Charter. A few weeks later (June 21st, 1842), a motion was made calling for the adoption of the secret ballot. Since very few were in attendance in the House, the Government decided to give it the silent treatment. Sheil, an Irish M.P., was angered by this strategy, and denounced Graham as an 'Aristocratic Whig graduating to high Tory principles'. Graham replied that since the Reform Committee of 1832 had fully discussed and then voted against the secret ballot he considered that action final. The secret ballot, he declared, was inconsistent with English character, a danger to the Monarchy and harmful to good government.[57] When he was criticized for this 'finality' stand, he wavered a little and declared that if he could be convinced that by granting the ballot, 'we should be erecting a barrier to further change', he would support it; but he believed that opening the door to the ballot would inevitably lead to universal suffrage — a radical nostrum which he could never sanction.[58]

Having opposed the secret ballot and an extension of the suffrage, Graham also opposed the Chartist demand for annual parliaments on the grounds that it took a new M.P. at least a year or two just to become acquainted with procedures in the House. Nor would he agree to a proposal that all parliamentary oaths be abolished, because he did not want to disturb the settlement reached in the Catholic Emancipation Act of 1829. On the debit side of the ledger must also be placed his opposition to Russell's proposed Bill to extend the principles of the Municipal Corporations Act to all remaining corporations and to abolish eighty-three of the smallest of them.[59]

On the other hand, Graham recognized that the existing political

[56] *Hansard*, 3rd Ser., LXII, 42.

[57] *Ibid.*, LXIV, 401 et seq. For this statement he was taken to task by the *West. Rev.*, XLI, 341, and the *Globe*, June 22nd, 1842, p. 4. In the debates, Graham said that he was opposed to the ballot, but that if he could be shown that granting the ballot would be a barrier against further change, he 'might vote for it'. The *Chronicle* (June 24th, 1842, p. 5), didn't think much of this. 'Where then is the compact?' it asked. 'Where the pledge of finality? Which of the two allegations is humbug, for the purposes of debate — the pledge against ballot [which Graham had made when a member of Grey's cabinet] or the freedom to support the ballot, or both? What an elastic thing is unprincipled inconsistency.'

[58] *Hansard*, 3rd Ser., LXIV, 403.   [59] *Ibid.*, LXVIII, 987 et seq.

machinery was in need of a thorough overhauling. As a member of the committee which had drawn up the Reform Bill of 1832 he had sponsored the requirement that every legally qualified voter prove his qualification and have his name put on the electoral list.[60] He was also the author of the Bill's registration clauses which provided for the formation of a register of voters, the division of constituencies into convenient polling districts and the limitation of polling to two successive days.[61] The purpose of these clauses was to prevent fraud, to protect the rights of *bona fide* voters, and to decrease the expense of elections. The task of seeing to it that all legally qualified voters had a fair opportunity to get their names on the registers was entrusted to the overseers of the poor.[62] In practice the system worked about as follows. In the counties, registration began each year on June 20th, when the overseers requested each duly qualified voter to send in a notification of his claim. When the claim was received, and not until then, the name was inserted on the list. It was the only claim needed and was not repeated unless an objection was raised to the placing of the name on the list, and unless the voter had changed either his qualification or his residence. In the county, the voter had to prove his qualification; in the borough, the rate-book was sufficient.[63] By July 20th the overseer's list of names of those who claimed the right to vote had to be ready. The list was kept open for inspection and any elector could object to the name of any other on the list provided he did so before August 25th. Interestingly enough, the objector was not required to state the grounds of his objections. Then, if the claimant failed upon notification to appear to defend his claim against the objection, his name was struck from the list.

The requirement in the boroughs was that the electors had to have paid their rates up to the commencement of the registration period. By July 20th the assessors and tax-collectors were required to have a list prepared of all who were in arrears and their names

[60] For an excellent analysis of this question see CHARLES SEYMOUR, *Electoral Reform in England and Wales*, Chap. v.

[61] *Statutes at Large*, 2 and 3 Will. IV, c. 45.

[62] It was an easy matter for the overseers of the poor to keep correct lists since they kept the rate-books and knew who paid the rates as well as the value of all houses. They also were personally acquainted with everyone in the parish and so could check any fraudulent claims. See SEYMOUR, *op. cit.*, 109.

[63] For further information on the Act of 1832 see *Statutes at Large*, 2 and 3 Will. IV, c. 45, Sec. 36 et seq.

were struck from the list by the overseers. A list of all duly qualified voters was then made out and published on the last day of July, and, as in the counties, any elector might object to any other name on the list. Anyone whose name had been omitted and who felt he was qualified to vote could present his claim to the overseers. A list of such claimants was published along with another containing the names to which objection had been made.

'After the preliminary lists were thus compiled and the objections entered', writes Seymour, 'the process in counties and boroughs was identical. The lists were handed over to the clerical officials, the clerks of the peace in the counties and the town clerks in boroughs, and copies made out for the courts constituted to revise the lists.'[64] The task of hearing claims and settling objections was entrusted to specially chosen barristers who held court for the purpose in each of the counties and boroughs. These revising barristers were chosen by the senior judge in the commissions of assize[65] and they could not be M.P.s nor could they hold 'any Office or Place of Profit under the Crown'.[66]

The courts conducted by the revising barristers were held in September and October and all overseers and town clerks were required to be present. The barristers then corrected the lists and struck off 'the names of all those who were shown to have died during the year and of those whose qualification was proved insufficient, or who had failed to comply with the stated conditions of residence or payment of rates',[67] or who had been found guilty of bribery or like offences.

The elector who had objected to a name on the list had to appear before this court and state his objections or the name remained on the list. If the claimant could not prove that he was a legally qualified voter, or if he failed to appear to defend his claim, his name was taken off the list. So each claimant, regardless of how clear his claim, had to bear the expense and trouble of proving his qualification. If he failed to appear, regardless of the reason, he lost his vote.

[64] SEYMOUR, *op. cit.*, 112.
[65] However, in Middlesex and the Metropolitan boroughs, the revising barristers were chosen by the Lord Chief Justice. See *Statutes at Large*, 2 and 3 Will. IV, c. 45, Sec. 41.
[66] *Ibid.*   [67] SEYMOUR, *op. cit.*, 113.

The revised lists were then sent to the clerks of the peace in the counties and to the town clerks in the boroughs where they were transferred to books, copies of which were sent to all sheriffs and returning officers. These books then formed the voting register for the succeeding year. Graham's object in drawing up this plan had been to secure as cheaply as possible lists of all qualified voters and to prevent the registration of those not qualified. But the scheme did not work very well. It was new and difficult for the voters to comprehend; many voters were apathetic about it;[68] overseers were frequently lax in their work and compiled inaccurate lists; and too many frivolous objections were raised to names on the list.

Bills to remedy these defects were passed by the House in 1834 and 1835 but were thrown out by the Lords. Then it was discovered that the provision requiring each elector to swear that he had not moved from his property disfranchised an increasing number of voters each year. And even though many, so disfranchised, had moved to property of greater value, they nevertheless lost their right to vote. The inevitable result was a great increase in the personation of voters as well as additional expense to the Government in having to investigate the character of removals. Bills introduced in 1839 and in 1842 to correct these evils were abortive.

It was these problems which Graham sought to solve by the Registration of Voters Bill which he introduced on February 20th, 1843. One of the clauses provided that the clerk of the peace in the counties and the town clerk in the boroughs should issue a 'precept' i.e., a directive, ordering the overseers to prepare on July 31st of each year an alphabetical list of all qualified voters. The laxness of the overseers in making out proper electoral lists would, as a result, be corrected.[69]

Furthermore, the Law of 1832, which had disqualified many voters because it required rates to be paid up to the time the claim was made, was altered and the ratepayer was given three months' leeway by the stipulation that rates due up to April 6th were to be paid when the claim was made. The Bill also ordered the overseers to warn by June 20th the occupiers of premises of a yearly value of

---

[68] Voters 'had always voted without being registered and did not see why they should have anything of the kind done now'. *Edin. Rev.*, LVI, 545.

[69] *Statutes at Large*, 6 and 7 Victoria, c. 18, Sec. 3 et seq.

£10 that their rates had to be paid within a month if they intended to register.[70]

In addition, in order to reduce the great number of trifling objections arising from the unwillingness of many claimants to spend time and money attending the courts of revision, the Bill provided that the costs would have to be borne by the persons who raised the frivolous or unwarranted objections.[71]

Then, to prevent the names of unqualified persons from appearing in the electors' lists, the Bill stipulated that the overseers must publish lists of all persons who had not paid the rates or who had been guilty of corrupt or illegal practices. From this list the revising barristers were to select the names to be expunged from the register. Furthermore, the Bill simplified procedures by permitting objectors to protest in writing, and hence obviated the necessity of a personal appearance.

Barristers were to be of three years' standing and the total number was reduced from 160 to 85. This would result not only in greater efficiency but would, Graham proudly told the House, accomplish an annual saving of about £15,000.[72]

Clause 58 of the Bill (Section 60 of the Act) allowed appeals from the decisions of the barristers to go directly to the Court of Common Pleas instead of to the House of Commons as heretofore. When the House was considering this clause, Russell objected on the grounds that it gave to judges the right to judge of the election of M.P.s (a long-established right of the House) and that it would make judges too partisan. Graham, to the satisfaction of the House, replied that appeals were to be granted not on questions of fact but of law, and Russell's objection was beaten by the decisive vote of 154 to 51.[73]

Finally, the Bill made it a misdemeanour punishable by two years' imprisonment at hard labour to personate a voter. Almost everyone admitted the necessity of this regulation, for the personation of voters had become scandalous. On June 9th, 1834, Walter had reported to the House that he had had to bear the expense of 'the humbug claim of thirty-seven fictitious voters, who had

---

[70] *Statutes at Large*, 6 and 7 Victoria, c. 18, Sec. 11.

[71] *Ibid.*, Sec. 46; *Hansard*, 3rd Ser., LXVII, 767.

[72] *Statutes at Large*, 6 and 7 Victoria, c. 18, Sec. 28; *Hansard*, 3rd Ser., LXVII, 1084. The cost of 160 revising barristers had been £32,000, of the 85 it would be £17,000.   [73] *Ibid.*, LXVIII, 340 et seq.

registered themselves in fourteen different parishes; thus he had 518 objections to take against parties who had not the slightest claim in the world'.[74] In February 1841 Liddell, describing the election in Walsall, said that 'the leaguites polled nine dead men, three of whom were decided Conservatives'.[75]

The House regarded this measure as a non-partisan one and Graham had little difficulty in securing its adoption. But while the House regarded it as a non-partisan measure, the *Westminster Review* took the opposite view and argued that it restricted popular rights and was so constructed as to benefit 'those tenants-at-will who are supposed to be the most subservient to the interests of the Tory aristocracy'.[76] The *Quarterly Review* thought that the Bill should have provided for a greater decrease in the costs of elections.[77] On the other hand, the *Manchester Guardian* probably best reflected popular opinion when it wrote: 'the proposed changes are likely to operate beneficially and to diminish the trouble and annoyance which have resulted from the operation of the existing law'.[78]

This Act did not, however, solve all the electoral problems, for weaknesses in the system continued to crop out in succeeding years. The increased powers and diligence of the overseers did not stimulate interest in voting and the general apathy continued until it was discovered some years later that political power in Parliament was to a large degree dependent upon the registers of voters. Then it was seen that Peel had been unusually prescient in 1838 when he wrote:

> There is a perfectly new element of political power — namely, the registration of voters, a more powerful one than either the Sovereign or the House of Commons.
> That party is strongest in point of fact which has the existing registration in its favour. It is a dormant instrument, but a most powerful one, in its tacit and preventive operation.
> . . . .
> The registration will govern the disposal of offices, and determine the policy of party attacks; and the power of this new element will go on increasing. . . .[79]

[74] *Ibid.*, XXIV, 343.
[75] *Ibid.*, LVI, 323.
[76] *West. Rev.*, LXXVIII, 528.
[77] *Quart. Rev.*, LXXI, 486-488
[78] *Manchester Guardian*, March 1st, 1843, p. 4.
[79] Peel to Arbuthnot, November 8th, 1838, in PARKER, *Life of Peel*, II, 368

But none of the parties paid much attention to the registers as a lucrative source of power until the Anti-Corn Law League began to realize its potentialities. The Reform Act of 1832 had given the county franchise to tenants-at-will at an annual value of £50, as well as to the 40-shilling freeholders. This favoured the landowners because it admitted their tenants-at-will to the franchise on easy terms, and therefore made it possible to fabricate a number of votes by putting together many partners in a tenancy-at-will. As Harriet Martineau put it: 'Brothers, sons, uncles, and every kind of relative, were made partners, and had votes under this clause.'[80] To offset this advantage of the landowners, Richard Cobden had his free traders, according to Trevelyan, 'qualify as county voters by purchasing property worth 40 shillings a year. Fifty or sixty pounds could make a man a county voter. In this way they would more than outnumber the faggot votes created by the landlords . . .'[81] The Anti-Corn Law League exploited this opportunity with a vengeance, and in 1845 Cobden, one of its leaders, exultantly exclaimed: 'In vote-making we are doing great execution. It is now the towns against the squires and the towns will win.'[82]

Not only did Graham's measure fail to stop the personation of voters, but it also failed to lessen materially the complexities in the electoral system. 'The granting of costs for vexatious objections', concludes Seymour, 'proved so innocuous that the raising of objections on wholly unjustifiable grounds soon became a party weapon that was utilized with impunity as well as with success. On the other hand, many facilities for unfair and often fraudulent claims were still offered.'[83] Graham's registration system was therefore neither complete nor pure, and complaints were so numerous that in 1846 Parliament insisted upon the appointment of a committee of investigation.

It was Graham's intention in framing this measure to interfere as little as possible with the system established by the Reform Act. By nature gloomy and pessimistic, he was fearful of ill-advised

[80] HARRIET MARTINEAU, *History of England*, IV, 433.

[81] GEORGE M. TREVELYAN, *Life of John Bright*, 122. See also, SEYMOUR, *op. cit.*, 122 et seq.

[82] TREVELYAN, *op cit.*, 123. A great amount of money was spent by the League in buying property for the creation of qualifications.

[83] SEYMOUR, *op. cit.*, 122.

schemes of political reform and continually reminded himself that he must be on guard against any radical tampering with the *status quo*. Change, of course, was inevitable but it must be moderate and gradual.

It was with this attitude that he faced the problem posed by the Friendly Societies. These societies, formed for the purpose of providing burial, accident, and sickness benefits, had also, says Fay, 'educated their members in self-government. They were a part of the corporate life of the workers'.[84] In the late 1830s and 40s their membership increased greatly. Graham was fearful of these associations, even when the purpose was charitable, because they had begun to use a great deal of ritual, such as annual feasts and processions to churches. He would not object, he told the House, to a combination of masters to reduce wages, or of workmen to raise them by legal means, 'but if workmen were to enter into friendly and mutual benefit societies to maintain themselves during a strike, though it might not be illegal in itself, he nevertheless doubted whether it would be the policy of the State to extend the advantages of these societies to men engaged in any such object'.[85]

Thomas Duncombe had proposed a Friendly Societies Bill the object of which was to legalize friendly societies 'for any purpose which is not illegal whether of the same description as is hereinafter mentioned, or otherwise'.[86] This was too loose for Graham and he succeeded in getting the words 'or otherwise' stricken from the Bill. Then he introduced one amendment after another. One of these compelled Friendly Societies to be enrolled by the Attorney-General. 'On being certified by the attorney general to be legal . . . there would be an application to the Secretary of State, and the society would be registered.'[87] Another provided for keeping a record of all societies enrolled as well as a statement of the objects of each society. He also objected to the transferability of shares in Friendly Societies and introduced an amendment to the Bill which provided that 'no party shall give his investment for the relief, maintenance, or endowment of any person' other than the person investing, his children, or kin.[88] This amendment, he hoped,

---

[84] CHARLES R. FAY, *Life and Labour in the Nineteenth Century*, 279. See also FAY, *Great Britain from Adam Smith to the Present Day*, Chap. XXII; CLAPHAM, *Econ. Hist. of Mod. Brit.*, I, 295-300.

[85] *Hansard*, 3rd Ser., LXXXIV, 107.

[86] *Ibid.*, 106.   [87] *Ibid.*, 930.   [88] *Ibid.*, LXXXV, 854.

would prevent 'strike-associations' from being able to hold out for a long time against employers. Finally, he suggested that all disputes affecting Friendly Societies be arbitrated by the Registrar of Friendly Societies, a post to be created when the Bill passed, instead of being decided by the Court of Chancery. This would save delay and expense. No wonder Duncombe announced that the Bill was no longer his, but the Home Secretary's. As finally passed, in 1846, the Bill transferred control of Friendly Societies from local authorities to a central authority known as the Registrar of Friendly Societies.[89] J. T. Pratt, who held the office for many years, used every effort to prevent fraud and mismanagement in these organizations.

Legal Reform

Another field in which reform was long overdue was the law. Because of the natural and timid conservatism of lawyers 'who see the social order', according to Smellie, 'only through the medium of individual cases of dispute', and in whose work 'there is little to . . . produce the administrator's sense of the need for continuous change',[90] they had neither asked for nor initiated reform in the courts. 'Scarcely ever', wrote the *Quarterly Review*, 'has any occupant of the Bench led the way to reform. Seldom, if ever, has the Bench collectively asked for . . . reform.'[91] As a consequence much-needed improvements in the common law courts had to be undertaken by Peel's Government. The preparation of these reforms should have been the responsibility of Lyndhurst, the Lord Chancellor, but because neither Peel nor Graham had much confidence in his ability the task fell to Graham, who, says Campbell, 'acted as Chief Minister of Justice'.[92]

It was the laws relating to bankruptcy and insolvency which most required immediate attention. The law of 1831 had established a Court of Bankruptcy consisting of a chief and three puisne judges to do the work formerly done by the Court of Chancery.[93]

[89] *Statutes at Large*, 9 and 10 Victoria, c. 27.
[90] SMELLIE, *A Hundred Years of English Government*, 121.
[91] *Quart. Rev.*, CCLXI, 41.
[92] LORD CAMPBELL, *Lives of the Lord Chancellors*, X, 140. Lord Lyndhurst's appointment as a member of Peel's cabinet was a concession to Wellington, who esteemed him highly.
[93] *Statutes at Large*, 1 and 2 Will, IV, c. 56,

But the law did not work well. It did not define 'traders', and did not distinguish between traders and non-traders though it applied only to traders. In addition, proceedings in bankruptcy depended upon the size of a trader's business. 'A petitioning creditor in bankruptcy', writes Walpole, 'was required to be a person to whom at least £100 was due; if two persons petitioned, their debts were required to amount to £150; if more than two persons petitioned, to £200.'[94] Furthermore, the application of the law was restricted to an area within forty miles of London. Therefore, since the welfare of the commercial community depends in large part on a reasonable law of bankruptcy, 'the great commercial world', says Bowen, 'avoided [this] court of bankruptcy as they would the plague . . . To the honest insolvent the bankruptcy court was a terror. To the evil-doer it afforded means of endlessly delaying his creditors, while the enormous expenses of bankruptcy administrations rendered it the interest of few to resort to the remedy . . . '.[95]

On the advice and constant prodding of Graham, Lord Lyndhurst introduced a Bill in the House of Lords in August 1842 to remedy these evils. After it had passed the Lords Graham piloted it through the House of Commons.[96] The Act abolished the country commissioners and turned country bankruptcies over to District Courts set up under the Act. In addition, Section 39 of the Act took away the power of the creditors to veto the grant of the debtor's discharge, and left the latter entirely at the discretion of the Court. The sums necessary to become a petitioning creditor were reduced from £100 to £50 for individuals, from £150 to £70 for two persons, and from £200 to £100 if more than two petitioned. The London metropolitan district was extended from 40 to 100 miles around the city. The district courts of bankruptcy established in various places throughout the country were given the same jurisdiction as that possessed by the London court, but were required to report all cases to the chief registrar of the Court of

[94] WALPOLE, *Hist. of Eng.*, IV, 419.
[95] BOWEN, 'The Reign of Queen Victoria', cited in A. V. DICEY, *Law and Opinion in England*, 122-123.
[96] 56 bankers and merchants and 537 traders had memorialized the Government to reform the existing law and to extend the London system to the rural areas. *Hansard*, 3rd Ser., LXV, 1082 et seq.

Bankruptcy, who was compelled to present annual reports to Parliament.[97]

One of the things which Graham liked about this law, he told the House, was that by it a creditor with an unsatisfied claim could summon a debtor to court and ask him: 'Do you acknowledge the debt you owe me or do you not?' If the debtor acknowledged the debt but refused to pay it, he committed an act of bankruptcy. If he then acted honestly and surrendered his property he was exempt from punishment. 'But, . . . if he concealed his property, and would not surrender it, or acted . . . with fraud, then his person would become, not on account of his poverty or misfortunes, but of his immorality, vice, and fraud, promptly and rightly subject to the law.'[98]

Having passed a bankruptcy law Parliament now found it necessary to take action in the matter of insolvency. Bankruptcy law was founded on the principle that the property of a debtor could be seized, while insolvency law provided for the seizure of the person of the debtor. But this imprisonment deprived the debtor of the opportunity of earning the money with which to pay his debts; he simply languished in jail while the creditor failed to obtain payment of his debt. To Graham this was not only stupid but unjust, for it often resulted in extorting from the debtor's relatives and friends 'the means of paying debts which they were not legally or morally called upon to liquidate'.[99] The Act which was passed by the Government to remedy these evils enabled both private debtors and traders whose debts were less than the sums named in the Bankruptcy Act, to become bankrupts, and abolished imprisonment for debts of less than £20.[100] Hence some of the worst evils of the old system were removed and many debtors were released from prison.[101]

Another cause of needless delay, expense, and fraud in the courts was the system of paying officials by fee instead of by salary. Not only were these fees often exorbitant but also the amounts charged for the same service varied in different localities. Officials simply took all the traffic would bear. To remedy this condition the

[97] *Statutes at Large*, 5 and 6 Victoria, c. 122.
[98] *Hansard*, 3rd Ser., LXV, 1087-1088.   [99] *Ibid.*, LXXVI, 1893.
[100] *Statutes at Large*, 7 and 8 Victoria, c. 96.
[101] *Annual Register* (1844), Chron. 87. The *Manchester Guardian* (May 6th, 1843, p. 4), described it as a 'very beautiful measure'.

Home Secretary introduced a Bill in August 1844 which provided for paying by salary instead of by fee the clerks of magistrates, clerks of peace, and clerks of assize.[102] Justice, he asserted, 'was better administered by public servants receiving salaries . . . than by [those] receiving fees'.[103] Economy would be achieved, too, for the magistrates would have power over county funds and could fix the salaries at a 'reasonable' sum. The country would have a uniform and controllable system. The Act incorporating this idea was passed in 1845.[104] So, too, was a similar Act abolishing fees on pleading and acquittal in criminal cases.[105]

Both laws met with universal approbation. The *Westminster Review* praised Graham very highly for his work and called him 'the patron saint of our new law reformers', [106] and even the hostile *Punch* declared that the Bills were the 'one white spot in Graham's life! and, like one white hair in a black cat, spoils what would otherwise be all of one colour'.[107]

Graham also secured the adoption of an act for expediting the settlement by local courts of means for recovering small debts (less than £20) by permitting additional local courts to try these cases. In addition, it gave the Home Secretary and the Lord Chancellor power to extend or to diminish, and hence to equalize, these courts.[108] However, an equally desirable Bill designed to overhaul completely the cumbrous and out-dated machinery of the county courts, which he introduced in 1844, met with so much opposition that he decided to drop it.[109]

In his labours on these legal reform measures, Graham did not receive much aid or encouragement from his colleagues, and therefore the credit for the constructive work done belongs to him. In 1842, when he first began to work on the problem, Peel wrote to him: 'We must approach this with great caution.' He admitted that a speedier and better administration of justice would result from Graham's projected reforms, but he feared that it would strike a blow at 'the useful influence of the best part of

---

[102] *Hansard*, 3rd Ser., LXXVI, 1940 et seq.
[103] *Ibid.*, LXXVIII, 762.
[104] *Statutes at Large*, 8 and 9 Victoria, c. 78.
[105] *Ibid.*, c. 114.
[106] *West. Rev.*, XXXIX, 224.
[107] *Punch*, VIII, 137.
[108] *Statutes at Large*, 8 and 9 Victoria, c. 127, Sec. IV. The *Globe* (March 20th, 1844, p. 4), described it as 'a great boon to the poorer classes of artisans, small tradesmen and shopkeepers'. See *Hansard*, 3rd Ser., LXXIII, 1672-1673; LXXIV, 193.
[109] *Ibid.*, LXXVII, 152. See also SMELLIE, *op. cit.*, 121.

the local and provincial aristocracy'. But while Peel was only cautious and undecided, Follett, Wellington, and Goulburn were positive in their opposition. They professed to see, as Goulburn put it, 'a growing tendency to withdraw the administration of business, judicial, financial, or administrative, from the hands of the upper classes of society and to vest it in paid officers of the government' with the likelihood that the landlords would 'degenerate into an idle and useless' class of society.[110] No wonder Graham complained that his 'ministerial friends' did not encourage him much.[111]

Poor Law Reform

But if the laws relating to bankruptcy, insolvency, and small debts were in need of corrective treatment so too were the laws relating to the poor. One of the most important sections of the Poor Law of 1834 was Section 52, which authorized the poor law commissioners to issue peremptory orders 'after which all relief in contravention thereof, save strictly guarded emergency relief, was illegal'.[112] The commissioners, provided for by the Law, acted on three general principles: the principle of less-eligibility, the principle of all-or-nothing, and the principle of national uniformity. By the first it was meant that the conditions in the workhouses, where, so far as possible, all relief was to be given, were to be made less desirable than the conditions existing among the lowest grade of independent workers.[113] By the second it was meant that to obtain relief an able-bodied man had to prove that he was totally dependent. And finally, national uniformity was to be achieved by incorporating all of the parishes in England and Wales into Poor Law Unions and placing them under the management of unpaid boards of guardians. Real power, however, rested in the hands of three central commissioners and their secretary, Edwin Chadwick. From 1834 to 1847 this Poor Law was, as the Hammonds have correctly observed, an interesting experiment in centralized administration which, like most such

---

[110] See PARKER, *Life of Graham*, I, 333-335.
[111] *Hansard*, 3rd Ser., LXXVIII, 762.
[112] FAY, *Great Britain from Adam Smith to the Present Day*, 341.
[113] See SIDNEY WEBB and BEATRICE WEBB, *English Poor Law Policy*, Chap. II.

experiments, worked well in some places and not so well in others. Good harvests in 1835 and 1836, plus the development of alternative sources of employment (such as railroad construction), eased the application of the Law in the southern rural districts and hence enabled the commissioners quickly to set up numerous unions and to supply them with boards of guardians. On the other hand, the violent fluctuations in employment prevented the Law from working well in the urban industrial centres and it was persistently criticized.[114] In years of poor harvests it was denounced in the southern rural areas as well.

The Law was to operate for a period of five years, and with each passing year the opposition to it became so bitter that the Melbourne Government was able merely to renew it annually in 1839 and 1840. It was therefore obvious to Peel and Graham that they would have to grapple with this problem — one that became increasingly urgent as the economic gloom deepened in 1840, 1841, and 1842. As applications for relief increased so too did criticism of the Law. On September 28th, 1841, while opposing Graham's request that the House extend the life of the Law for six months to afford time to prepare a new bill, Sharman Crawford succinctly summarized the criticisms directed at the union workhouses in these words:

> Under the present system five [sic—six] great evils were prevalent: first, the separation of families; secondly, arbitrary punishment and too severe discipline; thirdly, harshness to old age; fourthly, bad food; fifthly, difficulty of obtaining admission into the workhouse; and sixthly, the mixture of the virtuous and the profligate.[115]

These evils arose partly from the fact that neither the commissioners nor the guardians had ever defined the term 'pauper'. Hence the Law which was designed to compel the able-bodied to work, was often applied to the aged, to the infirm, and to children.[116] Report after report from the union workhouses criticized the 'bastilles', as the workhouses were called, and denounced

[114] These fluctuations in employment in the Midlands were due to the periodic influx of migrants from the southern rural areas and from Ireland. See SIR GEORGE NICHOLLS, *A History of the English Poor Law*, II, 305-306.

[115] *Hansard*, 3rd Ser., LIX, 927.

[116] For an excellent treatment of this phase of the problem see the WEBBS, *op. cit.*, II, 12 et seq.

the commissioners as 'the three bashaws' of Somerset House.[117]

Having received hundreds of suggested improvements from the boards of guardians,[118] having been a member of a board of guardians himself, and having served on the Poor Law Committee,[119] Graham was now well prepared to frame a new bill,[120] and on May 11th, 1842, he presented it to the House. It called for an extension of the Poor Law until 1847, and its guiding principle was stated in the following words: 'local administration, in conformity with the plan defined by law, placed in the hands of a mixed body, composed partly of persons chosen by the ratepayers, and partly of magistrates appointed by the Crown, checked and controlled by a central authority emanating from the Crown itself'.[121]

One of the clauses of the Bill called for the abolition of the Gilbert Unions.[122] Only fifteen of these remained, and since they permitted outdoor relief, while the Poor Law was based on indoor relief for the able-bodied, they were in obvious conflict with each other and Graham was acting on sound principle in proposing their abolition. The Bill also enabled parishes within fifteen miles of each other to unite to form schools, subject to the inspection of the committee of the Council on Education. A chaplain

---

[117] The criticisms were almost endless. No rules existed whereby loose women could be kept from the virtuous; strict silence was often imposed during meal-time; no smoking was permitted; no books, not even the Bible, were provided in some; aged couples were compelled to live separately; children were kept from their parents; hateful work such as stone-breaking and bone-crushing was enforced on all.

[118] *Home Office Papers* (Domestic Book), 43/62.

[119] In 1838 Peel wrote to Croker: 'It was our support of the Poor Law that enabled the Government to pass it without fearful resistance . . . The defender of the Poor Law on the Committee was Sir James Graham, not the Government.' CROKER, *Corr. and Diaries*, II, 337.

[120] He was ably assisted in preparing the Bill by Sir Edmund Head, a Whig whom he had appointed to the Poor Law Commission. In making this 'creditable appointment', says Greville, Graham threw over 'all party considerations, and having, after strict inquiry, satisfied himself that Head is the ablest and fittest man, he has given him the situation'. GREVILLE, *Journal of the Reign of Queen Victoria*, II, 60-61. Actually the Poor Law question had never really been a party issue. Graham supported it as a Whig and then again as a Conservative. Also, at no time were all the members of the commission from one party.

[121] *Hansard*, 3rd Ser., LXIII, 433.

[122] Gilbert's Act, passed in 1782, permitted parishes to group themselves into unions and provided that the able-bodied poor were to be given work by the local authorities or else maintained in their own homes. It was an optional act, and less than 1,000 of the 16,000 parishes in England adopted it.

was to be appointed for each school, but parents of dissenting children were permitted to choose a minister of their own persuasion for the purpose. To secure more humane treatment for children in the workhouses, the Bill provided that they should be examined every six months by the relieving officers in order to detect cases of mistreatment. The number of assistant Poor Law Commissioners was reduced, but no change was made in the Law of Settlement except to provide that those who were sick could receive relief 'and not be liable to removal on that account, unless they receive relief for forty consecutive days'. As to bastardy, the Bill stated that the father could be imprisoned for three months, but only when the mother and child were in the workhouse. Finally, it established the elective principle for choosing guardians.[123]

The Bill was subjected to furious attacks in the press as well as in Parliament. Admitting that Graham had introduced the Bill in a speech of 'considerable tact and artful presentation' the *London Morning Herald* attacked him for proposing to prolong 'the despotism of the Somerset House triumvirate'.[124] The *Chronicle* declared that the Bill did not go far enough to protect pauper children apprenticed to employers.[125] The *Standard*, which had given its support to Peel's Government, asserted that the Poor Law had caused *more* destitution and resulted in *less* relief because of the workhouse test. Declaring that if the Bill passed, the Conservative party would lose the support of the labouring classes, it urged all Conservatives to vote against it.[126] *The Times* took the same view but in addition declared that the chief evil of the Bill was that it regarded poverty '*as a crime punishable by death, or the pains of the workhouse*'.[127] The Whig *Globe*, on the other hand, thought it was a good measure because it would mitigate the severity of the old law and 'obviate some of its inconveniences by diminishing the distances which applicants for and recipients of relief have had to travel to relieving officers'.[128]

While these same criticisms were voiced in the House of Commons, the chief argument advanced by the parliamentary

[123] *Ibid.*, 442-446. Both the owner and the occupier, up to a rating of £50, had one vote; up to £100, two votes; up to £300, six votes.
[124] *Herald*, May 12th, 1842, p. 4.   [125] *Chronicle*, May 13th, 1842, p. 5.
[126] *Standard*, May 13th, 1842, p. 2; May 16th, p. 2; May 17th, p. 2; July 13th, p. 2.
[127] *The Times*, May 12th, 1842, p. 2.   [128] *Globe*, May 12th, 1842, p. 2.

N

opponents of the Bill was that it concentrated too much authority in London. Graham answered this charge by saying that if central control were removed, 'the effect will be to put an end to control and to introduce confusion; and having introduced confusion you will not be likely to mitigate the law'.[129] It was a perfectly sound argument. Furthermore, as he pointed out, the Poor Law Commissioners were after all responsible to the Government and it in turn was responsible to Parliament and to the country. Equally sound, whether one agrees with the basic philosophy or not, was his reply to those who opposed the Poor Law altogether. Do the poor have an absolute and indefeasible *right* to relief? Was an able-bodied man entitled to relief without some kind of test? If so, it was not relief at all but rather 'subsistence upon the industry of others'.[130]

The Bill passed its second reading on June 17th, but on July 19th Graham announced that due to the lateness of the session and to the fact that the clauses relating to the Gilbert Unions and the schools required more detailed discussion, he had decided to withdraw them for the present and to bring them up at a later time. Divested of these clauses the Bill was read a third time and passed on July 23rd.[131]

Throughout the following year Graham was compelled to answer numerous questions asked by members of the House about reported abuses in various union workhouses. That flagrant injustices existed is true; that they were often exaggerated by such opponents of the Poor Law as Ferrand and Duncombe is also true. But Graham's boast that in all the world there did not exist a law 'which provides so humanely, so charitably, so largely, for the sick, the needy and the destitute in their hours of affliction'[132] is an exaggeration.

No changes were proposed in 1843,[133] but in February 1844

---

[129] *Hansard*, 3rd Ser., LXIV, 158.   [130] *Ibid.*, 152-153.
[131] *Statutes at Large*, 5 and 6 Victoria, c. 57.   [132] *Hansard*, 3rd Ser., LXVI, 1180.
[133] *The Times* (September 8th, 1943, p. 4) criticized Graham for not doing so and declared that he was as responsible as any man for the unhappy lot of the poor, 'whom the Poor Law Commissioners seduced from ... the "over-peopled" rural districts of the south, where work was said to be scarce and labour abundant, into the "under-peopled" manufacturing districts of the north where work was said to be abundant and labour scarce'. Greville was quite right in stating that *The Times* had now assumed a hostile and offensive tone 'towards the Government generally, particularly Peel and Graham'. GREVILLE, *Memoirs*, V, 132.

Graham introduced a carefully prepared Poor Law Amendment Bill. It was cleverly done, too. He had given notice that the Bill would be brought in on February 9th, but on that day there was no House and so the notice became technically a 'dropped notice'. The House met on the following Saturday and Graham, according to *The Times*, 'stole a march very silently and very unexpectedly upon the opponents of the Poor Law' by going ahead as if it had been the order of the day. 'By that manœuvre he got rid very dexterously of a preliminary inquiry . . . into the operation of the existing law. The Bill thus clandestinely and surreptitiously brought in was read a first time without opposition.'[134] It was read a second time on the 23rd and Graham, addressing the House 'with his usual creamy smoothness', as *The Times* ironically put it,[135] asked the House to read it *sub silento*, promising to go into committee on it at five o'clock on whatever day the House desired. It was an adroit move and the Bill was read a second time without opposition. From then on it was so skilfully piloted through the House that even Captain Pechel, one of its chief opponents, thanked Graham for the courteousness and conciliatory spirit he had shown throughout the debates.[136]

The main innovations in this Bill, which incorporated many of the recommendations made by the parliamentary committee of inquiry of 1838, were the clauses relating to bastardy. The machinery provided by the Act of 1835 for 'affiliating a bastard child upon the putative father was such as to render the requisite proof of paternity a matter of great difficulty'[137] and therefore the task of maintaining her illegitimate offspring was imposed entirely upon the mother. Graham's Bill, which easily passed into law, corrected this evil by removing the law of bastardy from the Poor Law and by not only enabling the mother to recover from the father the cost of maintaining the child but even fixing the weekly amount the putative father had to pay.[138]

---

[134] *The Times*, June 29th, 1844, p. 6; *Hansard*, 3rd Ser., LXXII, 479-480.

[135] *The Times*, June 29th, 1844, p. 6.

[136] *Hansard*, 3rd Ser., LXXVI, 1443-1444.

[137] *Annual Register* (1844), 219. For a good analysis of the situation from 1835 to 1844 see THOMAS MACKAY, *A History of the English Poor Law*, III, 315-318.

[138] *Statutes at Large*, 7 and 8 Victoria, c. 131, Sec. 1-11. The magistrates in many unions had been compelling women to tell whether they were the mothers of illegitimate children, but Graham wrote to them that he did not believe they had such compulsory powers. *Home Office Papers* (Domestic Book), 43/63, p. 198.

Section 12 of the Act took up the very important question of the apprenticing of pauper children. It authorized the Poor Law Commissioners to prescribe the duties of the masters to whom poor children were apprenticed as well as 'the Terms and Conditions to be inserted in the Indentures by which such children may be so bound as Apprentices'.[139] Any master who then neglected to fulfil these conditions was liable to a fine of £20. The Poor Law Commissioners, under authority vested in them by this Act, then drew up an elaborate order which provided that pauper children were no longer to be apprenticed by the overseers but by boards of guardians; no child under nine was to be apprenticed at all; no one over fourteen was to be apprenticed without his consent; and none were to be bound out for more than eight years.[140]

To facilitate administration of the Act parishes were divided into election wards; the scale of voting between owners and rate-payers was equalized; parishes and unions were combined into districts for purposes of audit; schools and asylums were to be erected for the casual poor; and a married woman whose husband was at sea, in jail, or in a lunatic asylum, was to be treated as though she were a widow.[141]

In addition, Sections 64 and 65 provided that a parish with a population in excess of 20,000 should not be joined to any other unless such union was approved by two-thirds of the guardians. Likewise, when two or more parishes in the Metropolitan district, containing a combined population of more than 20,000, united for purposes of settlement or rating under a local Act, and not united in a Poor Law union, such united parishes were not to be included in any district for auditing purposes.[142] These exemptions, writes Nicholls, 'were conceded to the representations

[139] *Statutes at Large*, 7 and 8 Victoria, c. 101, Sec. 12, p. 605.

[140] *Ibid.* See also *Hansard*, 3rd Ser., LXXVI, 438-439, and NICHOLLS, *op. cit.*, II, 360.

[141] *Statutes at Large*, 7 and 8 Victoria, c. 101, Sec. 19 et seq. When the clause providing for the equalization of the scale of voting was being debated, Thomas Duncombe proposed an amendment calling for the abolition of plural voting. Graham resolutely opposed this amendment because 'he could not with justice to the rights of property make a great alteration; he had already gone as far as justice would allow'. *Hansard*, 3rd Ser., LXXVI, 443. The clause providing for an independent audit was a great improvement on the previous practice of each board appointing its own auditors and provided what Graham liked so much, i.e., a centralized, efficient checking of all accounts.

[142] *Statutes at Large*, 7 and 8 Victoria, c. 101, Sec. 64 and 65.

of the Metropolitan members and their constituents, who were naturally averse to the introduction of a new power into affairs which they had long been accustomed to manage entirely themselves'.[143]

Conditions among the poor in Scotland had become so bad by 1843 that a parliamentary commission was appointed to inquire into the cause of the distress.[144] The poor relief system in use in Scotland was of the outdoor variety and consequently there were few workhouses. In some places the poor were simply boarded out; in some they were kept in the town hospital; in others charity workhouses were used. To make matters worse these agencies provided only for the 'enrolled' poor, not for the 'occasional' poor.[145] The committee report recommended the construction of more workhouses; the acceptance of voluntary relief contributions instead of compulsory assessments; and the charging of medical and educational assistance to the poor relief funds. On the basis of this report a Bill to amend the Poor Law in Scotland was easily carried through the House.[146] It created a board of supervision, three of whose members were to be nominated by the Crown, with power to sanction, though not to compel, the union of parishes. In all burghal parishes and parish unions there was to be an elective board of managers of the poor. In those parishes which had adopted assessment, the local board was to be partly elective and partly *ex-officio*; in parishes having no assessment, the board was to be chosen from the old authorities, i.e., the heritors and the Kirk sessions. The Law also provided that parishes with a population in excess of 5000 could build a poor-house if they so desired. If they did so they had to hire a qualified medical man to serve it. Those parishes which had no poor-house had to provide medical 'comforts' for the poor

---

[143] NICHOLLS, *op. cit.*, II, 364.

[144] Out of a total of 5716 operatives in Paisley, there were 2588 unemployed. *Home Office Papers* (Disturbances Book), 40/59. The same situation existed in Glasgow and other cities and many emigrant-aid societies were formed which petitioned the Government to aid the unemployed to move to Canada and other countries. *Home Office Papers*, 45/O.S. 512. In many places the daily relief allowance was cut from 1½d. to 1d. Graham expressed sympathy with the poor, but insisted that they must not under any circumstances disturb the peace. *Ibid.*, (Scotch), 103/10.

[145] See CLAPHAM, *op. cit.*, I, 586.

[146] *Hansard*, 3rd Ser., LXXXI, 425 et seq.; LXXXII, 426 et seq.

wherever they were kept. Finally, there was to be an inspector of the poor in each parish.[147]

This Law, it is clear, left the initiative in each case with the parish itself and hence incorporated Graham's principle of leaving the law 'to be governed by local circumstances, and the local knowledge of the parties'.[148] But it did not work very well, not because it was a weak law but because conditions prevented it. The failure of the potato crop in 1845-46, the influx of Irish labourers and the inability to obtain adequate medical assistance prevented it from functioning adequately. As a result, by 1848, according to Clapham, 'only eight new poor-houses had been approved — not built'.[149]

In 1845 *Punch* dedicated an 'Ode on the Opening of the Session' to Sir James Graham which contained the following lines:

> Meanst thou to mitigate the Law
>   Whose fangs the poor of England rue?
> Or tighter yet its clauses draw,
>   And closer drive the legal screw?
> The Law of Parish Settlement
>   To settle, is it thy intent?
> Or houseless lab'rers to resign
>   To those who thrust them off and cry,
>   'No child of mine?'[150]

To 'settle' the Law of Parish Settlement was precisely Graham's intent. He fully realized that the Poor Laws could not be made to work unless this law was changed. The Statute of 1662 which had 'authorized the magistrates', as Fay puts it, 'upon complaint made within forty days of arrival, to remove all persons, likely to become chargeable, to the parish where they were last legally settled',[151] had resulted in checking the migration of labour from over-populated areas and so kept it from going to its natural markets. The theory on which this parochial legislation was based was that each parish should support its own poor and keep out the poor of other parishes. It was manifestly unjust to the

---

[147] *Statutes at Large*, 8 and 9 Victoria, c. 83.
[148] *Hansard*, 3rd Ser., LXXXII, 426.
[149] CLAPHAM, *op. cit.*, I, 588.
[150] *Punch*, VIII, 76.
[151] FAY, *Life and Labour in the Nineteenth Century*, 99.

migrant[152] and the Law was therefore modified so as to protect persons from removal until actually chargeable. But this did not solve the problem since the overseers of each parish continued to see to it that no artisan was hired for a year because that would give the artisan a settlement, i.e., the right to relief in the new locality.[153] The parliamentary committee on agricultural conditions reported in 1833 that the Law of Settlement tended 'to prevent the free circulation of Labour, to chain it to the spot where it is not wanted, and to check its natural flow into the place where it is required'.[154] But the Poor Law of 1834 gingerly bypassed this phase of the question, except to abolish settlement by service,[155] and the evil remained until Graham attacked the problem in 1844.

In his customary methodical manner Graham attacked the problem along three lines: first, the right of settlement; second, the power of removal; third, the right of appeal on removals. As to the first, he proposed that 'where the settlement had been ascertained by a past order, fixing the settlement, which had been confirmed by a competent authority, or by an admission in writing, such a settlement should not be disturbed, but be held final'.[156] He next suggested that all the existing ways of settlement (parentage, apprenticeship, renting a tenement of a given value, officeholding, payment of rates, birth and marriage) should be abolished and that birth alone should establish a settlement and the place of birth should be the place of settlement. Derivative settlement, he recommended, should be allowed to legitimate children by admitting the father's settlement, and failing that, by the mother's. In the case of illegitimate children, 'the place of birth should first determine the settlement, which on failing to be proved, the

---

[152] See J. REDLICH and F. W. HIRST, *Local Government in England*, I, 104; G. D. H. COLE and R. POSTGATE, *The British Common People* (1939 ed.), 116-117; A. SMITH, *The Wealth of Nations*, Book I, Chap. IX. On the other hand, Hasbach does not think that the law was 'so black as it has been painted'. W. HASBACH, *A History of the English Agricultural Labourer*, 173.

[153] Cottages were often pulled down to make it harder for a newcomer to establish a settlement. See A. REDFORD, *Labour Migration in England*, 77-80. Part of the immobility of the labourer was due to transportation inadequacies and to the natural aversion of peasants to moving about.

[154] *Parl. Papers* (Report on Agriculture), 1833, p. vii.

[155] *Statutes at Large*, 4 and 5 William IV, c. 64, Sec. 64.

[156] *Hansard* , 3rd Ser., LXXVI, 1933.

mother's settlement should determine the question'.[157] Furthermore, he proposed to relieve every destitute person until the
destitution ceased, or until a settlement were found.

Then, Graham proposed the following changes:

1. A man who had ordinarily resided in or near a parish for
   five years and had not been convicted of a felony or mis-
   demeanor should not be removed.
2. No woman, living with her husband at the time of his death,
   should be removable to her own parish after his death.
3. No widow, living in her husband's parish or elsewhere,
   should be removable for twelve months after his death.
4. No legitimate child, under sixteen years of age, should be
   removable from its father.
5. No legitimate child, after its father's death, and no illegitimate child under sixteen, was to be removable from its
   mother.
6. No person, becoming chargeable by sickness or accident,
   was to be removable until he had received relief for forty
   consecutive days.

Finally, methods of appeal from the removal acts were simplified
and applied to Scotland and Ireland as well as to England.

Most of the objections to these proposals were directed against
the first. Graham admitted that irremovability after five years
might very well be favourable to the rural districts at the expense
of the towns and therefore agreed that birth alone should confer
a settlement. Furthermore, he recommended that the 14,500
parishes and townships in England and Wales be deprived of the
power to confer settlements and that this power be transferred to
the 620 Poor Law unions. This would not only greatly simplify
the Law but would also be a benefit to the ratepayers.[158]

The last proposal raised a veritable storm of protest from the
press. Most of this criticism took the line advanced by *The Times*,
which denounced it as 'a wanton' and 'audacious' scheme for
'disrupting the social frame of the country', and therefore was
'indefensible'. To achieve a simplification of the Law was not,
it declared, sufficient grounds for wiping out all of the parochial

---

[157] *Hansard*, 3rd Ser., LXXVI, 1933-1934.
[158] *Ibid.*, LXXVII, 317-319.

settlements in favour of union boards the members of which were opposed to the poor.[159]

Because of the 'contrariety of opinion' Graham decided not to go on with his Bill in that session of Parliament and it was allowed to stand over until 1846. But, on February 19th, 1846, he announced that he would not go on with the Bill until the Corn Law Bill had been disposed of.[160] When the question came up again, on July 13th, Graham was no longer in office, but, in response to a question, he stated that he sincerely hoped that Russell's Government would proceed with the measure. The latter agreed to do so with the result that the Poor Removal Bill was passed into law. The new Law applied only to England and decreed that no person should be removed from a parish in which he had lived for five years, but that during those years he must not have received relief from the parish, a hospital, or an asylum. No widow was to be removed for twelve months after the death of her husband, nor should any widow be removed who had been relieved on account of sickness or accident. The Law incorporated, therefore, most of Graham's proposals and he must be given whatever credit is due for the passage of this Law. By the same token he must assume a large part of the responsibility for its weaknesses, the chief of which were that it did not alter the conditions of settlement but rather dealt only with removal, and that it worked unjustly against the town parishes.[161]

One of the integral parts of Poor Law administration was that which dealt with the workhouses. The first one had been built at Bristol in 1697 and it was here that the 'workhouse test' was first applied. Willingness to enter was taken as the sole test of destitution. So successful was this scheme that it was adopted by a great number of parishes and was incorporated in the Poor Law of 1723, which authorized withholding relief from any person who

---

[159] *The Times*, March 3rd, 1845, p. 4, and May 6th, 1845, pp. 5-6. The *Illustrated News* (February 15th, 1845, VI, No. 140, p. 102), admitted the need for reform but predicted the defeat of the measure because it abolished parochial settlements.

[160] *Hansard*, 3rd Ser., LXXXIII, 1166-1167.

[161] According to Redford, parishes had avoided the necessity for poor removal by the payment of non-resident relief to the 'settled' poor living elsewhere. The Act had tried to secure that this should not be used to transfer settlement liability. But the Law was not clear and 'many parishes which had been paying non-resident relief stopped their allowances'. This resulted in 'a sudden increase in the burden of pauperism in many towns'. REDFORD, *op. cit.*, 110.

refused to enter the workhouse.[162] During the next few decades this test effectually diminished the number of applications for relief, but at the same time, criticism of the workhouses became so general that the Gilbert Act of 1782 repealed the act which had created them and conversely legalized out-door relief. From 1783 to 1834, then, no new workhouses were built. Those which continued in operation differed in every conceivable manner. There was no uniformity as to size, food provided, work required of inmates, discipline and punishment, or provision for separation of males from females.[163]

The Poor Law of 1834 retained the workhouses on the principle that they were an effective means of securing national uniformity in the treatment of the destitute. It was this principle of national uniformity that was the very basis of the Poor Law and its central authority. It provided relief for the destitute in workhouses in which each person was to be put to work. The type of maintenance was left to the discretion of the central authority. According to the Webbs, it was the intention of Parliament that each union should have several small institutions and that different classes of the poor should be assigned to each.[164] But the Poor Law authorities pursued an opposite course, erecting one large union workhouse in each union for all paupers.

In order to discourage pauperism, conditions in the workhouses were made as disagreeable as possible. Destitution became in general the sole ground on which relief was given. Not only was this system objectionable, but its administration was imperfect. 'Masters of workhouses', writes Walpole, 'interpreting their orders strictly, committed excesses which the Commissioners had never foreseen. Adult girls were flogged for misconduct; old people were washed in cold water; and sick people . . . were refused the food which was essential to their recovery'.[165] Pauper lunatics, idiots, or imbeciles were not segregated; children were separated from their parents; married persons were kept separated from each other. And, of course, criticism of these 'bastilles' grew apace, criticism directed particularly against the inadequate

[162] See the WEBBS, Eng. Local Gov't. (Eng. Poor Law Hist.), part I, 243 et seq.
[163] See CLAPHAM, op. cit., I, 357-362.
[164] See the WEBBS, Eng. Poor Law Policy, 55.
[165] WALPOLE, Hist. of Eng., V, 69.

diet, the nature of the work required of all inmates, the unsanitary
conditions,[166] and the severe discipline.[167]

As Secretary of State for the Home Department, Graham was
compelled to face a running barrage of questions from parliamentary opponents of the Poor Law. When, on February 23rd,
1843, Walter protested that the quantity and quality of food
provided in the workhouses was inadequate, Graham replied that
the destitute were given better treatment in England than in any
other country.[168] A few weeks later Ferrand denounced the
guardians for having erected tread-wheels in some of the workhouses. Did Graham sanction this? It was not a 'tread-wheel',
said Graham, but a 'hand-mill' for grinding corn. The erection of
a tread-wheel he would not sanction.[169] The guardians at Mans-
field had directed that anyone who sought shelter for a night
should be forced to work at a wheel for four hours the next day.
The wheel did no work at all and was therefore just a labour-
making device. Graham did not approve of this, he told the
House, and had directed the Poor Law Commissioners to have it
stopped at once.[170]

The most serious case of this type, brought to the attention of
the public and Parliament, concerned the Andover union. The
master of this workhouse was charged by Wakely with having so
starved the inmates that they fought among themselves for the
marrow and fetid meat left on the bones they were given to
crush.[171] Graham promised an immediate investigation and,
finding the charge to be true, instructed the commissioners to
issue an order forbidding bone-crushing in union workhouses as
of April 1st, 1846. But on March 6th Etwall had asked for a

[166] For a description of the foul conditions in the St. Pancras workhouse see *The
Times*, September 11th, 1846.

[167] James Jarvis, a pauper 75 years of age who had refused to work at a pump in
the Barrow-on-Soar workhouse, was sent to prison at hard labour for 21 days. He
died within a few days of his arrival at the workhouse. *Hansard*, 3rd Ser., LXXXVI,
225.

[168] *Ibid.*, LXVI, 1180 et seq.

[169] *Ibid.*, LXVII, 427.   [170] *Ibid.*, LXXXII, 1320.

[171] *Ibid.*, 1321. *The Times* (August 14th, 1845, p. 4), wrote a scathing denunciation
of the Poor Law Commissioners for permitting such 'sickening' things to go on and
said that the centralized control, so dear to Graham, was supposed to prevent this
sort of thing. 'It is quite evident', it said, 'that they are just as likely, and indeed more
likely, to happen where centralization is substituted for local management.' For an
interesting defence of this practice, see NICHOLLS, *op. cit.*, II, 368-369.

parliamentary committee of inquiry into conditions at Andover. Graham, admitting that the conditions complained of were true, declared that responsibility for these conditions rested with the local authorities, not the central board. The latter had protested to the Andover authorities but they had ignored the protest. If the Poor Law Commissioners had the necessary authority, it would have been stopped long ago. Andover, he said, was a good illustration 'of what local management was, when unchecked by any proper superintending authority'.[172] He agreed to the appointment of the committee of inquiry but opposed a proposal to extend the inquiry to the conduct of the Poor Law Commissioners. The proposal was carried over his objections and the committee of inquiry, which was appointed, ultimately reported that the conduct of the commissioners was 'irregular and arbitrary'.[173]

Ecclesiastical Reform

Reform was the order of the day and increasing numbers of people were applying the pragmatic test to all institutions. The Established Church, 'wrapped in her own virtue or indifference, . . . seemed to be preparing to meet the blow in haughty silence'.[174] or, as Mozeley put it, 'was folding its robes to die with what dignity it could'.[175] Its leaders knew, or should have known, that it could not remain changeless in a world of change. The repeal of the Test and Corporation Acts in 1828 and the Catholic Emancipation Act of 1829 had opened office-holding to non-Anglicans and had permitted Roman Catholics to serve in the Army, Navy, and Parliament. These acts did not materially weaken the position or power of the Church, but the Reform Bill of 1832, which gave political power to the Dissenting middle classes, increased the power of the class opposed to the Established Church. The Whigs, who represented this class in Parliament, secured the passage of the Tithe Commutation Act in 1836 by

---

[172] *Hansard*, 3rd Ser., LXXVII, 307.
[173] *Report of Select Committee on the Andover Union*, 1846, part II, p. 22620. The *Manchester Guardian* (March 11th, 1846, p. 4), said that the Government's defeat was due to the hatred of the landed interests who wanted to get even with Peel and Graham because of their willingness to see the Corn Laws repealed.
[174] HENRY O. WAKEMAN, *History of the Church of England*, 7th ed., 461.
[175] Cited in WILFRID WARD, *Ward and the Oxford Movement*, 49.

which tithes were commuted for a rent-charge on land made payable to tithe-owners, whether clerical or lay, and made payable in money. The Court of Delegates was deprived of its appellate jurisdiction and the judicial committee of the Privy Council was made the final court of appeal in matters of church discipline. Then a Church Temporalities Act forbade any clergyman to hold more than two livings, and another statute created a permanent Ecclesiastical Commission to administer church revenues. An effort was also made to abolish church rates, but this was unsuccessful.

By 1841, therefore, the general attitude in the country was, as Woodward puts it, that this legislation had 'set the church in sufficiently good order; there were further anomalies to be removed, but, for the time, nothing to cause a scandal'.[176] And, with Peel and Graham in office, the Church felt safe because both were regarded as loyal churchmen and because it knew that the Conservative party needed its support. But it was impossible for Graham to carry out reforms in almost every phase of government and not touch one of the country's most inefficient institutions. His attitude on this question was clearly enunciated in a letter to Peel:

> By judicious measures we may *gradually* propagate the saving knowledge of Christian truth; we may . . . render the property of the Church more available for sacred uses, and less subservient to temporal interests. All this may be done *gently*, almost *silently*, and from time to time public aid may be obtained. But if . . . we attempt any large measure general alarm will be excited, a spirit of resistance will be generated, failure will ensue, and the good which might otherwise be effected will be rendered impossible.[177]

This was clear enough: the fundamental doctrines of the Established Church must be kept pure and inviolable; flagrant abuses which brought discredit to it must be gradually and quietly removed. Dicey has put the case very well: 'Here we have the policy of conservatism combined with concession which has coloured the whole of modern ecclesiastical legislation.'[178]

---

[176] E. L. WOODWARD, *The Age of Reform, 1815-1870*, p. 492.
[177] Graham to Peel, September 17th, 1842, in *Peel Papers*, CCLXVII, 162-167 (Br. Mus. Add. MSS. 40447). Italics are mine.
[178] DICEY, *op. cit.*, 335.

Reforms, when made, were to preserve and strengthen, not basically to alter, the Establishment.

Early in 1842 Sir John Easthope introduced a Bill for the abolition of church-rates. The Government opposed it on the ground that if there ought to be an Established Church at all that Church had an absolute right to church-rates; Easthope's motion was beaten by a vote of 160 to 80.[179]

But on May 20th Graham himself brought in the first of his reform measures in the form of the Ecclesiastical Corporations Bill, which proposed to give to ecclesiastical corporations, aggregate and sole, the right to grant leases for ninety-nine years for corporation purposes. The object of the measure was to increase the value of these properties. To the Opposition argument that the Church already possessed enough wealth, Graham replied that the increased revenues so earned were to be used for ecclesiastical purposes only, i.e., for the augmentation of small livings which, he said, 'were so shamefully insufficient', and for establishing 'cures of souls in destitute districts'.[180] The Bill stipulated that the income derived from the increased value of ecclesiastical property, above certain specified amounts, was to be paid to ecclesiastical commissioners empowered to use the revenue for the above purposes. The Bill was easily passed and became law on August 12th, 1842.[181]

Early in the following year, Peel introduced a Bill the object of which was to endow additional ministers and to augment small livings.[182] While Peel was successfully piloting this Bill through the House, Graham was hard at work on his Ecclesiastical Courts Bill. The object of the Bill was to abolish about 380 inefficient, petty diocesan courts and to concentrate in London jurisdiction over wills.[183] Opposition to the Bill was greater than Graham had anticipated. Objections made were that the reform was too

---

[179] *Annual Register* (1842), 209-211.

[180] *Hansard*, 3rd Ser., LXV, 933. According to the Hammonds, 'Churches were, like members of Parliament, most numerous where least needed'. *Age of the Chartists*, 221.

[181] *Statutes at Large*, 5 and 6 Victoria, c. 108.

[182] *Annual Register* (1843), 203-209. The Dissenters could not object very strenuously because the Bill did not provide for the building of additional churches. *Statutes at Large*, 6 and 7 Victoria, c. 37.

[183] *Hansard*, 3rd Ser., LXVIII, 805 et seq.

inconsequential to bother with; that it interfered with vested rights; that it concentrated too much authority in London.[184]

Because of this opposition Graham did not proceed with the Bill during that session, but in 1844 he re-introduced it in a slightly modified form. Admitting that he did not like this Bill as well as the first one, he promised that if the House would pass it, 'he was not likely again to meddle with this thorny subject during the remainder of his life'.[185] The amended Bill provided for transferring jurisdiction over wills from the Courts Peculiar to the Court of Arches and to the Diocesan Courts as well as for the abolition of both the Courts Peculiar and the Consistorial Courts. But the opposition was again so great that he abandoned it altogether, announcing to the House that he despaired of being able to frame a measure respecting ecclesiastical courts which would be acceptable or satisfactory to Parliament.[186]

While Graham was thus attempting to strengthen the Church by reforming its worst abuses and by sweeping away an accumulation of evils, the Church itself remained divided into factions. One group felt that the State had no authority to legislate on ecclesiastical matters and that the Church must resolutely resist encroachments on its authority. This faction, known as the Oxford Movement, led by Keble and Newman, argued that only the Church had the right to reform its own body.[187] Their object was, as Laski has put it, 'if not to free the Church from the trammels of an Establishment, at any rate to minimize its consequences in the direction of secular control . . . It was emphatically against Erastianism that [they] were contending'.[188] This Oxford Movement was therefore another phase of the struggle that was going on in all other fields of government — a struggle against a State which claimed a supreme authority against which 'no part of itself might contend'.[189]

---

[184] See the *Globe*, April 12th, 1843, p. 2.

[185] *Hansard*, 3rd Ser., LXXIV, 170.

[186] The *Edin Rev.* (LXXVIII, 527), was glad the Bill had failed because it did not abolish those courts (diocesan) which everyone knew ought to be abolished. See also Vol. LXXIX, 488.

[187] See JOHN W. FIGGIS, *Churches in the Modern State*.

[188] HAROLD J. LASKI, *The Problem of Sovereignty*, 87-88; R. W. CHURCH, *The Oxford Movement*, Chap. VI.

[189] LASKI, *op. cit.*, 113.

Another faction, the Broad Church group, led by Thomas Arnold, headmaster of Rugby, wished the Church to sink all doctrinal differences and to comprehend all except Roman Catholics, Quakers, and Unitarians. While not neglecting occasionally to speak up for social reform, their real interest was in spiritual and moral reform. Their aim was to restore the Church to the position it had held in the 'Golden Age' of Edward VI.[190]

The Ecclesiastical Reformers, on the other hand, led by Bishop Blomfield, sought to forestall reform of the Church from without by reform from within. They were quite willing to work with the State in doing so and thus pursued a policy at one with that of Peel and Graham.

Finally, there were the High Churchmen, committed to all that was meant by an 'Establishment' and interested chiefly in educational and parochial problems.

Outside the Church were the Roman Catholics and the Dissenters. The former were a decidedly minority group and therefore argued for religious freedom. They were increasing in numbers, especially in the industrial north, but not at such a pace as were the Dissenters. Since the Established Church had, in the words of the Hammonds, 'no patience with emotion, no curiosity about doctrine, no prejudice against "this wicked world"',[191] it did not appeal to the working classes, who found their spiritual needs better satisfied by the Dissenting groups. Their main concern was in the salvation of souls and as a rule they paid little attention to the environment in which people lived. However, the Established Church was guilty, in their eyes, of inhumanity and of sanctioning injustices and for this reason they often took part in Chartist meetings, aided striking labourers, and permitted reform groups to use their chapels as meeting places.[192] Concentrating their attention on heavenly rather than earthly pursuits, they were in fact non-humanitarians in an age of increasing humanitarianism. Only in their being rugged individualists in an age of individualism were they in keeping with the spirit of the times.

The Oxford Movement, as we have seen, were interest in freeing

---

[190] See S. C. CARPENTER, *Church and People, 1789-1889*, p. 63.
[191] HAMMONDS, *The Town Labourer, 1760-1832*, 191.
[192] See R. F. WEARMOUTH, *Methodism and the Working Class Movements in England, 1800-1850*, p. 212 et seq.

themselves from the trammels of State control, but the real leaders in this field were the Scottish Presbyterians. And the famous non-intrusion controversy within the Church of Scotland proved to be the most complex problem Graham was called upon to handle in his whole public career. The controversy grew out of the demand of the evangelical group in that Church that the intrusion of ministers on unwilling congregations be stopped.[193] The patrons,[194] who had been accused of intruding unsatisfactory ministers on parishes, insisted that the presentee must be accepted by the parish unless valid objections were raised to his theology, literary style, or moral character. On the other hand, the more zealous of the laity and clergy insisted that the presentee must also be personally acceptable to the congregation. To some, in fact, this acceptability was the chief consideration.

An understanding of the use and meaning of the 'call' in Presbyterian Scotland is a prerequisite to a proper comprehension of this question. When a parish fell vacant, the patron nominated, i.e., 'presented', someone to the living. The congregation then took the presentee on trial, i.e., heard him preach, questioned him as to his theological orthodoxy, invited him to their homes, and subjected his moral principles to careful scrutiny. Then the presbytery (ministers of the region plus the elders who represented the sessions of the churches) decided whether the number of signatures to the call from the congregation was sufficient to entitle it to proceed with the settlement. If so, the call was extended to the presentee. If the latter accepted, he was then installed as the minister, but, if the decision was negative, did the patron have the right to intrude his nominee on the unwilling congregation? It was this question that was to split the Church of Scotland, result in a large secession from that Church, and lead to the formation of the Free Kirk.

The roots of this controversy go back to the sixteenth century

[193] For a more detailed discussion of this subject see my article in *Church History*, XI, 302-325. The legal aspects of the problem are discussed by Charles R. Mullett in volume XII of the same journal.

[194] Parishes were often co-terminous with landlord's estates upon which churches were built for themselves and their dependants. The Church conceded to the landlords the right to appoint the minister of the church and it therefore became a part of their estates. The landlord, i.e., the patron, could therefore transfer or sell the right of 'presenting' the minister whenever he sold his estate.

o

when Scotland accepted Calvinism. The theocracy then formed insisted upon complete sovereignty in matters it considered purely spiritual.[195] Many refused to accept this claim, however, and from 1567 it was the subject of much angry disputation.[196]

Those who claimed for the Church at least co-ordinate jurisdiction in determining whether cases appealed to it were spiritual or temporal, and final authority in all cases it considered spiritual, based their claim on the Act of 1592, which had given the Church full authority over ecclesiastical matters.[197] Furthermore, lay patronage — the core of the problem by 1832 — was abolished in 1690 and ministerial appointments were given to the male heads of the families of the congregations.[198] The Act of Union of 1707, in turn, specifically pledged the State to maintain the Acts of 1592 and 1690. Consequently, when Parliament in 1712[199] restored lay patronage, the General Assembly of the Church protested vigorously.[200]

After 1712 bickering about this patronage question subsided, for the Age of Reason produced a large measure of moderatism[201] in which, says Hetherington, 'secular principles [and] cold legal and moral preaching and uncensored immorality' held sway.[202] Consequently, control of the General Assembly passed into the hands of the Moderates. When moderatism arose, therefore, it

---

[195] The real rulers of the State, and through it, the Church, were, says Smith, 'the ministers and elders elected by the people. The democracy of the kirk consisted in the rise of most of these men from the lower ranks of the people; its theocracy in the claim of these men . . . to interpret the commands of God'. PRESERVED SMITH, *The Age of the Reformation*, 364.

[196] The basic question, says Laski, was: 'Can the State tolerate alongside itself churches which avow themselves *societates perfectae*, claiming exemption from its jurisdiction even . . . when they traverse the field over which it ploughs? Is the State but one of many, or are those many but parts of itself the one?' LASKI, *op. cit.*, 28. The State answered in the negative; the Church in the affirmative.

[197] *Acts of the Scottish Parliament*, III, 541.

[198] *Ibid.*, IX, 196-197.

[199] *Statutes at Large*, 10 Anne, c. 12.

[200] *Acts of the General Assembly* (1712), p. 23 et seq. In a letter to Graham, Thomas Chalmers declared that the Act of 1712, passed with undue speed while Scottish M.P.s were absent from Parliament, was the infidel Bolingbroke's way of 'punishing the Church and people of Scotland for their adherence to the House of Hanover'. In PARKER, *Life of Graham*, I, 380. On the other hand, the *Quart. Rev.* (LXVII, 249-250), and *Blackwood's Magazine* (XLVI, 580), state that the Act of 1712 was passed because the Act of 1690 had caused only 'heats' and dissensions.

[201] See ARTHUR P. STANLEY, *History of the Church of Scotland*.

[202] WILLIAM W. HETHERINGTON, *History of the Church of Scotland*, 405.

corresponded to the dominant note of the age, but in the early nineteenth century evangelicalism triumphed. The Evangelicals, led by such men as Wellwood, Thompson, and Chalmers, immediately denounced lay-patronage as the chief evil in the Church of Scotland.[203]

The controversy came out into the open simultaneously with the passing of the Great Reform Bill in 1832.[204] As soon as Chalmers, the Moderator, called the General Assembly together, eight presbyteries and three synods placed on the table an overture begging the Assembly to put an end to the settlement of unacceptable ministers on the grounds that it alienated the people, corrupted the ministers, and weakened the Church.[205] But the Moderates, still in control of the Assembly, carried a counterresolution by 45 votes and the issue, now clearly joined, ushered in a bitter ten-year struggle.

In 1833 a motion put by Chalmers, that the dissent of a majority of a congregation, with or without the assignment of reasons, should set aside a presentee, was beaten in the Assembly by only twelve votes.[206] The following year, as a result of prodigious efforts on the part of the Evangelicals, the General Assembly, by a majority of 46 votes, passed the famous Veto Act[207] which

[203] An anti-patronage society had been founded by Andrew Thompson in 1825. See Ibid., 396; Quart. Rev., LXVII, 205 et seq.

[204] While it is true that the Reform Bill, giving the franchise to thousands who had not formerly had it, led some to reason that if they should have a voice in the selection of M.P.s they should also have a determining voice in the selection of their spiritual guides, it had, as a matter of fact, little effect on the non-intrusion controversy. It did, however, give such an impetus to the public mind, sending it into every channel of thought, that henceforth no institution, civil or ecclesiastical, could 'be long in a state of safety, which could not stand the most searching scrutiny'. HETHERINGTON, op. cit., 391. In 1839 Chalmers wrote to Graham: 'This is in no shape a political question.' Cited in FRANCES BALFOUR, Life of George, Fourth Earl of Aberdeen, II, 49 (Hereinafter cited as Life of Aberdeen). Most of the Evangelical leaders were Conservatives and were opposed to the Reform Bill. See HANNA, Memoirs of Chalmers, III, 298 et seq. The Quart. Rev. (LXVII, 205), attributed the opening of the non-intrusion struggle to 'the feverish longing for innovation', engendered by the Reform Bill.

[205] Acts of Assembly (1832), 41-42.

[206] Ibid. (1833), 45-46. See also HENRY COCKBURN, Journal, I, 44-45.

[207] Quart. Rev., LXVII, 211. The Veto Act reads as follows: 'It is the fundamental law of this Church, that no pastor shall be intruded on any congregation contrary to the will of the people; and, . . . it shall be an instruction to Presbyteries, that if, at the moderating in a call to a vacant pastoral charge, the major part of the male heads of families, members of the vacant congregation, and in full communion with

stated that no pastor should be intruded on an unwilling congregation, and hence clearly put an end to intrusion. As the *Quarterly Review* complained, it 'converted the right of the patron to *present* into a mere right to propose'.[208]

But was the General Assembly competent to so decide? Could it legally pass an act which in effect set aside the Statute of 1712? Lord Brougham thought so;[209] the Crown lawyers approved the action; the clergy were certain about it since they rested their case on the Act of 1690.

In less than a year the matter was put to the test, for in August 1834 Lord Kinnoul nominated Robert Young to the living at Auchterarder in Perthshire. 287 out of a membership of 300 refused to accept him[210] and the presbytery upheld the congregation and refused to sustain the call. Young immediately appealed to the synod and, when it affirmed the decision of the presbytery, he appealed to the General Assembly. The latter rejected the appeal and Lord Kinnoul thereupon raised an action on behalf of his presentee in the Court of Session on the grounds that legally the power of the presbytery was limited solely to the question of qualification. The court, by an eight to five vote, decided that the Veto Act was contrary to the Act of 1712 and that the General Assembly had acted illegally. In announcing the decision, the President of the Court of Session stated that the Presbyterian claim that Jesus and not Parliament was the sole head of the Church in temporal and legislative matters was an absurdity.[211] Graham put the attitude of the Presbyterian Church very suc-

---

the Church, shall disapprove of the person in whose favour the call is proposed to be moderated in, such disapproval shall be deemed sufficient ground for the Presbytery rejecting such person, and that he shall be rejected accordingly, and due notice thereof forthwith given to all concerned; but that, if the major part of the said heads of families shall not disapprove of such person to be their pastor, the Presbytery shall proceed with the settlement according to the rules of the Church: And further declare that no person shall be held to be entitled to disapprove as aforesaid, who shall refuse, if required, solemnly to declare, in presence of the Presbytery, that he is actuated by no factious or malicious motive, but solely by a conscientious regard to the spiritual interest of himself or the congregation.' Quoted in HETHERINGTON, *op. cit.*, App. 491.

[208] *Quart. Rev.*, LXVII, 211.   [209] He later changed this opinion.

[210] Objection was not made to his character or conduct but to the 'feebleness' of his preaching and to some physical deformities. See P. H. BROWN, *History of Scotland*, III, 427.

[211] See WOODWARD, *op. cit.*, 508.

cinctly when he said that it 'acknowledged the right of no authority
to interfere with their ecclesiastical government. They recognize
not the Sovereign of these realms as the head of their Church'.[212]
Chalmers, spokesman for the Evangelicals, said bluntly that the
Church was 'amenable to no higher power on earth'.[213] The
General Assembly took the same view and refused to recognize
the Court of Session as a superior court. The case was therefore
taken to what Balfour called the 'Laodicean atmosphere' of the
House of Lords.[214] On the principle that church courts could
reject a presentee only because he was not qualified in a literary,
doctrinal, or moral sense, the Lords rejected the position of
the Assembly and upheld the decision of the Court of Session.
It meant, as the *Westminster Review* pointed out, that the clergy
were 'bound to *ordain* at the bidding of the civil courts'.[215]
The Evangelicals were naturally incensed that their Church 'had
been sacrificed to English prejudices;'[216] the Moderates were
pleased that the Lords had decided in their favour; the Dissenters
were happy because they calculated that the decision would make
converts to their cause.[217]

A similar case — that of Marnock in Strathbogie, Aberdeenshire
— in 1837, added fuel to the fires of revolt. It was clear to all that
the ordination of ministers, as well as the judgment of their
qualifications, was a spiritual function. The enjoyment of the
benefice, on the other hand, was a clearly secular one. If the two
were inseparable, then, as the Duke of Argyll pointed out, 'either
the civil courts must coerce the Church in the function of ordination, or else the Church could abolish the statutory right of
patronage in parochial benefices'.[218] The civil courts held to the
doctrine of the inseparability of the cure and benefice, and consequently dictated to the Church in the purely spiritual function of
ordination. The problem quite obviously could not be solved
without changing the law of patronage.

To obtain a change in the law a deputation was sent by the
General Assembly to interview spokesmen for the Government of

---

[212] *Hansard*, New Ser., XXXV, 581.   [213] HANNA, *op. cit.*, IV, 45.
[214] BALFOUR, *op. cit.*, II, 48.   [215] *West. Rev.*, XL, 199-200.
[216] See COCKBURN, *Journal*, I, 226.
[217] 'Its [the Church] buttresses are falling every hour', wrote Cockburn. *Ibid.*,
169.
[218] ARGYLL, *op. cit.*, I, 166.

Melbourne and for the Opposition.[219] Chalmers was the one who interviewed Melbourne, Brougham, Peel, Graham, and Aberdeen. He first saw Melbourne, the Prime Minister, but the latter's party was really helpless in 1840 and Melbourne, 'utterly ignorant' of the Church question, preferred to 'let it alone'.[220] Brougham, whom Chalmers saw next, refused to make any concessions to the Church for fear the result would be to 'end all Church Establishments'.[221]

Chalmers then turned to the Conservative leaders. Peel he found 'very bland' and possessed of such 'extreme caution and coldness' that it 'damped' Chalmers' spirits. Graham, on the other hand, was 'fine, hearty, honest', and a man of 'practical sense'.[222] Aberdeen, though friendly as always, took the same stand as Peel and Graham[223] and 'refused to pledge himself'.[224]

It was natural and logical that the Conservatives, who championed the supremacy of the law as interpreted by the courts,[225] would not pledge aid to the Non-Intrusionists, who openly declared that if the civil law and divine law were in conflict they owed first allegiance to God. To the Conservatives this was a secular question; to the Non-Intrusionists, it was purely ecclesiastical. Realizing that Melbourne's party neither could nor would do anything, Aberdeen, himself a patron whose nominee had been rejected, introduced a Bill making the presbytery competent to decide upon objections to a nominee providing the objection was made in specific terms.[226] The General Assembly upon learning of its terms immediately rejected this Bill and the opposition in Scotland was so great that Aberdeen withdrew it. There were three reasons, he said, for this action: first, Melbourne's

[219] The deputation was headed by Chalmers, Bruce, Gordon, Candlish, Muir, and Smythe. Although suspecting that their errand would be fruitless, they clung to the slender hope that some concessions would be gained from either the Whigs or the Conservatives because an election was not far off and both parties would no doubt like to have the clerical influence on their side. See COCKBURN, *Journal*, I, 235.

[220] See *Melbourne Papers*, ed. by Lloyd C. Sanders, 416.

[221] *Hansard*, 3rd Ser., LIV, 362.

[222] HANNA, *op. cit.*, IV, 120, 121.

[223] See Graham's letter to Chalmers in PARKER, *Life of Graham*, I, 378-379.

[224] BALFOUR, *op. cit.*, II, 49.

[225] Brougham, commenting on the Lords' decision, said he 'had never seen a clearer case. It seemed to be all one way'. *Hansard*, 3rd Ser., L, 374.

[226] *Ibid.*, LIII, 1209-1229.

Government opposed it as contrary to the right of patronage;[227] second, the General Assembly declared that it was 'an attempt to dethrone the Redeemer from His seat'; third, it was now obvious that the aim of the Non-Intrusionists was to abolish patronage and since his Bill did not so provide, it was useless to proceed with the measure.[228] The Duke of Argyll next attempted to settle the question by proposing a Bill by which Parliament would sanction the veto, but the Conservative party, having just come into office, refused to support it.[229]

Meanwhile the situation in Scotland was becoming more critical. In the summer of 1840 the Non-Intrusionists organized a league called the 'Evangelical Covenant' to counter the efforts of the 'Moderate League' which had just been formed. The battle cry of the Covenanters was non-intrusion or dissolution. In the same year the chair of theology at the University of Glasgow fell vacant, and Chalmers, by general agreement, was the logical choice for the post. But to the amazement of many Graham, Lord Rector of the University, made a special trip to Glasgow to oppose the election of his former friend.[230] This unexpected and wholly unusual procedure, Peel's speech in the House of Commons accusing the Evangelicals of openly defying the law,[231] plus the withdrawal of Aberdeen's Bill and the failure of Argyll's, showed unmistakably where the Conservatives stood. But the Non-Intrusionists acted with equal celerity. The Assembly of 1842 immediately passed two resolutions: the first condemned patronage as a grievance and as unscriptural although it was found easier to

[227] The *Quart. Rev.* (LXVII, 233), praised the Bill highly but said that it left too much power to the Presbyteries. 'We feel no surprise', it said, 'that Government should not have supported Lord Aberdeen's Bill . . . They opposed it because it went too far rather than not far enough.'

[228] *Hansard*, 3rd Ser., LVI, 1207-1210. By July 10th, about 265,000 persons had petitioned Parliament against the Bill and only about 4000 for it. See ROBERT BUCHANAN, *The Ten Years Conflict*, II, 121.

[229] The Duke of Argyll blamed Aberdeen for the Government's rejection of his Bill. He asserts that Aberdeen was unduly influenced by John Hope, one of the leaders of the Moderates, and a bitter opponent of non-intrusion. His pamphlet denouncing the Non-Intrusionist's claim of co-ordinate jurisdiction was very widely read. See ARGYLL, *op. cit.*, I, 178.

[230] In a letter to Peel, September 2nd, 1840, Graham said that because of his vote, Chalmers and his friends had declared war on the Conservative party. *Peel Papers*, CXXXVIII, 222 et seq. (Br. Mus. Add. MSS. 40318).

[231] *Hansard*, 3rd Ser., LV, 1058-1060. The same stand was taken by the *Quart. Rev.*, LXVII, 226.

argue the former than to prove the latter;[232] the second was a resolution to petition both Parliament and the Queen.[233] Then the Assembly adopted the famous 'Claim, Declaration, and Protest'.[234] This document traced the question at issue from its inception, re-stated the unconstitutional proceedings of the Court of Session, and concluded that the invasions of the State into the spiritual realm had been such that 'the Church of Scotland had ceased to be a Church of Christ'.[235] Convinced that the Government would undoubtedly meet their petition with a decided negative, positive steps were taken to meet the situation. After they had covenanted together to secede from the Church if the Government did not abolish patronage, they organized committees to collect money and supplies with which to build their own churches.[236]

After carefully studying the Claim and Protest, Graham sent the Government's answer to the Moderator of the Church.[237] This letter, skilfully written, stated positively that the Government would not abolish patronage, would not give a popular veto, but would accept a 'judicially used' presbyterial veto.[238] Since this was precisely the position taken by Aberdeen, a position from which the Evangelicals had already dissented, their answer to the Government declaration was immediate and decisive. They denounced Graham's letter as extremely Erastian and resolutely denied his insistence that all questions of jurisdiction had to be decided in the law courts. Hetherington thought Graham's letter the work of 'a galled partisan, rather than the grave and deliberate

[232] This difficulty was clearly pointed out in *Blackwood's*, XLVI, 587 et seq.

[233] *Acts of Assembly* (1842), 25, 62.

[234] *Ibid.*, 35-48.

[235] BROWN, *op. cit.*, 430.

[236] Cockburn states that the Moderates had told the Government that if it remained firm there would be no secession because the Scottish clergy would not willingly surrender their benefices. That the Government could actually believe that the Evangelicals would not do as they had threatened was almost incomprehensible to Cockburn. He also declared that the 357 ministers (out of the 427 at the meeting), who had pledged themselves to secede, 'contain the whole chivalry of the Church'. *Journal*, I, 337.

[237] This letter was first published in *The Times*, January 14th, 1843. It is given in full in the *Annual Register* (1843), pub. doc., 463-470.

[238] Cockburn insists that Aberdeen was the author of the letter. But, while the ideas may have been largely Aberdeen's, the language and phraseology are certainly Graham's. In a letter to Peel, on December 30th, 1842, Graham said that there was 'not one harsh expression or offensive argument' in the letter. *Peel Papers*, CCLXVIII, 164-165 (Br. Mus. Add. MSS. 40448).

thought of a wise statesman'.[239] Hanna condemned Graham for having taken advantage of the fact that the Assembly had sent two addresses to the Crown, one praying for the abolition of patronage, the other for the spiritual independence of the Church, and had 'mixed the two together, giving one answer to both, to the inevitable and injurious confounding of topics which the Church had been at so much pains to keep distinct'.[240] He denied Graham's charge that the Claim and Protest was comparable to Papal pretensions and maintained that the Church of Scotland took a position midway between that of the Erastian State and the Catholic Church. The *Westminster Review* excoriated Graham for logic-chopping when 'he ought to have warded off a great national calamity'.[241] It went on to assert that the Church ought to have known better than to have expected 'from men [Graham and Aberdeen] of aristocratic principles and passions, concessions to ecclesiastical democracy', and from a cabinet composed of men who possessed a 'double hatred to what we call evangelical democracy'. The result, it concluded, was that 'the life has fled from the Kirk. The spirit of John Knox has left it'.[242] Fox Maule, an eminent Scottish M.P., also took up arms against Graham. He insisted that the Church courts had an equal right with the Court of Session in deciding the limits between civil and ecclesiastical functions in cases brought before it.[243]

But while Graham and his letter were bitterly denounced by some, they were highly praised by others. The conservative *Fraser's Magazine* described the letter as

> a State-paper ... which, for lucid analysis, kind and conciliatory feeling ... and closeness of thought, ... will be treasured up in the archives of England ... This document, so decisive on the supremacy of the law, as becomes its author and his office ... exterminates quietly, but most triumphantly, the ridiculous pretences of the Non-Intrusionists.[244]

[239] HETHERINGTON, *op. cit.*, 454.

[240] HANNA, *op. cit.*, IV, 321. If this charge be sound, it would tend to prove that Graham was the author because in that type of composition Graham was a master with few equals and no superiors — save possibly Gladstone. *Home Office Papers*, 45 O.S., $\frac{505}{3}$.

[241] It had been hostile to Graham ever since he left the Whig party in 1834.

[242] *West. Rev.*, XL., 205 et seq.   [243] *Hansard*, 3rd Ser., LXVII, 357.

[244] *Fraser's*, XXVII, 366-367, passim.

Similar praise came from the *Morning Chronicle*[245] as well as from Graham's friends and associates.[246]

After disposing of the question of the *quoad sacra* ministers,[247] the General Assembly of 1843 adopted a series of resolutions which pointed out the basis of their disagreement with the Government's position, and then for the last time petitioned Parliament. This petition was presented by Fox Maule, who asked for a committee of the whole house to consider the petition. A long debate ensued in which Graham, denouncing the Church's claim to equality in jurisdiction as 'unjust and unreasonable', refused to deviate from the position he had taken in his letter.[248]

The State having met the Church's claims and petitions with a decided negative, dissolution of that Church was inevitable and immediate, and with the passage of the Act of Separation and Demission, on May 24th, 1843, the ecclesiastical revolution was accomplished.[249] On that day four hundred and seventy clergymen withdrew from the Established Church of Scotland, leaving their manses and stipends just as they had vowed to do.[250] Many of the congregations left with their pastors and the secession was soon constituted into a body which called itself the Free Kirk of Scotland. This Free Kirk immediately took the lead among Presbyterian Dissenters, and within four years of the disruption, despite the fact that times were unusually hard, it had raised £1,254,000, had built 654 churches, and had organized, on a national scale, a system of schools and theological colleges that rivalled those of the Established Church. On its side, the Government finished its work by passing Aberdeen's Bill 'enslaving the people', as the Non-Intrusionists put it, to the presbytery and it to the Court of Session,[251] and Graham's Bill on the endowment of

---

[245] *Chronicle*, February 24th, 1843.

[246] See COCKBURN, *Journal*, I, 338-339; PARKER, *Life of Graham*, I, 389-390.

[247] The Court of Session had decided that these ministers were not entitled to full ministerial privileges. In keeping with that decision, Cook, leader of the Moderates in the Assembly, moved that their names be stricken from the roll of the commission. But this motion was defeated by a vote of 115 to 23. See BUCHANAN, *op. cit.*, II, 414-415.

[248] *Hansard*, 3rd Ser., LXVII, 378-394.   [249] *Acts of Assembly* (1843), 19-29.

[250] The list of ministers who signed it is given in full in *Home Office Papers*, 45 O.S., $\frac{505}{10}$.

[251] The Moderates claimed that Aberdeen's Bill was a farce since it modified the Act of 1712 and in so doing had virtually set aside the decision of the House of

quoad sacra parishes, excluding the ministers of these parishes from participation in church government. Hence the Government succeeded in establishing the supremacy of the civil arm over the ecclesiastical.

The disruption of the Established Church of Scotland was inevitable from the moment a quickened evangelical fervour made itself felt in that country, for a good deal of 'the same stubborn and indomitable spirit which worked in the minds of the old Covenanters'[252] was now revived in those leaders who took up the cause of the spiritual independence of their beloved Church. Claiming final authority for that Church in all purely spiritual concerns, and holding the abolition of patronage an indispensable condition of the integrity of that Church, they assumed so stern, distinct, and uncompromising language that it should have been evident to all that there was no alternative but for the State to accede to their demands or to face a secession.

In view of this fact, frankly avowed by the Non-Intrusionist leaders, whose characters afforded, as the *Annual Register* put it, 'full assurance that the resolution which they avowed was no idle menace, and that they would deem no sacrifice too great for the assertion of their principles',[253] why did this question occasion so much controversy and strife? One reason is that to the Evangelicals this was basically and almost exclusively a religious question upon which they thought sincerely and felt deeply. The Scottish temper on religious subjects was such as to preclude the possibility of concession to the State which was now challenging their doctrine of Christ's headship. Over and over again they promised that rather than see their 'Redeemer dethroned from His seat', as Aberdeen lightly put it, they would leave their manses and glebes and throw their stipends to the winds.[254]

In the second place, the Scots were firmly convinced that the lukewarmness in their Church, the lack of apostolic zeal in the

---

Lords in the Auchterarder case. *Blackwood's* (LIV, 547), on the other hand, argued that Aberdeen's Bill limited, but did not destroy, patronage. The *Edin. Rev.* (LXXVIII, 535), was very critical: 'A legislative declaration of the law is made, contrary to the law as decided by the House of Lords on appeal; and thus the legislature has been called upon to stigmatize by statute, a judgement of the highest court of the land.'

[252] *Annual Register* (1843), 240.   [253] *Ibid.*
[254] *Hansard*, 3rd Ser., LVI, 1208; *Chronicle*, August 11th, 1843, p. 4.

Master's cause, was due to patronage. This was the root of all evil. It was patronage that had caused the numerous secessions and swelled the ranks of the Dissenters; it was patronage that had prevented the return of these bodies to the true Church.

It was indeed unfortunate that such a question had to be settled in the British Parliament because there existed in that assembly opposing concepts of life, doctrine, and ecclesiastical agencies. 'The whole subject', as Buchanan so aptly put it,

> was new and strange to the mass of British senators and statesmen. Accustomed to contemplate the relations of church and state through the medium of the English Establishment, where the supremacy in all matters and causes ecclesiastical is vested in the crown, and where the queen in council ... regulates almost everything, and the church herself regulates nothing — it was easy to foresee how little prepared or predisposed they were likely to be to appreciate or acknowledge claims to which they had nothing similar among themselves.[255]

When the disputed Veto Act first reached the House of Lords the Whigs were in office; at the time of dissolution, the Conservatives were. But it made little or no difference, because the Whigs, who had no real love for any church establishment, could not have done anything if they had wanted to, and the Conservatives would not if they could.[256] Furthermore, few people in England ever really understood this question. Melbourne honestly admitted being utterly ignorant of it and proved his ignorance by confounding 'admission of ministers with presentation'.[257] The Duke of Argyll asserts that he had never met an Englishman 'who could understand, or even conceive, that idea of the relations between Church and State which was embedded and embodied in the Constitution of Scotland'.[258] Cockburn thought the ignorance of Whigs and Conservatives on this subject was profound,[259] and even Gladstone admitted that there was no subject more difficult for him to understand.[260] Perhaps the best proof of their ignorance

[255] BUCHANAN, op. cit., II, 122.

[256] In a pamphlet, 'What Ought the Church and People of Scotland to do Now?' Chalmers declared that the difference between Whigs and Tories was in 'having no principle, or in having a principle that is wrong. In either way they are equally useless'. Cited in HANNA, op. cit., IV, 174.

[257] BALFOUR, op. cit., II, 74.   [258] ARGYLL, op. cit., I, 174.

[259] COCKBURN, Journal, II, 37.

[260] See his letter to Graham, in PARKER, Life of Graham, I, 374-375.

lies in the fact that even though dissolution was by 1839 almost as certain as death, neither the Whigs nor the Conservatives really believed it and both still thought that firmness alone would win the day. In addition, many proved themselves totally ignorant of the character of the Scottish Presbyterians by doubting the seriousness of their threat to leave the Church. To make matters worse, Scottish Presbyterianism was not a religion for English gentlemen and they would not take the question seriously enough,[261] nor could they understand why the Scots made such a *furor* over the matter. Many, in fact, sorely bored by the whole business, did not really care what happened in the Scottish Church[262] other than to deprecate the impetus which the dispute gave to dissent in England.[263] Some were stupid enough to imagine that the Evangelicals were leagued with the Chartists in a grand conspiracy to pull down the pillars of society,[264] while others felt that the patrons had not been guilty of abusing their rights and that only a slight reform of patronage was necessary.[265] Then, too, most of the English M.P.s were thorough-going Erastians to whom, as the *Westminster Review* cynically, but accurately, commented, 'relations of the clergy to the State imply no greater independence of control than those of soldiers and sailors'.[266]

Throughout the entire controversy Graham assumed towards the non-intrusion question a purely legal attitude,[267] and declared

[261] In 1839 the Earl of Galloway predicted that popular selection of clergymen would result in a kind of 'preaching match' which would be won by those who could best reproduce the sermons of the eminent London preachers. See *Hansard*, 3rd Ser., L, 376. The *Quart. Rev.* (LXVII, 217), declared that it would result in 'scenes of riot, profligacy, and fraud which characterize a Westminster election'. Such ignorance and prejudice was equalled by the stupidity of Collett, who declared in the House of Commons, that he was for 'free trade in corn; . . . free trade in machinery; . . . and . . . free trade in parsons'. *Hansard*, 3rd Ser., LXXI, 530.

[262] Aberdeen notes in his Journal, on January 4th, 1841, that everyone was interested in the ministerial crisis and that 'beyond a passing joke it [Scottish Church] is scarcely ever mentioned'. Cited in BALFOUR, *op. cit.*, II, 90.

[263] *Chronicle*, November 16th, 1843, p. 2.

[264] Most of the Evangelical leaders were Conservatives and had opposed the Reform Bill of 1832. See HANNA, *op. cit.*, III, 405; BUCHANAN, *op. cit.*, II, 181.

[265] *Quart. Rev.*, LXVII, 203 et seq.; PARKER, *Life of Graham*, I, 381 et seq.

[266] *West. Rev.*, XL, 208.

[267] Such journals as the *Quart. Rev.* and *Blackwood's* considered this a legal question in which the chief issue was not the Church but whether or not the law of the land was to be enforced. See also, *Hansard*, 3rd Ser., LI, 356; LXVII, 394.

that obedience to the law as laid down by the courts of the realm was the first duty of all citizens. To him and his colleagues, the Church was an institution 'established by civil law, represented by strictly legal courts, and having the political Sovereign as over all persons and in all causes supreme'.[268] They alleged, therefore, that the Presbyterian system, as interpreted by the Non-Intrusionists, involved an inroad on the civil authority and hence was a menace to the liberty of the State.

But while the English Government held to the majesty of the law and the sovereignty of Parliament, the Non-Intrusionists appealed to a 'higher law' — the Bible, and to a higher sovereign — God. Viewing the question as a theological one, the uncompromising Scots charged that the Erastian State was impinging on the spiritual authority of the Church and therefore menaced its liberty and freedom.

In a larger sense, the English Government, which in the mid-nineteenth century was rapidly becoming a strongly unitary state, found itself opposed by the Scottish Non-Intrusionists, who, like the Jesuits on the Continent, were fighting for the principle of federalism — a principle which stressed the impossibility of confining sovereignty to any one of its constituent parts.[269] Hence, they insisted, neither the spiritual courts nor the civil courts should coerce the others in their own sphere.[270] But since the English Government held to the view that in questions of conflicting jurisdiction it was the civil courts that must decide whether cases were spiritual or temporal, compromise was impossible. If, theoretically at least, the State was victorious in 1843 it admitted in 1874, when it abolished patronage by law, that it had sustained a moral defeat.

Educational Reform

Another facet to this problem of the relations between Church and State to which Graham directed considerable thought and

---

[268] ARGYLL, op. cit., I, 175. Blackwood's (XLVI, 579), asserts that, as an institution established by law, the Church of Scotland was nothing but an incorporation whose powers and privileges 'rest exclusively on statute law; and the Court of Session is the proper and legally constituted interpreter of a statute'.

[269] See JOHN N. FIGGIS, The Divine Right of Kings, preface vii-viii.

[270] BUCHANAN, op. cit., II, 286. According to Blackwood's (XLVI, 575), the Church Courts had no power of execution, could not ordain payment, provide a remedy, or redress wrongs. Only the civil courts could do so and they were therefore superior courts.

effort was that of education. The extremely meagre educational facilities available to British children were in the hands of religious societies and voluntary workers who were activated by religious, charitable, or similar motives. Because neither the Anglicans nor the Dissenters wanted to leave the field in the hands of the other, they competed in establishing schools for the poor. In 1814 the Dissenters organized the British and Foreign School Society while the Established Church founded a rival institution — the National Society for Promoting the Education of the Poor.

No government action was taken, however, until 1833, when the paltry sum of £20,000 annually was voted for educational purposes. The money was divided between the two rival societies, who were directed to use it for building schools. While only a few were built and the quality of education remained very low, interest in the subject was steadily increasing, as seen by the fact that in 1834, 1835, and 1837 select committees were appointed by Parliament to inquire into the subject. In 1839 the Government created a Committee of the Privy Council to supervise elementary education, provided for the appointment of school inspectors, and increased the annual grant from £20,000 to £30,000. But when it proposed to build a teacher-training school, the opposition from both Churchmen and Dissenters was so great the Government decided to let well enough alone and dropped the matter.

Graham, it has already been pointed out,[271] was one of the opponents of this programme, but by 1843 he was willing to try his hand at reform in this field too. 'Let me entreat and conjure you', Brougham wrote to him in October 1841, 'to direct your attention to education.'[272] In his reply, Graham declared that education could not be separated from religion; that public funds could not be used to teach the Established Creed without irritating the Dissenters. Education was a necessity, he willingly admitted, for, as he put it, 'the peace and order of society are involved in it, and ... a wise policy on this subject may promote the temporal and eternal happiness of millions'. The difficulty, however, lay in the fact that 'religion, the keystone of education, is, in this country, the bar to its progress'.[273] But Brougham continued his importunities on the subject and in 1842 submitted to Graham two

[271] Supra., 202.
[272] In Parker, Life of Graham, I, 337.
[273] Ibid., 339.

plans for national education. These plans Graham discussed with Peel, but the latter did not like either one and wrote to his Home Secretary: 'A more rapid advance in promoting good education will be made by the cautious and gradual extension of the power and the pecuniary means of the Committee of the Privy Council than by the announcement at present of any plan by the Government.' He went on to say that 'there would be great jealousy of the taxing powers of corporate authorities, almost universal. Here the Dissenters would object, there the Church, just as one party or the other might happen to prevail in the corporation'.[274] The answer which Graham had proposed to send to Brougham was thought 'too favourable' by Peel and so the question was dropped.

Early in 1843, however, the question was brought up in Parliament and the Government was consequently forced to deal with it. Lord Ashley, in broaching the subject, declared that 'the public mind should be enlightened by means of a sound, moral, and religious education, so that the working-classes might acquire that sober self-control, which would enable them to govern and repress the workings of their passions'. He deplored the 'terrible wilderness of spiritual destitution' which existed and stated that in England and Wales there were 1,014,193 persons capable of receiving an education who received none at all.[275] He was absolutely correct. The ignorance of the working classes was appalling. 'Many of them had never heard of London,' says Walpole, 'had never heard of Scotland, had never heard of America. Many of them had never heard the name of Christ . . . Many colliers had never heard the name of God except in an oath.'[276] The evil everyone admitted, but few would agree on the necessary remedy.

Some of the advocates of educational reform had declared that education would have a salutary effect in checking Chartist agitation, riots, and strikes. Graham did not think much of this argument. 'Cheap bread, plenty of potatoes, low-priced American bacon, a little more Dutch cheese and butter', he wrote to Peel, 'will have a more pacifying effect than all the mental culture which any Government can supply.'[277]

[274] Peel to Graham, January 18th, 1842, in PARKER, *Life of Peel*, II, 533-534.
[275] *Annual Register* (1843), 53.   [276] WALPOLE, *op. cit.*, IV, 373.
[277] Graham to Peel, August 25th, 1842, in PARKER, *Life of Peel*, II, 541.

On the other hand he admitted that mental culture was a necessity too and he therefore prepared a Bill providing for the compulsory education of pauper and factory children. District schools were to be established in London and other large towns. Superintendence of the schools was to be vested in the hands of the clergy of the Established Church but provision was made for the instruction of the children of Dissenters by ministers of their own persuasion. The schools were to include an area of fifteen miles (ten in London), and were to be financed by a rate not exceeding one-fifth of the annual assessment for the three preceding years. The employment of factory children (between the ages of eight and thirteen) was to be limited to six and one-half hours per day to be worked either in the morning or afternoon, because if they had to work longer than that they would be too tired to study. Certificates of attendance at school were to be granted to the National and British and Foreign School societies and by the Roman Catholic schools for Catholic children. All were to be open to inspection by officers appointed by the Educational Committee of the Privy Council, and to be financed by grants from the Government supplemented by a sum of 3d. per week of the earnings of each child retained by the employer for the purpose. Religious instruction was to be given in the Authorized Version of Holy Writ, together with portions of the Liturgy, under the supervision of clergy of the Established Church, but safeguards would be set up to protect the children of Dissenters from proselytism. The schools were to be taught by masters appointed by the bishops in each diocese and to be managed by seven trustees — the clergyman of the district, two church wardens and four elected trustees, two of whom were to be freeholders. This was the general scope of Graham's proposed measure as he outlined it to the House, and he concluded his statement by saying that he was about to present a Bill on the subject.[278]

True to his promise, he brought in such a Bill, but it was immediately attacked by extreme churchmen, like Robert Inglis, because it made too many concessions to Dissenters; by Roman Catholics, who declared that no Catholic child could conscientiously attend the new schools; and by the Dissenters, who claimed that it violated the principles of religious liberty. Despite

[278] *Hansard*, 3rd Ser., LXVII, 75-91.

P

this opposition, however, the Bill was supported by Russell, Viscount Sandon, Charles Buller, and others and passed the first two readings.

Graham sincerely believed that he had produced a compromise 'consonant with the principles of the Established Church, and at the same time to the utmost extent consistent with the honest principle of toleration'.[279] He knew it was not going to be easy 'to uphold the just authority of the Church and to respect the honest scruples of the Dissenters';[280] he suspected, so he told Gladstone, that the Dissenters would perhaps defeat it, 'at least in the sense which led me to propose it, as a scheme of comprehension and concord';[281] but he did not imagine that the opposition would be quite so violent.

Nonconformists of all types held protest meetings, publicly castigated Graham, and literally flooded the House with petitions against the Bill.[282] They objected to the appointment of a clergyman as the chief trustee; to approval of the masters by the bishop of the diocese; to the inspectorate which they assumed would be exercised on behalf of the Established Church; and to the 'teaching' of the Scriptures, which, they said, would inevitably become an exposition of doctrines distasteful to Dissenters.[283] The press took up the issue also. The Whig *Globe* denounced the Bill as a High Church plot against the Wesleyans and other Dissenters,[284] while the *Morning Post* professed to see in it 'a movement towards the overthrow of the Established Church'.[285]

[279] *Annual Register* (1843), 195.

[280] Graham to the Rev. R. Burgess, November 22nd, 1842, in PARKER, *Life of Graham*, I, 342.

[281] Graham to Gladstone, in *Ibid.*, 344. At the same time he wrote to Stanley that he thought the Dissenters would be 'too much for us'. *Ibid.* MACCOBY (*op. cit.*, 247-248), says that how Graham could have expected the Dissenters to accept the scheme 'passes comprehension'. On the other hand he did have a reasonable right to expect that his 'measure of peace' would, with some concessions, be accepted at least as a step in the right direction. See Graham to Peel, December 27th, 1842, in *Peel Papers*, CCLXVIII, 150-151 (Br. Mus. Add. MSS. 40448).

[282] See *Annual Register* (1842), 196. According to MACCOBY (*op. cit.*, 248), there were 13,369 petitions with 2,068,059 signatures against the Bill. See also HODDER, *op. cit.*, I, 457.

[283] *Annual Register* (1843), 193-195.

[284] *Globe*, April 20th, 1843, p. 2.

[285] *Post*, March 18th, 1843, p. 4. It also declared that the Bill was 'only a step in the mighty march of free trade'. The *Chronicle* (March 1st, 1843), on the other hand, thought it a good Bill and praised Graham for not treating it as a party question.

Had the opposition been less violent and the hostile petitions fewer, Graham would no doubt have proceeded with the Bill, but the animosities engendered were so fierce that in May he proposed a series of amendments which he hoped would go far enough in the way of concession to the Dissenters. The original Bill had provided that parents whose children were employed in factories should send them to the Sunday Schools established by the Act instead of to other schools. He now proposed to make such attendance voluntary instead of obligatory. In addition, if parents so desired, their children could be exempted from doctrinal teaching, which was to be offered before or after regular school hours three days each week. Furthermore, Dissenting ministers were to be permitted to give the children of Dissenters religious instruction for three hours on one of the week-days at some place other than the school-house. Changes were made also regarding the selection and responsibilities of trustees. One was now to be the clerical trustee, one was to be elected by donors, one was to be selected by the clerical trustee, and four were to be elected by the £10 ratepayers. To ensure minority representation it was provided that 'no ratepayer shall vote for more than two trustees, the effect of which will be that in every case where the majority does not preponderate to the extent of more than two-thirds, the minority [party] will return two representatives in the trust. It will be thus seen that five out of seven trustees will be elected'. Finally, Graham proposed that only the head master should be subject to dismissal by the bishop of the diocese; that all the assistant masters should be appointed by the trustees and be subject to no veto. Three trustees should have to concur before any child could be dismissed from school (i.e., from factory employment), any trustee could appeal to the Privy Council against any decision of his colleagues with respect to books used, and the Privy Council could reverse any decision of the trustees. In other words, the educational committee of the Privy Council was to control the schools.[286]

While these concessions to the Dissenters were very considerable and though he made them, he said, as a 'peace-offering in the spirit of concord, and of Christian charity and goodwill',[287] the stream of criticism and denunciation continued with unabated

---

[286] *Hansard*, 3rd Ser., LXVIII, 1104 et seq.
[287] *Ibid.*, 1118.

fury.[288] The Dissenters claimed that despite these concessions the ascendancy of the Established Church was still maintained. *The Times* put their case quite well when it wrote that despite 'considerable' concessions, Graham's statement that the schoolmasters would now be merely 'expositors' rather than 'commentators' on the 'true meaning' of the Scriptures was 'a deliberate and intolerable absurdity'. The master would always give the Anglican view of the Scripture and hence continue to 'Church-of-Englandize' the pupils.[289] The Globe took the same view, declaring that no Bill would be preferable to one which provided that the head masters must belong to the Established Church.[290]

In the House, Roebuck denounced the Bill as a Churchman's Bill since the whole machinery was in the hands of the Church, while Hawes, a spokesman for the Dissenters, demanded perfect equality in religious teaching. Graham disagreed with both and declared that so long as an Established Church existed at all it ought to have 'a few preferences'. One of these was that the master of a factory school should belong to the Established Church.[291]

Since bitter sectarian controversy had been the result of his 'measure of peace' Graham decided to bow before the storm and give up the battle. On June 15th, 1843, he announced to the House the withdrawal of the educational clauses of his Bill. 'I am bound to say', he concluded, 'that I feel great disappointment at this result.'[292]

There were three reasons for the failure of Graham's educational proposals. In the first place, there was the fierceness and strength of the opposition. 'The Government are right [Shaftesbury wrote in his diary], it could not have been carried in the House except by forced and small majorities; it could not have been reduced to practice in the country without fierce and everlasting collisions ...'[293] The Dissenters objected to the Bill on both economic

---

[288] Hume estimated that there were 25,535 petitions with over four million signatures against the Bill compared to 170 petitions with 312,669 signatures in favour of it.

[289] *The Times*, May 3rd, 1843, p. 6.

[290] *Globe*, May 2nd, 1843, p. 2. The *Herald* (March 27th, 1843, p. 4), however, looked upon this argument as a 'mere exhibition of hostility to the Established Church'.

[291] *Hansard*, 3rd Ser., LXIX, 564. The *Edin. Rev.* (LXXVIII, 532), thought this attitude was 'wholly indefensible'.

[292] *Hansard*, 3rd Ser., LXIX, 1568.   [293] Cited in HODDER, *op. cit.*, I, 459.

and on religious grounds. To have opposed it because it might have lowered the earnings of the pauper and poor children in the factories, by reducing their hours of labour, deserves nothing but censure. To have opposed it on religious grounds was equally reprehensible because the Bill was a step in the right direction and from time to time could, and no doubt would, have been extended and broadened. Out of pure sectarian animosity they opposed the measure because it gave a slight preference to the Established Church. The criticism of the conduct of the Dissenters made by the *London Morning Herald* is very much to the point: 'If religion . . . is to be made the pretext for inflicting this deadly blow on the country, let us abase ourselves, be humble, and take lessons in morality and common sense from the conquered Chinese.'[294]

A second reason for the failure of Graham's educational proposals was the fact that neither the Conservatives nor the churchmen, lay and clerical alike, did much to support it. This apathy *Fraser's Magazine* attributed to the 'coldness and reserve of the ministers'.[295] They had, consequently, to assume part of the blame for the defeat of the Bill.

Finally, there was the inevitable political angle to the question. With the Nonconformists solidly arrayed against them,[296] the Government could not establish a national system of education unless the Established Church was permitted to control it. The Dissenters, as G. M. Young has put it, 'would not stand the parson in a State school. The Establishment would not stand anyone else'.[297] The Government could not, therefore, afford to bring in a measure that would excite the distrust and enmity of the Church. 'Since the Dissenters refuse to cooperate,' Graham wrote to Stanley, 'we must assist the Church, and rely on her increased exertions.'[298]

Though this controversy stimulated both sides to found new

[294] *Herald*, April 27th, 1843, p. 4. The *Manchester Guardian* (May 3rd, 1843, p. 4), was equally critical.

[295] *Fraser's*, XXVIII, 369-378.   [296] See the *Globe*, April 20th, 1843, p. 2.

[297] YOUNG, *Early Victorian England*, II, 465.

[298] In PARKER, *Life of Graham*, I, 344. Greville expected the Government to 'cast themselves entirely on the Church' and said it would be wise for them to do so because they would then have the support of 'the most powerful and influential interest there is', instead of none at all. GREVILLE, *Journal of the Reign of Queen Victoria*, II, 212.

schools,[299] and though the Government later provided small sums of money for use in building houses for masters and mistresses, for provisioning schools with furniture and other materials, and for adding to the staff of inspectors,[300] nevertheless, in defeating Graham's proposed measure, the Dissenters had won what Peel correctly called 'a sorry and lamentable triumph',[301] for the price paid, as Smellie has well stated it, was that 'England entered the fierce economic competition after 1870 with artisans the least trained, and a middle class the worst educated in Europe'.[302]

Social Reform

The first three years of the Peel administration, it has already been pointed out, were years of widespread distress, unemployment, declining wages, and steady worsening of the conditions of labour. Reform was therefore imperative in this field too. As early as 1802 an Act had been passed limiting to twelve hours per day the labour of apprentice children in cotton and woollen mills, and in 1819 another Factory Act forbade the employment in cotton mills of children under nine years of age and limited to twelve hours per day, exclusive of meal time, the labour of those between nine and sixteen. A more important Act, however, was that passed in 1833. It forbade the employment in textile factories of all children under nine; limited the employment of children from nine to thirteen to 48 hours per week; limited to 69 hours per week the employment of persons between thirteen and eighteen years of age; required that these hours be worked between 5.30 a.m. and 8.30 p.m.; directed that all children under thirteen attend school for two hours each day; and provided for inspectors to see that the law was enforced.

In 1840, Ashley, one of the leaders in this movement, secured the appointment of a committee of inquiry to look into the operation of the Act of 1833 as well as into conditions in trades and industries other than the textile. The committee which studied con-

---

[299] According to Kay-Shuttleworth, by the end of 1844 the National Society had raised £160,000; the Congregationalists £70,000; the Wesleyans £70,000. See FRANK SMITH, *Life of Kay-Shuttleworth*, 157.

[300] See *Ibid.*, 197.

[301] Peel to Stanley, June 16th, 1843, in PARKER, *Life of Peel*, II, 560.

[302] SMELLIE, *op. cit.*, 33.

ditions in the collieries reported that in nearly every district children were employed underground at the age of six, in some places at five and in a few even at four.[303] They also reported that children of these tender years were compelled to pull trams along passages too small for grown men; were poorly paid and ill-treated by the mine owners; that women and young girls often worked in the mines in a semi-nude state; that the general environment of the women and children was equivalent to 'solitary confinement of the worst order'.[304]

On the basis of this Report, which was immediately made public,[305] as well as of his own extensive investigations, Ashley drew up the famous Mines Act of 1842. After describing to the House the appalling conditions in the mines, he outlined the provisions of his Bill, and Graham, speaking for the Government, promised Ashley every assistance in carrying it through the House. But the promise was better than the performance. Ashley had wanted to prohibit the employment in mines of boys under thirteen, but Graham would not agree to that and insisted upon a ten-hour limitation. Not only did he thus weaken the Bill, but in addition he did nothing to assist Ashley in carrying it through the House. For this inaction, he was taken to task by Palmerston.[306] The Bill, as finally passed, prohibited the employment of girls and women in underground mines, set the age limit for boys at ten, forbade the apprenticing to mines of boys under ten, and fixed the maximum term of apprenticeship at eight years. The Law also provided for a corps of inspectors who were regularly to report to the central authority, and forbade the payment of wages in beer shops and public houses.[307]

It was a good law and a very important step in the right direction, but it was difficult to enforce. In 1843, for instance, Graham directed H. L. Tremmenheere, the Inspector of Mines and Col-

---

[303] *Parliament Papers* (Report of the Commissioners on the Employment of Children in the Mines), April 21st, 1842, Part I, pp. 9, 15 et seq.

[304] *Ibid.*, 26, 256.

[305] This annoyed Graham because he had not wanted the Report made public until he had carefully studied it. *Home Office Papers* (Commissions of Inquiry — Children), 74/1, pp. 294-295.

[306] *Annual Register* (1842), 175. Members of the Government did not support the Bill as a Government, but individual members could support it if they wished. See the *Herald*, February 24th, 1843, p. 4.

[307] *Statutes at Large*, 5 and 6 Victoria, c. 99.

lieries, to investigate the report that wages were, contrary to the Law, still being paid in beer shops and public houses, and that payment in truck 'continued in full force'.[308] The report was correct and a conviction was obtained against all the mine owners. Nevertheless, the Law was still violated and, as late as December 1845, Tremmenheere reported to Graham that in Monmouthshire this part of the Mines Act was 'very generally disregarded'.[309]

The provisions respecting the employment of women and children in mines were also disregarded in both England and Scotland.[310] Responsibility for this situation must be shared by the mine-owners, inspectors, and the miners themselves. In the first place, the Inspector, Tremmenheere, would notify a coal-mine owner that he was going to inspect his mine on a certain day. By that time, of course, the Law was being 'scrupulously observed'.[311] In addition, the colliers themselves were often to blame. When a mine owner discharged the women and children, the loss of family income was keenly felt, and as a result 'the women disguise themselves as men, and as they usually . . . proceed in company with several men to and from the pits, detection is difficult'.[312] One mine manager reported that he had often seen fathers drive their daughters, and husbands their wives, to the pits and that he could not stop it.[313] Furthermore, where the Law was enforced, the colliers, having to support their families on their own incomes, found their wages to be inadequate and therefore formed unions and struck for higher wages.[314]

From the reports of the factory inspectors Graham discovered that the Factory Act of 1833 was also violated with impunity, particularly during the years of distress, when as Inspector Horner pointed out, 'it is employment on any terms or starvation'.[315] Mill and factory owners had moved the clocks backwards and forwards; compelled the operatives to come fifteen minutes

[308] Home Office Papers (Inspectors of Factories), 87/1, pp. 287-288.
[309] Home Office Papers, 45/511 O.S.
[310] Ibid., December 23rd, 1844; October 6th, 1845; July 25th, 1845, etc.
[311] Ibid., June 10th, 1844; February 14th, 1844.
[312] Ibid., August 4th, 1845. But the Duke of Buccleuch wrote to Graham that if the overseer was honest and vigilant this could easily be detected.
[313] Ibid., July 25th, 1845.
[314] Ibid., Disturbances Book), 45/644, O.S.
[315] Parliament Papers (Report of Factory Inspectors), June 30th, 1842, p. 3.

early in the morning and stay after quitting time at night; fraudulent certificates as to the age of children and young persons were made out by the owners; the repair and greasing of machinery was done after closing hours and for this no pay was given.[316] In order not to stop the machines, the operatives were often compelled to eat while working,[317] and during rush seasons no attention was paid to the legal limit of hours of labour.[318] Apprentices were cruelly mistreated and holidays were seldom observed, so that, 'with the exception of two or three days at Christmas . . . there are no regular holidays . . . They go from bed to work and from work to bed'.[319] It is unnecessary to prolong this list. Suffice it to say, therefore, that as a consequence of these conditions the inspectors discovered a frightful amount of illness and accidents due to fatigue, lack of safeguards on machines, faulty ventilation in shops, lack of toilet facilities (men, women, and children using the same ones publicly), and as a consequence of males and females working scantily clad in overheated rooms, the open prevalence of prostitution.[320]

But while these conditions prevailed in the flax, cotton, wool, and silk mills and factories, they were every bit as bad in such other trades and industries as weaving, pin-making, nail-making, bleaching, calico-printing, paper-making, tobacco-manufacturing, porcelain-making, and agriculture.[321]

To correct the most glaring and obvious of these evils Graham introduced a new Factory Act on February 6th, 1844.[322] 'Children' were now defined as persons between the ages of nine and thirteen, whereas it had previously been eight to twelve. They

[316] *Ibid.*, December 31st, 1842, p. 18 et seq.

[317] *Ibid.* (Children's Employment Commission), App. to Second Report, Part I, Vol. VII, p.b. 21; F 3; B 15, etc.

[318] R. J. Saunders reported a case of girls of fourteen having worked from 7 o'clock Friday evening straight through until 3 o'clock Sunday morning — a total of 32 hours.

[319] *Ibid.*, F 14, 41.

[320] This prevailed, according to Inspector Graiziger, 'to a most awful extent in Nottingham'. *Report*, F 9; Q 15.

[321] See (Report of the Commission on Hand-Loom Weavers); (Report of Assistant Poor Law Commissioners on Employment of Women and Children in Agriculture) in *Parliament Papers*, 1843; *Hansard*, 3rd Ser., LV, 1262; *Home Office Papers* (Domestic), 44/39; *Ibid.*, (Scotch), 103/10.

[322] The Bill of 1843 had been withdrawn because of opposition to the education clauses.

were not to work more than six and one-half hours per day, a period to be worked wholly in the morning or afternoon. 'Young persons', those between thirteen and eighteen, were not to work more than from five in the morning to seven in the afternoon in the summer and from six-thirty to eight in winter, in the silk, cotton, woollen, and flax industries; and of the thirteen and one-half hours, one and one-half hours were to be set apart for meals and rest. No limit was placed on the labour of adults except that in these four trades women were not to work more than twelve hours in every twenty-four. To be sure that these restrictions on working hours were enforced, the Bill provided that all labour be stopped between midnight and five-thirty in the morning. Finally, employers were made liable for those injuries to the operatives which resulted from failure of the employer to install safeguards around dangerous machinery.[323]

As soon as the House went into committee on the Bill, Ashley moved a resolution reducing the working day for women and young persons from twelve to ten, in order, he said, to give them 'a slight relaxation of toil, a time to live, and a time to die; a time for those comforts that sweeten life, and a time for those duties that adorn it'.[324] But Graham, who owned some cotton mills and who sold considerable quantities of larch and birch to the J. and P. Coats Company for use in making bobbins and spools and who was not at heart an advocate of factory legislation, immediately opposed this resolution. A ten-hour day, he said, would be fatal to employers, employees, and country. It would be fatal to employers because production would decline and consequently profits would also decline. It would be fatal to employees because employers would be forced to improve machinery and to accelerate the speed at which machines were run and hence increase the severity of labour. In addition, a reduction in hours of labour would obviously mean an equivalent reduction in wages, i.e., 25 per cent.[325] It would be fatal to England in the industrial race with the rest of the world, which race was now so close that

---

[323] *Hansard*, 3rd Ser., LXXII, 277-278. In general, the provisions of the Bill followed the recommendations of the Committee of Inquiry of 1840. See *Parliament Papers*, Sixth Report, February 18th, 1841, pp. 1-33.

[324] *Hansard*, 3rd Ser., LXXIII, 1101.

[325] This was Horner's estimate. See *Peel Papers*, CCLXIX, 351 (Br. Mus. Add. MSS. 40449).

'a feather would turn the scale; an extra pound weight would lose the race'.[326]

Despite Graham's opposition, Ashley's amendment was carried by a majority of nine, many landlords, according to the *Morning Chronicle*, voting for the resolution 'out of personal antipathy to Graham'.[327] Shortly thereafter, Clause Eight of the Bill came up for consideration and Ashley again proposed a ten-hours amendment. This time Graham made full use of party pressure, i.e., of the threat that both he and Peel might resign, and, as a result, Ashley's amendment was beaten.[328] The House would undoubtedly then have compromised on eleven hours, but Graham would not agree to that either, and instead withdrew the Bill altogether with the announcement that he would prepare a new one.

Meanwhile this labour question was being debated in the country at large and Graham received numerous petitions both for and against his Bill. The Manchester School opposed all legislative interference with industry. They argued that the Bill would deprive people of the right to work where, when, and for how long they chose; that reduced hours of labour would force a reduction in wages and consequently cause hunger and suffering; that a ten-hour day for women and young persons was just an entering wedge and would soon be extended to men also; and that unless a free play of economic forces was permitted English industry would lose out in the race with European countries where no ten-hours restriction existed.[329] To the Whig *Edinburgh Review*, cheaper food was the real solution to the problem, and therefore the Government ought to cease interfering with industry and instead repeal the Corn Laws. With cheaper food, parents would not have to rely on the labour of their children.[330] On the other hand, *Fraser's Magazine*, speaking for the landed classes, declared that

[326] *Hansard*, 3rd Ser., LXXIII, 1109.

[327] *Chronicle*, May 13th, 1844, p. 4. See also GREVILLE, *Memoirs*, V, 169; *Manchester Guardian*, March 27th, 1844, p. 4.

[328] *Hansard*, 3rd Ser., LXXIII, 1460-1463. Many M.P.s from the agricultural districts also voted with the Government because they feared that if Ashley's amendment was carried the Corn Laws would have to be repealed.

[329] The views of the Manchester School were clearly stated in such papers as the *Manchester Guardian* (March 20th, 1844, p. 4), and the *Chronicle* (March 20th, 1844, p. 4), and the *Leeds Mercury*.

[330] *Edin. Rev.*, LXXIX, 149 et seq. See also, HODDER, *op. cit.*, II, 29.

if the economic prosperity of England was really based on the labour of women and children it would be better if it fell right away,[331] while the *London Morning Post* asserted that the idea that a ten-hour day would ruin England, was 'stark, staring nonsense'. In addition, it said, reducing the hours of labour would result in greater employment and hence cause wages to rise.[332]

The new Bill which Graham brought to the House on April 22nd, 1844, was similar in most respects to the first. It proposed to limit the hours of employment of children from eight to eleven years of age to six and one-half hours a day in silk mills, and of children from eight to thirteen years in cotton, woollen and flax mills to the same number (to be, in each case, worked either in the morning or in the afternoon); forbade the employment of women for more than twelve hours a day; empowered surgeons to certify not only the ages of the children but also their health and strength;[333] and ordered safeguards to be placed on all dangerous machinery.[334]

On the third reading of this Bill, Ashley again tried to reduce the hours of employment by proposing that for three years there should be an eleven-hour limit and thereafter ten. Graham obstinately refused to budge an inch. Ashley's proposal, he said, was equivalent to giving workers another Sabbath each week (two hours each day for six days). This would total six weeks per year and England could not afford such a withdrawal of productive industry.[335] The amendment was defeated and the Bill was finally passed by a vote of 136 to 7.

It is interesting to note that the discussions on this question, both in Parliament and in the country, cut across class and party lines. In the northern part of England, Oastler and Sadler, who led the ten-hours movement,[336] were Tory Democrats;[337] Fielden, a manufacturer and Radical, also supported it;[338] so, too, did the Chartists, Socialists, and political economists like Francis

---

[331] *Fraser's*, XXIX, 621.   [332] *Post*, May 13th, 1844, p. 5.

[333] There had been numerous cases of fraudulent certificates of baptism, etc., *Home Office Papers* (Inspectors of Factories), 27/1.

[334] *Hansard*, 3rd Ser., LXXIII, 1667.

[335] *Ibid.*, LXXIV, 917 et seq.

[336] G. D. H. COLE, *Chartist Portraits*, Chap. III.

[337] The label is Trevelyan's. GEORGE M. TREVELYAN, *John Bright*, 157.

[338] COLE, *Chartist Portraits*, Chap. VIII.

Place.[339] In Parliament, Ferrand, a protectionist, supported the ten-hours proposals as did O'Connell and Macaulay who were free traders. Russell and Palmerston, who were Whigs, also supported it, while Melbourne and Brougham of the same party opposed it.[340] Finally, many members of the Conservative party, as has been pointed out, favoured the Ashley proposal until forced into line by Peel's and Graham's threats to resign.[341]

While this Factory Act was not as liberal as many wished it to be, and as it perhaps should have been, it was nevertheless a substantial step forward. In addition to the desirable clauses already discussed, the Law provided that all protected persons had to begin work at the same time in the morning and to take meals at the same time, and therefore went far towards establishing the principle of a 'normal' working day.

Since few people believed that the passage of the Act of 1844 had disposed of the question of factory legislation, little surprise was expressed when Ashley sought, in April 1845, to extend the provisions of the 1844 Act to the operatives engaged in calico-print works and in bleaching and dyeing.[342] Graham assented to the introduction of the Bill but reserved the right to amend it as he saw fit. Before the second reading he had made extensive inquiries on the subject and had discussed it with factory inspectors, labourers, and employers. On April 2nd he explained to the House the provisions to which he had agreed. There was to be no employment for children under eight; no night work for any

---

[339] GRAHAM WALLACE, *Life of Francis Place*, 173-175.

[340] According to Greville, Russell's support of the ten-hours clause, 'filled the world with amazement, and many of his own friends with indignation'. GREVILLE, *Greville's Diary*, P. W. Wilson, ed., II, 173. For Brougham's views, see *Annual Register* (1844), pp. 131-133.

[341] 'Such is the power and such the exercise of Ministerial influence', Ashley wrote in his diary. Cited in HODDER, *op. cit.*, II, 50. Opposition to Graham's plans was often purely personal and for which Graham had no one to blame but himself. The *Examiner*, edited by Leigh Hunt, was a free-trade journal which referred to Ashley's proposed ten-hours scheme as an example of 'Jack Cade' legislation. Graham had seen this statement and at a propitious moment in the debates taunted Ashley with fostering 'Jack Cade' legislation, with the result that Ashley's followers 'flew at him like Tigers', and, according to John Bright, 'Graham was at once regarded as the arch-enemy of the labouring classes'. In Hodder's opinion, he became 'one of the most unpopular men in the country'. See GREVILLE, *Memoirs*, V, 169-170; JOHN BRIGHT, *History of England*, 98; HODDER, *op. cit.*, II, 37.

[342] *Hansard*, 3rd Ser., LXXVIII, 958. The *Chronicle* (April 4th, 1845, p. 6), praised Ashley's Bill, which, it said, was 'framed with caution and judgement'.

females; for purposes of education, children between eight and thirteen were to be treated as agricultural instead of as factory children because the work was unsteady (fluctuating with changes in styles), and were therefore to attend school four hours daily during slack seasons. Deleted entirely from Ashley's Bill were the provisions for regulating conditions of employment in the dyeing and bleaching trades.[343] Though Ashley was so displeased with what Graham had done that he let Graham proceed with the Bill as his own, he did not oppose it and the Bill was easily passed and became law on June 30th, 1845.[344]

Early in 1846 Ashley and Fielden proposed a Bill limiting to ten hours a day the labour of 'young persons' working in factories. But, since Graham refused to take any action on this Bill until the corn law question had been decided, the Bill was defeated. A final effort at factory legislation was Duncombe's proposal to prohibit the employment of children under eight years in all lace factories. Graham successfully opposed this too, on the grounds that since much of this work was done in homes and small shops it would be too difficult to enforce; that if this trade were regulated it would also be necessary to regulate such trades as pin-making, nail-making, etc. Once this was done, he said, the State would have to regulate all labour and even pass minimum wage laws. Woe to England when that should be done, for capital would fly away to countries where no such restrictions existed, and England would lose its position as a manufacturing nation and consequently cease to be a great power.

All in all, Graham's policy in the field of factory legislation can best be described as 'piecemeal'. The *Westminster Review* caustically described it as a policy of '*charity*, never *justice*; — always the *open purse*, never the *equal measure*'.[345] There were both advantages and disadvantages in such a policy. It was, in the first place, slow, and therefore prolonged obvious and patent injustices. It was, furthermore, unequal in its incidence, affecting first one industry and then another, and consequently necessitated the passage of many laws instead of just one over-all law. On the other hand, making reforms cautiously, gradually, and at the same time slowly, to use Graham's own words, prevented any

---

[343] *Hansard*, 3rd Ser., LXXVIII, 1372-1376.
[344] *Statutes at Large*, 8 and 9 Victoria, c. 29.   [345] *West. Rev.*, XLIII, 449.

sudden violent shock in the nation's industrial system. In addition, errors which developed in the regulation of one trade could be avoided in the next. Slow changes also enabled industries to prepare for regulation (if not actually to prevent it by setting their houses in order), and hence cushioned the blow when it finally came.

While he was opposed to legislative interference with the industrial life of the State, Graham did agree to placing restrictions on the labour of women and children, always provided that it be done with moderation and caution. A ten-hours Bill was too much for him to stomach. It would, he was certain, result in decreased production, lower wages, and declining morality. He was wrong in each case. It has been demonstrated over and over again that as much, and often even more, can be produced in ten hours as in twelve; that fatigue leads to accidents, illness, shoddy workmanship, and spoilage of material; that most labourers husband their physical energy and work at a pace geared to the number of hours they must work. He was equally wrong in the matter of wages, for as hours of labour were subsequently reduced, wages, both real and money, continued to rise. His professed belief that reducing the working day for women and children would result in lower moral standards is too absurd to necessitate refutation.

Considering all the facets to this problem of factory legislation, real progress was made during the years from 1842 through 1846, for besides the salutary laws passed in 1842, 1845, and 1846, it was clear that though Ashley's ten-hour proposals were defeated, the regulation of hours of labour for 'young persons' really meant regulation for all persons because it was impossible to organize the working day in a factory so as to combine a twelve-hour day for some workers with a ten-hour day for others. For practical purposes, therefore, the ten hours day was achieved in 1845 even though it did not become the legal working day until 1847.

In a much larger sense, these laws were a recognition of the philosophy that the regulation of labour is the concern of the State, and therefore laid the basis for the whole subsequent system of government regulation, inspection, and control.

The distressed and diseased state of society in the early 'forties called attention to the need for a great amount of remedial legislation. This was especially true with respect to England's penal institutions, for, according to Walpole, in 1842 one out of every 500 of the population was committed and one in every eleven persons was a pauper.[346] This alarming increase in the amount of crime, due to the shift of population from rural to urban areas, to increased destitution, to improved police efficiency in the detection of crime, plus the agitation for penal reform by such persons as John Howard, Samuel Romilly, Francis Burdett, and Elizabeth Fry, plus the fact that Peel's successors at the Home Office had not continued the work of penal reform he had so nobly begun, meant that Graham had to take the problem in hand. It was a very real problem which few people understood. 'It was obvious', writes Woodward, 'that prisons ought not to be centres of disease; that the prisoners should not live under conditions harsher than those required by the law; that young offenders should not be contaminated by contact with hardened criminals. Yet there was not even a clear idea about the purpose of punishment; most people failed to distinguish between retributory, deterrent, or reformatory punishment.'[347]

Since 1779 the national government had assumed the duty of maintaining places of confinement for certain classes of convicted criminals. To accommodate those who had been convicted but for whom there were not enough jails, it was decided to transport them to penal settlements abroad. While waiting to be transported, they were confined on prison hulks, i.e., old vessels fitted out for the purpose, and compelled to labour in the dockyards and arsenals. These soon became, according to the Webbs, 'the most brutalizing, the most demoralizing, and the most horrible' of all forms of penal servitude.[348] Many, therefore, wished the transportation system abolished, but Graham was not one of them. 'Abolishing' was not his method: 'I desire to regulate it,' he wrote to Peel, 'to correct the evils proved by experience to exist in the old system; ... to graduate the punishment in conformity with the sentences which shall be passed here.'[349] In keeping with this principle he began to clear out the hulks by shipping the convicts to various places in the Empire. In 1841, for instance, 1000 were sent to Gibraltar to labour on the improvements being made at the fortress. Then, together with the Admiralty, he made

---

[346] WALPOLE, op. cit., VI, 386.   [347] WOODWARD, op. cit., 449.
[348] The WEBBS, Eng. Local Gov't., VI, 45-46.
[349] Peel Papers, CCLXVI (Br. Mus. Add. MSS. 40446).

plans to send a considerable number to Gambia. He hoped, he told the House, to continue this policy.[350]

As soon as he took office as Home Secretary, Graham ordered the prison inspectors to add an appendix to their reports in which they should indicate matters to which Graham should direct his attention, and matters to which the attention of Parliament should be called. Their reports revealed the existence of frightful conditions in the jails and prisons. In some the dark cell or 'cage' was absolutely unfit for human habitation; some had no written rules whatever; in some, no employment was provided; many had no chaplains though the law required it; some had no doctors or surgeons; female prisoners were attended by male officers; male prisoners often had to sleep two in a bed; many keepers charged the inmates for the food given them; some jails had not been cleaned for twelve months; in all the food, clothing, and accommodation were appalling.[351]

Through the efforts of Romilly and George Halford the Government had purchased some marshy ground from the Marquis of Salisbury and had constructed on it the famous Millbank penitentiary as a 'model' institution. But the inadequate food and ventilation, the irregular and irksome life within its walls, the unhealthy prison site, the system of solitary confinement and the rule of absolute silence, caused epidemics of illness as well as riots to break out at frequent intervals.[352] In 1838 it was denounced in Parliament as a total failure. In 1842 Graham called a meeting of all the prison inspectors. Each was directed to come prepared to discuss and to recommend necessary reforms and changes in the management of prisons, in prison diets, discipline, type of labour performed, educational and religious instruction, and so on.[353] The conference was held at the Home Office on November 29th and as a result of it Graham prepared a Bill for the better regulation of Millbank and other prisons.

This penal reform Bill provided for the classification of all

[350] *Hansard*, 3rd Ser., LX, 147.
[351] *Home Office Papers* (Domestic Book), 43/61; (Penitentiary and Prison Book, vol. II), 21/8.
[352] For a good description of Millbank see ARTHUR GRIFFITHS, 'Millbank Penitentiary, an Experiment in Reformation', in *History and Romance of Crime*, III, Chaps. I, III and v.
[353] *Home Office Papers* (Penitentiary and Prison Book, vol. III), 21/9, pp. 72-75.

Q

prisoners. Parkhurst prison was to be used only for juvenile offenders; Pentonville (the new prison just about ready for occupancy) for adults; while transportation was reserved for older and hardened offenders. The latter group were to be divided into three classes: 'The first was to consist of those who could get tickets of leave on their arrival on account of their general good conduct. The second class was to consist of those whose reformation was certain and to whom tickets of leave would be granted after some probation in the colony if their conduct should be satisfactory. The third class was to consist of those who were completely depraved and who would suffer the utmost punishment awarded to them.'[354] To make the classification, a term of probation was required and this was the use to which Millbank prison was to be put. It was to be used as a kind of depot for nine to twelve months during which time some opinion could be formed as to the character of the prisoners. From this depot the juveniles among the group would be sent to Parkhurst, adults (from 18 to 35) would be sent to Pentonville, and all others would be transported. The Bill providing for this system, as well as for the completion of Pentonville, was approved by the House with very little opposition and became law in 1842.[355]

Parkhurst, to which juveniles were to be sent, had been established in 1838 as a reformatory. While here, many were taught trades and given the rudiments of an education, but at the conclusion of their sentences they could not find employment. As a consequence they soon drifted back into crime. Graham carefully studied this problem and then proposed a new plan to Lord Stanley, the Colonial Secretary. It provided for sending the 'reformed' boys to the colonies, where they would be effectually cut off from their former haunts and associates and where they could find work. The boys selected for emigration were to be divided into two classes: free emigrants and apprentices. The first class would be confined to older boys who had distinguished themselves by good conduct and who, on arrival in the colony, should be aided in finding employment by the colonial authorities. The second class would consist of younger boys, who, he wrote to Stanley, should also be of good character, 'but whose youth and inexperience render it desirable that they should be subjected for

[354] *Hansard*, 3rd Ser., LXIX, 842.   [355] *Statutes at Large*, 5 and 6 Victoria, c. 29.

some time to come to the restraints of an apprenticeship'. Lord Stanley agreed. Nineteen boys were selected in 1842 and sent to Western Australia and ninety-two were sent to New Zealand. Specific instructions were issued by Graham to the captains of the ships directing them to provide educational and religious instruction for the boys en route and to employ them in the same trades they had learned at Parkhurst. The colonial authorities were directed to see to it that the masters to whom the boys were apprenticed supplied them with good clothing, food, and lodging, provided for their education, and paid them. Part of each boy's earnings was to be deposited in a savings bank so he would have some money on the expiration of his apprenticeship. On arrival in the colonies the boys would all receive Royal pardons and at the end of their apprenticeship would become free men.[356]

Parkhurst, then, was to be a prison of probation and instruction for juveniles. Pentonville, which was ready for occupancy in December 1842, was to serve the same purpose for the adults sent to it from Millbank. On December 16th Graham sent instructions to the commissioners at Pentonville who had been appointed to superintend the experiment. 'No prisoner', he wrote, 'shall be admitted to Pentonville without the knowledge that it is the portal to the penal colony, and without the certainty that he bids adieu to his connections in England, and that he must look forward to a life of labour in another hemisphere.' As soon as a prisoner arrived at Pentonville he was to be told that his eighteen months of incarceration were purely probationary. At the end of this year and a half,

> When a just estimate can be formed of the effect produced by the discipline on his character, he will be sent to Van Diemen's Land, there, if he behave well, at once to receive a ticket of leave, which is equivalent to freedom . . . if he behave indifferently, he . . . will receive a probationary pass which will secure to him only a limited portion of his own earnings and which will impose certain galling restraints on his personal liberty; if he behave ill . . . he will work in a probationary gang without wages, deprived of liberty — an abject convict.[357]

[356] *Home Office Papers* (Criminal), Ser. I, 21/2, pp. 267-301.
[357] *Parliament Papers* (Letter of Sir James Graham to the Commissioners for the Government of Pentonville Prison), App. No. 4, pp. 25-27; *Home Office Papers* (Penitentiary and Prison Book), vol. III, 21/9, pp. 102-107.

The commissioners at Pentonville would decide in which class each deportee should be placed. Pentonville, then, was to be like Parkhurst, except that discipline was to be much more severe because the solitary system was to be used. After eighteen months of this, 'a better frame of mind will have been moulded, or the heart will have been hardened, and the case will have become desperate'.[358]

Crawford, the Inspector of Prisons, carried out Graham's 'solitary' or 'separate' system to perfection. Prisoners wore masks along the passages; while in chapel they sat in separate cells; they were separated by partitions while they worked at the tread-wheel; they took their exercise of one hour each day in a triangular area surrounded by high walls. And this was the system Graham had ordered for Pentonville. It was, he said, 'the best system of imprisonment'.[359] The discipline was military; labour from 6 a.m. to 7 p.m. was difficult and broken only for meals; exercise and attendance at chapel were taken in total silence.

How did this 'model system' work? Jebb, the Surveyor-General, considered the system so successful that he could not 'too strongly recommend its general adoption'.[360] Most officials naturally liked the system for it gave them little trouble and few cared about its mental or moral effect on the inmates. The public regarded it in the same light, i.e., as highly successful, even enlightened and, by 1848, 54 new prisons were built on this cellular isolation model. On the other hand, statistics painted a different picture. In 1853 it was reported that out of 60,000 confined at Pentonville, there were 220 cases of insanity, 210 of delusions, and 40 suicides.[361] The system was so depressing that even if an inmate did not actually lose his mental balance, his wit and will were both rendered limp and flabby.[362]

Discipline at Pentonville was severe, vexatious, and often, when administered by a martinet, unbearable.[363] The same can be said

---

[358] *Home Office Papers* (Penitentiary and Prison Book), vol. III, 21/9, pp. 102-107.
[359] *Hansard*, 3rd Ser., LXXVI, 267.
[360] *Parliament Papers* (Report of Surveyor-General), March 10th, 1844, p. 3. The *Chronicle* (September 10th, 1844) claimed the same excellence for Parkhurst.
[361] A. CREW, *London Prisons To-day and Yesterday*, 88; G. IVES, *History of Penal Methods*, 186.
[362] See W. L. CLAY, 'Our Convict Systems', 19, cited in the WEBBS, *Eng. Local Gov't.*, VI, 177.
[363] The worst forms of punishment were hard labour at the tread-wheel and the crank. For a description of each see *Ibid.*, 146 *n.*, and 96 et seq.

for the prison diet. After carefully studying this subject, Graham drew up a dietary system the object of which was to give each inmate enough food to maintain health, but not more than that. The plan, generally known as the 'Graham Dietaries', was made public in the summer of 1843. It provided a specific diet for all persons in prison and the amount of food given depended on the term of imprisonment and on whether the inmate was sentenced to hard labour or not. Each was to receive a specific amount of solid and liquid food. Those sentenced for seven to twenty-one days, not at hard labour, were to receive 168 ounces of bread and fourteen ounces of gruel, but no soup, no cocoa, no potatoes, and no meat, while those sentenced to hard labour received an additional pint of soup daily. Those incarcerated for more than four months without hard labour were to receive 168 ounces of bread, 32 of potatoes, 12 of meat, 3 pints of soup, and 14 of gruel; those at hard labour were allowed 154 ounces of bread, 112 of potatoes, 16 of meat, 3 pints of soup, 11 of gruel, and 3 of cocoa.[364] It was subsequently discovered at Pentonville that this minimum diet was inadequate and an extra ration had, from time to time, to be granted the inmates.

The system was easily enforced at Pentonville, but Graham ran into difficulties in other prisons. He ordered the governors of all prisons to send him lists of the diets used and he would then approve or disapprove them. He never saw one that was too good but many times he discovered hopelessly inadequate ones and was forced to order them to be increased.[365] Furthermore, some governors refused to adopt the system altogether while others modified it in either direction as suited the desires of the locality Their reasons for so doing were that they felt that the new diet system was 'an unnecessary increase of the comforts of prisoners'; that by its adoption, 'the terror of imprisonment will be decreased'; that it acted as an impetus to crime; that it cost the ratepayers too much; that it was superior to workhouse diets.[366] Graham's answer to these complaints was that two years' experience (1843-1845) had shown that there had been no increase in commitals, that the

[364] *Parliament Papers* (Second Report of Surveyor-General of Prisons), App. H. vol. III, 58.
[365] *Home Office Papers* (Penitentiary and Prison Book), vol. III, 21/9, p. 1 passim,
[366] *Ibid.* (Domestic Book), 43/68, pp. 310-311.

health of prisoners had been greatly improved, and that the increase in expense had been very small and when considered in the light of its beneficial effects was unimportant.[367]

This improved prison bill-of-fare, plus improved sanitation and a new ventilating system which secured adequate amounts of fresh air, resulted in a reduction in the mortality rate at Pentonville from 18.52 per cent in 1838-1842 to 9.13 per cent for the years from 1842-1846.[368] Furthermore, the prison commissioners reported that the improvement in the morals of inmates was 'without parallel in the history of prison discipline'. Admitting that the 'separate' system was 'safe and efficient', nevertheless it had serious weaknesses. Not only did it drive many completely insane, but those who survived without the loss of reason arrived at Van Diemen's Land, according to the Governor, with 'a sluggishness of intellect, [and] a slowness of thought and action' which took years to wear off.[369]

When on board ship bound for Van Diemen's Land, or in the case of the 'incurably bad' for Norfolk Island, the convicts were under the jurisdiction of the Admiralty.[370] Upon arrival at Van Diemen's Land they became the responsibility of the Colonial Office. Here they were subject to regulations drawn up by Stanley and Graham, known as the probation system. 'The bulk of the convicts', as Walpole describes the system, 'were in the first instance to be employed on public works . . .; they were to pass from public works to private service; from private service they were to be released on a ticket-of-leave, and the ticket-of-leave was ultimately to be terminated by a conditional pardon.'[371] Theoretically this was a good scheme but it broke down in actual practice because the convicts, working in gangs, were not effectively supervised. In addition, the acute commercial depression in Van Diemen's Land in 1843 and 1844 reduced the demand for convict labour. Finally, in 1846, because of the protests of the governor against the sending of additional convicts, the Govern-

[367] *Home Office Papers* (Domestic Book), 43/68, pp. 310-311.
[368] *Parliament Papers* (Second Report of Surveyor-General), III, App. 73.
[369] *Ibid.*, 25.
[370] Elizabeth Fry, an active prison reformer, had succeeded in persuading Graham to send two female officers on each ship to take charge of the female convicts. See ELIZABETH FRY, *Memoirs*, II, 438 et seq.
[371] WALPOLE, *op. cit.*, IV. 414.

ment suspended transportation to this colony and the convicts were thenceforward put to labour on various public works in England.

Early in 1843, Graham, seeking to establish some uniformity in prison rules, directed Crawford, the Rev. W. Rupell, and Bethune, prison inspectors, to draw up a new set of prison rules. This done, the rules were sent to the governors of all the prisons and their criticisms and suggestions were solicited.[372] When finally corrected and amended, copies of these prison rules and by-laws were sent to all prisons, jails, and houses of correction and the magistrates were told that they were to be put into effect at once. The object of the new rules was to establish a uniform practice in the treatment of offenders as well as to have as many prisons and jails as possible built, or remodelled, on the plan of the 'model' at Pentonville. It was understood that modification in the rules would probably have to be made to fit them into the variations in conditions in the different localities, and therefore local authorities continuously sent to the Home Office for Graham's approval their plans for new jails, prisons, and houses of correction as well as for changes in prison rules. Graham studied these carefully and then either approved or disapproved them. The keeper of Queen's Prison, for instance, objected to having to attend chapel each day, but Graham said that it was compulsory. At Holywell, the prisoners were denied the right to be visited by ministers of their own persuasion and Graham had to order the officials to permit prisoners this legal privilege. At Welchpool, the amount of tread-wheel labour imposed on the inmates was 31,500 feet of ascent, whereas, Graham told them, it must not exceed 12,000. Some plans for jails and prisons were not approved because they did not provide adequate lighting, ventilation, or heating; others because the plans did not provide for solitary confinement; still others because the exercise yards were either too big or too small.[373]

From Graham's point of view, one of the great advantages of this uniformity was that it would achieve greater efficiency and hence be more economical. He lost no opportunity to insist on

---

[372] *Home Office Papers* (Penitentiary and Prison Book), vol. III, 21/9, p. 1 passim; 154-155; (Domestic Book), 43/63, p. 436.

[373] These examples are from the *Ibid.* (Domestic Book), vol. III, 43/62; 43/64; 43/65; 44/65.

economy in the management of prisons and jails. When the
authorities in Arbour Square requested Graham's approval for
the purchase of carpets for the police court, Graham replied that
he would like to know which rooms were to be carpeted and the
amount of carpet needed as well as the cost per yard. At Union
Hall, he said, too much was spent on trimming lamps; at Greenwich Court, three newspapers were bought daily and Graham
ordered it to be cut to one; when the police court at Clerkenwell
bought new carpets and furniture Graham demanded to know how
the old furniture had been disposed of; to another police court
Graham wrote that he 'did not approve of an ornamental building', and that no such court or jail needed mahogany furniture —
wainscot would do just as well. In 1845 twenty-six subordinate
officers at Parkhurst asked Graham for an increase in salary and
he replied that their wages were high enough, but that 'if they are
dissatisfied with their situations, they may resign: — and that if
they are not zealous in the discharge of their respective duties, they
will be instantly dismissed'.[374]

As we have seen, Graham had hoped and planned to have the
prisons at Millbank, Parkhurst, and Pentonville serve as real
reformatories in which the inmates would be turned from a career
in crime and made into useful citizens. By 1844, however, he knew
that it was not working out that way. 'Imprisonment, I fear,' he
wrote to Peel, 'under the best regulations can only be regarded as a
means of exemplary punishment, not of moral improvement.'[375]
For this reason, too, he believed that to be effective executions
should take place before 'a large multitude of spectators' sufficiently near the scaffold so that the spectators could hear any
'words of warning' the condemned might utter.[376] On the other
hand, he disliked the jailer's practice of selling seats to those who
wished to hear the sermons to the condemned because he considered
such things 'disgraceful and demoralizing'. But, he wrote to the
Queen, it was a practice of long usage in which the community had
a keen interest and caution should be used in proposing to change
it.[377] Caution was used, too, for it was not until 1868 that such

[374] *Home Office Papers* (Criminal), Ser. I, 21/3, pp. 145-146.
[375] *Peel Papers*, CCLXX, 250-251 (Br. Mus. Add. MSS. 40450).
[376] *Home Office Papers* (Domestic Book), 43/67, pp. 293-294.
[377] A. C. BENSON and VISCOUNT ESHER, *The Letters of Queen Victoria*, II, 44-45.

public exhibitions were stopped. In taking this stand Graham feared that if the public was denied admission to such 'events' they would demand lurid press accounts and, if denied this, they would demand the abolition of capital punishment.

Another class of unfortunates for whom an ameliorative reform measure was long overdue was the lunatics. In 1828 two Acts had been passed, one enabling justices at quarter-sessions to provide county asylums, the other regulating the treatment of lunatics kept in private houses. Both Acts, however, were merely permissive and enabling Acts and remained dead-letters with the result that lunatics continued to be horribly mistreated. A reform bill brought in in 1842 by Lord Lyndhurst was dropped because of the stress of other business and was not again considered until 1845, when Ashley introduced the Bill which eventually became law. Graham seconded Ashley's motion 'in a very kind and fervid speech, and announced the full support of the government'.[378] It provided for a permanent commission with detailed power of visitation and authority to place all asylums under proper regulations, such as that compelling asylum wardens to keep complete records, provide inmates with proper food, permit friends of inmates to visit them, etc. County asylums were to be built, and when a lunatic's friends could not care for him, he was to be housed in a pauper asylum. Those lunatics cared for in the houses of friends were to be examined by doctors, who were to make quarterly reports to the commission.[379] To be sure that 'uniformity ... should be observed in the rules' throughout England, Graham ordered the commissioners in lunacy to draw up a standard code. When this code had been prepared and then approved by Graham, copies were sent to all asylums.[380]

As Home Secretary, Graham was frequently called upon to decide cases appealed to the Government for executive clemency. In Staffordshire, according to charges made in the House by Thomas Duncombe, two girls, one eleven years of age and the other thirteen, had been arrested for stealing; the first, a penny's worth of coal; the second, a waistcoat. The constable chained them to a grate in the kitchen and refused to provide them with a

[378] HODDER, op. cit., II, 112; Hansard, 3rd Ser., LXXXI, 199.
[379] Statutes at Large, 8 and 9 Victoria, c. 100.
[380] Home Office Papers (Domestic Book), 43/70, pp. 176-178.

bed or with water with which to wash themselves. When, on investigation, Graham found the charges to be correct, he reprimanded the Lord-Lieutenant of the county, stating that this conduct was reprehensible and unjustifiable and must not happen again.[381]

In 1839, three Chartists — Frost, Williams, and Jones — had each led a column of men who attacked the town of Newport, overpowered the military and stopped the mail. This was a signal for other groups to take other towns and to hold them for the purpose of establishing the Charter. The police arrested the leaders, who, when found guilty, were sentenced to death. In cases of this type — treason — the law required that the accused be given a copy of the indictment as well as a list of witnesses. But the Crown Solicitor had not given the accused both documents at the same time, and on appeal nine of fifteen judges held the Crown Solicitor's action to be improper and the sentence was commuted from death to transportation for life. When Frost, Williams, and Jones had served five years a request was made that they be pardoned. Graham positively refused. 'Why, Sir,' he said to the House, 'a person transported for seven years for a minor offence would not, in the ordinary course of the administration of justice in this country, have his sentence commuted at so early a period.'[382]

Then there was the case of the soldier who had broken down the door of Mary Brown's apartment and had assaulted her. The culprit was duly arrested, tried, found guilty, and sentenced to pay a fine of ten shillings. Horsman found out about it and told the House of Commons that a mere fine of ten shillings was a miscarriage of justice. After investigating the facts, Graham admitted that the fine was not an adequate one, but, on the other hand, he said, the door to Mary's apartment was an old one, the hinges were rusty, and it had not offered much resistance![383]

These cases illustrate Graham's policy, except in case of the indisputable miscarriage of justice, of upholding the decisions of the authorities. This occasionally resulted in hardship to some, but it is difficult to see how he could have pursued any other course unless he wanted to spend all his time reviewing cases. Since about 4000 such cases were appealed to him each year he simply had to

[381] *Hansard*, 3rd Ser., LXXXII, 673.
[382] *Ibid.*, LXXXIV, 887.   [383] *Ibid.*, LXXIV, 718-719.

assume that the courts had made proper decisions and let the law take its course.

In 1842 Graham secured the passage of the Public Houses Bill, the purpose of which was to prohibit the sale of wines, spirits, and other excisable liquors on board boats or other vessels lying at anchor on the Thames within the Metropolitan police district during hours of divine service on Sundays, Good Friday, and Christmas Day, when licensed victuallers had to keep their shops closed. Those who felt the need of spirituous liquors during those hours obtained them at the bars on the river boats. During the debates on the Bill, an effort was made to introduce a clause preventing the working class from going to the public houses during these hours for tea or coffee. Graham successfully opposed this proposition. He could see no reason why the working class should be prevented from 'regaling themselves with bread and cheese and a glass of ale . . . He knew of no objection . . . to their having the innocent gratification of reading the newspapers in those houses'.[384]

Closely related to the subject of public houses was the question of gambling. Gaming houses, apart from clubs, were forbidden, but a large number existed just outside the city boundaries. Few police dared interfere and those who did were frequently beaten by the thugs hired to guard the houses. But the greatest amount of gambling occurred at the race-tracks. In 1844 Graham ordered the police to break up some gambling games going on at Epsom. For this action he was taken to task by an M.P. who objected to the Government's interfering with these 'harmless games of chance'. He had no objections to games of chance or of physical dexterity, replied Graham, but these were not games of chance at all, for there was no chance in them. He then threw on the table of the House a set of dice which could not roll out a deuce ace. Then came another set in which eleven and twelve could be thrown with equal certainty. Roulette, he said, was equally crooked. 'They could not be considered games of chance, but perfect acts of pillage and robbery', and he would like to exterminate the whole nefarious business.[385] While this was impossible, he did secure the passage in 1844 of an Act to indemnify witnesses who testified

before Parliament about illegal gaming practices,[386] and the
following year of an Act fining any gaming-house keeper on whose
premises illegal games were played,[387] and in 1846 of an Act to
strengthen the Law of 1836 against advertising foreign lotteries in
the press.[388] These laws, said Graham, 'might not be good for the
publican, but . . . would be good for the public'.[389]

Many people, however, were beginning to feel that town-dwellers
would not attend these gaming houses at all, nor the public houses
either, if they had anything else to do in their spare time. In some
parts of England, the labourer who had been driven off the enclosed
commons had sometimes found compensation in allotments and
potato-patches provided for him by philanthropic squires, parsons,
and farmers. Why not apply this idea in the towns and give to the
poor small allotments where they could profitably amuse themselves planting gardens? Work in the fresh air would be healthful
and the vegetables grown would augment their diet. Graham,
though not entirely sympathetic to the idea because he regarded it
as a system of maintaining the poor out of the rates, did not oppose
Cowper's Bill, introduced in 1844, which provided for giving an
acre of land to each of the poor. But he thought that one acre was
too much, for the real purpose should be to provide the poor with
amusement and recreation, not subsistence. Because of the lateness of the session the Bill was postponed until 1845. When it was
brought up again, Cowper had cut the acreage to one-half at
Graham's insistence. During the debates Graham stated that he
hoped that employers, seeing labourers augment their diet in this
fashion, would not therefore reduce wages nor landlords increase
their rents. As finally passed Cowper's Bill was a weak one and
was rejected by the House of Lords. The only result of this allotments agitation, then, was a very meagre clause inserted in the
Enclosure Act of 1845. Clause Thirty of this Act gave authority to
the commissioners whose duty it was to administer the Law, to
require as a condition of enclosure, provision of an allotment for
the 'Exercise and Recreation [of] the inhabitants of the Neighbourhood'. The amounts fixed were as follows: for towns of
10,000 population, ten acres; those of 5000 to 10,000, eight acres;

---

[386] *Statutes at Large*, 7 and 8 Victoria, c. 7.
[387] *Ibid.*, 8 and 9 Victoria, c. 109.   [388] *Ibid.*, c. 74.
[389] *Hansard*, 3rd Ser., LXXXII, 795.

those of 2000 to 5000, five acres; those of less than 2000, four acres. Clause Thirty-one of the Act gave the commissioners power to provide garden plots for the labouring poor in amounts the commissioners thought necessary. If they allotted none at all, they had to state the reasons in their reports. While this was a step in the right direction, it was just a short step, and, as the Hammonds correctly point out, it 'proved [to be] miserably inadequate'.[390]

Closely related to this problem was the question of public health, about which very little had been done. Typhus, cholera, small-pox, and other diseases had spread throughout the land with annoying regularity. This was only natural, of course, in view of the fact that public hygiene, practically non-existent, was regarded by the State as a private matter. Conditions in the towns were frightful. Cesspools were placed in the gardens or in the basements of houses; the water-supply was both inadequate and impure since it was usually obtained from a nearby well or river into which the city sewer and the seepage from the cesspools flowed;[391] streets were rarely paved and hardly ever cleaned. The urbanization of the country resulted in the crowding of whole families, and sometimes more than one family, in a single room. Houses were built back to back with no drainage or ventilation. To avoid paying the window tax, owners built houses, writes Young, 'with as few openings as possible, and closets, privies, passages, cellars, and roofs were left unventilated'.[392] In such crowded towns as Manchester, Liverpool, and others, a large part of the population lived in cellars.[393] It was a natural product of the system of free enterprise. Each owner built as many houses as he possibly could upon his land, built them as cheaply as possible and collected as much rent as the traffic would bear.[394] Under a system which permits a man to climb to the top of the highest hill and say, 'All I see is mine; I saw it first', dung-heaps grew like mushrooms, slaughter-

[390] The HAMMONDS, *Age of the Chartists*, 141.

[391] In Bristol, for instance, 1300 out of 3000 houses had no water. See YOUNG, *op. cit.*, I, 85-86.

[392] *Ibid.*, 141, 166-167.

[393] In Manchester, one family out of every ten lived in cellars; in Liverpool, one out of every five. *Ibid.*, 167.

[394] The trouble, says Fay, was that 'in the short run slums paid. Shaftesbury found that the vilest houses made the biggest profits'. CHARLES R. FAY, *Great Britain from Adam Smith to the Present Day*, 365.

houses were built anywhere, the dead were buried in the over-crowded cemetery, the family lot, or even under the floors of houses.

That these evils had to be attacked was common knowledge — but how? And, who should do it — the State or local authorities? A start was made in 1840 when, on the basis of the Report of the Health of Towns Committee, three Bills were introduced in the House: the Regulation of Buildings Bill, the Drainage of Buildings Bill, and the Borough Improvement Bill. But, before any positive action could be taken, the Whig Government fell from power and the problem was dumped into the laps of Peel and Graham.

Goaded into action by Fox Maule's proposed Building Regula-tions Bill of 1842, which was dropped on Graham's promise to bring in one of his own, and by MacKinnon's Health of Towns Bill of 1843, Graham appointed a scientific commission to study the whole subject.[395] Before this commission had completed its survey a demand was made that the Government bring in a Bill to prohibit interments in towns.[396] But Graham refused. He had evidently had enough trouble with religious passions for he declared that 'any prohibition of interment within the walls of a city would not be in harmony with the feelings of a great body of people'.[397] When the subject again came up for discussion in the House in April 1845 Graham refused to admit that the existing system endangered public health. Nor would he admit that living near a churchyard was unhealthy. When the Bishop of London had been the rector at Bishopsgate, his family had lived next door to the churchyard and they 'had never enjoyed better health!' If the House should now decide that.

> Churchmen and Dissenters should not bury in the accustomed places of sepulture, but at a distance from towns, then every poor individual wishing to attend his friend to his long home must forego a day's wages; and in winter he must travel four or five miles from home and back. To attend a funeral would be extremely

---

[395] See *Peel Papers*, CCLXVII, 285-287 (Br. Mus. Add. MSS. 40447); *Home Office Papers* (Domestic Book), 117/5, p. 229.

[396] A campaign was being waged by such journals as the *Westminster Review* (XXXVII, 108-116) and the *Lancet, Journal of British and Foreign Medicine* (Herein-after cited as *Lancet*), (New Ser., I), to have cemeteries built outside town limits.

[397] *Hansard*, 3rd Ser., LXXVIII, 325. See the article on 'Funerals and Funeral Expenses', in *Quart. Rev.*, LXXIII, 439 et seq.

inconvenient, unless conveyances were provided; and if they were provided, the cost to the poor would be oppressive. There was a desire in the human breast of laying our bones beside those of our departed relatives and friends. This feeling we could not reason on; it was stronger than reason, and was connected with the best sentiments of human nature.[398]

Political expediency no doubt dictated this ridiculous opposition of Graham and as a consequence nothing was done on a national scale. However, the impetus given by the discussions on the subject, plus the publication of the Report of the Public Health Commission, resulted in local legislation and ultimately the passage of the Public Health Act in 1848.

A very important facet to the problem of public health was the practice of medicine. Graham had long been interested in this subject and had carefully studied the Report of the Select Committee on Medical Education of 1834, had assiduously read the reports of the doctors associated with the Poor Law Authority, and had corresponded with the president of the Royal College of Surgeons and the masters of the Society of Apothecaries.[399] And he kept at this subject so steadfastly that the *Morning Chronicle* declared in 1845 that he had pursued this 'hobby' with 'an indefatigable perseverance as regards the end, and a pliancy and versatility in his choice of means, the union of which is as admirable as it is real'.[400]

It was indeed a subject which needed to be pursued with indefatigable zeal. According to the census of 1841, as reported in the *Westminster Review*, there were in the United Kingdom 1776 physicians, 19,106 surgeons and apothecaries, and 2152 medical students, making a grand total of 23,034. Of this total there were 16,435 in England, 2849 in Scotland, 2900 in Ireland, 632 in Wales, and 168 in the Islands.[401] But in addition to these practitioners, who had at least the rudiments of a technical education, there were, as Traill puts it, 'a group of nondescript persons calling themselves surgeon-apothecaries, men-midwives, cuppers,

---

[398] *Hansard*, 3rd Ser., LXXIX, 357-358.
[399] *Home Office Papers* (Domestic Book), 43/62, p. 21 et seq. Graham had undoubtedly read the widely-circulated pamphlet: *Observations on the Present System of Medical Education with a View to Medical Reform*, 1834.
[400] *Chronicle*, July 8th, 1845, p. 4.
[401] *West. Rev.*, XLV, 30.

tooth-drawers, compounders, and dispensers of medicines'.[402] This group had gained what little knowledge it possessed by actual practice, had little if any schooling, 'were subject to no controlling body, and were unrecognized by law'.[403] To be sure, Parliament had in 1815 passed the Apothecaries Act authorizing the Society of Apothecaries to examine all apothecaries in England and Wales, but the Act did not affect druggists or chemists, and exempted the universities of Oxford and Cambridge, the Royal College of Physicians, and the Royal College of Surgeons from its provisions. In addition, much to the annoyance of the physicians and surgeons who saw in it the loss of their monopoly in the field, hospitals had begun to establish private medical schools.

To bring order out of chaos in this profession and to establish some uniformity in the education, the theory, and the practice of medicine, Graham introduced into the House, on August 7th, 1844, a Medical Reform Bill which he had carefully prepared. In doing so, he pointed out that there were seventeen colleges granting degrees and licences to practise medicine and that there existed over these colleges no regulatory or controlling agency of any kind; that they had lowered their already meagre standards in competing for students; that some had even been guilty of selling degrees. He did not wish to place restrictions on the private practice of medicine, but he did want a law passed stating that no one 'should be eligible to fill a medical or surgical office in any public institution unless his qualification had been tested by competent authority'.[404] All acts of Parliament relating to medicine and surgery should be swept away and a uniform centralized system established for the United Kingdom.

The central and arresting feature of his scheme was the establishment of a council of health in London responsible to the executive government. 'Thus the present great anomaly of a number of rival bodies possessing powers capable of being exercised without any responsibility would be abolished',[405] and instead there would be this council of eighteen members (eleven *ex-officio* members

[402] H. D. TRAILL, *Social England*, VI, 64.   [403] *Ibid.*

[404] *Hansard*, 3rd Ser., LXXVI, 1898.

[405] *Ibid.*, 1899. Lucius, an office bearer in the Royal College of Physicians, states that of these licensing bodies, 'no two agree in the course of study prescribed, in the strictness of execution, nor in the amount of privilege conferred'. LUCIUS, *Remarks on Medical Reform and on Sir James Graham's Medical Bill*, 7.

consisting of university professors, surgeons, and physicians, and seven to be appointed by the Crown) which would meet periodically, control all examinations, and regulate and equalize all fees to be paid for licences to practise medicine. The council was to keep a register, which was to be published annually, of all physicians and surgeons licensed to practise. The names of licentiates were to be sent to the council by the various licensing bodies and the council would divide them into three classes: the vendors of medicine, the surgeons, and the physicians. No one was to be licensed as a vendor who was not at least twenty-one years of age, as a surgeon who was under twenty-five, as a physician who was under twenty-six. Those who had no college training and who wished to practise had to be forty years of age and to pass an examination given by the Royal College of Physicians; those who had both a physician's and a surgeon's licence could become general practitioners.

In addition, the council of health was to be empowered to inspect and to supervise the courses of study in the licensing bodies so as to achieve uniformity in qualifications, requirements, and fees. It could refuse to register any persons it thought unfit, and no one whose name was not on the register could hold any medical or surgical office in any public institution, the Army, Navy, or East India Company, nor give testimony in a court of law. All persons were to be given one year in which to register.

As soon as Graham had concluded his adroit address, Macaulay arose, praised the whole plan, and promised Graham the support of the University of Edinburgh, the College of Physicians, and the College of Surgeons, to whom the Bill, he said, 'would give great satisfaction'.[406] Wakley, a spokesman for the general practitioners on the other hand, denounced the Bill on the grounds that the proposed council of health did not adequately represent the general practitioners, and promised Graham that almost all 30,000 of them would resolutely oppose the Bill.

Leave to bring in the Bill was given just before the House recessed and therefore before the next session the members of the medical profession had an opportunity fully to apprise themselves of its provisions. And it soon became apparent that both Macaulay and Wakley had correctly diagnosed the situation. The general

[406] *Hansard*, 3rd Ser., LXXVI, 1899.

R

practitioners at once opposed the Bill. On August 27th, 1844, the general practitioners of London held a meeting in Exeter Hall and unanimously adopted a resolution condemning the Bill *in toto*.[407] In the first place, it was denounced as a 'Quack Protection Bill' since it repealed the Apothecaries Act of 1815 and so threw open the medical practice to unqualified persons. The *London Medical Gazette*, proud of its record of having laboured to maintain the old professional tabernacles in their integrity and of its opposition to change, was particularly critical of the Bill on this score. It argued that quackery ought to be made illegal and 'made punishable, upon prosecution, as a high crime and misdemeanour, which it certainly is'. This could be done, the *Gazette* recognized, only by making it illegal to advertise patent medicines in newspapers. But such advertisements were a lucrative source of revenue to the papers and therefore Graham, said the *Gazette*, would do nothing to stop it. 'We should indeed like to see', it wrote, 'with what countenance the Right Hon. Baronet could face the editor and proprietor at least of the *Cumberland Chronicle*, or the *Carlisle Independent* in the prospect of an election, had he been accessory to cutting off supplies to the amount of several hundreds per annum in the shape of quack advertisements.'[408] The comic touch to this argument against the proposed law was supplied by *Punch*:

> And unto quackery ope the door?
> Have Galen's sons offended thee?
> Or lov'st thou quacks from sympathy?
> Ah! hold, Sir James, thy ruthless hand,
> Nor meddle with affairs thou dost not understand.[409]

In the second place, they did not like the registration scheme whereby all medical practitioners were to be alphabetically listed as physicians, surgeons, and licentiates in medicine and surgery. 'Thus', wrote the *Lancet*, their leading journal and spokesman, 'nineteen-twentieths of the medical practitioners of the country will . . . be branded with the mark of *inferiority*, and be classed at the *lowest* figure in the scale of professional qualification and rank.'

---

[407] See *The Times*, August 27th, 1844, p. 7.

[408] *The London Medical Gazette, A Weekly Journal of Medicine and the Collateral Sciences*, New Ser., XXXIV, 666-667 (Hereinafter cited as *Medical Gazette*). The same view was taken by *The Medical Times, a Journal of English and Foreign Medicine* (Hereinafter cited as *Medical Times*).

[409] *Punch*, VIII, 76.

It assumed that the names of physicians would head the list, then would appear the names of surgeons, and at the bottom would appear the names of the general practitioners, who would thus be marked as 'a degraded caste; the lowest order'.[410] At the same time, they objected to the registration fees, which were fixed at £5 for physicians and surgeons, and £2 for the general practitioners. 'Having already paid handsomely for our diploma, license, or certificate,' wrote the *Medical Gazette*, 'we peremptorily object to this proposition to pay any more.'[411]

Some criticized the Bill as a 'job' done by Graham at the behest of the Scottish and Irish physicians and surgeons and hence was 'un-English'.[412] *Lancet* declared that it was 'the dirty work of the *monopolists*', i.e., the physicians and surgeons of the entire United Kingdom.[413] Others objected to the spirit of centralization and uniformity implicit in the Bill. To them, centralization was synonymous with tyranny and they did not wish the medical profession tyrannized over, as the *Medical Gazette* put it, 'by the Secretary of State for the Home Office and his obsequious nominees'.[414] The *Quarterly Review*, while praising the other features of the Bill, complained that it did not regulate midwifery together with the other branches of medical practice.[415]

The main opposition, however, was directed against the proposed council of health. As the *Lancet* put it, thirteen of the eighteen members would 'derive their seats from the Crown, and the other five will be chosen by the close and corrupt medical corporations. Oh, rare institution'.[416] The general practitioners desired a council of health the membership of which was to be elective rather than appointive. They professed to see a union of the medical profession and the State resulting from Graham's Bill, comparable to that between the Church and State. 'Subject the medical government of this country', wrote the *Lancet*, 'by means

---

[410] *Lancet*, II, July 11, 1843, p. 667; New Ser., December 7th, 1844, pp. 322-323.

[411] *Medical Gazette*, XXXIV, 778. The same criticism was made by the *British and Foreign Medical Review or Quarterly Journal of Practical Medicine and Surgery*, XIX, 202 (Hereinafter cited as *Br. and For. Med. Rev.*). The *London and Edinburgh Monthly Journal of Medical Science* (IV, 843), objected to 'our ill-paid and ruined profession [being] taxed to the enormous amount of £75,000'.

[412] See *Medical Gazette*, XXXIV, 837.   [413] *Lancet*, New Ser., II, 167.

[414] *Medical Gazette*, XXXV, 293. *The Times* (August 31st, 1844, p. 4; September 10th, p. 4; October 8th, p. 4) criticized the Bill on the same grounds.

[415] *Quart. Rev.*, LXXV, 26.   [416] *Lancet*, New Ser., II, 228.

of such [a council], to the control of a minister of the Crown, and the independence of the profession is gone forever'.[417] *The Times*, now violently anti-Graham, incessantly harped on this point. The Bill, it said, would make the Home Secretary virtually a dictator over the medical profession, since all schemes for examinations conducted by the College of Physicians and the College of Surgeons (assisted by the Apothecaries Company) were to be approved by the Home Secretary's council 'with its quorum of seven nominees of the Crown, and therefore the ultimate power of nominating all examinees is virtually vested in the Home Secretary'.[418] The *Lancet* concluded that 'Chadwick and Company' had concocted the scheme of having the council of health so chosen as to place the medical profession 'at the mercy of the poor-law commissioners and the Secretary of State for the Home Department'.[419]

To be sure that their interests would be safeguarded, the general practitioners formed, in December 1844, the National Association of General Practitioners. Early in 1845 this association sent a long letter to Graham protesting against the Bill and asking that they be incorporated by charter 'into an independent college ... and placed in every respect on a footing of equality with the existing colleges of physicians and surgeons'.[420] In addition, numerous meetings were held at which memorials, pleas, and protests were drawn up and sent to Graham. Almost every town in England soon had a 'Medical Protective Society' dedicated to the task of defeating the Bill.[421] All of which proved, gibed the *Illustrated News*, that Englishmen 'did not like to take their *salts* from a Senna-tor like Sir James'.[422]

But Graham's Bill was received with a great deal of praise as well as criticism. The *Edinburgh Medical and Surgical Journal*, chief spokesman for the physicians and surgeons, declared that it was 'as perfect as the present state of the profession admits, and remarkably well suited to remove and rectify the abuses and evils of which the members of the profession have long complained'.[423]

---

[417] *Lancet*, New Ser., II, 264.
[418] *The Times*, October 8th, 1844, p. 4.   [419] *Lancet*, New Ser., II, 87.
[420] *Ibid.*, I, 135. Graham agreed to accept their request if they themselves drew up a detailed plan and signed it. *Home Office Papers* (Domestic Book), 43/68, p. 224.
[421] A list of these meetings, though not a complete one, is given in *Lancet*, I, 135.
[422] *Illustrated News*, VI, No. 144, p. 75.
[423] *Edinburgh Medical and Surgical Journal*, LXIII, 196; LXXII, 543.

If this Bill did not pass, predicted the *Journal*, a long time would elapse before another would be drawn up. The council of the Medical Association of Ireland drew up a resolution supporting the measure;[424] the usually anti-Graham *Chronicle* grudgingly supported it; [425] and even the *London Medical Gazette*, by October, was apologizing for its earlier opposition.

But the proponents of the measure did more than merely praise the Bill; they replied to each of the objections that had been raised by the opposition. They admitted that Graham's measure did not regulate or abolish quackery, but agreed with Graham that this could not be done. People, when sick, would seek aid from anyone they wished, and, in any event, who was a quack? What was quackery? When the Government had said who was and who was not a regular practitioner, the rest had to be left to the will of the individual. All that could possibly be done, wrote the *Edinburgh Medical and Surgical Journal*, was to prohibit the sale of patent medicines 'which have put hundreds silently to death'.[426] Crook, in a pamphlet entitled *The Proposed Scheme of Medical Reform in Reference to Chemists and Druggists*, declared that it would be impossible to find one person 'who could not prescribe some remedy for some disease — many of them for all diseases'. This could be stopped only by making it a felony 'for any man to take a dose of physic without prescription from a regular practitioner'. This, of course, was manifestly impossible and John Bull would strenuously resist such a law as 'unconstitutional!'[427] With respect to midwifery, proponents of the measure declared that it was right of Graham not to regulate the practice, for if a woman wanted a female instead of a male to deliver her baby she ought to be allowed that privilege. And, in 1844, it must be admitted, the majority of midwives were probably as proficient in this art as were most of the medical men.

The physicians and surgeons also regarded the registration scheme as an immense improvement on the old system because it would introduce uniformity and order into a profession where there had been, as the *Chronicle* put it, no 'gleam of order, arrange-

[424] *Home Office Papers* (Ireland), 122/18, p. 301.
[425] *Chronicle*, September 10th and 20th, 1844.
[426] *Edinburgh Medical and Surgical Journal*, LXII, 544-545.
[427] G. CROOK, *The Proposed Scheme of Medical Reform in Reference to Chemists and Druggists*, 162-163.

ment, or regularity'.[428] They did not even bother to answer the charge that the registration fees were too high.

To the criticism that the new measure introduced too much centralization and gave to the Home Office despotic power over the profession, the proponents answered that this was one of its best features because it delivered the profession, as the *Medical Times* put it, 'from ten or twelve beggarly corporations, who had the power of admitting into our Profession anybody at any price, with any attainments', and that it would end the competition between the 'different diploma factories'. With respect to the Bill's giving the Home Office despotic power, the same journal declared this to be 'simply moonshine', because 'no government have an interest in injuring or degrading the medical profession'. Furthermore, the Home Secretary was, after all, responsible to both Parliament and public.[429]

It was also pointed out that centralized control would accomplish a decent standard of education for all members of the profession with the result that no one in the future would be licensed to practise who could not prove himself qualified to do so.[430]

Finally, proponents of the measure defended the proposed council of health on the grounds that the members chosen by the Government could have no earthly interest in or desire to harm the profession; that the presence of non-medical men on the council would benefit, not hurt the profession;[431] that since the duties of such a board would be judicial and executive, laymen should serve on it as well as professional men. The *British and Foreign Medical Review* even went so far as to suggest that the Home Secretary ought to appoint *all* the members of the council at his own discretion and on his own responsibility.[432] To those medical practitioners who opposed the creation of a regulating government board because they preferred to have the profession govern itself, the *Edinburgh Medical and Surgical Journal* was very critical: 'This is ... what has been going on in this country ... for the last century, and what is the result? Most complete anarchy, or no government at all; all confusion, disorder and irregularity. The

---

[428] *Chronicle*, September 10th, 1844, p. 4.
[429] *Medical Times*, X, 388, 429, 518. See also the *Edinburgh Medical and Surgical Journal*, LXIII, 187.
[430] *Ibid.*   [431] See *Medical Times*, X, 518.
[432] *Br. and For. Med. Rev.*, XXX, 220.

idea of the medical profession governing themselves is completely Utopian.'[433] And those who objected to the council because it was a nominated rather than elected one, the same journal accused of doing so merely because the representative or elective system had become popular in the political arena and because it sounded well.[434]

In addition to those who opposed and those who favoured the Bill there were a considerable number who opposed some parts of it and favoured others, felt that despite its weaknesses and shortcomings regulation of some kind was necessary, and were therefore willing to accept it.

Because of the criticisms, pro and con, which his proposed measure had evoked, Graham decided to frame a new Bill which he hoped would be acceptable to all. This Bill, which he presented to the House on February 25th, 1845, exempted the universities of Oxford and Cambridge and hence secured to them all of their privileges; permitted the Apothecaries Company to prosecute all unregistered practitioners who practised without a licence from their body; made it a penal offence for any person falsely to assume the title of physician, surgeon, apothecary, or doctor; and provided for compulsory examinations for all midwives. The Bill proposed to retain both the registration system and the council of health provided for in the first measure, although Graham did not agree to recommend to the Crown the appointment of general practitioners to the council.[435]

But the new Bill was still not palatable to the general practitioners. They admitted that it was a vastly improved one; that it was 'a just concession to reason, justice, and humanity';[436] that Graham had sought to conciliate all parties; but that it still gave too much power to the Home Secretary and so destroyed the independence of the profession. Furthermore, they objected to the registration system, which created, according to the Lancet, 'an aristocracy amongst the medical practitioners'.[437]

The physicians and surgeons, since they lost none of their vested rights, continued to support the measure. In a pamphlet entitled,

[433] Edinburgh Medical and Surgical Journal, LXIII, 181.   [434] Ibid., 184.
[435] See Hansard, 3rd Ser., LXXVII, 1211 et seq.
[436] Lancet, New Ser., I, 241. See also Medical Gazette, XXXV, 717.
[437] Ibid., 296.

Observations on the Education and Examination for Degrees in Medicine as Affected by the New Medical Bill, Richard Quain defended the registration system on the grounds that it would serve to encourage the general practitioners 'to labour for the acquisition of additional honours' such as the title of Doctor of Medicine.[438] Lucius, another pamphleteer, defended the council of health declaring that it was 'impossible to conceive a Board better calculated by its constitution to answer the purposes for which it is intended'.[439]

The reaction of the press was equally contradictory. The *Globe* opposed the whole scheme because it did not specifically abolish quackery.[440] The *London Morning Chronicle* mildly approved the Bill because it provided for examinations for midwifery.[441] The *Illustrated News* supported the measure because it protected the profession from 'false pretenders' and the public from uneducated practitioners. [442] The *Edinburgh Review* was loud in its praises, stating that 'the thanks of the medical profession, as well as the country at large, are due to him [Graham] for the address and success with which he has reconciled conflicting interests'.[443]

But the conflicting interests had not been reconciled and Graham knew it. To achieve that goal he agreed to meet with a deputation from the Medical Protective Assembly. The latter at once asked Graham that they be allowed to form a college of their own to be known as 'The Royal College of General Practitioners in Medicine Surgery and Midwifery'. Graham agreed on the following conditions:

1. That the general practitioners agree unequivocally to accept such a charter if granted,[444]
2. that the college have two representatives on the council of health,
3. that the course of education to be established be subject to the approval of the council of health,
4. that everyone, physicians, surgeons, and general practitioners must submit to a general examination given by a board of

[438] RICHARD QUAIN, F.R.S., *Observations on the Education and Examination for Degrees in Medicine as Affected by The New Medical Bill*, 56.
[439] LUCIUS, *op. cit.*, 13.   [440] *Globe*, April 3rd, 1845, p. 2.
[441] *Chronicle*, February 26th, 1845, p. 5.
[442] *Illustrated News*, VI, No. 148, p. 129.   [443] *Edin. Rev.*, LXXXI, 271-272.
[444] *Home Office Papers* (Domestic Book), 43/69, p. 167.

physicians and surgeons. Those who passed the exam. and wished to be physicians must be twenty-six years of age and pass a test given by the College of Physicians before they could register as physicians; those wishing to be surgeons had to be twenty-six and pass an exam. given by the College of Surgeons; those wanting to be general practitioners had to be twenty-two and pass an exam. given by their college,

5.   that all colleges require five years of study,

6.   that the penal clauses of the Apothecaries Act be retained.[445]

The deputation agreed to these terms and on May 7th, 1845, Graham asked leave to recommit the Bill incorporating the new terms. If it did not then pass, he said, 'I confess I shall absolutely despair'.[446]

During the debates on the recommitted Bill, Graham made three more alterations in it. First, instead of an examination before a joint board of physicians and surgeons, the first, or general exam. should be given by a board of general practitioners to be followed by one by the joint board. Those who passed both were to be recognized as general practitioners and to be members of the College of Surgeons. Secondly, one who moved from one part of the kingdom to another should be admitted to the corresponding college there. Finally, the council of health was to be cut to thirteen members.[447]

These changes, which, in the opinion of The Times, were so great that the Bill now 'bore no resemblance to the original',[448] and which made the Bill 'extremely satisfactory', in the opinion of the Chronicle,[449] did not make it acceptable to the profession. The general practitioners still did not like it because the membership of the council of health was to consist of one secretary of state and twelve others appointed by the Crown. As a consequence, said the Lancet, 'the leaden weight of patronage and courtly sycophancy will exercise its pernicious effect'.[450] Furthermore, it still objected to the 'degraded position' assigned to them in the registration list.

---

[445] Three Reports by the Joint Deputation of the Society of Apothecaries and the National Association of General Practitioners Appointed to Confer with the Secretary of State, etc., Report I, 10-14. At the same time he continued to refuse to grant a charter to the Apothecaries Society or to appoint any of that group to the council of health. Home Office Papers (Domestic Book), 43/69, pp. 66-70, 165-166.

[446] Hansard, 3rd Ser., LXXX, 257.

[447] Ibid., LXXXII, 1169-1170.   [448] The Times, July 28th, 1845, p. 4.

[449] Chronicle, June 9th, 1845, p. 4.   [450] Lancet, New Ser., II, 185.

Graham, on the other hand, would not change the registration plan nor 'consent to give up in any point the principle of Nomination by the Crown as it now appears in the Bill'.[451]

And now the physicians and surgeons, 'incurably obstinate in their resolve to live on at all hazards as private clubs', as the *Chronicle* put it, joined in the opposition to the Bill. In the first instance, they objected to the creation of a college of general practitioners, for, according to the *Edinburgh Medical and Surgical Journal*, '99 in 100 [of the general practitioners] are most imperfectly educated, all engaged in the trading, money-making parts of the profession, and not one in 100 of them distinguished by anything like science or liberality of mind'.[452] The physicians objected to having to take an exam. given by general practitioners and to the permission given to that group to fill all medical and surgical offices, because the general practitioners were not only the youngest (22 years of age) but also the least educated of all medical men. The surgeons protested against the new colleges being made 'co-ordinate in professional rank and importance with the existing Colleges of Physicians and Surgeons',[453] as well as to the clause by which general practitioners were deemed capable of practising surgery.

Completely discouraged, as well as disgusted, with the reception accorded his efforts at reform, Graham gave up the struggle and dropped his reform Bill with the announcement that he would not again introduce a Bill on the subject unless there was 'a reasonable probability of its giving satisfaction to the Profession generally', and that he did not then 'entertain any such expectation'.[454]

And so the first major effort at reform in the medical field ended in failure. It failed partly because the physicians and surgeons, who already had all they wanted or could get, had nothing to gain by the proposed reform and did not want to weaken their favoured position by acceding to the general practitioner's demands for equality.[455] Corporations like these are inherently selfish and

---

[451] *Home Office Papers* (Domestic Book), 43/68, p. 340.

[452] *Edinburgh Medical and Surgical Journal*, LXIV, 255.

[453] *Three Reports by the Joint Dep. of Apoth., and the Nat. Assoc. of Gen. Pract.*, No. II, 18.

[454] *Home Office Papers* (Domestic Book), 43/70, pp. 360-361.

[455] See the *Medical Times*, XIII, 282, and *The Medico-Chirurgical Review and Journal of Practical Medicine*, New Ser., IV, 239-240.

automatically oppose any changes which they think will alter their favoured position. The masses, for their part, were completely apathetic since they knew little about the subject and cared less. It was not a popular type of reform in which public support could be used to break down the indifference of legislators. Furthermore, the profession as a whole really did not want reform, objected to government interference, and insisted that when reform was needed it should come from the profession itself — to be planned and executed by medical men. Experience has abundantly shown, however, that if the initiative is left to the profession, little reform beneficial to the public is likely to result. This, of course, is due not only to their 'let alone' attitude, but also to the fact that the members of the medical profession were, and are yet, a divided body torn by dissensions, jealousies, and clashing opinions about medical polity. Finally, the medical profession, like other groups and 'interests', were opposed to increasing the power and authority of the central government. They preferred local health boards,[456] which they could more easily control, to a national council of health. Local anarchy was preferable in their minds to the centralization, order, and efficiency which could be achieved in the type of unitary state towards which Peel's Government was inexorably moving.

Economic and Fiscal Reform

In addition to administering the Home Office and carrying reform into as many fields as possible, Graham performed yeoman service in helping Peel frame and carry through the House those economic and fiscal reforms for which this administration is justly famous. Here Graham was assuredly the rod and the staff which comforted Peel. 'Your cordial support and entire and unreserved confidence have been my chief stay',[457] was Peel's own admission of his reliance on Graham. It was natural that it should have been so, for few men knew as much about business as did Graham.

[456] See the article, 'The Medical Policy of the United Kingdom', in *West. Rev.*, XLV, 29-46.
[457] Peel to Graham, July 5th, 1846, in *Peel Papers*, CCLXXII, 142-143 (Br. Mus. Add. MSS. 40452).

Business acumen and the ability to think objectively were priceless assets to Peel and Graham for when they took office the country was in the throes of a serious depression. Not only was there widespread unemployment and low wages, but defective harvests combined with the Corn Laws to keep the price of bread too high. From almost all of the industrial centres came endless tales of unemployment, suffering, starvation, and crime. As a consequence, many of the lower classes went in for direct action. Strikes occurred in scores of places, Orange processions were held in such places as Liverpool, Chartist meetings grew in number, while the National Complete Suffrage Union and Anti-Corn Law League gained numerous adherents.[458]

Economic and fiscal reform was Peel's remedy for this state of affairs. By it he hoped to stimulate industry, alleviate distress, and balance the budget. And since cheaper and more abundant food was the most urgent need of the moment, the Corn Laws, which regulated both the price and the supply, had to be revised. Prior to 1815 the Corn Laws had been primarily regulative rather than protective, but the Law of 1815 had introduced the protective principle by forbidding the importation of foreign wheat until the home price reached 80s. a quarter. But the Law did not work well. It did not stabilize prices; it did not stabilize agriculture. It was, therefore, bitterly denounced by the commercial and industrial classes. To correct this situation Peel had introduced, in 1828, the principle of the sliding scale. Its purpose or aim was to keep the price at about 70s. a quarter. If the price rose above 73s., the import duty would be reduced to 1s. If the price fell below 62s., imported wheat was dutiable at 25s. 8d. Then, for every increase of 1s. in price there was 1s. off the duty until the price reached 73s. But this plan did not work well either, because it made trade too speculative and did not relieve the consumer. The economic distress in 1840, 1841, and 1842 caused Peel again to 'operate' on the Corn Laws. The Bill, which he introduced to the House on February 14th, 1842, retained the principle of the sliding scale. When the price of wheat was at or above 73s., importation would be subject to a minimum duty of 1s., when it fell to 50-51s. there would be a maximum duty of 20s. Between these two poles

[458] *Home Office Papers* (Domestic Book), 43/62, p. 355; 43/63, p. 424; (Disturbances, London), O.S. 252; (Law Office), 49/8, pp. 430-433.

there was a carefully graduated scale of duties which rose when prices fell and declined as prices rose.[459]

On the second day of debate on Peel's Bill, Graham defended it in a long and able speech. It was not, he said, a question of protection or no protection, but the *kind* of protection desired. He supported this Bill 'because it abandoned a high scale of protection; because . . . it would diminish greatly the frauds in the averages . . . by diminishing . . . temptation; . . . because it would give a degree of certainty to the speculation in Corn by fixing a maximum duty . . .; and because it would enable the holders of foreign Corn to bring it to market before the shipping duty had reached its highest point'.[460] The principle here enunciated is to agree to the lowest duty consistent with adequate protection for agriculture. This was not to be considered a final measure, he said, for the term 'finality' was just a phantom when applied to legislation. 'A very virtuous resolution', wrote the *Morning Chronicle*, because the question now became one of expediency and time.[461] Graham admitted, as he had put it in his celebrated *Corn and Currency*, that the landlords were entitled 'to a liberal protecting duty',[462] and he was not *yet* quite convinced of the necessity nor desirability of total repeal. At the same time both he and Peel would unquestionably have gone further in that direction than most of their colleagues.

While, therefore, Graham was not in favour of total repeal he was, by 1842, well on the way towards free trade. He was becoming convinced that cheaper food was the only remedy for the suffering caused by low wages and unemployment. Not only that, but the safety of the country was unstable, he wrote to Peel, 'when it depends on sunshine and passing clouds'.[463] He attributed the concentrated violence which had been brought to bear against the Corn Laws to the fact that the introduction of machinery had increased industrial production faster than the means of consumption.[464] By the end of the year, Graham was convinced that

[459] See PEEL, *Memoirs*, II, App. 327-357.
[460] *Hansard*, 3rd Ser., LX, 515 et seq.
[461] *Chronicle*, February 17th, 1842, p. 5.   [462] *Corn and Currency*, 14.
[463] *Peel Papers*, CCLXVII, 51 (Br. Mus. Add. MSS. 40447).
[464] *Ibid.*, CCLXVI, 60-61 (Br. Mus. Add. MSS. 40446). To pretend that machinery was the cause of distress instead of the Corn Laws was a piece of 'despicable trickery', in the opinion of the *Manchester Guardian* (March 2nd, 1842, p. 2).

free trade was inevitable. 'It is a question of time', he wrote to Peel. 'The next change . . . must be to an open trade; . . . But the next change must be the last; it is not prudent to hurry it; next Session is too soon; and as you cannot make a decisive alteration, it is far wiser to make none.'[465] Free trade was inevitable but the time was not yet ripe. According to Trevelyan, had Peel and Graham attempted total repeal in 1842, 'the Protectionist crew would have cut the throats of their officers before they had perfected their arrangements for handing over the ship to the enemy'.[466]

Early in 1843 Graham openly announced that the principles of free trade 'were those of common sense' and were now disputed by few people.[467] Conditions were steadily improving by the autumn of the year and the anti-Corn Law agitation subsided, but Graham had already concluded that the Corn Laws could not survive another year of hard times. England was now a commercial and industrial country, and unless these classes were prosperous the agricultural classes could not be. Like Peel, he was impressed by the inexorable logic of statistics — statistics of population which revealed that while the rural areas were certainly not being depopulated, nevertheless the town population was increasing by about 200,000 annually. This meant that total repeal of the Corn Laws was, as Graham put it, only a matter of time.

On February 7th, 1842, Graham had written to Lord de Grey: 'We shall succeed with our corn; our great difficulties will be taxation and finance.'[468] He was right on both counts. The Corn Bill was passed on April 5th, by substantial majorities, but the 'Free Trade' budget encountered fierce opposition. It provided for a reduction of duties on 769 articles, chiefly raw materials. The resulting loss of revenue, aggravated by the fact that the Melbourne Government had bequeathed to the Peel ministry huge deficits, was to be made up by the imposition for five years of an

---

[465] Graham to Peel, December 30th, 1842, in PARKER, *Life of Peel*, II, 551.

[466] TREVELYAN, *Life of Bright*, 87.

[467] *Hansard*, 3rd Ser., LXVI, 687. The *Herald* (February 16th, 1843, p. 4) described this speech as 'the speech of the night'. But, the *West. Rev.* (XLI, 348), bitterly assailed Graham for changing his opinions on this subject. See also, *Chronicle*, February 20th, 1843, and *Post*, March 13th, 1843, p. 4.

[468] See PARKER, *Life of Graham*, I, 316.

income tax of about 3 per cent. Peel estimated that this tax would furnish a revenue of about £4,380,000, which would enable him to liquidate the deficit in the treasury (about £2,469,000), reduce the tariffs, and give the country a surplus for the first time in years.

Despite strenuous opposition from Hume, Russell, Baring, and others, Peel was able to carry the measure because it had retained the duties on corn and was therefore approved by his own party.

While distress was still prevalent at the commencement of the year 1843, and disturbances such as the Rebecca riots in Wales[469] agitated and alarmed many people, it was not long before decided improvements were discernible. The harvests were good, business picked up, prices rose steadily[470] and the national revenue increased. 1844 was even better, but 1845 was to be the year of trouble. It started out peacefully enough. In February the Bill relieving sugar of taxation to the tune of £1,300,000 was passed and the duties on 430 other articles were taken off entirely.[471] Graham was willing to go even further along the free trade line by suggesting a reduction in the tea duties, but Peel did not think the budget could stand this loss of revenue.

Early in March the troubles started. It was proposed that in applying any surplus revenue to the relief of taxes due regard be had for helping the agricultural classes. Graham stoutly resisted this motion and in doing so he claimed that he was a friend of agriculture. It was entitled to 'some' protection, he said, but such protection would have to be 'consistent with the interests of the entire community'. If the population of the country continued to increase, 'must not also the importation of corn increase, since the quantity produced by the land has been admitted to be inadequate to the demand for some years past?' It followed,

[469] Poverty, occasioned by three successive crop failures, was the chief cause of these riots. They took the form of opposition to tolls, church-rates, workhouses, the Poor Law, etc. Hard physical labour and a deficiency of food, causing what Lord Bacon once described as a 'rebellion of the belly', was the underlying trouble. See *Home Office Papers* (Commission of Inquiry), 74/1, pp. 342-343; (Domestic Book), 117/5, p. 264.

[470] TOOKE, *History of Prices*, IV, 14, 50.

[471] Graham was certain the Bill would pass since the Radicals would protect the Government from the Whigs. The only thing he feared, he wrote to Stanley, was that 'the Country Gentlemen do not desert in sullen sadness'. Graham to Stanley, February 14th, 1845, in *Graham Papers*.

therefore, as night the day, that the sliding scale had to be abandoned, because

> the effect of the sliding scale . . . is to lay the market open . . . to the operation of speculation in corn at the critical juncture immediately preceding the harvest. Between the periods when the stock of old corn runs short, and the corn of the approaching harvest has not yet been brought to market, there are a variety of means taken to run the prices up to a high pitch to the detriment of the community at large, in order that advantage be taken of the sliding scale to introduce a quantity of foreign grain at the lowest possible duty and at the highest possible price.[472]

So, since the sliding scale did not work, and since he did not believe in a fixed duty, free trade was the only alternative. Hearing this speech of Graham's, Bright said he did not know whether it was designed 'to give more hope to the Opposition, or more consolation to the Ministerial side of the House'.[473] The Country Party was dismayed and angered. Croker, long a friend of Graham, wrote that they were 'out of temper' with him, and Graham, now also out of temper, replied:

> We have laboured hard, and not in vain, to restore the prosperity of the country, and to give increased security to the aristocracy, by improving the condition and diminishing the discontent of the great masses of the people. We have effected this object without inflicting any real injury on the landed proprietors; yet we are scouted as traitors, and we are denounced as if we were time-serving traders in politics seeking to retain place by the sacrifice of the interests of our friends.
> The country gentlemen cannot be more ready to give us the death-blow than we are to receive it. If they will rush on their own destruction, they must have their way; we have endeavoured to save them, and they regard us as enemies for so doing.
> If we have lost the confidence and good will of the country party, our days are numbered; and the time will come when this party will bitterly deplore the fall of Sir Robert Peel, and when in vain they will wish that they had not overthrown a Government which its enemies could not vanquish, but which its supporters abandoned and undermined.[474]

On May 26th, in order to widen the growing breach in the

---

[472] *Hansard*, 3rd Ser., LXXVIII, 993.   [473] *Annual Register* (1845), 98.
[474] CROKER, *Corr. and Diaries*, III, 31.

Conservative ranks, Lord John Russell introduced a series of resolutions on the state of the nation. It was high time, he said, that some specific action be taken on the Corn Law question. Graham assumed the task of answering Russell and he did so most convincingly. The country was now prosperous; wages had increased while the price of such necessities as wheat, barley, oats, beef, pork, sugar, and coffee had gone down; crime and pauperism had declined sharply; the cost of poor relief had been cut by at least 20 per cent; the amount spent on education had increased from £30,000 annually in 1841 to £75,000; new churches had been built; there had been £5,000,000 bullion in the treasury and £16,400,000 of Bank of England paper in circulation in 1841 while now the amounts had increased to £16,000,000 in the treasury and £21,163,000 of paper. At the conclusion of this speech, in which, wrote the *Manchester Guardian*, he sounded like 'the special pleader for the Anti-Corn Law League',[475] he moved the previous question and carried the House by a vote of 182-102.[476]

A week or so later, Villiers brought in his usual motion for total repeal. Graham, who was now doing most of the speaking on all manner of subjects for the Government,[477] opposed Villiers's motion and it was defeated by a majority of 132. In opposing it, Graham declared that a high duty on corn would check imports in years of scarcity when corn was most needed. A low duty, on the other hand, was no protection at all. England had reached a point where the next change must be to total repeal. The present law was working, he said, but it might not if a bad harvest should come.[478] So, by the summer of 1845, Graham was willing to accept total repeal if there was a diminution in the production of corn in England. All that was needed, then, was a bad harvest. He did not have to wait long. On July 30th, the *Morning Chronicle* reported that the crops did not look good and that if they failed, Peel's Government would have to repeal the Corn Laws 'with' the

---

[475] *Manchester Guardian*, June 4th, 1845, p. 4.

[476] *Hansard*, 3rd Ser., LXXX, 896-920.

[477] Gladstone, Stanley, and Follett had left the cabinet. According to Greville (*Memoirs*, V, 202), the whole weight of government labour now 'fell on Peel and Graham'.

[478] The *Chronicle* (May 30th, 1845, p. 5), argued that this speech proved the necessity for repeal.

s

landlords or 'against' them.[479] A few days later the Duke of Norfolk told the Duke of Argyll that a blight had hit the potato crop in Sussex and a potato merchant told Peel that the crop was ruined in the Isle of Wight as well as in most of the south-eastern counties.[480] On August 5th Russell forecast a deficient harvest, but Graham, in order to quiet the fears of many, chided Russell with being alarmed by 'some mist that hung over the Surrey Hills'.[481]

By mid-August the weather was the chief concern of virtually the entire country. A rainy spring was followed by a very cold summer, the mean temperature of every week from July 6th to September 28th being four degrees below average.[482] 'I know not that the state of affairs is exactly sound', wrote Graham, 'when Ministers are driven to study the barometer with so much anxiety.' He knew of no law by which twenty-five million people crowded in a narrow island could be fed when 'Heaven denies the blessing of abundance'. And then came the fatal question: 'What is the legislation which most aggravates or mitigates this dispensation of Providence?'[483] Peel and Graham, wrote the Duke of Argyll, 'were like men standing on a watch-tower, and seeing all around the horizon the distant gloom of a great but slowly invading host'.[484] Part of this 'host' came from Ireland where the effects of the failure of the potato crop was reported to Graham by the Lord-Lieutenant in a steady stream of letters.[485] On getting this information, Peel wrote to Graham that in his opinion, 'the removal of impediments to import [was] the only effectual remedy'.[486] On the same day, their letters crossing, Graham wrote to Peel that the crops had failed in Holland and Belgium and that they had opened their ports to foreign grain. Should England do the same? 'Could we with propriety remit duties

---

[479] The *Chronicle*, May 30th, 1845, p. 5.
[480] ARGYLL, *op. cit.*, I, 271; *Home Office Papers* (Domestic Book), 43/70, p. 14; *Peel Papers*, CCLXXI, 169 (Br. Mus. Add. MSS. 40451).
[481] *Hansard*, 3rd Ser., LXXXII, 1489.
[482] *Illustrated News*, VII, No. 186, p. 326.
[483] Graham to Peel, August 15th, 1845, in *Peel Papers*, CCLXXI, 182-183 (Br. Mus. Add. MSS. 40451).
[484] ARGYLL, *op. cit.*, I, 272.
[485] *Home Office Papers* (Potato Failures in Ireland), 45/1080; (Ireland), 122/18, etc.
[486] Peel to Graham, in PARKER, *Life of Peel*, III, 223.

in November by Order in Council, when Parliament might so easily be called together? Can these duties, once remitted ... be ever again imposed? Ought they to be maintained in their present stringency, if the people of Ireland be reduced to the last extremity for want of food?'[487] Both knew that the Corn Laws had to go, but because the protectionists in their party accused them of free trade tendencies, they waited until the seriousness of the situation was common knowledge. Then, on October 31st, Peel summoned a cabinet meeting. At this meeting, and at subsequent ones held in November, the cabinet split on Peel's proposal that the Corn Laws be repealed. Only three members supported Peel: Graham, Aberdeen, and Herbert. Stanley agreed to a suspension of the Corn Laws for the duration of the emergency provided Peel would agree to re-impose them when it was over. Since Peel would not consent to this proposition, Stanley and the Duke of Buccleuch resigned. Failing to carry the cabinet with him, Peel, on December 6th, surrendered the seals of office and Lord John Russell was summoned by the Queen to form a government.

To do so proved to be a gigantic task. Russell had himself to blame for this because on November 22nd he had published his celebrated Edinburgh Letter to the electors in the City of London in which he had said that while Peel's Government was not responsible for the blight, it was responsible for retaining the Corn Laws. He favoured a policy of free trade. It was, as Barnes has pointed out, typical Whig policy, for 'now when it became obvious that public sentiment against landowners and the aristocracy was becoming more of a menace than the Corn Laws were a benefit, Russell prudently went over to Free Trade'.[488] It was easier to do that than to form a government. Furthermore, his party did not control the Commons and Russell knew very well that he could not carry a repeal bill through the Lords against Wellington's opposition. The latter would agree to repeal only if carried by Peel because he thought that only Conservatives knew how to govern the country. Consequently Russell wrote to both Peel and Graham asking them for a pledge to help carry a repeal bill.[489] Both refused. It amused Graham to see Russell

---

[487] *Peel Papers*, CCLXXI, 378-379 (Br. Mus. Add. MSS. 40451).
[488] BARNES, *Hist. of the Corn Laws*, 275.
[489] See *Later Corr. of Lord John Russell*, I, 104; GREVILLE, *Memoirs*, V, 261.

so confused, not knowing whether to form a government or not, making proposals and arranging plans 'as if he were in possession of royal authority'.[490] Unable to get the desired pledge from Peel and Graham and unable to get Lord Grey to serve in the same cabinet with Palmerston, Russell was unable to form a government and, as Disraeli put it, 'handed back with courtesy the poisoned chalice to Sir Robert Peel'.[491]

Peel and Graham were back in office in December and had at once to grapple with the problem. The Corn Laws had to go in spite of the fact that repeal would wreck the party. 'We have a nation to carry, as it were, in our arms, and no very great assistance on which we can rely', wrote Graham.[492] By the end of January 1846 their minds were made up and Peel proposed to the House a total repeal of the Corn Laws. The debates on this Bill were unusually bitter. The Protectionist party, which Bentinck and Disraeli had been forming out of the dissentients in the Conservative party, attacked the Bill and the traitors — Peel, Graham, et al., — who had 'sold out' the landed classes. Night after night the debates went on and it was not until February 10th that Graham made his famous speech in defence of repeal. It was perhaps the greatest speech of his career and according to the London Globe, was superior even to that given by Peel.[493] The Government, he said, had been asked to own up to the fact that they had changed their opinions. 'I answer that challenge. I do frankly avow my change of opinion, and by that avowal I dispose of whole volumes of Hansard, and of all the speeches that have been made on the charge of inconsistency.' Was this change of opinion intended to promote his own personal interests? Did it arise out of selfish personal motives? Not at all. 'All that I possess', he declared, 'is as a landlord . . . I have inherited that property, and I may add, that it is a large tract of inferior quality; and I congratulate myself that, by my position as a landlord, if the

---

[490] Graham to Fremantle, December 18th, 1845, in PARKER, Life of Graham, II, 27.

[491] BENJAMIN DISRAELI, Lord George Bentinck, A Political Biography, 221. Greville was irked: 'If Peel and Graham would communicate frankly with J. R., . . . the work would not be difficult, but there is always a great difficulty when it is necessary to deal with such men as Peel and Graham — the one cold, reserved, suspicious, and insincere, the other slippery.' Memoirs, V, 257-258.

[492] Peel Papers, CCLXXII, 90-91 (Br. Mus. Add. MSS. 40452).

[493] Globe, February 11th, 1846, p. 4.

proposed change be dangerous, it exposes me to as great risks as any landed proprietor in the three kingdoms.' Was his change of opinion occasioned by a desire for political advancement or prestige? Far from it. Had not he and Peel almost wrecked their own party? Finally, had he changed his opinion merely to exclude the Opposition from office? Not at all: 'With my entire concurrence [Peel] frankly tendered to her Majesty the office which he held . . . I concurred in that resignation; and I can truly and sincerely say, it was my earnest desire that this measure should be brought forward by the noble Lord opposite [Russell] in whose hands I think it would have been more properly placed.' He agreed to repeal because he now believed in free trade and had it not been for the unforseeable crop failure he would have favoured gradually but progressively diminishing protection to agriculture until repeal was achieved. He was now frankly opposed to any fixed duty and since the sliding scale 'would neither slide nor move', total repeal was inescapable.

What had caused him to change his mind since 1842? In the first place, a careful study of statistics had proved to him that wages did not fall with falling prices. Secondly, he no longer believed that England could feed herself. Thirdly, importing more grain would increase England's exports and so promote the prosperity of all classes. It had been openly stated in the debates that the Conservative party had been broken up, social relationships destroyed and the administration dissolved. He deeply regretted all that, but he had the satisfaction of believing in his conscience 'that this proposal will rescue a great and powerful nation from anarchy, from misery, and from ruin'.[494]

The resolutions passed the first reading on February 27th by a majority of ninety-seven. In the debates on the second reading, in March, Graham added new arguments in favour of free trade. The Corn Laws, keeping food prices high, prevented the masses from buying manufactured goods and so were harmful to industry. In addition, free trade made for peace in the world. He concluded his speech by quoting the following lines from Pope's *Windsor Forest*:

> The time shall come, when, free as seas or wind,
> Unbounded Thames shall flow for all mankind,

[494] *Hansard*, 3rd Ser., LXXXIII, 710-725.

> Whole nations enter with each swelling tide,
> And seas but join the regions they divide;
> Earth's distant ends our glory shall behold,
> And the new world launch forth to seek the old.[495]

On March 23rd the second reading was carried by a majority of eighty-eight, and the third, on May 15th, by a majority of ninety-eight, after two great speeches by Peel and Graham.[496] Wellington, even though he disliked the measure, piloted it safely through the Lords and it finally became law on June 25th. Thus England became a free-trade area.

Wellington attributed the end of the Corn Laws to rotten potatoes, saying that 'they put Peel in his d—d fright'.[497] Croker, on the other hand, insists that Peel and Graham were driven to repeal by fear of the Anti-Corn Law League.[498] It is true that Graham considered the political principles of the League dangerous, that he feared it in that sense and therefore was happy at the prospect that repeal would end the League. He was, like Peel, influenced by the potato rot, but the fact is that by the summer of 1845 he was already a free trader. It was not fear, therefore, but the irresistible logic of facts carefully studied that caused him to take the final plunge. For the repeal of the Corn Laws, therefore, Graham must be given credit at least equal to that given Peel. In fact, Peel himself admitted that Graham's responsibility was equal to his.[499] It was an act of political courage and wise, disinterested statesmanship. Both knew that repeal would mean the dissolution of their party and the end of political power, and yet they were willing to sacrifice that, as well as long-established personal friendships, in order to carry out a policy they believed beneficial to the country.

Foreign Policy

While the years from 1841 to 1846 were years of tremendous activity on the domestic front, they were years of peace and tranquillity in foreign relations. With relative ease the Canadian

---

[495] *Hansard*, 3rd Ser., LXXXV, 162-185.

[496] CHARLES MACKAY, in his *Forty Years Recollections, 1830-1870* (I, 293), says Graham's speech was the 'most remarkable', and the *Chronicle* (March 30th, 1846, p. 4) described it as having been given with 'admirable skill and power'.

[497] See GREVILLE, *Memoirs*, V, 282-283.

[498] CROKER, *Corr. and Diaries*, III, 66.   [499] See PARKER, *Life of Graham*, II, 22.

border controversy with the United States was settled in 1842 by the Webster-Ashburton treaty; in 1846 the Oregon squabble was brought to a satisfactory conclusion; and in 1842 the unlovely war with China was concluded by the signing of the Treaty of Nanking. Graham had no part in the solution of any of these problems.[500] But he did concern himself with developments in India and New Zealand.

In the matter of India he opposed the 'forward' policy of Lord Ellenborough just as he had opposed it when Lord Auckland had been the Governor-General. As a member of the cabinet he agreed to the annexation of Sind in 1843 because it had already taken place, but he did not like it. When Ellenborough, despite his being censured for his aggression against Sind, perpetrated a similar attack on Gwalior in 1844, the Government decided to recall him. Rumour had it that Graham was going to resign from the cabinet and take over the now vacant India Office,[501] but there was no truth to it. However, Ellenborough had to be given a post of some kind and Graham suggested that he be given the office of Postmaster-General, but, he wrote to Stanley, Ellenborough got 'on his high horse' and insisted upon the Presidency of the Board of Control.[502] To keep peace in the party ranks it was found necessary for Peel to accede to Ellenborough's demand.

The New Zealand difficulties concerned the New Zealand Company. This joint-stock company had been formed in 1838 and under Wakefield's driving leadership had decided to colonize New Zealand. When the French showed signs of interest, the British Government sent Captain Hobson to negotiate with the native Maoris for the cession of the islands. The resulting Treaty of Waitongi (1840) caused heated controversy wherever it was discussed. To the Maoris it was a good treaty because in exchange for ceding sovereignty to England the Maori chiefs received a guarantee of their lands with the right of preemption for the British Crown if any of this land were sold. Before the New Zealand Company settlers arrived, the British Government had therefore

[500] He wrote to Peel that England should have taken the port of Chusan rather than Hong Kong because it had a better harbour and superior climate. *Peel Papers*, CCCLXXIV, 20 (Br. Mus. Add. MSS. 40554).
[501] See *The Times*, April 13th, 1844, p. 4, and *Globe*, April 12th, 1844, p. 2.
[502] *Graham Papers*, Letter to Stanley, October 22nd, 1844.

become the sovereign power. The settlers almost immediately began to speculate in lands and consequently found themselves in conflict not with the natives but with the English Crown. The settlers, irked by the depression of 1843, defective land titles, native interference, and the indifference of the Company, accused the Government of defending native rights (in living up to the treaty) against those of Englishmen. In June 1845 the conflict which had been raging between the Company and the Colonial Office was brought out in public when spokesmen for the former accused Stanley of bungling the problem.

Graham immediately defended Stanley's actions. The difficulties in New Zealand could all be traced, he said, to two things: disputed land titles and the lawless spirit in the islands. The Treaty was a sacred obligation and had to be 'religiously observed'. This being so, all claimants to land, native or English, must prove their titles. Those who did not forfeited those titles and claims, and 'the right of the Crown to all unregistered lands is indisputable'. As to local government in New Zealand, the Treaty of Waitongi gave to the natives the rights and privileges of Englishmen and 'if you adopt a representative form of government, you must, either admit the natives to a share in the representation, or exclude them'. To admit them would be premature; to exclude them would cause civil strife. Consequently, since no definite policy could, nor should, now be announced, Stanley's authority must of necessity continue to be flexible.[503] Charles Buller's motion of censure, which had caused the debate, was easily defeated and Stanley's conduct thereby vindicated.

But Graham found it easier to defend Stanley's conduct than to defend his own actions in an incident which related to foreign affairs in the first instance but which ultimately became a first-rate domestic issue. On March 1st, 1844, he issued a warrant to the officials at the Post Office authorizing them to open the letters of Mazzini, the Italian patriot, then a political exile in England, and to make copies of such letters for his inspection.[504] Mazzini had been corresponding with the Bandierra brothers (deserters from the Austrian Navy), who were shot by the Austrian Government for having participated in the Neapolitan insurrection. It was

---

[503] *Hansard*, 3rd Ser., LXXXI, 914 et seq.
[504] *Home Office Papers* (Post Office), 79/4.

then incorrectly deduced by many that Lord Aberdeen, the Foreign Secretary, had sent the information obtained by opening Mazzini's letters to the Austrian Government for use in the trial.

The right to open letters at the Post Office, conferred during the reign of Queen Anne, had been confirmed by the Post Office Act of 1837. On the request of Aberdeen, Graham had then merely exercised his legal prerogative in opening Mazzini's letters. On June 14th, 1844, a petition on behalf of four persons (two foreigners, including Mazzini, and two Chartists) was presented to the House begging for the appointment of a commission of inquiry. Thomas Duncombe, who presented the petition, demanded a full explanation. This Graham refused to give saying merely that the charge was partly untrue, that the letters of three of the petitioners had not been opened at all, while in the case of Mazzini, the letters had been opened at Aberdeen's request under authority vested in him by the Act of 1837. Despite Duncombe's charge that it was an odious and unjustifiable thing to do, Graham refused to give a more explicit answer.[505]

But Duncombe could not so easily be silenced. On June 24th he proposed the appointment of a select committee to inquire into the practice of opening letters at the Post Office. Graham objected to the motion saying that while he did not like the power vested in him, it was a necessary one and that his office imposed upon him silence. Thanks to very fine speeches in his defence by Peel, Sandon, and Gladstone, the motion of Duncombe was defeated.

The House having begun the discussions, the public took up the issue and subjected Graham to such fearful abuse that Archer is undoubtedly correct in saying that 'perhaps no politician of the Gladstone Era incurred so much odium as he [Graham] did'.[506] Palmerston's mouthpiece, the *Morning Chronicle*, described Graham as the best English minister the Holy Alliance had yet discovered and one compared to whom 'Lord Castlereagh was a novice and a liberal'.[507] The *Globe* accused Graham of having converted the Post Office into an inquisition where the fraudulent process of opening and re-sealing letters went on in a spirit alien

---

[505] *Hansard*, 3rd Ser., LXXV, 893.
[506] T. ARCHER, *Gladstone and His Contemporaries*, I, 336.
[507] *Chronicle*, June 26th, 1844, p. 5.

to English traditions of fair play.[508] *Punch* dedicated the whole of Volume VII to Graham. 'I protest,' ran one of its quips, 'that henceforth I shall never think of that crowning pile of St. Martins-le-Grand, without seeing you [Graham] in imagination working away with a crow-bar, smashing red and black wax — or, by the more subtle agency of steam, softening wafers, that the letter may open its lips, and yield up the contents of its very heart to the Secretary of the Home Department.' It concluded by suggesting Graham's elevation to the peerage as 'Lord Letterreading'.[509]

On July 2nd, 1844, Duncombe advanced to the attack once more by proposing a select committee to inquire into a department of the Post Office called the 'secret' or 'inner' office where, he charged, many letters had been opened. Graham, fed up with the whole question, countered this proposal with a demand for a full inquiry by a secret committee. It was a shrewd move, for he knew perfectly well that his own record would not suffer when compared to that of his predecessors at the Home Office and that neither he nor Aberdeen had exceeded their legal rights. He proposed that the committee should consist of nine members five of whom were to be from the Opposition. But this move did not satisfy nor silence his opponents, and the press, especially *The Times*, carried a running barrage of criticism. So, too, did the *Westminster Review*, which asserted that Graham was merely hoping to prove that he was no worse than his predecessors and that as soon as that was done, 'the petitioners might be unceremoniously dismissed'.[510]

The Committees (one in the Lords and one in the Commons) met immediately and called upon Aberdeen, Graham, and their predecessors to testify. Both committees completely exculpated Graham. The House Committee reported that very few such warrants were issued (in fact, since 1799 the annual average was only eight), and that Graham and Aberdeen had not exceeded their constitutional powers.[511]

Graham, convinced that the purpose of the investigation had been to ruin him personally, rejoiced that 'the hot iron had burnt

[508] *Globe*, July 1st, 1844, p. 2.   [509] *Punch*, VII, 2 et seq.
[510] *West. Rev.*, XLII, 236.
[511] 'Report from the Secret Committee on the Post Office', in *Graham Papers*. August 5th, 1844.

the fingers of some who were most eager to handle it',[512] and that the odious subject could be dropped. His rejoicings were short-lived, however, for in February 1845 a proposal was made by Howick in the House to inquire into the allegation of Duncombe that his own letters had been opened. Stung to the quick by Duncombe's gibe that he did not have the courage to avow having done so, Graham replied that he had ordered Mazzini's letters to be opened because there was a conspiracy on foot to attack Italy: if it had succeeded the peace of Italy and of all Europe would have been disturbed; in that case, 'England could not have remained a spectator to the conflict'. He had had the letters intercepted and without reading them had turned them over to Aberdeen. The purpose was to preserve the peace of Europe which he and Aberdeen thought threatened. It was now up to the House to decide what to do: either revoke the statute, hedge it about by legal checks, or stop criticizing those who used the power.[513] Peel and Herbert immediately defended Graham, declaring that all the members of the cabinet were equally responsible for the exercise of the power, and even Russell and Disraeli admitted that he should not be blamed for doing what all his predecessors had done.

Howick's motion was voted down by a majority of seventy-five but the question would not stay down. On April 1st, Sheil proposed that the House adopt an expression of regret that Mazzini's letters had been opened. Graham, now not a little piqued that Aberdeen was letting him take all the blame, reviewed the whole case. In October 1843 he was only one of three secretaries then in the country and he had had to do the work of all three. In August and September movements of considerable importance and danger took place in Bologna, information about which he had obtained from Lord Holland at Venice. In October the Austrian Minister, Nieuman, told him that encouragement to insurrection was being given by Mazzini (whose name, Graham said, he had never even heard before). Nieuman had also given him a paper, the *Giovanena Italia*, which contained an inflammatory article written by Mazzini. From that date until January 1844 he had heard no more about Mazzini. By then Aberdeen was back in England and told him that London was the focal

[512] Graham to Croker, *Ibid*.
[513] *Hansard*, 3rd Ser., LXXVII, 699-710.

point from which the Italian movements were directed. During February Mazzini was discovered in England carrying on an extensive correspondence with revolutionists. Consequently it was decided to ascertain just who Mazzini was and what he was doing. They discovered that he had established a secret society while in asylum in Marseilles, France, and that this society had killed three Italian refugees. The sentence of death had been signed by Mazzini, and the King of France had therefore ordered him to leave the country. From Marseilles, Mazzini had subsequently gone to Switzerland, to Belgium, and at last to England where Graham had ordered Mazzini's letters to be opened. He thought it was to England's interest to do so. If he was mistaken, he could not help it, for 'wisdom after the event is not very valuable'.[514]

Having heard this frank and complete explanation and become thoroughly tired of the subject, the House defeated Sheil's motion and dropped the matter. Early in April, however, Marriotti, a friend of Mazzini, wrote to Duncombe that Graham's allegation that Mazzini was responsible for the death of the three refugees was 'a foul, base, and dastardly lie'.[515] Duncombe took it up with Graham and when the latter, after investigation, found that he had been wrong, publicly apologized to Mazzini who did not even have the graciousness to accept the apology.[516]

The memory of this interesting case died slowly and years were to pass before Graham was free from insulting innuendoes and insinuations that he had tampered with the letters of a persecuted exile. His opponents, out of party and personal malice, failed to consider the other side of the question. Mazzini was sheltered in England on the assumption that he would not involve England in any danger by using the sanctuary thus afforded him as a shield behind which he could develop plots and organize revolutionary movements against other governments. But that was precisely what Mazzini had done. At the time, opening his letters seemed like an odious trick, but as Justin McCarthy has so aptly put it, 'It would in the end be to the heavy injury of all fugitives from

---

[514] *Hansard*, 3rd Ser., LXXVIII, 1342-1353.
[515] For Marriotti's letter to Duncombe, see *Life and Correspondence of Thomas Slingsby Duncombe*, ed. by his son, T. H. Duncombe, I, 335.
[516] See Mazzini's letter to Duncombe, in *Ibid.*, 322-323.

despotic rule if to shelter them brought such consequences [revolution] on the countries that offered them a home.'[517]

In the Mazzini case Graham's conduct had been proper. He had used a legal prerogative as his predecessors had done. He was correct also in refusing in the first instance to discuss the case in the House because if in each such case, upon challenge, a full disclosure had to be made, the power itself would become largely useless and inoperative. Furthermore, he honestly believed that Mazzini's actions were a threat to the safety and peace of Europe, including England. As for Duncombe's charge that his own letters had been opened, it is not clear why Graham did not frankly state that a warrant to open them had been issued on August 19th, 1843, but that it was rescinded on the twenty-third without any having been opened.[518]

Brougham may have been right when he wrote that Graham had 'come out of the fire unsinged',[519] but Graham did not think so and once jocularly remarked that 'he would go down to posterity famous only for having opened letters at the Post Office'.[520]

Ireland

When the Melbourne Government was overthrown in 1841 the Whigs were entirely discomfited and could only hope that the prevailing distress would cause discord and dissension in the Conservative ranks. 'Above all,' wrote Greville, 'they look to Ireland as a great and constant source of difficulty, and they evidently hope that O'Connell's influence will now be successfully exerted to render the Government of Ireland impossible.'[521]

The first hurdle which had to be got over was not O'Connell, however, but the personnel of the Irish Government. The post of Lord-Lieutenant was given to Earl Grey. It was not a good choice for Grey was too Protestant for that post. In addition, his brother-in-law, the Earl of Enniskillen, was an Orangeman. Lord Eliot, who was appointed Chief Secretary, was inclined to the Catholic side, and so too was Lord Sugden, the Lord Chancellor.

---

[517] JUSTIN MCCARTHY, *History of Our Own Times*, I, 211.

[518] *Home Office Papers* (Post Office), 79/4.

[519] Brougham to Graham, February 21st, 1845, in *Graham Papers*. That was also the view of Croker, Normanby, and others.

[520] In PARKER, *Life of Graham*, I, 447.   [521] GREVILLE, *Memoirs*, IV, 394.

To make matters worse, the latter did not have a reputation for impartiality. All that can be said in defence of these choices is that Grey, Eliot, and Sugden may have been the least offensive to O'Connell.[522] Selecting a Viceroy connected with one party and a Secretary who had the confidence of a different party guaranteed weakness and divided counsels where unity of command was seriously needed and was to prove a constant source of embarrassment to Peel and Graham. The likelihood of an open rupture between Eliot and Grey continually haunted Graham.

It was an unruly crew and one which caused trouble immediately. Grey gave almost all the patronage to Protestants and angered Eliot by not even consulting him; Lucas, the Under-Secretary, did not agree with Eliot; Sugden had more zeal than judgment. To make matters worse, now that his allies, the Whigs, were out of office, O'Connell was ready to declare war on the Conservatives because of their oft-avowed adherence to the Legislative Union, i.e., to Protestant ascendancy. Now sixty-five years of age and obviously unable to wait for another Whig Government, he decided to use his 'nuisance value' and to wring from Peel and Graham as large a measure of concession as he had wrung from Peel and Wellington in 1828-1829.

In 1840 he founded the Repeal Association, which, together with the Temperance Society,[523] began agitation for repeal of the Act of Union. Each year thereafter it became more formidable as the business depression deepened and as increasing numbers of priests joined the movement. Huge mass meetings were held at frequent intervals; the whole island went on an emotional spree. O'Connell took care not to incite his followers to the use of force, but his language was equivocal to say the least and that he was trying to intimidate the Government was apparent to all.

How to handle these meetings was a question about which Graham quickly made up his mind. 'There must be', he wrote to Peel on October 21st, 1841, 'a steady and marked discountenancing of the Repeal party, and a decided preference [for those] who advocate the British connection; an impartial and liberal policy; and equal justice administered to Roman Catholics . . .'[524] And

---

[522] This is the view taken by the *West. Rev.*, XLI, 263.
[523] This society had been founded by Father Mathew, a Capuchin Friar.
[524] Graham to Peel, in PARKER, *Life of Graham*, I, 350-351.

how best to uphold the Legislative Union in face of O'Connell's repeal agitation? Simply by taking no official notice of it, for, 'If we wait, the Repeal movement will subside; or, if our forebearance be mistaken for timidity, the Repeal Party will become more daring and give us an opportunity of striking a blow which the occasion will justify in the eyes even of moderate men.'[525]

But when this policy was pursued, the repeal movement grew in magnitude instead of subsiding because O'Connell and his followers mistook the Government's forbearance for timidity. As a result, and to warn O'Connell that forbearance came from strength instead of weakness, in May 1843 the Government passed an Arms Act. This Law required the possessors of arms to have a licence to own them, to have them branded by government officials, and to have them properly registered. Anyone who possessed unlawful arms such as pikes, daggers, and spears was to be punished by imprisonment.[526] The Law was not materially different from others which had been passed on previous occasions of trouble in Ireland but it was hotly debated in Parliament and in the country at large.

Whigs, like Russell and others, attacked the Bill as unnecessary and as likely merely to aggravate the situation. This opposition was to be expected and Graham took it gracefully enough. What annoyed him was that there were differences of opinion within his own party. Wellington and Stanley supported Graham's insistence upon a 'strong' policy; Peel desired a more moderate programme; Disraeli opposed the Bill as a 'contemptible and futile' measure. Graham therefore decided to close the ranks and by a vigorous statement in the House force the party, including Peel, to fall into line behind a forceful policy. Conciliation had reached its limits, he told the House, and at a time like this 'it would be madness and cowardice' not to pass the Bill.[527]

The strategy worked perhaps too well, for when Peel acquiesced in Graham's speech, some assumed that he had surrendered his

[525] Graham to Peel, November 6th, 1841, in *Peel Papers*, CCLXVI, 115-116 (Br. Mus. Add. MSS. 40446).

[526] *Statutes at Large*, 6 and 7 Victoria, c. 74. It was hoped that the Law would quiet the fears of those people in Ireland who felt compelled because of the troubled times to keep themselves armed, but who feared that these arms would be seized by the agitators.

[527] See *Annual Register* (1843), 143.

leadership of the party to Graham. 'When till now,' asked the *Morning Chronicle*, 'did a subordinate so overlay his chief as did Sir James Graham ... The Graham ascendancy is too much established in the Cabinet to talk even as he [Peel] pleases.'[528] Graham deeply regretted this reaction to his speech and wrote apologetically to Peel:

> We are not only colleagues but intimate friends, and in the present state of affairs the least reserve between us would be most unfortunate. My conscience told me that you thought my speech imprudent, and you should not hesitate to warn me, for you know my reliance on your judgment.[529]

Disraeli, on the other hand, did not fall into line, and for his party perfidy received an appropriate reward. On December 20th he wrote to Graham asking the latter for a position for his brother.[530] Graham, who preferred to have Disraeli in the ranks of their open enemies,[531] replied: 'I foresee no opportunity of complying with your wish.'[532] It was a cold but civil snub which Disraeli never forgot nor forgave.

In addition, in saying that conciliation to Ireland had reached its limit, Graham had meant that no concessions in the direction of the disruption of the Union, the overthrow of the Established Church, or the confiscation of property would be made. But his opponents took it to mean that *no* concessions would henceforth be made and that the Government's policy would be one of coercion. They therefore denounced his statement as a gratuitous insult to Ireland.[533]

The passage of the Arms Act added more fuel to the fires O'Connell had been setting in Ireland. Huge mass meetings were held in various cities at which the Government was denounced and demands made for the repeal of the Union. A monster meeting was scheduled to take place at Clontarf, three miles from Dublin, on Sunday, October 8th. The Repealers planned no violence but the preparations for the meeting were carried on with a military

---

[528] *Chronicle*, June 23rd, 1843, p. 5.

[529] Graham to Peel, June 18th, 1843, in PARKER, *Life of Graham*, I, 363.

[530] Disraeli to Graham, December 20th, 1843, in *Graham Papers*.

[531] See Graham's letter to Croker, August 23rd, 1843, in CROKER, *Corr. and Diaries*, III, 9.

[532] Graham to Disraeli, December 21st, 1843, in *Graham Papers*.

[533] See the *Chronicle*, June 21st, 1843, p. 5, and the *Herald*, June 21st, 1843, p. 4.

air and the Government decided to stop it — to strike the blow
Graham thought justifiable. The cabinet's decision is contained in
the following note which Graham wrote to Stanley on October 4th:

> We have had incessant meetings for the last two days. . . .
> We determined that de Grey and Sugden should go to Dublin
> tomorrow with full authority to apprehend O'Connell and leading
> members of the League, on a charge of treasonable conspiracy. . . .
> When you read this note of preparation for military array, you will
> agree with us that a meeting thus assembled during Church time
> on Sunday in the metropolis of Ireland is clearly illegal. We have
> resolved so to consider and treat it. De Grey will proclaim it on
> Saturday, prohibit the assembly, and disperse it by force if
> necessary.[534]

In getting the cabinet to approve his policy, Graham had the
powerful backing of Wellington, who was enchanted with the
prospect of using a little force in dealing with O'Connell and
the Repeal Association. But Graham was convinced that force
would not have to be resorted to, that the mere show of force
would cause O'Connell to back down, and that they had found
the best method of ruining O'Connell and of breaking up the
Repeal Association without bloodshed.

On October 7th Sugden prohibited the meeting at Clontarf and
ordered the arrest of any who attended. O'Connell therefore had
to choose between inaction and open insurrection. Not made of the
stuff of martyrs, O'Connell yielded, called off the meeting, told his
followers to go home and even posted guards at the approaches to
Clontarf to keep Repealers out of the city.

Having won the first round and completely taken the wind out
of O'Connell's sails, the Government, and Graham in particular,
should have let well enough alone. This they did not do. Rather,
thinking to even up past scores with the Irish leader, they ordered
his arrest along with his son and eight other accomplices, on a
charge of conspiracy, sedition, and unlawful assemblage. The law
officers of the Crown had assured Graham that the Government
had a good case against the defendants,[535] but the trials were
frightfully bungled. In selecting the jury sixty names of qualified
householders, as a result of negligence or fraud, or both, were

[534] Graham to Stanley, October 4th, 1843, in PARKER, *Life of Graham*, I, 398.
[535] *Home Office Papers* (Ireland), 45, O.S., 793.

T

omitted from the official list. Worse than that, all the Roman Catholics who had been members of the Repeal Association were struck from the list. Graham was furious: 'It is hardly credible', he wrote to the Lord-Lieutenant, 'that such a mistake at such a moment could have been accidental . . . It is hard that the public interest should be endangered by such gross negligence.'[536] When Eliot wrote that the case was being handled properly and that the Government had the right to challenge jurors, Graham replied: 'I cannot consider the explanation satisfactory. The negligence appears to me gross and palpable. If an inquiry be desired in the House of Commons, I see no reason why we should resist it. On the contrary, such neglect of duty ought not to be passed over.'[537] But Eliot stood his ground, ridiculously insisting that there could be no Roman Catholics on the jury because *all* Roman Catholics were Repealers and that the acts of the Association were now the main subject of the trial.

The trial began in Dublin on November 2nd, 1843, before the Court of Queen's Bench. The defendants were charged with conspiring to abolish the Legislative Union, with inducing persons to desert from the Army and Navy, with usurping the Royal prerogative by establishing arbitration courts, and with soliciting funds for anti-Union purposes.[538] The grand jury brought in a true bill and the trial was fixed for January 15th, 1844. At its conclusion all were declared guilty. O'Connell was sentenced to serve one year in jail, fined £2000, and required to give bail of

[536] Graham to the Lord-Lieutenant, in PARKER, *Life of Graham*, I, 403.
[537] *Ibid.*
[538] *Home Office Papers* (Ireland), 45, O.S., 793. The charge was based on articles written by O'Connell and others which were published in such papers as the *Freeman's Journal*, the *Pilot*, and the *Nation*, and on public speeches he had given. In his speeches he had solicited funds for anti-Union purposes and had been supported in this campaign by the Temperance Union as well as by some of the Catholic clergy. *Home Office Papers* (Ireland), 100/257; (Report of Outrages), 45 O.S., 874. The pertinent statements in the newspaper articles which O'Connell had signed were as follows: 'We have applied in vain to the legislature for redress; our complaints are unheeded, our remonstrances unavailing.' 'It is admitted by all . . . that unless we redress ourselves we can have no succour from any other quarter; but we suffice for ourselves . . .' 'From the English Parliament there is neither redress nor even hope.' 'Irishmen . . . stand together and Ireland shall have her Parliament again.' He also had intimated that he had under his command 'a force superior . . . to that which the Duke of Wellington had at Waterloo'. *Ibid.*, 45/793 and (Law Office Reports), 119/18. O'Connell had advised the Irish to ignore the regular courts of law and to set up arbitration courts of their own to try cases involving landlords and tenants.

£5000 as a guarantee of good behaviour for seven years. Lesser sentences were meted out to the other defendants and all were packed off to Richmond prison.[539]

The day after the jury's verdict was announced (May 30th, 1844) Russell proposed to the House the appointment of a committee to investigate conditions in Ireland. In doing so he denounced the jury-packing of the Irish Government and accused the Government of treating Ireland as a conquered province. Graham replied that the use of force was justifiable because O'Connell's mass meetings had assumed a military air. Then he tamely defended Eliot's conduct by saying that only those Roman Catholics who were Repealers were struck from the jury list. The real issue in Ireland, he insisted, was a religious one — it was not political nor economic. He, and the Government of which he was a part, believed in the maintenance of the Established Church and the Union. 'I stand upon the choice', he said, 'made by this country at the Reformation, confirmed at the Revolution, sealed by the Act of Settlement, and ratified by the Act of Union ... I do not believe it will be overthrown by any Repeal Association, or any body of Conspirators such as we have succeeded in convicting.'[540] The House agreed with him and rejected Russell's motion by a majority of 109.

In the meantime O'Connell had appealed the case to the House of Lords. Here, the judges whose opinions were requested, upheld the decision of the Irish court, but the law lords voted three to two in favour of O'Connell. Furthermore, the three who supported O'Connell (Cottenham, Campbell, and Denman), were all Whigs. This action of the Lords was galling to Graham even though he had expected that it would be decided by political considerations. In a letter to his friend, Croker, he complained:

> The decision really rests on technicalities, which, triumphing over the merits in the last resort, bring law and reason and justice into contempt ... I fear that no Irish juries will ever again convict in

---

[539] *Ibid.*, (Trial of O'Connell), 45 O.S., $\frac{793}{5}$. The governor of the prison permitted the convicted men to have as many guests as they wished and they had such a good time that it became known as the 'Richmond Picnic'. They received great quantities of food and drink and O'Connell rarely had fewer than thirty guests to dinner. Management of Richmond prison was in the hands of a board over which the Home Office had no control.

[540] *Hansard*, 3rd Ser., LXXII, 786.

a political case; and it will be hard to find judges bold enough to do their duty when the House of Lords betrays its trust; and no public prosecutor will have the heart to proceed with boldness and confidence, when having triumphed over minor difficulties and dangers, he is exposed to certain failure in the supreme tribunal, and from the malice of political adversaries, in defiance of justice and of law.[541]

Campbell, Cottenham, and Denman may, as Graham believed, have acted from personal or party motives, and yet it was perfectly proper for them to condemn the Crown's exercise of its right to set aside unfit jurors (in this case Roman Catholics) as a practice which could very easily make a mockery of the whole jury system if allowed to continue unchecked.

This celebrated case had clearly demonstrated the need for a change in the Irish Government. As early as December 1841 Eliot and Grey were in open disagreement, and Graham wrote to Grey telling him to discuss the situation with Eliot and saying that if they could not come to some agreements he (Graham) would have to take it up with Peel 'for we cannot', he said, 'attempt to govern Ireland with a Ld. Lieutenant and his Secretary in open variance on such a subject [concessions to Catholics]'.[542] The following year Eliot and Grey differed so sharply on the former's advocacy of fixity of tenure for Ireland that Graham proposed to Peel the abolition of the office of Lord-Lieutenant.[543] By August 1843 cordial co-operation between Grey and Eliot was no longer possible and Graham and Peel began to consider possible choices to fill Eliot's post. Ashley, Sidney Herbert, the Duke of Richmond, and Lord Canning were all considered, but the choice finally settled upon, in July 1844, was Lord Heytesbury.[544]

While the Government had been proceeding with a forceful policy in Ireland, Graham and Peel both knew that the application of force alone would do nothing to remedy the social evils of that island. 'An insurrection may be subdued by the sword; but a military government and free institutions cannot permanently

---

[541] Graham to Croker, in CROKER, Corr. and Diaries, III, 20. For the opinion of the judges, see Home Office Papers (Law Officers Reports), 119/10, pp. 1-32.

[542] Graham to Peel, in Peel Papers, CCLXVI, 164 (Br. Mus. Add. MSS. 40446).

[543] See correspondence on this subject in Ibid., CCLXVII, 325-328 (Br. Mus. Add. MSS. 40447); and CCLXVIII, 71-79 (MSS. 40448).

[544] Home Office Papers (Queen's Letters, Ireland), 101/9, p. 140-150.

coexist; and Ireland must at last be treated', Graham concluded, 'as a rebellious colony, or reconciled to Great Britain on terms, which will command the hearts and affections of her people.'[545] The Union and the Established Church must be preserved, laws must be enforced, and peace, order and security achieved. Having done that, it was the Government's duty to reform existing evils and by good administration eliminate criticism and discontent.

One of the best methods of putting an end to agitation and unrest in Ireland was, thought Graham, to give offices to loyal Roman Catholics. In January 1842 he told Greville that he regretted not having 'some offices of profit that he might now bestow upon Catholicks',[546] and he urged Peel to let no opportunity be lost of 'admitting them to a share of patronage'.[547] Peel was perfectly willing, but the trouble was that Grey would not give effect to their oft-repeated requests. Graham had frequently to remonstrate with de Grey. 'I am afraid', he wrote to him in 1843, 'that the unbroken series of Protestant appointments for the past two years to all posts of rank and authority in the police will give rise to invidious comment, if not to angry feelings. Surely wherever an honest and loyal Catholic can be found he ought at least to have an equal chance with the Protestant in the public service in Ireland; his exclusion from the superior ranks of the Constabulary cannot be defended.'[548]

The following year the Government brought in a Bill for the better administration of charitable and religious trusts. From the beginning of the century these bequests, three-fourths of which were for Roman Catholic endowments, had been administered by a predominantly Protestant board and the arrangement had not worked well. The Bill now before the House provided that two of the three legal members of the board should be Catholics, and that ten additional members should be appointed to the board of whom five were to be Catholics. All questions relating to the doctrine and discipline of the Church of Rome were to be referred only to the Catholic members of the board. Clause Ten guaranteed the application of donations according to the will of the donor and so

---

[545] Graham to Peel, October 20th, 1843, in *Peel Papers*, CCLXIX, 111-112 (Br. Mus. Add. MSS. 40449).

[546] GREVILLE, *Memoirs*, V, 6.

[547] Graham to Peel, in PARKER, *Life of Graham*, I, 363-364.

[548] Graham to de Grey, September 3rd, 1843, in *Ibid.*, 366.

abolished the doctrine of 'expediency', by means of which the will of donors had previously been often set aside. Clause Twelve permitted bequests to the Church for the purpose of maintaining Roman Catholic residences and chapels. The measure was tendered as a peace-offering and, according to the *Morning Chronicle*, was received 'with decided expressions of satisfaction,[549] and easily passed into law.[550]

But the Bill was not accepted as a peace-offering by O'Connell, who, on September 7th, was released from Richmond prison and then promptly renewed the Repeal agitation. Peel and Graham expected that this Charitable Bequests Act, because it was a more liberal measure than they themselves had requested in 1842, would split the Catholics in Ireland and detach the moderates from O'Connell's Association. But, since many Catholic bishops refused to serve on the Commission, and since O'Connell was openly denouncing the Act,[551] Graham urged Peel to have the Ambassador at Rome sedulously cultivate the Pope, to convince him that O'Connell's conduct was hurting the Catholics of Ireland, and if possible to get the Pontiff to issue a rescript to the Archbishops in Ireland ordering the Irish clergy to cease political agitation. It was a shrewd move, for when the rescript was issued O'Connell lost the support of the clergy and with it the support of thousands of his former adherents.[552]

During the same year three Bills intended for the pacification of Ireland were all dropped because of stiff opposition in the House. One of these would have granted compensation to tenants for improving lands by fencing, building, and draining; another would have provided for increasing the number of voters in Ireland by about 30,000 through giving the franchise to all who paid a poor-rate of £30; the third, a Municipal Corporation Bill, would have given the franchise to all householders who had occupied a house for three years and had paid the rates.

Despite the unfortunate defeat of these desirable measures, Peel and Graham continued their policy of reform and pacification by

[549] *Chronicle*, August 3rd, 1844, p. 4.
[550] *Statutes at Large*, 7 and 8 Victoria, c. 97.
[551] *Peel Papers*, CCLXX, 231-232 (Br. Mus. Add. MSS. 40450); *Home Office Papers* (Report of Outrages), 45 O.S., 874.
[552] Graham to Peel, December 23rd, 1844, in *Peel Papers*, CCLXX, 434-437 (Br. Mus. Add. MSS. 40450).

proposing, early in 1845, to increase the annual grant to Maynooth, an Irish college for the education of priests. Peel first brought up the question on February 11th, 1844, in a Cabinet minute in which he asked whether or not the annual grant to Maynooth should be increased.[553] It was discussed frequently thereafter but no action was taken because of the intransigeance of Gladstone. By January 2nd, 1845, he had decided to resign from office if the cabinet proposed an increased grant to Maynooth.[554] This threat posed a serious problem for Peel and Graham. Stanley, one of the best debaters in the House, had just gone to the House of Lords, and Peel and Graham, already overworked, now had to face the prospect of losing the brilliant Gladstone. But neither Graham nor Peel, regarding the Maynooth grant as the most important part of the Government's Irish policy, would abandon it. Gladstone therefore left the cabinet, not so much because he was opposed to the measure itself, as because he had just argued a contrary principle in his book, *The State in Its Relations With the Church*, and would be accused of inconsistency if he remained. His letter of resignation was a typical Gladstonian essay and Peel was unable to understand it. Graham, to whom Peel sent the letter, admitted that it was 'obscure' but assured Peel that it meant that Gladstone had quit.[555]

On April 3rd, 1845, Peel brought to the House his carefully prepared Maynooth Bill. It provided for increasing the annual grant to Maynooth from £9000 to £26,000. This would make possible a doubling of the salaries of the professors and improvements in the physical plant of the college. It was an opportune time to bring in this measure, for the year 1844 and the spring of 1845 was a time of prosperity for all classes. There was scarcely a single cloud on the political horizon when Peel proposed this Maynooth grant, but clouds, very dark clouds, gathered almost at once, and according to Harriet Martineau it became 'the subject

[553] For the memorandum see PARKER, *Life of Peel*, III, 101-103.
[554] See MORLEY, *Life of Gladstone*, I, 272-275.
[555] Graham to Peel, January 4th, 1845, in *Peel Papers*, CCLXXI, 7-8 (Br. Mus. Add. MSS. 40449). Either through carelessness or design, Gladstone had not sealed the letter. This amused Graham who declared that it did not matter much because he doubted whether there was 'a postmaster in England who after reading the letter would understand one word of it'. The Earl of Dalhousie replaced Gladstone at the Board of Trade, Sidney Herbert became Secretary for War, and Cardwell Vice-president of the Board of Trade.

on which society seemed to be going mad'.[556] Thousands of petitions against the Bill were sent to Parliament; meetings of protest were held throughout the country (chiefly in the Dissenting districts); Peel was even denounced as the Anti-Christ. This Protestant criticism became so bitter that Queen Victoria declared that she was compelled to 'blush for Protestantism'.[557]

In the House of Commons it was the same story. Ultra-Protestants like Inglis, Plumptre, and Colquhoun opposed it because they said it would destroy Protestant ascendancy and endow the false church of Rome; the Independent, Duncombe, opposed the Bill because he was against all religious establishments; the Dissenters opposed it on the grounds that Ireland did not need money for education so much as it needed cheaper food. The Bill looked to Bright like 'a sop given to the priests. It is *hush-money* given that they may not proclaim to the . . . world the sufferings of the population to whom they administer the rites and consolations of religion'.[558] On the other hand, Catholics like Sheil, and Whigs like Russell, warmly supported the proposal.

Night after night the debates went on, all the while becoming more heated and acrimonious. It was on the fifth night that Graham took complete charge of proceedings. Sir George Grey, a Whig who supported the Bill, asked Graham if he did not now think that he ought to retract his previous statement that concessions to Ireland had reached their limit. To everyone's surprise, that is exactly what Graham did. He got up and made a sincere retraction and apology: 'I admit the expression', he said, 'and I avow my regret at having used it . . . I say that I am sorry for the use of that phrase; it has given offence in Ireland; I deeply regret it; and I can only say, conscientiously and from the bottom of my heart, that my actions towards Ireland have been better than my words.'[559] From this gracious recantation Graham proceeded to a vigorous defence of the proposed grant to Maynooth. Thus far, he said, England had been unable either to correct or to extirpate the 7,000,000 Roman Catholics in Ireland. They were now willing

[556] HARRIET MARTINEAU, *History of England*, IV, 387.

[557] Queen Victoria to the King of the Belgians, April 15th, 1845, in *Letters of Queen Victoria*, II, 42-43. The majority of Protestants objected to the application of English money to support Irish Catholic schools. See *Fraser's*, XXXI, 628.

[558] See TREVELYAN, *Life of Bright*, 161.

[559] *Hansard*, 3rd Ser., LXXIX, 921.

to accept a grant of £27,000 annually to provide for the better education of their spiritual guides and the House certainly should grant such a moderate sum. Maynooth, as it stood, was a disgrace: the professors were inadequately paid; the classrooms were too small; the buildings were old and dilapidated. The college should be renovated, repaired, and improved, or else abolished.

This speech drew from all sides of the House prolonged cheers. Lord John Russell declared that Graham's apology was 'admirable'; Sheil, speaking for the Irish Catholic members, accepted it with gratitude; O'Connell, speaking at a Repeal Association meeting in Dublin, praised 'the manly spirit and straightforwardness with which he delivered his speech', and stated that Graham deserved 'the highest commendation'.[560]

Despite the storm of controversy which the Bill had engendered, it passed all readings with majorities exceeding a hundred. Party lines were completely ignored. Non-party members (Liberals), Whigs, and Irish Catholics supported it on the principle that the Government of England, having admitted Roman Catholics to civil and political privileges, could not very well continue to outlaw their religion. The bulk of the Conservatives also voted for the Bill rather than risk being thrown out of power.

But, though the Bill passed easily enough, it widened and deepened the schism in the Conservative party.[561] About a hundred members voted against it and Graham was convinced that it was the death-knell of the party. 'The Bill will pass,' he wrote to Lord Heytesbury, 'but our party is destroyed.'[562] Even though both Peel and Graham were literally worn out from the staggering amount of labour they had been doing, this prospect of seeing their party destroyed did not deter them. They had no thought of surrender. They intended to persevere in their Irish policy until they were driven from power.

And persevere they did. Notwithstanding the clamour which

---

[560] Cited in *Illustrated News*, April 26th, 1845, p. 267. The *Chronicle* (April 19th, 1845, p. 5), praised Graham very highly and said that during Graham's recantation, Inglis 'sat thunderstruck and Lord Ashley quivering with astonishment'.

[561] It also split Disraeli's Young England Party and was one of the rare occasions on which Cobden and Bright voted on opposite sides. MONEYPENNY and BUCKLE, *Life of Disraeli*, II, 330; TREVELYAN, *Life of Bright*, 162.

[562] Graham to Heytesbury, April 12th, 1845, in PARKER, *Life of Graham*, II, 10.

the Maynooth Bill had occasioned, and indifferent to party or personal feelings, Graham, on May 9th, introduced the Academical Institutions Bill. It provided for the establishment of three colleges in Ireland: one at Cork, one at Belfast, and one at Limerick. Provision was made for financing the building of these institutions and for obtaining administrative and faculty personnel. Each college was to have a principal, vice-principal, and from ten to twelve professors. The latter were to be nominated and removable by the Crown because 'security must be taken that in the lectures — not theological — opportunities are not seized of making these lectures the vehicle of any religious tenets'. Interestingly enough, there was no provision for a faculty of divinity, but private persons were to be permitted to endow chairs of theology subject to the supervision of the Crown. Roman Catholics could therefore obtain religious teaching in their faith and Protestants in theirs. Under no circumstances was there to be compulsory attendance at theological lectures. Trinity College, since it had been founded by a Protestant Sovereign for Protestant purposes, was to retain all its rights and property.[563]

Only the High Churchmen, led by Robert Inglis, opposed the Bill, declaring it to be 'a gigantic scheme of Godless education'. The Irish M.P.s neither opposed nor approved the Bill. Sheil merely objected to the continuance of Trinity College because it was 'a memorial to Ascendancy';[564] O'Connell pointed out that Protestants, who were rich, would immediately endow chairs of divinity, while Catholics, who were poor, would be unable to do so;[565] and other Irish M.P.s requested that Roman Catholics be allowed to have Roman Catholic chaplains in the colleges. To this Graham would not agree because if that was allowed, Presbyterians would have to be permitted Presbyterian chaplains, Anglicans Anglican Chaplains, and Jews rabbis.

Supported by the Liberals in their own ranks as well as by the Whigs,[566] the Bill was passed by a majority of 151 in the House and was readily accepted by the Lords. It received the Royal

---

[563] *Hansard*, 3rd Ser., LXXX, 345 et seq.
[564] *Ibid.*, 385.
[565] *Corr. of Daniel O'Connell*, II, 358.
[566] The Whig *Globe* (May 12th, 1845, p. 2), described it as a Whig measure carried out by the Tories. See also *Manchester Guardian*, May 14th, 1845, p. 4 and *Illustrated News*, May 22nd, 1845, vol. VII, No. 151.

assent on July 31st, 1845,[567] and Commissions were appointed to carry it into effect.[568]

When Parliament was prorogued on August 9th, the Peel ministry was firmly in the saddle. The country was prosperous and the opposition disorganized. The High Church group and the Dissenters effectively neutralized each other and the Whigs had no chance of getting back in office so long as Peel and Graham continued to propose measures which they themselves were bound to support.

Both statesmen knew, however, that their days in office were numbered. It was not England, but Ireland that continued to worry them and both practically despaired of bringing peace and good government to that island. To Peel, it was a state which seemed 'to preclude honest and impartial government',[569] while Graham told Croker that it had ruined many administrations and caused the downfall of many great statesmen. 'It has not lost its malignant influence', he said, 'and will do its accustomed work again.'[570]

The 'accustomed work' came very quickly. The distress in Ireland, occasioned by the failure of the potato crop in the fall of 1845, was accompanied by a serious increase in crime. It was decided therefore to attack the problem from two sides: to relieve the suffering from hunger, a Free Trade Bill would be proposed; to protect life and property, a Preservation of Life Bill would be proposed. Both Bills were 'musts'. Agrarian crimes of a kind resulting from high-priced food had increased alarmingly, particularly in the counties of Clare, Leitrim, Limerick, Roscommon, and Tipperary.[571] The Preservation of Life Bill, designed to protect life and property, was introduced in the House of Lords by Lord St. Germans on February 13th, 1846. It proposed giving to the Irish Government authority to 'proclaim' any county or district, i.e., the Government could appoint additional magistrates and police at local expense. In such 'proclaimed' districts victims of outrages, or their representatives, could be compensated for

---

[567] *Statutes at Large*, 8 and 9 Victoria, c. 66.
[568] *Home Office Papers* (Queen's Letters, Ireland), 101/9, pp. 245-253.
[569] Peel to Graham, October 5th, 1845, in PARKER, *Life of Graham*, II, 19.
[570] Graham to Croker, February 18th, 1846, in *Ibid.*, 34-35.
[571] See *Annual Register* (1846), p. 124; *Peel Papers*, CCLXXI, 1 (Br. Mus. Add. MSS. 40449).

such outrages from taxes collected in such districts; persons found out of doors at night were to be liable to transportation for seven years; any person attending a public meeting or carrying arms was liable to arrest.

Since most of the members of the House of Lords were men of property and since the Bill was identical to previous coercion Bills passed by both parties, it was quickly carried through the Upper House. Much time was to elapse, however, before Graham presented it to the Commons. In fact, he did not present it to the House until March 30th. This delay was due to a dilemma into which the Government had fallen. If it proceeded with the Protection of Life Bill first, it would be accused of indifference to the famine; if it proceeded with the Corn Bill first, it would be accused of indifference to crime and violence. Peel and Graham finally decided to propose the second reading of the Corn Bill and then to proceed with the first reading of the Preservation of Life Bill. The former was not passed until March 28th and so Graham could not bring in the latter until the thirtieth. In presenting the Bill Graham declared that the Government had done everything within its power to improve conditions in Ireland. The Charitable Bequests Act had been passed; the Maynooth and Academical Institutions Bills had become law; the Corn Bill, if passed, would give Ireland cheaper food. It was the frightful increase in crime, and only that, which had made this Bill necessary. [572]

Whigs, Irish M.P.s, and 'malignant Tories', as Greville called them, subjected the measure to a running cross-fire. The Whigs supported the Government so long as the Corn Bill was under consideration but were determined to drive Peel and Graham out of office as soon as it was carried. About 120 Radicals and Irish M.P.s opposed it because they were opposed to coercion on principle. The 'malignant Tories', hating Peel and Graham because of their conversion to free trade, had decided to throw them out of office regardless of consequences and so did everything they could to delay the measure. Greville was right in saying that their sole object was to get revenge on Peel and Graham because they were

---

[572] See *Hansard*, 3rd Ser., LXXXV, 297-360. The *Globe* (March 31st, 1846, p. 4), admitted that he had made out a good case for the Bill, but the *Chronicle* (March 31st, 1846, p. 5), poked fun at his sending 'a pack of extra magistrates and constables' to solve the problem that was really economic.

the very group who intrinsically believed in the philosophy of coercion. Their leaders, Lord George Bentinck and Disraeli (the latter suffering from the longing of unfulfilled desires and thirsting for revenge), surpassed the bounds of propriety in their splenetic attacks on Peel and Graham. As a result, it was not until May 1st that the Bill passed the first reading. Two weeks later the Corn Bill was passed by a slim majority and sent to the House of Lords, where, with Wellington pointing out that it was useless to delay the issue (since they couldn't defeat it), the Bill was read a third time without a division on June 25th.

Meanwhile Graham had been equally busy administering relief to a starving people. In December 1845 the Lord Lieutenant of Ireland was directed to consult with the landed proprietors in destitute districts as to the best type of public works which could be begun as a means of furnishing employment.[573] Relief which had to be given before public works projects could be begun was to be limited. 'Our object', he wrote to Twisleton, the Commissioner, 'is ... to save the people from starving, but not to render reliance on the Public Purse an *attractive* habit. Want must be *extreme* and *very severe* before gifts even in kind can be administered with prudence.'[574] Maize was then admitted duty free and Graham urged the Irish executive to exert all possible efforts to get it from the ports to the people with as much dispatch as possible.[575] One thing more needed doing and that was to throw open all the ports and to establish free trade. This, as we have seen, was done by June 25th.

With the Corn Bill having passed, Graham knew very well that the Protection of Life Bill was doomed.[576] But even so he did not give up the battle. Night after night he successfully fought off one amendment after another, nailing the Whigs to the cross of inconsistency by incontrovertibly demonstrating that this Bill was even less coercive than those they had passed in 1833 and 1834. Graham's skill in handling this Bill and Peel's in handling the Corn Bill amazed both friend and foe. 'See how those two men do

---

[573] *Home Office Papers* (Ireland), 122/19, pp. 8-9.
[574] Graham to Twisleton, February 16th, 1846, in *Graham Papers*.
[575] Graham to Lord Lincoln, March 22nd, 1846, in *Ibid*.
[576] Peel and Graham had previously decided that if they had to go out of office, it should be on this Bill instead of on the Corn Bill. See PEEL, *Memoirs*, II, 292; *The Times*, June 9th, 1846, p. 4.

their business and understand it', declared Charles Villiers.[577] But it was of no avail. With the Corn Bill passed, the Whigs, Protectionists, Radicals, and Irish M.P.s united to defeat the Protection of Life Bill by a majority of 73 and the Government promptly resigned.[578]

The men who had just given up their seals of office constituted, in many respects, the greatest ministry of the nineteenth century. Practically every phase of English life was affected by the reforms which it carried out. The extremely able and effective leadership of Peel is known and recognized by all students of English history, but for the tremendous amount of constructive work done Graham deserves equal praise. No other member of the cabinet was as able or as tireless a worker; none a more loyal colleague. The best statement of Graham's sterling worth is that given by Peel himself:

> I have now completed the task which I have undertaken. One word before I bring it to a close. In the course of this Memoir I have acknowledged the deep obligation which I owe to the colleagues with whom I acted in the administration of public affairs — to those in particular who were united with me in the service of the Crown after the failure of Lord John Russell's attempt to form a Government.
>
> But I should do injustice to one of those colleagues, with whom, from the nature of our respective offices, my intercourse in regard to the transactions which form the subject-matter of the Memoir was the most frequent and the most intimate, and whose responsibility was equal to my own, if I did not express, in the strongest terms, my grateful acknowledgements for the zealous support and able assistance which I uniformly received from Sir James Graham.
>
> The correspondence which I maintained with him (whenever there was not the opportunity of daily personal intercourse) during the whole period of our official connection contains ample proof of the unreserved confidence which subsisted between us, and of the obligations which I owe to him for that cordial co-operation which is the most valuable and most effectual when it is prompted by warm feelings of personal regard as well as by the sense of public duty.

[577] Cited in Duchess of Northumberland to Arbuthnot, June 8th, 1846, in PARKER, *Life of Peel*, III, 352.

[578] Queen Victoria was greatly touched by Graham's 'great emotion' on resigning. *Letters of Queen Victoria*, II, 101, 104.

Sir James Graham has had his full share of the obloquy with which
I have been assailed; and I close this Memoir with the hope that
the evidence incorporated with it may serve to rescue his name, as
well as my own, from some degree of unjust accusation and un-
merited reproach.[579]

Graham's fundamental political philosophy was that laws
should be enforced impartially, honestly, and efficiently; revolutionary changes should be stoutly resisted, but salutary reforms
which would remedy evils and improve the machinery of government, should be conscientiously encouraged. Never a real
doctrinaire, he was, like Peel, willing to change his ideas when
circumstances and the indisputable logic of facts dictated a change.
Like Peel, too, he became progressively more liberal while in
office.

Generally speaking the political philosophy of the early nineteenth century was that the extension of individual freedom and
the elimination of oppression could cure existing evils and hence
obviate the necessity for a further extension of democracy. But in
the 1840s this philosophy was often found inadequate. It was
discovered that problems had arisen which affected the entire body
politic and which were so national in scope that they could be
solved only by collective action. And each time that Peel and
Graham proposed to reform an existing institution, therefore, an
individualist versus collectivist conflict developed. The individualists protested against collective action on the grounds that it was
fatal to individual freedom. Factory owners, doctors, and edu-
cators, for instance, refused to believe that labour problems,
health, and education could not be left to the mercy of the interested parties themselves. Individualists objected to what they
called the tyranny of central authority. Graham appreciated the
fact that central control resulted in the loss of some personal free-
doms but argued that it was more than compensated for by the
increased efficiency which centralized authority made possible.

The argument advanced by lawyers, doctors, industrialists,
Evangelicals, Churchmen, and others was that they should be let
alone, that in the proper time and manner they would themselves
introduce the necessary reforms. It was not the public welfare
which they sought but the welfare of their own vested interests,

[579] PEEL, *Memoirs*, II, 324-325.

and local anarchy was to them preferable to an efficient, centralized State. Graham, often taking the opposite point of view, was therefore subject to constant attack from all of these quarters. He was respected and admired as an efficient, hard-working public servant, but he was not popular. His was the fate of most efficient public administrators.

Part of the criticism of Graham on this score was unavoidable. Control of party patronage had been gradually shifting from the party whip to the Secretary of the Home Office and it appeared to many that the Home Secretary was becoming far too powerful. It is true that his office was becoming an increasingly important one and that the number of appointive offices at its disposal was constantly increasing. This state of affairs, however, must be attributed to the character and ability of the Home Secretaries themselves (like Peel and Graham) and to the fact that each of the great reform measures passed since 1827 had provided for a central administrative or regulative board and for inspectors, supervisors, and other officials all under the control of the Home Office, rather than to any conscious plan or desire on the part of the Home Secretary. Graham did not hold party advantage nor political power in such high esteem. In fact, he had never been what we should call a 'party man', and a good deal of the opposition to him within his own party (in 1830-1834 and in 1841-1846) was attributable to the fact that in making appointments he too frequently ignored party interests altogether.

Graham's chief weakness as a public servant, and as a Home Secretary in particular, was that the machinery of government was more important to him than the human beings for whom government exists. The penal reform which he carried out, for instance, was directed towards achieving an efficient, businesslike, and economical administration rather than towards helping the unfortunate inmates of penal institutions. Improving man's physical environment as the best means of solving the problem of crime did not enter sufficiently into his philosophy. In fact, in the field of factory legislation, he displayed a rather callous indifference to the welfare of the human beings who were making England the workshop of the world.

CHAPTER IX

THE 'GRAHAMITES'

A LONG period of confusion and instability produced by the shifting sands of party politics followed the break-up of the Conservative party.[1] Issues were confused and confusing; party distinctions seemed to be fading away. The Whigs, led by Russell, were in power, but as the *Illustrated News* put it, they occupied a throne which was theirs 'rather by the voluntary abdication of their predecessors, than by conquest'.[2] It followed, therefore, that Russell could stay in office only so long as the Conservative party remained divided. To keep it divided, Russell wisely decided to offer posts in his cabinet to three members of Peel's Government — Lord Dalhousie, Lord Lincoln, and Sidney Herbert. But all three refused on the grounds that it was too early to unite with the Whigs,[3] and Russell was finally driven to select a cabinet most of the members of which succeeded to office by what Marriott calls 'the Divine right of Whiggism'.[4]

Queen Victoria, admiring Graham's business knowledge and his administrative proficiency,[5] was sorry to see him out of office.[6] Graham, on the other hand, was glad to be rid of it. He was weary of labouring twelve to thirteen hours a day at the Home Office;[7] he was weary of the intolerable abuse to which he had been forced to submit; and he was weary of party strife. At the same time, he told Gladstone, he had served many years in the House of Commons and wanted to continue there, not as a party man, but as an independent member. He could then take part in the debates and spend his leisure time at Netherby with his family and his books. He felt no bitterness towards the Whigs; they were fairly in

---

[1] From 1846 to 1867 there were nine administrations.

[2] *Illustrated News*, August 29th, 1846, vol. IX, 130.

[3] See CROKER, *Corr. and Diaries*, III, 130; PARKER, *Life of Peel*, III, 455.

[4] JOHN A. R. MARRIOTT, *England Since Waterloo*, 184.

[5] She appointed him to the Duchy of Lancaster Council, but Graham accepted the position, says Greville, only when the Queen made it a matter of personal favour to her and to Prince Albert. GREVILLE, *Memoirs*, V, 358.

[6] See *Queen Victoria's Letters*, II, 103.

[7] Labouchere, the Irish Secretary, said that Graham did more work in the years 1841-1846 than did either Peel or Russell. See Hobhouse to Graham, August 6th, 1846, in PARKER, *Life of Graham*, II, 49.

possession of power. But with those Conservatives who had 'displaced the late government by a factious vote' he would have nothing more to do. It would be impossible, he told Gladstone, ever to unite with them.[8] To continue to serve as a Member of Parliament but to refuse to sit with the Whigs or the Protectionists posed a problem for Graham and his friends,[9] which they finally solved by deciding to sit as Independents on the Opposition side of the House.[10]

Efforts had been made by Lord Lincoln, Lord Dalhousie, and Cardwell to keep the free-trade members of the Conservative party together and to unite them in a third party, but neither Peel nor Graham gave them any encouragement. The latter did not want to commit himself to any specific course of future action. But though they formed no formal party they certainly voted and acted as though they had. Queen Victoria diagnosed the situation perfectly when she wrote on July 7th, 1846: '[They] *will* come together again, whether under Peel or someone else.'[11] The necessary elements for united action were present: loyalty to Peel, the leader; close personal ties; a common determination to resist any and every attempt to return to Protection; and a common dislike of the Bentinck-Disraeli party. It was not long, therefore, before the members of this group, consisting of moderate, progressive politicians of liberal-conservative principles, who had acted with Peel, were known as 'Peelites'.

The Peelites having gone over to the doctrine of free trade, there was not much difference now between their views and those of the Whigs. For that reason, in the next few months Graham voted with the Government as often as he voted against it, in spite of the fact that technically he was a member of the Opposition. It was the support of Graham, Peel, and their colleagues that enabled Russell to carry his Sugar Bill in the autumn of 1846.[12] In like manner Russell's Irish policy was generally supported by

[8] See MORLEY, *Life of Gladstone*, I, 296.

[9] Graham to Peel, January 3rd, 1847, in *Peel Papers*, CCLXXII, 203-204 (Br. Mus. Add. MSS. 40452).

[10] *Manchester Guardian*, January 23rd, 1847, p. 6.

[11] Queen Victoria to King of the Belgians, in *Letters of Queen Victoria*, II, 103.

[12] This Bill proposed that duties on foreign and on slave-grown sugar from the British Colonies be immediately reduced to 21 shillings and then gradually reduced from that amount to 14 shillings. A similar reduction was applied to molasses and to refined sugar.

Graham and the other Peelites. And it was fortunate that Russell had this support, too, for Ireland was worse off in 1847 than it had been in 1846. Famine, pestilence, and crime stalked the land and Russell proposed to meet the problem by continuing Graham's public works projects while making certain that the wages paid on these projects were lower than those paid on private works. Graham supported the measure but only as a temporary policy. He advised the Government to stop such relief as quickly as possible. It was then February and there were about 580,000 people engaged on those projects. Since almost all of this number were ordinarily tillers of the soil, and planting usually began in March, it was desirable that they get back to the soil. If not, he said, the calamities then existing in Ireland would be only 'a prelude to calamities still more awful'.[13] This was sage advice, for much of the work done on public projects was non-productive — 'the making of superfluous roads . . . and the levelling of innocuous hills', as Low and Sanders put it.[14]

The Government met Graham's suggestion that aid be given only to productive labour on land by proposing a Drainage of Land Bill which provided for loans up to £15,000 to landlords to be used for this purpose. But Graham did not like the idea of making such large loans to landlords who already possessed enough money as well as credit. 'It was the yeomanry and the small proprietors who found a difficulty in borrowing money; their credit did not stand so high as that of their wealthier neighbours, while their estates needed improvement quite as much.'[15] Therefore, Graham proposed that the loans be limited to £10,000 and the Government accepted his suggestion.

In March he supported the Government's proposed revision of the Irish Poor Law to enable widows with children to receive relief outside the workhouse. Two months later he supported a Government Bill providing for a loan of £600,000 for Irish relief. But while Graham voted for it, he told Russell that the Government ought to make it clear to the Irish landlords that the whole sum would have to be repaid.[16]

---

[13] *Hansard*, 3rd Ser., LXXXIX, 967-969.
[14] SIDNEY LOW and LLOYD C. SANDERS, *History of England During the Reign of Queen Victoria (1837-1901)*, 73.
[15] *Hansard*, 3rd Ser., XC, 1121.   [16] See *Ibid.*, XCII, 1355-1357.

Thus far Graham had supported all of Russell's Irish measures, but when the latter proposed to advance a sum of £620,000 from the Consolidated Fund to three Irish companies for railway construction he demurred. Employing labour on railroad building took too many men away from agricultural labour just when it was needed most. He would not have been averse to spending money on land-reclamation projects or on colonization schemes designed to drain off some of Ireland's excess population (in terms of food supply), but he did not like to spend it on railway schemes. Was Russell sure that the object of this loan was not to relieve the destitute so much as to favour speculators in railway schemes? If the three to which the loans were to be given were entitled to public aid, why not all the others? 'Believing the measure wrong in principle, impolitic, and unnecessary', he therefore voted against it.[17] Then, 'to be consistent', he also voted against a proposed grant of £150,000 for the building of the Argyll Ship Canal.[18]

On January 26th, 1847, Fielden introduced a Ten-Hours Bill calling for a 58-hour week for all females over eighteen and for all young persons from thirteen to eighteen years of age. For five days each week ten hours would be worked; on Saturdays, eight. Three groups attacked this Bill: those who opposed any legislative interference with business; those who would limit it to children; those who would limit it to females. Graham was one of the first group. To his way of thinking the question was simply this: 'Shall you by indirect legislation restrain industrious men from working twelve hours a day for the purpose of earning their livelihood, though they are willing to undergo the fatigue?' He didn't like to have to say so but after all 'the lot of eating, drinking, working, and dying must ever be the sum of human life among the masses of a large portion of the human family'. Furthermore, since existing hours of labour were not injurious to the health of workers, shortening those hours was unnecessary. Finally, if he could believe that this would be the *last* bill of this kind, it would not be so bad, but he knew it would not be and that 'year after year we shall have regularly to discuss this matter'. If the Bill passed, the cotton, woollen, linen, and silk trades would surely be ruined and the masters in those trades would be forced

---

[17] *Hansard*, 3rd Ser., XCII, 1020-1027.   [18] *Ibid.*, XCIV, 6.

to submit to lower profits, or raise prices and/or lower wages, or go out of business, or leave England for other lands 'where no such absurd restrictions' existed. The Bill was supposed to aid the labourer, but was it just or fair 'to prevent him from pushing his industry to the utmost, and labouring long hours if he pleases'? The Government had just removed prohibitive tariff duties, repealed the Corn Laws, and suspended the Navigation Acts, and he did not now want 'to impose fetters hardly less galling than those which we have struck off'.[19]

The argument that it was neither just nor fair to prevent a person from working 'to the utmost' if he so desired was of course absurd. Few, if any, would have done so had it not been necessary in order to sustain life. Equally absurd was his argument that a reduction in hours of labour must inevitably result in less profits and lower wages. It would mean less profit only if productivity declined as a result of shorter hours; men like Robert Owen had proved that this was not a necessary consequence.

On the other hand Graham was certainly consistent in this opposition to the Bill. He had aided in striking off the Corn Laws, which many landlords regarded as essential to their way of life, but which were restrictive of the free play of the market, and he could not therefore now approve of placing restrictions on the manufacturing classes. This was *laisser-faire* philosophy pure and simple. But Parliament was inconsistent for having just repealed the Corn Laws in the name of *laisser-faire*; it now passed the Ten Hours Act in flat defiance of that doctrine.

Did business desert England, did profits fall, did wages fall as Graham had so dolefully predicted? Not at all. In fact, even though 1847 was not a very good year, industry survived, and labour was actually better off, for the cost of living went down and real wages therefore went up.[20] Graham, seeing these facts, naturally contended that his predictions *would* have been correct had it not been for the effects of the repeal of the Corn Laws on the cost of living.

In April 1847 the Government brought in a Bill by which a grant of £100,000 was to be made in aid of education in England. Graham, while favourable to the principle of the measure, and

---

[19] *Ibid.*, C, 773-781.
[20] See CLAPHAM, *Econ. Hist. of Mod. Brit.*, I, 527.

while he voted for it, strenuously objected to the clauses which provided that all sects could apply for aid from the fund but that such aid could be given only to those schools in which the Authorized Version of the Scriptures was used. This meant, of course, that Roman Catholics could not receive aid. He did not like this at all: 'I say that the time to do justice is now; and I never can believe that it is good policy to postpone any concession which justice, and equity, and the spirit of liberty and freedom irresistibly demand.'[21]

In May, the Home Secretary, Grey, brought in a Bill to amend the Poor Law. Since 1834 the Poor Law Commissioners had laboured under the disadvantage of not having a responsible representative in Parliament and it was now proposed to remedy this by creating a Poor Law Board two of the members of which were to represent the Commission in the House. Once again Graham voted with the Government. The Poor Law, he said, had prevented destitution and idleness too, and all that was required to make the system function perfectly was a centralized, responsible authority. This Bill provided for such authority and therefore he was now supporting it.[22]

We have already seen that Graham was an advocate of justice to Catholics, but when the Russell Government proposed to abolish transportation as a form of punishment, his sense of justice took another turn. He agreed that it was desirable to try to reform criminals; but reformation was only a secondary consideration. The primary one was punishment and it ought therefore to be so severe that it would act as a deterrent to crime. Punishments had been steadily diminished, he said, and crime had increased. If the country was not more careful in its sympathy for the sufferings of criminals, 'we shall, practically, so break down the severity of all our punishments for the gravest offences, that crime will be committed with impunity'.[23] He was convinced that separate confinement with transportation was the best system but the House, fortunately, did not agree with him.

[21] *Hansard*, 3rd Ser., XCI, 1208.   [22] See *Ibid*., XCII, 1223-1235.
[23] *Ibid*., XCIII, 326-342. Since the death penalty had been abolished juries were no longer loath to return verdicts of guilty and the number of convictions had consequently increased. However, the actual number of crimes committed had not increased when the increase in population is taken into account. See *Illustrated News*, XI, 184.

By the summer of 1847 Graham and the other Peelites had so often supported the Russell Government that the *Illustrated News* declared it would require 'a subtle casuist to define what is the difference between the Ministry and the Opposition'.[24] The differences between the Whigs and the Peelites were so nebulous, in fact, that Russell was led to believe that he might be able to get some of them to join his government. This was particularly the case with respect to Graham, who had once been a Whig colleague of Russell. He therefore decided to offer Graham the Governor Generalship of India to succeed Hardinge. On June 16th he wrote the following letter to Ellice, who was to act as the go-between:

> After reflection, and communication with Lord Lansdowne and the Duke of Wellington, I have arrived at the conviction that there is no person to whom the destinies of India can be so safely confided as to Sir James Graham. The finances and financial system of India require the most vigilant application of sound principles, combined with caution. . . .
> Whether such a post, high and important as it is, would suit his domestic arrangements, I cannot tell. My duty is to offer my influence with a view to obtain the best man for the government of India, and Sir James Graham is that man.[25]

This, the fourth time the India Office had been offered to him, was an eloquent tribute to Graham's business ability. But he refused to accept the position because, he told Greville, the Whigs still hated him, and Russell did not really like him, and had made the offer, he was convinced 'at the suggestion of others, and not by his own free will'.[26] Graham also discussed the proposition with Peel, who advised him not to take it on the grounds that it would generally be accepted as an evidence that the Peelites intended to support the Russell Government.[27]

Nevertheless, while he refused to join the Russell Government he continued to give it his cordial support and advice. In March 1847, for instance, the Government proposed to create a new bishopric — that of Manchester — and, in the near future, three

[24] *Ibid.*, X, 322.
[25] Russell to Ellice, June 16th, 1847, in PARKER, *Life of Graham*, II, 57-58.
[26] For a full account of Graham's talk with Greville, see GREVILLE, *Memoirs*, V, 451-452.
[27] *Ibid.*

additional bishoprics. Graham approved of the first part of the
Bill, not because the existing bishops were overworked, but
because there was enough money in the Episcopal Fund to endow
the new See. What did bishops have to do that was so hard?
They had to ordain parish priests, but priests were ordained only
once a year during Ember Week; they had to visit the parishes,
but this was only done once every three years, and since great
improvements had been made in transportation facilities, this was
no difficult task; they had to consecrate new churches and attend
the House of Lords, but no one would be so fatuous as to believe
that these duties were difficult to perform. He knew a bishop who
was over eighty years of age, who performed all these duties
easily. It was all right to create the new See at Manchester, but
not to create three additional bishoprics. 'No additional orna-
ments' were needed by the Church, but rather 'buttresses to sustain
the tottering fabric of the Church itself'.[28] Available funds should
be used, he thought, to build more churches and to increase the
salaries of under-paid priests, not to build 'Episcopal Palaces'.[29]
The logic of these arguments was unassailable and the Government dropped the clause calling for the future creation of three
additional bishoprics.

On July 24th the Parliament which had been elected in 1841
was dissolved and writs were issued for a new election. It was
highly desirable that this should be done, for the majority returned
in 1841 were pledged to protection, and now that parliament had
ended protection, it was necessary to ascertain the opinions of the
electorate. Graham refused to stand for election in the East
Cumberland district or for Hull,[30] but he did accept Earl de
Grey's offer to aid him at Ripon,[31] on condition that he should be
at liberty 'to pursue the course that my own deliberate judgement
may dictate'.[32] In his address to the Ripon electors Graham
declared:

> I am conscious that my judgement may have erred on many
> occasions, but it has been my constant and honest endeavour to

[28] *Hansard*, 3rd Ser., XCIV, 348 et seq.
[29] Graham to Gladstone, July 22nd, 1847, in *Graham Papers*.
[30] See *Illustrated News*, XI, 22.
[31] See Graham's letter to Peel, July 22nd, 1847, in *Peel Papers*, CCLXXII, 220
(Br. Mus. Add. MSS. 40452).
[32] Cited in PARKER, *Life of Graham*, II, 57.

strengthen and uphold the institutions of our country by the application of timely remedies to their defects; and, without regard to my personal interests, I have laboured to promote the happiness and welfare of all classes of my fellow-subjects. I can only promise to adhere to the independent conduct which I have hitherto pursued; and, if you confide to me the trust of representing you in Parliament, you may rest assured that no party considerations shall prevail over my sense of public duty.[33]

The election at Ripon, as well as those in other parts of the country, was an unusually quiet one[34] and Graham was returned to the House of Commons. When the election was over it was discovered that there were to be 336 Liberals, 201 Protectionists and 117 Peelites in the new House.

The new Parliament met on November 18th, 1847, and since distress prevailed in both England and Ireland, the Government secured the appointment of a committee to inquire into the effect the laws regulating the issue of bank-notes payable on demand were exerting on economic conditions. Graham was appointed a member of the committee because he was highly regarded as a man of business, and because he had been a member of the committee of 1832 whose labours resulted in the Bank Act of 1833. After examining many witnesses — bankers, financiers, industrialists — the committee came to the conclusion that the crisis of 1847 was due to crop failures and to the speculative mania in railroad shares rather than to the banking laws.[35] It therefore concluded that it was 'not expedient to make any alterations in the Bank Act of 1844'.[36]

Conditions had been bad in 1846 and though slightly improved in 1847, they were to be worse in 1848. On January 3rd the 'Tobacco War' began in Milan, and by March revolutions against the 'European System' so carefully nurtured since 1815 by the astute Metternich, had broken out in Paris, Berlin, Budapest,

---

[33] Quoted in *Illustrated News*, XI, 55.

[34] The *Annual Register* (Chron., 1847, p. 95), attributed this to the fact that most of the great questions and issues of the day had already been laid at rest.

[35] Clapham, however, blames the Bank for failure 'to realize the amount of control that it might exercise over the market'. JOHN R. CLAPHAM, *The Bank of England*, II, 199. The chapter on the crisis of 1847 is excellent.

[36] *First Report from the Secret Committee on Commercial Distress with Minutes of Evidence*, June 8th, 1848, vi.

Munich, Naples, Prague, Venice, and Vienna. When the storm broke out in Paris, Palmerston, the self-confident and aggressive Foreign Secretary, was assailed by two fears: 'The first was that the rest of Europe should meddle with France; the second that France should assail the rest of Europe.'[37] To keep Europe from meddling in French affairs and to check the rumoured French designs on Belgium and Lombardy meant that England would have to get its own forces in readiness. The Government proposed, therefore, to increase the naval forces to 43,000 men and Graham whole-heartedly supported the measure. Since France was pursuing an aggressive policy and was a threat to the peace of Europe, England was forced to maintain her naval leadership. Unless England, he said, 'stands at the head of the maritime Powers of the world at all times and in every emergency — if she is not, without dispute, the mistress of the British Channel — . . . these intact shores . . . may be exposed . . . to a national invasion'.[38] Graham disliked war as much as anyone, but he was convinced that the peace of Europe, and therefore of England too, could best be guaranteed by a strong, adequately-prepared England. Palmerston was naturally delighted with Graham's 'impressive speech' and thanked him for his support.

Revolutions in Europe were having their counterpart in Chartist demonstrations in England, and in crime, born of despair, in Ireland. The Irish potato crop was poorer than it had been the previous year and the Government was forced to ask Parliament for a grant of £50,000 to relieve the distressed. The Opposition, preferring loans to gifts, opposed the measure but Graham once again came to the defence of the Government and helped them carry the Bill. Outright gifts, he said, were always preferable to loans which could not, and would not, be repaid. He warned the Government, however, that this was the last time (cries of 'Oh! Oh!' from the Protectionists) he would vote for a grant of this kind because the Government should by now be prepared to bring in a measure completely revising the taxing system in Ireland.[39]

In addition to aiding Russell by supporting this Irish grant, Graham championed his Health of Towns Bill[40] and his proposals

---

[37] WARD and GOOCH, *Camb. Hist. of Br. For. Pol.*, II, 307.
[38] *Hansard*, 3rd Ser., XCVII, 815.
[39] *Ibid.*, 1079-1080.   [40] *Ibid.*, XCVIII, 1246-1248.

for improving conditions at Parkhurst prison.[41] More important, however, was the unstinted aid he tendered that Government on its proposed Sugar Bill. The Protectionists, still smarting from 'the great betrayal' of 1846, obtained the appointment of a commission to inquire into conditions in the Sugar Colonies, and under Bentinck's leadership carried a Report virtually suspending the Free Trade Act of 1846 and retaining for six years a differential duty in favour of colonial sugar. Realizing that his Government could not prevent the adoption of the Report, Russell proposed a compromise by which colonial sugar would secure a slight preference. In supporting Russell's proposal, Graham declared that the West Indies planters were requesting that the Government, by legislative action, guarantee them a profitable cultivation. Such protective action would, if adopted, mean high prices to the consumers and 'high prices make low wages; and the effects of low wages fall most heavily on the working classes'. Sugar was 'the only little luxury' that many families could enjoy. 'It rendered palatable their rice, their gruel, their crout, their indifferent tea and coffee.' Instead of raising prices by protective duties he thought it was the duty of Parliament 'as far as possible, to cheapen everything'.[42]

Peel thought so too, but not all of the Peelites agreed with them. In fact, it was beginning to appear as if the party might break up.[43] Greville reported that some of them were 'disengaging themselves from their Chief, without joining the Tories, and . . . so conducting themselves as to make any junction with the Whigs very difficult'.[44] Chief among this group of dissident Peelites were Gladstone, Herbert, and Lincoln, who really saw eye to eye with the Tories on everything except protection. They were provoked with Peel and Graham for continuously supporting Russell's Government and were anxious to vote him out of office. Graham was willing that the rest of Peel's former cabinet join with Stanley, Bentinck, and Disraeli, but he would not do so. Rather than risk the possibility of a return to protection, he would continue to vote with the Whigs. But the latter were unpopular because Wood, the

[41] *Ibid.*, 1433.
[42] *Ibid.*, XCIX, 1235-1242. The *Manchester Guardian* (June 28th, 1848, p. 4), praised Graham's speech as 'candid, generous, and just'.
[43] See MORLEY, *op. cit.*, I, 353. [44] GREVILLE, *Memoirs*, VI, 89.

Chancellor of the Exchequer, was quite inept — his budget bills were ludicrous when compared with Peel's. By the early summer of 1848, therefore, it looked as if Russell would have to surrender his seals of office. Should that happen, Graham, says Greville, hoped that the Queen would summon Stanley to form a government. Then all the free traders could unite on the free trade versus protection issue and vote him out of office. Greville took this to mean that Peel would once more take office.[45] But Greville was mistaken because neither Peel nor Graham had any intention of doing so. In September 1848 Lord Londonderry asked Graham if he would try to reorganize the Conservative party and take an active part in leading it. Graham flatly refused. 'I said', he wrote to Peel, 'that with the High Tory and Protectionist party my differences on principle were irreconcilable; and that concord with Lord George Bentinck and Disraeli . . . was impossible.'[46]

Having declined Tory overtures, Graham, early in 1849, was offered a cabinet position by the Whig party. In January Lord Auckland, the First Lord of the Admiralty, died and Russell, needing strength and experience in his cabinet, offered the post to Graham. It was a wise decision on Russell's part for there was no one in England better qualified to handle Admiralty problems. Graham told Russell that he would see Peel before deciding. Then, according to Lady Russell's account, he changed his mind, decided not to bother Peel and refused the offer.[47] The reason for declining, Graham told the Prime Minister, was that the Whigs would not go far enough in the line of retrenchment to suit him.[48] But at the same time he told Peel that there were other reasons too: he could not defend Palmerston's aggressive foreign policy, nor the Government's weak-kneed Irish policy in which it had not attempted 'the redress of a single grievance'. Furthermore, the Government was spending far too much money in Ireland.[49] Russell had gone very far towards making his offer to Graham an attractive one. He could have a peerage (which he refused); he

[45] GREVILLE, Memoirs, VI, 85.
[46] Graham to Peel, September 25th, 1848, in PARKER, Life of Graham, II, 64. See also Fraser's, XXXVIII, 236. Graham would never agree to lead the Conservatives as long as Peel lived. See Graham to Peel, January 15th, 1848, in Peel Papers, CCLXXII, 252-255 (Br. Mus. Add. MSS. 40452).
[47] See WALPOLE, Life of Lord John Russell, II, 98.   [48] Ibid.
[49] Graham to Peel, January 12th, 1849, in PARKER, Life of Graham, II, 73.

would be consulted on all cabinet appointments; the corn duties would not be reimposed nor new taxes levied.[50] The difficulty was that Graham did not believe that Russell could make good on these promises and bluntly told him so: 'I endeavoured to impress on Lord John', he wrote, 'that it was not his supreme authority, but the absence of it, that I regarded with jealousy.'[51]

It was wise of Graham to reject this offer. Considering their past differences of opinion, he would have been uncomfortable in a Whig cabinet; he could not have worked well with Palmerston; having quit the Whig party once he could not very well re-join it unless he was sure he would be able to support its future policy. Greville, who anxiously desired Graham to re-unite with the Whigs, somewhat unjustly attributed his refusal to do so to his timidity: 'He pines for office, he dreads to take it; he knows he is an object of suspicion and dislike to people of all parties; . . . he is clear-sighted enough to perceive all its entanglements and difficulties.'[52]

Russell's cabinet had been unanimous in their desire to have Graham join them and were sorry that he had refused. The Conservatives, on the other hand, were overjoyed and once more tried to get him to help reorganize their party. Again he refused, saying he would not be a party 'to any new combination of his [Peel's] former colleagues and adherents in present circumstances to his exclusion. A Tory Government to which he is opposed cannot stand'. He also told Lord Londonderry, the go-between, that the differences between himself and the Whigs were not so great as those between himself 'and the leaders of the implacable Protectionists'.[53] To retire from party leadership, or even mere membership, was his privilege, but, as Hardinge acidly observed, attending the House of Commons and helping to decide questions of policy was not 'what I call "absolute retirement"'.[54]

Hardinge was right, for on all of the major issues of the Sessions of 1849 Graham certainly did play a leading role in deciding questions. The first of these was the question of the Navigation Laws, which Russell's Government proposed to strike from the

[50] *Ibid.*, 74-75.　　　　　　　　　　　　　　　[51] *Ibid.*
[52] GREVILLE, *Memoirs*, VI, 152.
[53] Graham to Londonderry, January 20th, 1849, in PARKER, *Life of Graham*, II, 80-81.
[54] *Ibid.*, 82.

statute books. Graham cheerfully supported the proposal. He told the House that these laws had long since outlived their usefulness and that Adam Smith, the 'Newton of Political Economy', was correct in saying that these laws diminished the number of sellers and buyers with the result that England was forced to sell cheaper and buy dearer than it would under a system of free trade. He pointed out that Huskisson, than whom there was no better authority, had stated that the Navigation Laws operated to the detriment of the country with the largest merchant marine. In the final analysis, said Graham, these laws were merely 'a tax on the commerce and navigation of the country'. Repealing them at this time would 'increase our imports and exports; . . . stimulate trade and consumption . . . [which would] immediately lead to an increase in the number of our seamen and of our ships'.

It was Graham's firm belief that repealing these laws would benefit all classes of society. It would give the merchant lower freight rates; it would enable the manufacturer to purchase raw materials at lower prices and therefore to sell at lower prices thus stimulating trade; it would prove a boon to sailors because more trade would mean an enlarged demand for their services and would result in higher wages and better working conditions; consumers would benefit from lower prices; and even the ship-owners would be helped because their existing monopoly exercised a 'withering effect' whereas competition would result from repeal and this competition would 'vivify' that industry.

So much for England. What about the colonies? Antigua, Ceylon, Jamaica, and Trinidad had all remonstrated against the Navigation Laws. Canada, said Graham, would be lost to England if they were not repealed. And, had not Bancroft, the American historian, just declared that these laws had been the real cause of the American Revolution?

Graham then concluded his speech in these words: 'Here therefore is the issue joined. I say that protection or no protection is the point at issue; and I regard it as the battle-field on which the struggle must take place between reaction and progress . . . I take my stand here. I am opposed to reaction. I am favourable to progress tempered by prudence and discretion.'[55]

[55] *Hansard*, 3rd Ser., CIV, 658-676.

The *Manchester Guardian*, quite naturally, praised this speech as 'admirable and statesmanlike',[56] while Russell declared that Graham had so masterfully exhausted all the arguments for his Bill that he, Russell, felt 'great difficulty in addressing the House upon the subject'.[57]

Having helped the Government carry this measure, Graham also supported it in the Smith O'Brien case [58] in June, and in the Government of Ceylon question[59] in July. On the other hand, he opposed the Government on an issue respecting the prerogative of the House. It had just passed an Irish Poor Relief Bill and the Lords had amended Clauses One and Two which dealt with the levying and collecting of rates. Russell, anxious to avoid a conflict with the Lords, agreed to the amendments. Graham took the opposite view, arguing that if the Lords were permitted to amend this Bill they would soon begin to amend other bills relating to taxation, and he did not like to see the House gratuitously surrendering its long-established privileges in financial matters.[60]

Throughout the year Graham had carried on a lively correspondence with Peel in which they had considered what action should be taken in the event that Russell should decide to return to protection. But it was Disraeli, not Russell, who made the first major move in that direction. In February 1850 he proposed that the Poor Laws be revised so as to mitigate the distress of the agricultural classes. Trade and commerce were prospering but the price of agricultural products had decreased since 1846, and the Protectionists blamed this state of affairs on the free trade policy Graham had helped to carry. They knew that Parliament would not agree to a return to protection, so, under Disraeli's leadership, they proposed to compensate the agricultural interests by transferring part of the expenses then defrayed out of the rates to the general taxation of the country, i.e., to the Consolidated Fund.

[56] *Manchester Guardian*, April 25th, 1849, p. 4.
[57] *Hansard*, 3rd Ser., CIV, 682.
[58] O'Brien, together with Meaghre, M'Manus, and O'Donohoe, had been sentenced to death for high treason and the Russell Government, exercising its prerogative of mercy, had commuted the sentence to transportation for life. The House questioned the wisdom of this action.
[59] The question was whether or not Governor Torrington had exceeded his authority and also whether he had used proper means in suppressing a rebellion in Ceylon.
[60] *Ibid.*, CVII, 1057.

This proposal to aid the agricultural classes without returning to protection was a shrewd political move on the part of Disraeli. The Conservative party, since Bentinck's death in September 1848, had been without a leader or even a recognized statesman; the Peelites had been a group of statesmen more or less without a party.[61] It occurred to Disraeli, therefore, that Graham, who could not join the Whigs so long as 'two such men as Grey and Palmerston'[62] were members of the cabinet, might be induced to join the Conservative party if the latter would drop protection. But Graham entertained no such ideas. Not only did he refuse to consider the overtures made to him by Disraeli through Lord Londonderry in January,[63] but he now led the forces opposed to Disraeli's proposed compensation scheme.

On the third night of debate Graham and Peel both rose at the same time to speak on the proposal. Graham naturally proposed to give way to Peel, but the House cried 'No, No!' and Graham went on to speak.[64] Disraeli's motion, he said, was in reality a request that not only should the entire burden of the poor-rate be transferred to the Consolidated Fund, but the asylum tax, the land tax, and the malt tax as well. This would add up to about eighteen to twenty million pounds and would also be a reversal of the commercial policy the country had pursued since 1846. And why do this? Was it not, in the last analysis, just a clever ruse by which Disraeli sought to turn out the administration of Russell, dissolve Parliament, and return to protection?

> Let us suppose we adopt this motion. It is certainly a very clever device, and in itself is not unfair. But what would you do if you consented to it? You would go into Committee, and then, when you did so, the forms of this House would preclude the hon. Gentleman from moving any resolution of an operative or effective character to transfer local burdens to the Consolidated Fund.

[61] See *Illustrated News*, XVII, 7.

[62] GREVILLE, *Memoirs*, VI, 200.

[63] He distrusted Disraeli and refused to associate with the Protectionists. See *Letters from Benjamin Disraeli to Frances Anne Marchioness of Londonderry*, 1837-1861, p. 100; MORLEY, *Life of Gladstone*, I, 587.

[64] *Hansard*, 3rd Ser., CVIII, 1189. Greville says that this was the first time Peel ever rose to speak in the House and had to give way to another speaker. *Memoirs*, VI, 208. The Speaker had, undoubtedly, seen Graham first and therefore called upon him.

Without the consent of the Crown no such motion is possible. The hon. Gentleman can only move a resolution of opinion, and such a resolution . . . might as well be moved in full House as in Committee.

This was a clever political move on Graham's part, because everyone who differed from this resolution, 'thus slightly sketched and indicated', and anxious to move something else, was enticed by the manner in which Disraeli had put his resolution 'to place himself under the hon. Gentleman, and to vote with him'. Disraeli was trying to do the impossible, i.e., to reconcile two irreconcilable principles: to maintain the control of funds and at the same time to make a large reduction in the burden of the poor-rates. The first, said Graham, was obviously inconsistent with the latter.

But Disraeli's political chicanery was only a side-issue, for, said Graham, the real question which the House must now decide was: 'will you consent to a reversal of your recent policy in respect to taxation; and will you again take a large portion of the burdens now resting upon property, and place it upon labour and industry?' To do so would be both inequitable and unjust because the labouring classes still had to pay taxes on the timber and bricks 'of which their humble dwellings are composed', on butter and cheese, 'which, after bread, constitute a large portion of their food', on soap, tea, coffee, sugar, molasses, raisins, and currants. 'There remain four articles of the character of narcotics and stimulants by the help of which they seek to obtain a short oblivion of their sorrows and their cares. These are tobacco, spirits, British and foreign, and malt, the staple of their beer.' The taxes on these items amounted to £31,000,000 — more than the interest on the entire national debt. Under no circumstances, therefore, should the labouring class be loaded down with additional burdens.

If, as Disraeli had alleged, conditions in agriculture were so bad, why had not the number of applications for enclosure acts decreased instead of increased? In addition, land still enjoyed numerous exemptions from taxation: there was no duty on the descent of property; none on horses used in agriculture; none on insurance on stock and crops; none on servants, bailiffs, tax-carts, shepherds' dogs; none on tolls or lime or manure; no taxes on

x

windows of farmhouses under £200 yearly value. The agricultural interest, he said in conclusion, was not very wise in continuing to dissociate their condition from that of the entire body politic.[65]

Peel also opposed Disraeli's motion, but the Peelites as a group did not. Gladstone, for instance, though hesitating to answer Graham's powerful address, acquired 'the courage that proceeds from fear',[66] and supported Disraeli's motion. It was his contention that if the agricultural classes were relieved of the burdens referred to, they would have no more arguments against free trade. Goulburn and Aberdeen held similar opinions, and it looked to Greville, also to Disraeli, as though these three might now join with 'Stanley and Co.'[67]

Disraeli's motion was beaten by the small majority of twenty-one votes. It was now obvious to all that Russell could remain in office only so long as he had the support of Graham. And he had this support on every question[68] in the session of 1850 until Lord Palmerston's conduct in the Don Pacifico case drove him into the ranks of the Opposition.

Don Pacifico was a Portuguese money-lender living in Athens, Greece, who claimed to be a British citizen because he was born in Gibraltar. During disturbances in Athens, his house had been pillaged and he claimed compensation from the Greek Government. The latter, justly regarding the sum claimed to be excessive, did not pay it. Palmerston consequently ordered a blockade of the Greek coast and as a result was bitterly assailed in the House of Commons. Bright led the attack for the free trade Manchester Group, who believed that prosperity depended on a pacific foreign policy. Disraeli, seeing an opportunity to overthrow Russell's Government, led the assault of the Protectionist crew. Graham, Peel, and Gladstone carried the brunt of the Peelite attack. The latter group attacked Palmerston, whom they did not

[65] For the whole speech see *Hansard*, 3rd Ser., CVIII, 1189 et seq.
[66] A. T. BASSETT, *Gladstone to His Wife*, 81.
[67] See GREVILLE, *Memoirs*, VI, 209; *Disraeli to Lady Londonderry*, 79-80.
[68] In March, for instance, he supported Russell's Bill to set up a system of county councils to control county expenditures; in May he helped carry a measure to extend the franchise in Ireland to all £8 house-holders; in June, he aided the Government in defeating a proposal to require the reading of the Authorized Version of the Bible in *all* schools in Ireland. The proposal, he said, was tantamount to extinguishing the National System of Education, 'the only bright spot in the darkness which hangs over the face of that Country'. *Hansard*, 3rd Ser., CXII, 203-206.

like, but hesitated to vote against the Government for fear a defeat would bring in Stanley and a new Corn Law.[69]

The debates, however, soon shifted from the immediate question of Don Pacifico to the problem of the whole foreign policy of Palmerston. Under Aberdeen's leadership, the Lords carried a vote of censure on Palmerston's conduct of the Foreign Office. To repair this damage, the Government arranged to have Roebuck propose a resolution approving of Palmerston's actions. It was this resolution which began the long and heated debate that ended in Palmerston's triumph and which forced Graham to oppose the Government.

Graham began his very long attack on the foreign policy of Palmerston by saying that he was not personally hostile to the Foreign Secretary; that he had been his colleague in Grey's ministry. And he had been a very loyal colleague too, for he had collaborated with Palmerston in the blockade of the ports of Holland and in the expedition to Antwerp; he had approved the separation of Holland and Belgium; he had helped to expel Don Miguel from the Portuguese throne and to install Don Pedro. These were acts of intervention to be sure, but they had not resulted in any interruption in England's friendly intercourse with the Great Powers. It was obvious to anyone in the House, too, that he was not hostile to the Russell Government, for he had consistently supported its measures. But, try as he might, he could not sanction the foreign policy which Palmerston had pursued since 1846. His constant 'preaching of lessons' to the Spanish Government had resulted in the recalling of the British Ambassador from Madrid;[70] in Switzerland, he had sided with the ultra-Republicans in the Sonderbund schism in 1847; in France, he had taken the side of the opponents of Guizot because the latter had quarrelled with him in the Spanish marriage question, and for the revolution of 1848 which overthrew Guizot 'there will rest upon the conduct of the noble Viscount a heavy responsibility'; in Italy, in the fall of 1847, he had encouraged the nationalists to believe that England would aid them in expelling Austria from the peninsula, and some, like Piedmont, having

[69] See Graham's letter to Peel, April 3rd, 1850, in PARKER, *Life of Graham*, II, 104.
[70] Narvaez had returned to power in 1848 and Palmerston, through Sir H. Bulwer, 'advised' Narvaez to take more Liberals into office.

acted on this assumption, and not securing English aid, had failed. What was the result? Why, 'Rome is in possession of the French army. Lombardy is under the military rule of Austria. Venice was reconquered'. Furthermore, the English fleet had been sent to aid the Neapolitan insurgents in 1848, and when, despite this aid, they were defeated by the King of Naples and had fled to Malta, the Government had refused them asylum. In Russia, Palmerston's actions had been equally bad. The Czar had demanded that Turkey free its Polish refugees and the English Government had asked him to temper his demands. But, without waiting for a reply, the British fleet in direct violation of the Straits Convention of 1841[71] had been ordered into the Straits. When Russia had protested, Palmerston had replied that the Navy had gone in because of bad weather. Was this true? Not at all. Lord Hardwicke, an eye-witness, had publicly testified that it was a calm day and the waters were smooth. Again, in 1847, he had sent a note to the Greek minister, Glarakis, describing his Government as 'a system of illegality, of corruption, of injustice, and of tyranny, oppressive and disgusting to the Greek nation'. Was this the way to address the minister of a friendly state?

The result of this meddling in the affairs of other Powers, said Graham, was that both Austria and France had recalled their ambassadors from London, and Russia and Prussia were contemplating similar action. 'Narvaez is all-powerful in Spain; . . . Costa Cabral is all-powerful in Lisbon; . . . the French army is in occupation of Rome; . . . the Pope is much estranged from friendly intercourse with this country.' Give a vote of approval to such policies? Never.[72]

The next day Bernal Osborne castigated Graham for having first praised Palmerston and then blamed him. Such behaviour reminded him of those 'large serpents which are said to embroider their victims with their saliva before they make a meal upon their bodies'.[73] Palmerston, always dextrous, and in full command of the details of all his actions, chided Graham with having made the subject of foreign policy a matter of personal pique, and laughed

---

[71] This treaty had closed the Straits to warships in time of peace unless they had received a special firman from the Sultan. Canning, the Ambassador to Turkey, had received the necessary firman.

[72] *Hansard*, 3rd Ser., CXII, 304-325.   [73] *Ibid.*, 332.

at Graham for having blamed him for the French revolution of
1848. 'What will the French nation say', he asked, 'when they
hear that it was in the power of a British minister to overthrow
their Government? Why, Sir, it is a calumny on the French
nation.'[74] He concluded his own successful defence with a full
explanation of the Don Pacifico case that ended with his famous
civis romanus sum peroration.[75]

Graham's plan to keep the Whigs in office in order to save
free trade while at the same time delivering a 'blow in the
prestige' to Palmerston, backfired for the real victor in this
contest was not the Whig party, but Palmerston. Greville, who
disliked Palmerston, correctly observed that Palmerston was now
'more powerful than he was before; but whether they [the debates]
have strengthened or weakened the Government is another
question'.[76] As a matter of fact, Palmerston now had the upper
hand and Russell's plan to take Palmerston out of the Foreign
Office vanished into thin air.

The day after this famous debate, Peel, the closest friend and
colleague of Graham, was thrown from his horse and fatally
injured. Graham was with him when he died, was one of the
pall-bearers at his funeral, and was a member of the committee
selected to collect subscriptions for a suitable memorial.

Peel's death naturally had important political consequences.
Who was now to be the leader of the Peelites? It was obvious to
all that it would be either Aberdeen or Graham. Many, including
Russell and Disraeli,[77] were sure that it would be Graham, but,
according to Greville, Graham 'repudiated the notion of his
accepting any such position, and declared that he was quite unfit
to influence the opinions and regulate the conduct of other men'.[78]
This appraisal was only partly correct, for he had abundantly
demonstrated his power to influence the opinions of others on
numerous questions. But his strength to do so lay in his reputation
as a careful, efficient administrator, a master of detail, a sound,
though cool and impersonal, man of business. In short, he lacked
the warmth of spirit, the kindly personal touch, the genuineness in

[74] *Ibid.*, 422.

[75] See the excellent account of this subject in H. C. F. Bell, *Life of Palmerston*, II,
25 et seq.

[76] GREVILLE, *Memoirs*, VI, 232.

[77] See DISRAELI, *op. cit.*, 88-89.   [78] GREVILLE, *Memoirs*, VI, 244.

dealing with people that are required for leadership. Peel's followers admired and respected Graham; they loved Aberdeen. Consequently, the Peelites were now left without any publicly acknowledged leader. However, Graham's opinions so influenced those of the group, and his advice was so eagerly followed, that within a few months of Peel's death, the group were often referred to as the 'Grahamites'.

The balance of the session of 1850 was taken up with a discussion of three questions: the 'Jew Bill', the naval estimates and a proposal to compensate the depositors in a bank that had gone bankrupt. The first concerned the question of whether or not Baron de Rothschild, who had just been elected M.P. for London, should be sworn in according to the Old Testament or in accordance with the customary oaths. Graham suggested that Rothschild be asked to declare to the House what was binding on his conscience and if he would swear that it was his custom to use the Old Testament for oath-taking, it should be put on record. No questions should be put to him except by the Speaker and these should be in writing, moved and seconded and put from the Chair and carried before being put to Baron de Rothschild. This was agreed to and he was admitted to the House.

The question of the naval estimates was brought up when Joseph Hume proposed that the appropriation for officers on half-pay be reduced from £731,206 to £728,206. When Sir Francis Baring, the First Lord of the Admiralty, objected on the grounds that the saving was inconsequential, Graham, who as a member of the Committee on Naval Estimates in 1848 had recommended a plan for reducing the number of admirals from 150 to 100, sarcastically replied:

> If the reduction of one third in the number of admirals would affect no material saving in the half-pay of admirals, it was a case of despair. The right hon. Baronet appeared to think that it would not be possible to add any fresh youth, vigour, and activity to the list by means of selection. If they could neither reduce the expense, nor render this class of officers more efficient by infusing health and vigour into it, he thought the case of the admirals was desperate.[79]

But the House did not agree with Graham and rejected Hume's

[79] *Hansard*, 3rd Ser., CXIII, 471.

motion. Nor was Graham's opposition to the Government proposal to grant a sum of £30,000 to aid the depositors of the Cuffe-Street bank which had failed because of mismanagement, any more effective. His argument here was that if these depositors were to be aided, it would have to be done in all similar cases. If the grant of £30,000, when the depositors had lost £64,000, was founded on charity or sympathy, he said, 'it was too much'; if it was founded on equity, 'then the amount ought to be, not £30,000 but £64,000'.[80]

The comparative calm which had settled over the country in the summer of 1850 was suddenly broken in September by the publication of a Papal Bull establishing in England a hierarchy of bishops and dividing the country into twelve territorial Sees. Wiseman was elevated to the Cardinalate and consecrated Archbishop of Westminster; other Roman bishops assumed territorial titles. The country was in an uproar, 'meetings everywhere, addresses to Bishops and their replies, addresses to the Queen; speeches, letters, articles, all pouring from the press day after day . . .'[81] Russell, primarily an Erastian, was furious. In a letter to his friend, the Bishop of Durham, he characterized the Pope's action as ' "insolent and insidious" ' and denounced as 'unworthy sons of the Church of England' all those who approved of the adoption in England of 'the claim of infallibility for the Church, the superstitious use of the sign of the cross in baptism, . . . the muttering of the liturgy so as to disguise the language in which it was written, . . . and the administration of penance and absolution'. These things were simply 'mummeries of superstition'.[82]

The letter, made public with Russell's permission, occasioned a great deal of discussion. The *Quarterly Review* probably best reflected English Protestant sentiment when it wrote: 'The people of England . . . will not again place their necks beneath the sandals of monks.'[83] Roman Catholics, on the other hand, resented having their service described as 'mummeries of superstition', while the High Church group objected to being called 'unworthy sons of the Church'.

[80] *Ibid.*, 754.   [81] GREVILLE, *Memoirs*, VI, 259. See also *Punch*, XIX.
[82] Cited in WALPOLE, *op. cit.*, II, 120-121.
[83] *Quart. Rev.*, LXXXVIII, 264.

Unfortunately for Russell his letter alienated not only the High Church group but also Graham, who characterized it as 'hasty, intemperate, and ill-advised'. In a letter to Howard of Greystoke, he declared: 'Although I am a sincere Protestant, and resent the haughty tone assumed by the Pope in his Bull, and by Cardinal Wiseman in his pastoral letter, yet I am unwilling to join in the No-Popery cry, or to ask for the revival of penal laws or for any new enactment which might fetter the Roman Catholics in the full and proper exercise of their religious discipline within the realm.' He, too, was offended by the 'arrogance' and 'folly' of the Pope and Cardinal, but even so he could not agree to treat the religion of seven million of his countrymen with disrespect, 'or to contemplate for one moment the reversal of a policy which, in defiance of the No-Popery cry, I have supported throughout my life'.[84]

The 'Grahamites' were in different parts of the country at the time, but they all came to the same conclusion: though Pope and Cardinal had acted in an aggressive and impertinent manner, no penal enactments should be passed[85] and they must consequently oppose Russell's action.[86]

Disraeli and Stanley were overjoyed at this turn of events. Knowing that with Peel gone, and 'Graham and Co.' decidedly opposed to Russell on this question, and that the Whigs could not long remain in office, they sought to widen the schism by getting Graham to join them in a reconstructed Conservative party. Once again, however, Graham refused, because, he wrote to Londonderry, 'the policy of Protection, on which Lord Stanley insists, is an inseparable barrier between us'. He believed in a two-party system, he said, but he would not now join either one. Nor would he actively lead a third party: 'I do not presume to give advice to others: I have not courted any following; I have carefully abstained from all cabals and private negotiations.'[87]

As soon as Parliament met, in 1851, Russell introduced an Ecclesiastical Titles Bill the purpose of which was to restrain the Pope from organizing into territorial dioceses the congregations of Roman Catholics in the United Kingdom. Against this proposal

---

[84] Graham to Howard, November 23rd, 1850, in PARKER, Life of Graham, II, 113-114.
[85] See STANMORE, Memoirs of Sidney Herbert, I, 131.
[86] See BALFOUR, Life of Aberdeen, II, 160.
[87] Graham to Londonderry, January 31st, 1851, in PARKER, Life of Graham, II, 123.

the Grahamites fought a vigorous but losing battle, and as usual it was Graham who was the leader. He opposed the Bill on two grounds: first because it was a gratuitous interference with the principle of religious toleration; secondly, because it was a reversal of a policy which had been pursued since 1828. Was this what the House of Commons should expect from Russell? 'Is that the Russell chosen by the City of London as the champion of civil and religious liberty? Is it that Russell whose name will go down to posterity identified with the repeal of the Test and Corporation Acts?' The Bill was a bad one, he said, for it was equivalent to a declaration of war against seven million of the Queen's Irish subjects and if passed would render the peaceable government of Ireland impossible.[88] Graham's colleagues all joined in the attack and though the Bill was passed, they managed to carry one amendment after another until as Graham humorously put it, the Bill consisted of 'a preamble of more than usual length, and only three clauses'.[89]

The *Morning Chronicle*, *Post*, *Globe*, and *Manchester Guardian*[90] all agreed that Graham's had been the most masterful and exhaustive of all speeches on the question, but he nevertheless lost prestige by it, for many now came to look upon Graham as the confessed champion of the Court of Rome. Disraeli was convinced (happy thought!) that Graham was ruined. 'As a public man', he wrote, 'he is considered finished. A month ago, he was the proximate premier.'[91] The *Post* was of the same opinion and declared that Graham had 'knocked down his own wickets with his own bat', and that he now had no chance of ever becoming the Prime Minister.[92]

But Graham promptly recovered a great deal of his lost prestige. Disraeli drew attention to the acute distress among the agricultural classes, which he said had resulted from the Repeal Act of 1846, and asked the House to declare it to be the duty of the Government to introduce some relief measures without delay. Against this proposal Graham made one of his most effective speeches.

[88] See *Hansard*, 3rd Ser., CXV, 283-309.
[89] *Ibid.*, CXVII, 1358. Cook writes that the Bill was so watered down by these amendments that it became 'a dead letter'. EDWARD COOK, *Delane of the Times*, 42.
[90] *Chronicle*, March 1st, 1851, p. 5, and March 21st, p. 5; *Post*, May 31st, 1851, p. 4; *Globe*, February 14th, 1851, p. 4; *Manchester Guardian*, March 26th, 1851, p. 4.
[91] DISRAELI, *op cit.*, 102. [92] *Post*, May 31st, 1851, p. 4.

The time had gone, he declared, when any Government could by law artificially enhance the price of corn, for there was not 'a ploughboy who plods his weary way on the most distant and barren hill of Scotland; . . . there is not a weaver in the humblest cottage in Lancashire who has not fuller and cheaper meals without any fall in his wages than he ever had before — and he knows the reason why'. It was cheaper food! Disraeli's Bill was 'studiously elusive' and 'ambiguous', and the House ought to reject it. Disraeli had asked the House to forget the past, but that, answered Graham, was 'like administering a dose of chloroform before a capital operation'. He, for one, had recovered from the anodyne and would not forget the past.[93] Then he took up each of Disraeli's proposals and demolished them, doing it so well that the *Manchester Guardian* declared it had proved to one and all that Graham was 'the most practical and clear-headed of public men',[94] while the *Globe* asserted that he had effectively shut the gates of mercy on protection and given the *coup de grâce* to the Protectionists.[95]

It was, as Stanley admitted, a 'very telling' speech,[96] and enabled the Russell Government to defeat the motion. But Graham could not save Russell from himself. Locke King asked leave to bring in a Bill for equalizing the county with the borough franchise. Without consulting his cabinet, Russell promised to deal with the subject the following year. Resenting this conduct, many of Russell's own party deserted him and on February 22nd, 1851, Russell therefore resigned.

The Queen immediately sent for Lord Stanley, but when he told her that he could not form a successful government, she called in Aberdeen, Graham, and Russell.[97] After a long interview it was decided that Russell should once more attempt a junction with the Grahamites.[98] But the latter would not approve of the Ecclesias-

---

[93] *Hansard*, 3rd Ser., CXIV, 516-537.

[94] *Manchester Guardian*, February 22nd, 1851, p. 6.

[95] *Globe*, February 19th, 1851, p. 2. On the other hand, *Blackwood's* (LXIX, 599), denounced this speech as 'mockingly cruel' and 'bitterly unfeeling'.

[96] Cited in PARKER, *Life of Graham*, II, 126.

[97] See *Chronicle*, February 25th, 1851, p. 5; *Ill. News*, XVIII, 174-175.

[98] This annoyed the *Standard* which said that Graham and 'his dozen followers' could only bring to such a union 'the strength of their own characters — such as it is'. (February 26th, 1851, p. 2, and August 6th, 1851, p. 2). The *Globe* (March 1st, 1851, p. 4), and the *Manchester Guardian* (March 5th, 1851, p. 4), however, thought such a fusion would be a good thing.

tical Titles Bill, and since Parliament had voted solidly for that Bill, they refused to join a party committed to it. Russell therefore had to resign his commission and the Queen once more sent for Stanley, who, unable to secure the services of Canning and Gladstone, had to give up the task. Since Aberdeen had also refused to form a ministry because of his opposition to the Popery Bill, the Queen had to turn to Russell again.

This time Russell drew up and circulated a memorandum[99] in which he agreed to the following policies: 1, free trade would be safeguarded; 2, financial measures would be kept 'open'; 3, the Ecclesiastical Titles Bill would be modified; 4, a reform bill would be brought in after Easter; 5, a commission of inquiry into corrupt practices at elections would be appointed. But Graham refused to agree to numbers three and five, and, in addition, was sure that Russell would not go far enough in the way of economy so the negotiations broke down, and Russell had to form a wholly Whig ministry.[100]

Having refused to join the Whigs, Gladstone now desired Graham to place himself at the head of his own followers and help them pursue a course of their own, but Graham would not do this either, primarily because of his timidity and of his fear of assuming leadership. He was, as Greville correctly put it, 'generally afraid of everything, and sees many unnecessary and imaginary dangers'.[101] It was this fear and timidity which kept him from becoming Prime Minister at this time, and he was never again to have the opportunity. But while the free trade issue prevented him from joining Stanley, the Popery Bill made fusion with Russell impossible; and while his own timidity and fear made his own leadership of a separate party impossible, he could still exercise a great influence on the course of events by throwing his influence on one side or the other. Moreover, in the event that Russell's Government were defeated and Stanley were again unable to form a government, a Liberal government might be formed. In this case he could insist upon a large number of the Grahamites being given important posts.

[99] Unpublished memorandum quoted in *Edin. Rev.*, CLVIII, 554.

[100] Accounts of these negotiations can be found in *Hansard*, 3rd Ser., CXIV, 1044 et seq.; WALPOLE, *op. cit.*, II, 123-128; *Letters of Queen Victoria*, II, 44 et seq.; GREVILLE, *Memoirs*, VI, 268 et seq.; MORLEY, *op. cit.*, I, 406-407.

[101] GREVILLE, *Memoirs*, VI, 288. See also H. MAXWELL, *Life and Letters of the Fourth Earl of Clarendon*, I, 326 (Hereinafter cited as *Life of Clarendon*).

Russell's Government slid through the rest of the session without mishap but he, as well as everyone else, knew that this could be credited only to the lack of cohesion among the Opposition. He needed more strength in his cabinet if he was to hold office for long. With this in mind he renewed his efforts to get Graham and he thought that with the Popery Bill already passed there was no good reason for Graham not to join.

Since Graham had earlier refused the Admiralty Office,[102] Hobhouse, on February 15th, 1851, offered to give up the India Office to make room for him.[103] In September, he was offered the Board of Control and for his friend, Sir Frederick Peel, the Under-Secretaryship of the Colonies. These efforts to get Graham amused *Punch*:

> The Baronet of Netherby,
> Cold heart and ready tongue,
> Beheld himself, with wonder
> Towards Whig embraces flung.[104]

But Graham refused each of the proffered embraces because he could not get along with Palmerston, whom Russell could not get along without.[105] In addition, he told Lewis that he knew an extension of the suffrage was now inevitable and was afraid that Russell would go too far in that direction. Gloomy and pessimistic as usual, he was fearful that such a programme would have to be accompanied by a large disfranchisement and a redistribution of seats with the result that ' a war of classes and interests will commence, the end of which I cannot foresee'.[106] This running before popular clamour rather than leading and directing it was one of Graham's chief shortcomings and the main reason for his failure to achieve political leadership.

Soon after the last overture had been made to Graham, Palmerston ran into difficulties in two celebrated cases. First, he was compelled to agree not to receive Kossuth, the Hungarian revol-

[102] This was in January 1849 when Lord Auckland died.

[103] See F. Hobhouse to Russell, February 15th, 1851, in *Later Corr. of Russell*, I, 205.

[104] *Punch*, XX, 107.

[105] Graham would have preferred to see Palmerston as 'leader of the Protectionists opposite to him to having him on the Treasury Bench next to him'. Windsor MSS., c. 46, cited in BELL, *op. cit.*, II, 41.

[106] Graham to Lewis, September 20th, 1851, in PARKER, *Life of Graham*, II, 137.

utionist, in his home. But Palmerston did receive a public deputation and a complimentary address praising him for his efforts in Kossuth's behalf.[107] Then, when Louis Napoleon engineered his *coup d'état*, he disobeyed his instructions not to depart from a policy of neutrality, and signified to the French Ambassador his approval of Napoleon's action. Russell, to assuage the Queen's anger, dismissed Palmerston from the Foreign Office.

It was not Palmerston's dismissal that surprised Graham; it was that his presence in the cabinet 'had been endured so long'.[108] *The Times* thought that it had seen the last of Palmerston, but Graham did not think so because he was sure that Palmerston would now be bent on revenging himself on Russell. As to Napoleon, Graham was certain that he would soon pander to the vainglory of the French and embark on an aggressive war, and that England would eventually be involved in the fray.[109]

With Palmerston gone, Russell once more sought Graham's help. But Graham refused because he thought Russell's Government was doomed and that it was 'useless to add new materials to a tottering wall'.[110]

On all three counts Graham was right. The war he predicted came; Palmerston got his revenge; and the 'tottering wall' fell. On February 20th, 1852, Palmerston carried an amendment to the Government's Militia Bill, and Russell, taking it as a lack of confidence vote, promptly resigned, thereby affording Palmerston his 'tit for tat'.

On March 15th the new Prime Minister, Lord Derby, announced that although his party was still committed to protection he had decided to dissolve Parliament so as to let the country decide the issue in a new election. Graham at first decided not to stand for election at Carlisle: 'I have not sought for a seat in the next Parliament', he wrote to his friend, Mounsey, 'I know not that any one will be open to me. It is enough, at my age [60], to tender my services, if my countrymen require them.'[111] Later on, however, he changed his mind and became one of two Free Trade candi-

[107] See KINGSLEY MARTIN, *The Triumph of Lord Palmerston*, 68; *Letters of Queen Victoria*, II, 387 et seq.
[108] Graham to G. B. Roche, January 9th, 1852, in PARKER, *Life of Graham*, II, 148.
[109] Graham to Aberdeen, January 2nd, 1852, in *Ibid.*, 147-148.
[110] Graham to Cardwell, in *Ibid.*, 152. See also STANMORE, *op. cit.*, I, 146.
[111] Graham to Mounsey, January 27th, 1852, in PARKER, *Life of Graham*, II, 155.

dates.[112] In his speech to the electors he re-affirmed his opposition to protection, approved of an extension of the suffrage, but refused to accede to vote by ballot. Reaction to this speech followed the usual pattern. Free trade papers such as the *Manchester Guardian* and the *Morning Chronicle* thought it admirable, while such opposition papers as the *Standard* and *Blackwood's* thought it disgraceful.[113]

Shortly after his election at Carlisle, a city which the hostile *Standard* described as being made up of 'the least reputable population on the Islands',[114] Graham was given a reception to celebrate the victory. In his after-dinner speech, he said he was glad that protection was now dead because it was no more nor less than a system of 'outdoor relief to distressed landlords (great laughter and cheering)'.[115] He favoured the disfranchisement of decayed boroughs, a moderate extension of the suffrage, but not the grant of the ballot. The chairman, in introducing Graham, asked him, since he was not a Derbyite or a Russellite, what kind of an 'ite' he was, to which Graham replied: 'I have been a Peelite; but am now resolved not to bind myself in the fetters of any party, but will do my best as a private member of Parliament.'[116]

Why this decision to be free of party ties? The answer is to be found in the bewildering state of party confusion, especially in Graham's own group. For one thing, as soon as Derby assumed office, Graham and Cardwell had taken seats on the front Opposition benches next to Russell, while the 'Gladstonian sub-division' took their seats on the Opposition benches below the gangway.[117] In addition, Newcastle, Gladstone, and Herbert were High Churchmen and on Church questions did not agree well with the others. They were more conservative, too, than was Graham and were disposed to support the Derby Government if it would only abandon protection. If Derby would do this, they were sure that many Conservatives would desert Disraeli, and then a Liberal-

[112] The other was Joseph Ferguson, an 'advanced liberal'. The Derbyite candidate was W. N. Hodgson. See *Ill. News*, XX, 363.

[113] *Manchester Guardian*, July 7th, 1852, p. 6; *Chronicle*, July 6th, 1852, p. 4; *Standard*, July 16th, 1852, p. 2; *Blackwood's*, LXXII, 115-116.

[114] *Standard*, July 9th, 1852, p. 2.

[115] *Graham Papers*. The *Ill. News* (XXI, 67), carried a full account of this speech as did most of the newspapers.

[116] *Graham Papers*. The speech can be found in *Blackwood's*, LXXII, 260.

[117] See MORLEY, *op. cit.*, I, 420 et seq.

Conservative party could be formed which could easily take office. Sir James, however, would not agree, preferring, he said, a Liberal party 'animated by a Conservative spirit' to a 'liberally-disposed Conservative' party.[118] Finally, Graham and Gladstone were far apart on the question of political reform. In fact, Graham's opinions on this question appeared so liberal to Gladstone that he doubted whether they could continue to act together. Graham promptly informed Gladstone that he had never presumed to sway the judgment or to influence the counsels of his former colleagues in the Government of Sir Robert Peel. 'You intimate the decision that party connection must no longer subsist between us. I submit to your decision with regret.'[119]

These differences in the ranks of the Peelites were reflected in the election results. Only about forty were returned to Parliament, and Cardwell, Palmer, Mahon, and Smythe were among those defeated. 'It was often said', wrote the *Manchester Guardian*, 'that the Peelites were an army of officers without soldiers, and it now seems as if the officers had followed the privates.'[120] The *Illus-trated News* was convinced that the country would henceforth 'hear no more of the Peelites as a party', and that the group would split up and join either of the other parties.[121] *Blackwood's Magazine* was convinced that the country wanted men like Graham, Cobden, Bright, Cardwell, and Palmer in Parliament, but not in office.

At the same time, the Whig party had also split on this question of reform. Such leaders as Lansdowne and Palmerston were opposed to an extension of the franchise; Russell was irrevocably committed to it. He stood in the same position with respect to this question, to Lansdowne and Palmerston among the Whigs as Graham did to Gladstone and Herbert among the Peelites. Con-sequently, Russell and Graham were drawn closer together.[122]

But the election, except for decimating the ranks of the Peelites, did not materially alter the relative strength of the parties, and

[118] See STANMORE, *op. cit.*, I, 159.
[119] Graham to Gladstone, March 29th, 1852, cited in MORLEY, *op. cit.*, I, 421.
[120] *Manchester Guardian*, July 10th, 1852, p. 6.
[121] *Ill. News*, XXI, 33.
[122] Aberdeen stood with Graham on this question and as a result Russell, Graham, and Aberdeen were soon on intimate and cordial terms. See GREVILLE, *Memoirs*, VI, 355.

therefore, in view of the fact that Graham had advocated the ousting of the Derby Government in his Carlisle speech, it was generally expected that he would move a vote of want of confidence as soon as Parliament met. But who would replace Derby? Russell could not because of the lack of unity in his own party and his split with Palmerston. A Whig Government without Palmerston was out of the question. Many therefore assumed that the Peelites, led by Graham, would take over the job, supported by the Russell wing of the Whig party, the Radicals, and the 'Irish Popish brigade'.[123] *The Times* (now pro-Graham), the *Illustrated News*, the *Chronicle*, and *Blackwood's* were all certain that this would take place. 'The coming man', wrote the latter, 'to over-throw Lord Derby is Sir James Graham, and he [Graham] has taken uncommon pains to familiarize the public with him in that capacity.'[124] But they were all wrong, for Graham knew that he was not fit by temperament or disposition to lead a party, that he could serve his country best only as a 'first lieutenant', and that his tendency to boldness in language and timidity in action unfitted him for the premiership.[125] He knew, too, that the bulk of the Whigs would not support him and that the Derbyites disliked him. Furthermore, he had come to the conclusion that if a Liberal party was to be formed Aberdeen would have to be the leader.

A coalition was therefore clearly indicated. But what kind of a coalition? Sir James desired a Peelite-Whig combination in which the former would have at least half the power. The *sine qua non* of such a coalition, however, was the adhesion of Russell, but try as he might Graham could not make Russell understand that he could not be the leader of such a coalition because most of the Peelites would not support a Russell-led Government.[126] Russell, on the other hand, would not serve in any government of which he was not

[123] According to the *Standard* (September 8th, 1852, p. 2), the Irish were counting the number of places they would get when Graham formed his cabinet.

[124] *Blackwood's*, LXXII, 362.

[125] When, in July 1852 Roebuck, a Liberal M.P., implored him to lead a 'Liberal party', Graham replied that he would like to see a united Liberal party but that 'once for all, I declare that I cannot be "the Great Commoner" or "the leader" ... I am quite content with my station in the ranks'. Cited in PARKER, *Life of Graham*, II, 164.

[126] For the correspondence between Russell and Graham, see *Ibid.*, 165-169. See also, BALFOUR, *op. cit.*, II, 169; STANMORE, *op. cit.*, I, 161.

the leader, for it would be 'too degrading' to him. Graham then 'dangled the memory of Fox in 1806 before his eyes', but to no avail.[127] When Palmerston proposed a Whig-Peelite ministry headed by Lansdowne, Graham refused to join because he wished a government led by Aberdeen and because he did not want to see the Peelites 'absorbed in the Liberal party' — now often a designation for the Whigs.[128]

It was clear, therefore, that if the forty-odd Peelites held together as a unit (which they could do only if Gladstone, Herbert, and their friends did not desert to the Derby ranks), they could when Parliament met, continue to hold the balance of power. While this was a possibility, Graham did not think it probable because he could not see how any of Peel's former colleagues could join a party dominated by Disraeli, 'the bitterest and least sincere of Peel's assailants', and one whom the Peelites hated.[129] While this was doubtless the case, it was also true that many Peelites disliked Graham's friendliness to Russell. Therefore, to achieve unity in the ranks, Graham wrote Gladstone a friendly letter congratulating him on his election at Oxford and a little later on refused to attend a dinner given by Russell.[130] In addition, he wrote to Aberdeen, who passed the word around among the Peelites, that his allegiance to Russell was 'strictly limited to conjoint opposition to the present Government. I have changed no opinion, I have submitted in no degree my future course to his dictation . . . I have not promised to be his vassal . . .'.[131]

The breach in the Peelite ranks was consequently healed and on November 16th Aberdeen, Graham, Newcastle, Herbert, Gladstone, and Sir John Young met at Aberdeen's home and agreed to a resolution drawn up by Graham, which he had discussed with Palmerston and Russell, stating that Parliament intended to adhere to free trade. It was also agreed, on Graham's insistence, that Villiers, because of his long and zealous labours for free trade, should move the resolution as soon as Parliament assembled.[132]

---

[127] See GEORGE VILLIERS, *A Vanished Victorian*, 214; BELL, *op. cit.*, II, 66-67.

[128] See *Edin. Rev.*, CLVIII, 563. Gladstone took the same view.

[129] MORLEY, *op. cit.*, I, 432.

[130] See Graham's letter to Russell, November 1st, 1852, in PARKER, *Life of Graham*, II, 183.

[131] Graham to Aberdeen, October 9th, 1852, in *Ibid.*, 182.

[132] Russell had suggested that Graham make the motion. See *Ibid.*, 177.

In accordance with this agreement, Villiers, on November 23rd, moved a resolution that good times in England were due to the Repeal Act of 1846, 'a wise, just, and beneficial measure'.[133] Disraeli promptly admitted that the election had proved that the country was opposed to protection and that he was willing to accept that mandate, but that he could not accept those 'three odious epithets' (wise, just, and beneficial). He countered with a resolution to the effect that the Government acknowledged that free trade had benefited the working classes. But the Peelites would not accept this resolution because, as Graham wrote to Gladstone, free trade was ' "wise, just and beneficial" ' to *all* classes and not merely to the working classes, and because when free trade was at stake he 'would rather act with Charles Villiers than with Disraeli'.[134] Refusal of the Peelites to accept Disraeli's resolution meant the end of the Government. It would have fallen immediately had not Palmerston come to its rescue by proposing an amendment couched in the words of Graham's original draft. That draft had read as follows:

> That it is the opinion of this House that the policy of unrestricted competition, firmly maintained and prudently extended, will best enable the industry of the country to bear its burdens, and will thereby most surely promote the welfare and contentment of the people, and that the House will be ready to take into consideration any measures consistent with these principles, which, in pursuance of Her Majesty's gracious speech and recommendations, may be laid before it.[135]

Disraeli was willing to accept this resolution but the Manchester group would not abandon Villiers's motion. Graham therefore voted with Palmerston and his resolution was passed by a majority of 415.[136]

But the respite for the Government of Derby was short. On December 3rd Disraeli brought in his Budget Bill. It provided for taking off about half of the malt tax and half of the hop duty, and by stages reducing the tea duty from two shillings and twopence

[133] *Hansard*, 3rd Ser., CXXIII, 381.
[134] Graham to Gladstone, November 20th, 1852, in PARKER, *Life of Graham*, II, 186-187.
[135] Cited in *Ibid.*, 185-186.
[136] *Hansard*, 3rd Ser., CXXIII, 700-701.

to one shilling. It also provided for a re-shuffling of the income-tax rates, as well as for doubling the rate of the house tax. It was an ill-conceived measure which was immediately assailed on all hands, especially by Graham and Gladstone, and on the division was beaten by a majority of nineteen votes, and Derby promptly resigned.

CHAPTER X

'FIRST LORD OF THE ADMIRALTY AGAIN'

BUT who was to replace Derby? Graham was clearly out of the running; Russell was not acceptable to the Peelites nor to the Palmerston Whigs; Lansdowne had the gout and had been too outspoken against reform; Palmerston was not acceptable to the Russell Whigs nor to the Peelites. Therefore, since Aberdeen was acceptable to the Peelites, to the Whigs, and to many of the Radicals, the premiership fell to him.

Headship having been decided upon, a cabinet had to be selected consisting of both Peelites and Whigs. The major difficulty was what post to give Russell. First Russell told Aberdeen he would like the Foreign Office, but, thinking it over, he doubted, says Walpole, 'whether he had strength to discharge the heavy duties of the Foreign Office'.[1] Then he proposed an arrangement previously arranged only for Wellington: that he should lead the Commons and sit in the Cabinet without holding office. This surprised Aberdeen[2] and annoyed Graham who, attributing Russell's change of mind to 'the pride of the Whig party revolting at an act of submission to "an old Tory" ' and believing that the Duke of Wellington was 'an exception to all rule',[3] urged Aberdeen to refuse Russell's proposition. When Russell insisted on it, Graham wrote to Aberdeen:

> He will owe nothing to the favour of his sovereign, while he wields the whole power of the democratic body. He will not be on equal terms with his colleagues ... His power will be great, his immediate responsibilities small. He holds no office and presents no assailable front; yet he may sway the counsels of the State in the most fatal direction.[4]

These arguments were sound in every respect and Aberdeen, on Graham's advice, insisted that Russell assume some office. The

[1] SPENCER WALPOLE, *Life of Russell*, II, 161.
[2] According to the *Edin. Rev.* (CLVIII, 567-569), Clarendon, Lansdowne, and Macaulay all wrote to Russell urging him to keep his promise to Aberdeen.
[3] Graham's *Journal*, cited in PARKER, *Life of Graham*, II, 194, 195.
[4] *Ibid.*, 196.

latter eventually agreed to take the Foreign Office, which he had really desired from the first.

Palmerston, having a choice of office under Aberdeen, a role in Derby's opposition, or political solitude, accepted the Home Office. Newcastle took over the War Office; Gladstone the Chancellorship of the Exchequer. Graham, who had refused the Home Office, was strongly urged by Aberdeen and Gladstone to take the Exchequer.[5] It was a position he was ideally fitted for and which he could have handled to the satisfaction of all.[6] But he refused it point blank and instead went back to his first love, the Admiralty.

Graham's return to the Admiralty met with universal approbation. The *Illustrated News* complimented him on his spirit of self-denial in having taken the Admiralty when he had been urged to take the Exchequer, and said that the nation was fortunate to have so skilful an administrator at the Admiralty.[7] The *Globe* viewed his resumption of this office with '*unmingled pleasure*';[8] the *Post* took the same attitude;[9] *The Times*,[10] and the usually hostile *Fraser's*, echoed the same sentiment;[11] while the Duke of Argyll declared that Graham was 'a coalition in himself'.[12]

With these positions in the cabinet decided upon, the struggle for the remaining offices was intense and spirited. The Whigs claimed most of them on the ground that they would have to supply the bulk of the support on which the ministry relied. Russell, who thought Grey and Clarendon should be in the cabinet, wrote complainingly to Aberdeen: 'To this party [Peelites] of thirty you propose to give seven seats in the Cabinet, to the Whigs and Radicals five, to Lord Palmerston one.'[13] The Peelites, on the

---

[5] See A. T. BASSETT, *Gladstone to His Wife*, 97.

[6] Thomas Baring, who surely knew, said that Graham would make an excellent Chancellor of the Exchequer. See GREVILLE, *Memoirs*, VI, 433. So, too, did the *Manchester Guardian* which wrote: 'As an administrator, no statesman of the age stands so prominent as Sir James Graham.' (July 14, 1852, p. 4.)

[7] *Ill. News*, XXII, No. 602, p. 26.   [8] *Globe*, December 24th, 1852, p. 2.

[9] *Post*, February 22nd, 1853, p. 4.

[10] Graham told Lewis that this praise from *The Times* was precious to him 'on account of its rarity'. See Graham to Lewis, January 5th, 1853, in PARKER, *Life of Graham*, II, 205.

[11] *Fraser's*, XLVII, 332. See also *Chronicle*, December 24th, 1852, p. 4.

[12] ARGYLL, *Auto. and Memoirs*, I, 379.

[13] Russell to Aberdeen, cited in MORLEY, *Life of Gladstone*, I, 446. Of the 330 members in the Commons, 270 were Whigs and Radicals, 30 were the 'Irish Brigade' and 30 were Peelites.

other hand, claimed equal representation with the Whigs because of the unquestioned ability of their leaders. 'I have never passed a week so unpleasantly', wrote Graham. 'It was a battle for places from hostile camps, and the Whigs disregarded fitness for the public service altogether. They fought for their men as partisans. . . .'[14]

When this struggle for the pieces of a cake which was too small, as Disraeli sarcastically but accurately put it, was over, the cabinet consisted of six Whigs, six Peelites and one Radical (Molesworth). It was a very powerful ministry possessing great administrative ability, business acumen, parliamentary experience and formidable debating power. But, consisting of independent men of great ability, it lacked the cement of mediocrity which has held so many ministries together. It was, as Graham put it, 'a powerful team, but it will require good driving'.[15]

Just before the Christmas holidays the cabinet met at Aberdeen's and appointed a committee, of which Graham was a member, to draft a new income-tax measure. Then he went to Netherby for the holidays and to stand for election at Carlisle, where he promised his constituents that the Government would bring in a bill to extend the franchise.

True to this promise, Graham and Russell framed a reform measure providing for a considerable extension of the franchise and for the disfranchisement of many small boroughs. This proposal then became the subject of discussion in the cabinet, where Palmerston, Lansdowne, and Gladstone all opposed it. Despite this opposition, however, Graham insisted that they go ahead with it. 'We shall be ruined out of doors,' he wrote to Russell, 'if we dilute our measure to gratify squeamish tastes within the cabinet.'[16] Aberdeen agreed with Graham and Russell, but by February 1854 when Graham introduced the measure to the House, the Crimean War had begun, and he agreed to postpone the measure until the struggle was over.

This war, which involved Russia and Turkey, and England and France, now occupied all of the time and energy of the First Lord of the Admiralty. From the first, Graham, who felt that the war was unwise and unnecessary, attributed the difficulties in the Near

[14] Graham's *Journal*, in PARKER, *op. cit.*, II, 200.   [15] *Ibid.*, 197.
[16] Graham to Russell, November 25th, 1853, in *Ibid.*, 208.

East to the actions of Stratford de Redcliffe, whom Russell had appointed once again to the court at Constantinople 'to resist Russian designs'.[17] He suspected Palmerston, too, of concurring in Stratford's actions and of desiring the premiership should Aberdeen retire from office.[18] He was therefore strongly in favour of peace. So, too, were the Queen, Prince Albert, and the rest of the cabinet.[19] It was the general public who wanted the war and who openly supported it.[20] A like situation prevailed in Russia. The Czar was a pacifist and relied upon his friendship with Aberdeen to keep England peaceful. The Russian aristocracy, remembering their experience during Napoleon's campaigns, were opposed to war because it would result in their economic ruination and would also give an impetus to the serf-liberation movement. It was the liberals who wanted the war because they hoped it would discredit the czardom. And the masses followed the Church in desiring the spread of Orthodoxy to the Balkans. 'Holy Russia talked of war,' says Stephen Graham, 'war for the Sepulchre, for Bethlehem, for the cathedral of St. Sophia in Constantinople.'[21] In France, no group really wanted war. Napoleon III, in spite of his desire for 'la gloire', preferred to gain Catholic support for his regime by a diplomatic victory over Orthodox Russia.[22] The French people had had a surfeit of war and turmoil since 1789 and did not want a war in the Near East or anywhere else.

Graham, as we have seen, preferred peace, but war becoming each day more probable, he had to make the necessary naval preparations. On February 18th, 1853, he brought before the House his Naval Estimates Bill. It provided for the following increases: £193,211 for wages to seamen, £70,919 for victuals for

[17] WARD and GOOCH, *Camb. Hist. of Br. For. Pol.*, II, 340.

[18] Palmerston, though not the Foreign Secretary, had been corresponding with Stratford. See GREVILLE, *Diary*, P. W. Wilson, ed., II, 463.

[19] Aberdeen had met Czar Nicholas I on the latter's visit to England in 1844 and since that time had often been accused of being pro-Russian. Not even Palmerston wanted war. He was, says Martin, 'merely willing to risk more than other people'. MARTIN, *The Triumph of Lord Palmerston*, 82. See also, BALFOUR, *Life of Aberdeen*, II, 182; *Standard*, July 3rd, 1854, p. 2.

[20] According to Eych, the public was 'passionately eager for war'. E. EYCH, *Gladstone*, 85.

[21] STEPHEN GRAHAM, *Tsar of Freedom*, 30. See also, HAROLD TEMPERLEY, *England and the Near East*, 459 n.

[22] See ALBERT GUERARD, *Napoleon III*, 176 et seq., and F. A. SIMPSON, *Louis Napoleon and the Recovery of France*, 217.

these seamen, £140,516 for naval stores, including a small sum for steam machinery. He defended these increases because of the impending war, the increased number of seamen, and the increased cost of supplies. The Estimates met with approval and praise from all sides and were carried with scarcely a dissenting vote.[23]

During the discussions on the appropriation for the Admiralty Office, Graham was asked if he would not substitute confinement on bread and water for corporal punishment. He answered that he disliked corporal punishment, but that he would not agree to the request because most of the abuses in the system had been abolished by his regulation of 1833 and because, all hands on a ship being needed, to keep some in confinement would mean more work for those who had not misconducted themselves.[24]

In April orders were issued to all admirals, port officials, and others to maintain a discreet silence and under no circumstances to talk with newspaper men about naval matters.[25] Other orders directed that all ships be got in readiness for action, that the recruiting of seamen be begun and that all leaves be cancelled.[26] An extensive correspondence was carried on by the Admiralty with various architects, engineers, and others about new and different designs of ship-construction, improvements in guns, etc.[27] An assiduous search was instituted in June for competent pilots, particularly for those who knew the Baltic region.[28]

In addition, by August, Graham was ready to present to Parliament his plans for the creation of a new unit to be known as the Naval Coast Volunteers. In elucidating his plan he declared that there were a large number of men living along the coast (fishermen, bargemen, etc.) who would not object to being trained for a short time each year in 'the use of great guns'. He hoped that from this source and in this manner, he could obtain a force of about 10,000

---

[23] Joseph Hume said he was delighted to see Graham back at the Admiralty, a department that 'had received its greatest improvements through his agency'. *Hansard*, 3rd Ser., CXXIV, 321. Stafford joined in the applause saying that he had more faith in Graham 'than in anyone who had presided over the Admiralty in his time'. *Ibid.*, 324.

[24] *Ibid.*, 364.

[25] *Admiralty Papers* (Adm. Sec. Out-Letters; Home Stations, Military Branch), 2/1562.

[26] *Ibid.*

[27] *Admiralty Papers* (Adm. Comptroller Out-Letters), 9/15; 9/16; 9/17.

[28] *Admiralty Papers* (Adm. Secret Orders and Letters), 2/1697.

men. The training period would last for 28 days in each of five successive years. For each 28 days of training the men would receive a bounty of £6. They would be trained either on shore, at sea (not more than 60 leagues from the coast of Ireland and England) or both, and if danger arose the Government could call on them for one to two years of service. The result, said Graham, would be that England would always have a force ready to defend her coasts.[29] The Bill met with no real opposition and was quickly passed. At the same time Parliament also approved a Bill to give seamen higher pay if they enlisted for ten years instead of five.[30]

Then, in midsummer, the first grand naval review since 1814 was held off Spithead. It was an impressive display partly because steam was used to propel some of the new ships. Since they outran the sailing ships and were also more manœuvrable, a revolution in the whole character of naval warfare was clearly forecast.[31]

To secure adequate and reliable information about the Russian fleet, the First Lord sent a surveyor to the Baltic to visit Kronstadt and the Åland Islands. The surveyor, Captain Washington, found the Russian fleet in a 'wonderfully efficient state' and was 'thunderstruck at the general activity as well as the method of their proceedings'.[32] This was in sharp contrast to the prevailing view respecting Russia's naval strength and to that of Seymour, the British Ambassador to Russia,[33] and was therefore a source of perplexity to Graham.

However, a greater source of anxiety and a more pressing problem was that of securing able commanders. Seniority, which too frequently means senility, had been almost the sole basis of promotion in both branches of the military service, and no one was more anxious to remove the paralysis caused by this dead-hand than was Graham. 'There is no sense in it,' he had written to Peel in 1844, 'unless the wishes and feelings of worn-out admirals are to prevail over the interests of the public and the safety of the State.'[34] But the feelings of the admirals had prevailed. Lord

---

[29] *Hansard*, 3rd Ser., CXXIX, 1110 et seq.   [30] *Ibid.*, 745 et seq.
[31] A list of the ships in the review, including types, tonnage, number of men, and number of ships, was published in the *Ill. News*, XXIII, No. 640, p. 145 et seq.
[32] See Clarendon to Graham, September 27th, 1853, in PARKER, *op. cit.*, II, 223-224.
[33] Seymour to Graham, August, 18th, 1853, in *Ibid.* See also *Fraser's*, XLIX, 214-224.
[34] Graham to Peel, December 21st, 1844, in *Graham Papers*.

Dundonald was 79; Dundas was 69; Napier was 67. Justification for this state of affairs was to be found in the fact that the decades after 1814 had not been a time of competitive armaments and comfort could be found in the fact that other States had been equally negligent.

Early in 1853 Lord John Russell, the Foreign Secretary, persuaded Stratford to return to Constantinople as British Ambassador. Before he got there, however, events had transpired that pointed directly to trouble. The Czar, according to Temperley, believing that 'whatever happened, Aberdeen would prevent his colleagues from going to war',[35] incensed at the diplomatic defeat he had suffered in Montenegro,[36] and impressed with the imagined necessity of restoring the lost Russian ascendancy at the Straits, sent Prince Menshikoff to Constantinople. The latter's instructions were not clear, and he did not use the wide latitude given him with much discretion. Arrogant and high-handed, his first act on reaching Constantinople, on February 28th, 1853, was to so ostentatiously insult the Turkish Foreign Minister, Fuad Pasha, that 'the panic-stricken Sultan,' to use Seton-Watson's phrase, 'replaced [him] by the much more mediocre Rifaat Pasha'.[37] Alarmed by this development, the French and British Chargés d'Affaires, who were in charge of negotiations at Constantinople pending the arrival of the ambassadors, decided to call up the fleets. Benedetti telegraphed the French Government requesting the movement of the fleet to the Aegean, but Rose, who was very nervous and worried, instead of consulting the home Government, requested Admiral Dundas, Commander of the Mediterranean Fleet stationed at Malta, to send the fleet to Vourla. Dundas properly refused until he was specifically ordered to do so by the Admiralty.[38] Graham immediately called a cabinet meeting for March 20th at which Dundas's action was approved.[39] At the same time, Graham unsuccessfully opposed the suggestion of Palmerston and Russell that Stratford be given authority to call up the fleet if occasion demanded it, and Clarendon directed Stratford not to do so unless Russia displayed 'intentions of unmistakeable

[35] TEMPERLEY, *op. cit.*, 300.   [36] *Ibid.*, 198 et seq.
[37] SETON-WATSON, *Britain in Europe*, 308.
[38] *Admiralty Papers* (Adm. Sec. In-Letters), 1/5617, No. 479.
[39] *Admiralty Papers* (Adm. Secret Orders and Letters), 2/1697.

hostility', and even then, the fleet should not pass the Dardanelles except on 'the express demand of the Sultan'.[40] Dundas was therefore ordered by Graham, on June 2nd, to move the fleet to the 'neighbourhood of the Dardanelles' and to keep in touch with Stratford.[41] Fearful that the Ambassador might do something rash, Graham wrote to him in July that Dundas had been told to place the fleet at his disposal, but that he hoped Stratford would use this power with discretion for it would be 'a miserable end if Europe be convulsed in these latter days by a Holy War'.[42] But Stratford's letters to Graham were harsh and ominous, or so, at least, it seemed to Graham, and he therefore wrote to Clarendon on August 18th that Stratford was 'hardening himself to resist the proposed note from Vienna, and notwithstanding the peremptory order to the contrary, he is quite capable of advising the Turk to be refractory. In this case you should be ready to supersede him without the loss of a day'.[43] This opinion of Stratford was shared by Aberdeen and even by Clarendon, who, on July 8th had written to Lord Cowley at Paris: 'My fear is that he will never consent to any arrangement that does not humiliate the Emperor of Russia', which, he wrote a few days later, 'has become a necessity of his nature'.[44]

Stratford arrived in Constantinople on April 5th and promptly succeeded in separating the question of the Holy Places, in which he sided with Russia, from the demand of the Czar that recognition be granted to his claim to a protectorate over all the Greek Orthodox Christians in the Ottoman Empire, to which he would not agree. The French, Austrian, and Prussian Ambassadors agreed to advise the Porte to reject this demand of Russia. The baffled Menshikoff packed up and returned to Odessa whence, on May 31st, he informed the Sultan that unless his (Menshikoff's) note was accepted *in toto* within eight days the Russian armies would cross the Pruth. The Porte's refusal was supported by the British

---

[40] *Admiralty Papers* (Adm. Sec. In-Letters), 1/5620.

[41] *Admiralty Papers* (Adm. Secret Orders and Letters), 2/1697.

[42] Graham to Stratford, July 8th, 1853, in PARKER, *op cit.*, II, 222.

[43] Graham to Clarendon, August 18th, 1853, in *Ibid.*

[44] Clarendon to Cowley, July 8th, 1853, in *Secrets of the Second Empire, Private Letters from the Paris Embassy, from the Papers of Henry Richard Charles Wellesley First Earl Cowley*, F. A. WELLESLEY, ed., 27 (Hereinafter cited as *Secrets of Second Empire*).

Government, which, as stated above, ordered the Fleet to Besika Bay. This was a crucial and warlike step and for it the cabinet, not Stratford, must be held responsible.

The Russian forces crossed the Pruth in July, and when the Turks prepared to resist, the European diplomats sought to resolve the problem through the medium of the Vienna Note. This note, made public on July 27th, seemed to give the Czar support for his claim to the protectorate and he therefore accepted it. For the same reason, however, the Sultan refused, and despite Stratford's advice to the contrary declared war on September 26th. On October 20th, at the request of the Sultan, Stratford ordered Dundas to move the fleet into the Dardanelles. Two days later this was done.[45] When, a month later (November 30th), the Russians annihilated the Turkish fleet at Sinope, the British fleet was ordered into the Black Sea to clear it of all Russian ships of war.

During these days of diplomatic manœuvring, Graham had assiduously laboured to prevent war[46] but the Sinope attack so inflamed anti-Russian sentiment in England,[47] that Graham knew it was now inevitable. He therefore instructed Dundas to keep his eye on Sebastopol when he got to the Black Sea for that was 'a place where a blow might be struck which would be memorable in Europe, and which would settle the affairs of the East for some time to come'. If hostilities began, Dundas was to act with decision and promptitude 'so that the struggle may be ended in the Black Sea before the Baltic opens'.[48]

Since the aged and cautious Dundas wanted to retire, Graham sought a competent and aggressive officer to be second-in-command. Sir Edmund Lyons, whom he appointed, proved to be an excellent choice for he had been in the diplomatic service and also

---

[45] *Admiralty Papers* (Adm. Sec. In-Letters, Admirals), 1/5617.

[46] 'I hope you will not allow Europe to be involved in war,' he wrote to Clarendon on September 3rd, 1853, 'because Canning is resolved to embroil matters . . . in the hope of obtaining a triumph for his own morbid vanity and implacable antipathies.' MAXWELL, *Life of Clarendon*, II, 19. See also, MORLEY, *op. cit.*, I, 482.

[47] The vocal part of the British public felt that Sinope was a 'crime' and an 'unwarranted massacre' and that it justified a declaration of war against Russia. See *Ill. News*, XXIII, No. 659, p. 549. 'It amounted', says the Duke of Argyll, 'to a frenzy and seized all classes, all ranks, and all parties.' *Auto. and Memoirs*, I, 459.

[48] Graham to Dundas, in PARKER, *op. cit.*, II, 226. Lord Cowley thought this letter of instruction an excellent one and asked Clarendon for a full copy of it. See *Secrets of Second Empire*, 34.

knew the Black Sea region thoroughly. As to the command in the Baltic, Graham told the Queen that there were three possible choices: Lord Dundonald, Sir William Parker, and Sir Charles Napier. Dundonald was 79 years of age and the cabinet decided not to appoint him. And since Parker's health was failing, Napier had to be selected. Graham's recommendation of Napier was couched in these words: 'Though his appointment may be open to some objections, it is strongly recommended by many considerations.'[49] He was reputed to be a good seaman, was said to have plenty of courage and undoubtedly loved his country. But he had on several occasions been guilty of insubordination, and on October 6th, 1853, he had addressed a public meeting in London at which he criticized the peace policy of Aberdeen and said that 'instead of reviewing a grand fleet at Spithead, he would have treated the Russians to the old Nelson trick in the Baltic'.[50] His appointment proved unfortunate in every respect.

On January 4th, 1854, the British Mediterranean fleet entered the Black Sea; four days later it anchored at Sinope; and on March 28th, the Czar having refused to evacuate Moldavia and Wallachia, England and France declared war. But was the Navy ready for war? According to Graham, it was in better condition than it had ever been before,[51] and the London Times, echoing the same opinion, praised him for having got the fleet in readiness.[52] But it proved difficult to do because Graham insisted on strict economy at all times. For instance, he decided to transport cavalry horses in sailing vessels instead of steam vessels because if the latter were used, the horses would have to be put under hatches. This would require about 10 tons of space for each horse and so 15,000 tons would be required to transport 1500 horses. 6000 tons of coal would be used and the expense 'would be enormous'. He also refused either to increase the pay of sailors or to give them bounties.[53]

During the discussions on the estimates for the Navy in February and March, Graham explained to the House some of the problems the Admiralty had to face. He discovered that those who

[49] Graham to Queen Victoria, February 9th, 1854, in *Graham Papers*.
[50] *Ill. News*, XXIII, 333.   [51] *Hansard*, 3rd Ser., CXXX, 1313.
[52] *The Times*, January 23rd, 1854, p. 6.
[53] *Hansard*, 3rd Ser., CXXX, 1253; 1383.

had contracted with the forage department to supply the fleet with hay for the horses being sent to the East had been guilty of damping it so as to make it weigh more.[54] To obtain the necessary transports, he had agreed to pay the prevailing price for the alterations the shipping firms had to make in their boats, plus ten per cent. But the companies had submitted such outrageously high prices that he had, in many instances, refused to pay pending re-negotiation. One firm, for instance, asked for £2600 but settled for £900![55] In addition to these financial worries, Graham had other problems. He had been asked to define the status of coal and had decided that it was not contraband if used for purely commercial purposes, but was contraband if used for military and/ or naval purposes.[56] In May he had to explain the details of the sinking of the ship *Andes*. It was a 1200 ton ship with room for 500 men, but there were 800 in it. The powder on board caught fire and, while no lives were lost the cargo had to be dumped overboard. Only 500 men should have been put on board, said Graham, but both the port officer and the commander of the regiment had agreed to let 800 embark. In June he was forced to explain what had happened to the *Star*. According to a story in *The Times*, the sailors on this ship hated their officers so much that they had sent a round-robin to the Admiralty complaining of mistreatment by the Captain, asserting that all crew members had been flogged at least once and many of them three or four times. Graham told the House that the story was full of inaccuracies, that he had received no such round-robin, and that the few who had been flogged had deserved it because they had stolen a casket of wine and had got drunk. But, he admitted that the discipline on this ship was not good, and the Admiralty was considering changing its officers.[57]

Despite these problems Graham had done a magnificent job in preparing the Navy for war. The Black Sea Fleet had a complement of 32 ships, 1282 guns, and 12,740 men; the Baltic Fleet had 44 ships, 2200 guns, and 22,000 men.[58] Consequently Graham

---

[54] *Hansard*, 3rd Ser., CXXXI, 1070.
[55] *Report from the Select Committee on the Army Before Sebastopol, with Proceedings*, Vol. IX, Part I, p. 325 (Hereinafter cited as *Sebastopol Committee Report*).
[56] *Hansard*, 3rd Ser., CXXXIII, 38.
[57] *Ibid.*, CXXXIV, 47-48.
[58] See *Ill. News*, XXIV, No. 672, p. 203; No. 673, p. 246.

was the recipient of fulsome praise from all quarters and the Queen conferred upon him the honour of the Civil Grand Cross of the Bath.[59]

With the fleets in readiness it was agreed that England and France should attack Russia in the Black Sea region at Sebastopol, and defeat her there before the ice had cleared in the Baltic where the main naval operations were scheduled to take place. All members of the cabinet shared Graham's opinion that other enterprises were of secondary importance compared to the seizure of Sebastopol.[60] However, there was no unanimity of opinion as to how easily or how quickly this could be done. Lord Raglan and St. Arnaud, the timid and incompetent allied commanders, did not approve of attacking Sebastopol;[61] Admiral Dundas was loath to let his nice wooden ships attack stone forts of great strength which would fire 'red hot shells at them';[62] and Captain Drummond, who had reconnoitred the fort, declared it to be impregnable. On the other hand, Sir Edmund Lyons, the second-in-command, and a close personal friend of Graham, insisted that it could be taken although many lives would probably be lost. Palmerston shared this view and was certain the attack would succeed.[63]

While, therefore, the fleet was ready, action came incredibly slowly. The expedition to the Crimea was ordered in June but it did not arrive there until September 18th. Two days later the Russians were defeated at Alma and promptly retired to Sebastopol. Raglan and Lyons wanted to attack right away but St. Arnaud, now near death on his ship, urged caution and delay and the assault on Sebastopol did not actually begin until October 13th. This delay gave the Russians ample time heavily to fortify Sebastopol and to barricade the entrance by sinking ships in it. Graham was dismayed at this woeful lack of action and demanded that Dundas make a full report explaining why the Russian ships 'which were leisurely and deliberately placed in their positions and . . . sunk at the entrance to the harbour' were not impeded by his naval

---

[59] PARKER, op. cit., II, 229-230.
[60] See Graham to Lyons, June 13th, 1854, in Graham Papers; VILLIERS, A Vanished Victorian, 235; BALFOUR, Life of Aberdeen, II, 243; Clarendon to Cowley, in Secrets of Second Empire, 36.
[61] See ARGYLL, op. cit., I, 475.
[62] Admiralty Papers (Adm. Sec. In-Letters, Admirals), 1/5628, No. 754.
[63] See ARGYLL, op. cit., I, 477.

forces.[64] Dundas replied that the fleet was busy after the battle of Alma on the twentieth taking care of the sick and wounded; that no force could have prevented the Russians from sinking the ships; and that the fleet had 'to be kept ready to disembark the Army in case of a reverse' which was possible owing to 'the entire absence of all intelligence as to the real amount of the Enemy's force'.[65]

On October 13th Dundas was ordered by the Admiralty to blockade the Russian ports on the Black Sea and to attack all Russian ports from the Danube to the Isthmus of Perekop.[66] But he had not done so and on the 25th Graham protested against this failure to establish a blockade. 'Odessa is open; Kertsch is open; the whole coast from Sebastopol to the entrance to the Sea of Azoff has remained unmolested . . .' He concluded by ordering the blockade to 'be forthwith established!'[67] But, on November 17th, Dundas reported that Kertsch had not yet been blockaded,[68] and on December 8th, that Odessa had not yet been bombarded in deference to the wishes of the allied generals.[69]

Graham and the rest of the cabinet were naturally annoyed and angered by these evidences of incompetence; the public even more so. The *London Standard* thought that Sebastopol could and should have been taken as early as August 30th, and since 'no better administrator ever sat at the head of the Admiralty Board' it was obviously Dundas's fault.[70] On August 27th a public meeting was held at Newcastle at which a memorial was drawn up and sent to Queen Victoria demanding that 'effective and *bona fide*' steps be taken to force the prosecution of the war.[71] The outcry against Dundas increased in volume and intensity in each succeeding month. In December occurred the horrible bungling of the disembarkation proceedings at Balaclava during which two ships went down with their entire cargoes — including much-needed medical supplies. In addition, hospital supplies shipped

---

[64] *Admiralty Papers* (Adm. Sec. Out-Letters, Naval Book, Pol. and Secret Branch), 2/1702, pp. 43-47.

[65] *Admiralty Papers* (Adm. Sec. In-Letters, Admirals), 1/5628, No. 754.

[66] *Admiralty Papers* (Adm. Sec. Out-Letters, Naval Book, Pol. and Secret Branch), 2/1702, pp. 41-42.

[67] *Admiralty Papers* (Adm. Minutes), 3/265.

[68] *Admiralty Papers* (Adm. Sec. In-Letters, Admirals), 1/5628, No. 806.

[69] *Admiralty Papers* (Adm. Sec. Orders and Letters), 2/1699, No. 240.

[70] *Standard*, August 30th, 1854, p. 2.

[71] *Ill. News*, XXV, No. 700, p. 207.

to Constantinople were unloaded at Varna, reloaded and then shipped to Constantinople![72] And Dundas had made no reports at all. Layard, who was on board one of the ships, wrote to Cowley:

> The execution [of embarkation] would have been more successful had it not been for a sinister interference on the part of Admiral Dundas — who has been and is the curse of this expedition ... Our magnificent fleet is perfectly inactive ... From it, unless positive orders are received from England, we can expect no co-operation. Dundas's conduct has been such as to bring discredit upon our navy [and] ... he is ... the object of general disgust and indignation.[73]

Colonel Gordon, second son of Lord Aberdeen, wrote to his father: 'Some lay the blame on Admiral Dundas ... The Navy have only 70 rounds per gun — how is this? Surely Admiral Dundas should be called to account for not having enough for the service on which he is engaged.'[74]

Newcastle, the Secretary for War, urged that Dundas be recalled and that Lyons be given the supreme command. This decision would, of course, belong to Graham. He explained his attitude towards it in the following note to Aberdeen:

> I did not appoint him to his Command. I should not have selected him. I am not satisfied with his late proceedings. I should be glad to see Sir Edmund Lyons in his place ... Satisfy me that the public safety requires the immediate recall of Admiral Dundas, and show me any act of his which justifies this severity, and I will not shrink ... from the responsible discharge of the painful duty.[75]

He concluded that Dundas should be allowed to remain until the end of the year, when he would reach retirement age, and that the command should then devolve upon Lyons. This was sound reasoning because it is rarely wise to supersede an admiral in the midst of a war, because Dundas and Lyons were co-operating exceedingly well and the latter was consulted on all important matters anyway. Moreover, if Graham had removed Dundas

[72] *Admiralty Papers* (Adm. Sec. Out-Letters, Naval Book, Pol. and Secret Branch), 2/1702, pp. 310-318.
[73] Layard to Cowley, in *Secrets of Second Empire*, 61-62.
[74] Col. Gordon to Aberdeen, in BALFOUR, *Life of Aberdeen*, II, 244.
[75] Graham to Aberdeen, October 7th, 1854, in PARKER, *op. cit.*, II, 251.

before his incompetence was clearly proved he would have been accused of favouritism towards his friend Lyons. By December, however, it was clear to all that Dundas would have to be replaced. He had failed at Sebastopol and at Balaclava; he had failed to carry out the blockade as ordered; he had failed to provide hospital ships for the sick and wounded; he had failed to provide an adequate mail service; he had proved that he was timid, and psychologically unfit for the task, and Graham had even been compelled to defend him against imputations of cowardice.[76]

But, admitting the mediocrity or incompetence of Dundas and other military and naval personnel, it was not the men but the system that was really at fault. The fatal weakness of that system since Waterloo was its lack of a unified command. George Villiers describes it very well in these words: 'the nominal control of the Army was entrusted to the Secretary of State for the Colonies. The Ordnance was under a separate Administrative Board; the Commissariat was directly under the Treasury; while the Militia was under the Home Office'.[77] The inevitable consequence was confusion at the front and departmental jealousies at home.

Stratford and Dundas were at loggerheads from the beginning. On February 8th, 1854, Clarendon had been forced to write to Stratford: 'All Her Majesty's Government expect of you is to inform the Admiral of the service which you require him to perform, leaving to the Admiral to determine . . . in what manner it may be most advisable to give effect to your requisitions.'[78] Stratford, however, continued to give peremptory orders to Dundas and the latter continuously complained to Graham. 'I wish that peace could be restored at Constantinople', wrote Graham to Lyons, 'between the British Embassy and the Fleet. I fear nothing from the hostility of Russia . . . if the Civil and the Military can be induced . . . to pull well together.'[79] But peace was not restored and Graham finally wrote to Clarendon that either Dundas or Stratford would probably have to be recalled. Furthermore, despite orders from home,[80] Dundas and Raglan did not see eye to eye. The latter asked Dundas for a detachment of Marines to be

[76] See *Hansard*, 3rd Ser., CXXXVI, 411-412.
[77] VILLIERS, *op. cit.*, 238.
[78] *Admiralty Papers* (Adm. Sec. In-Letters), 1/5634, No. 55.
[79] Graham to Lyons, February 24th, 1854, in *Graham Papers*.
[80] *Admiralty Papers* (Adm. Minutes), 3/265.

used in a raid in the Crimea, but Dundas demurred and was supported by Graham, who wrote: 'They are not to follow the movements of the Army, nor to occupy positions in which they cannot be replaced at short notice if necessary.'[81] And, despite the urgent need for hospital ships, medical supplies, beds, and nurses, neither Dundas nor Raglan had even asked that supplies be sent until after the battle of Alma, and both had to be rebuked for not having done so.[82] Admiral Boxer, the superintendent of operations in the Dardanelles and the Bosporus, not only ignored orders from Dundas, his superior, but was both incompetent and inept. So, too, was Captain Christie, in charge of transports in the Black Sea. Each was informed whenever a convoy of supplies left England and each was ordered to be ready to receive them and to dispatch them promptly to their destination.[83] The former neglected to provide for the distribution of mail at Constantinople — even for letters of the fleet or the army — and on one occasion a packet of letters addressed to Constantinople had been 'inadvertently sent to Marseilles'.[84] Captain Christie, equally incompetent, had sent some Turkish troops to Balaclava instead of to Eupatoria.[85] And in May Graham was compelled to order Dundas to investigate responsibility for the fact that in the bombardment of Odessa empty shells had been used![86]

In addition, there were the French admirals and generals with whom to co-operate. 'There will be a magnificent power of troops and fleets collected in Turkey that might do great things if all under one master mind,' wrote Sir John Burgoyne to Lord Cowley, 'but when we find *three* Generals, *two* Generals, *two* Admirals, *two* Ambassadors, the instructions from *three* Governments, not to omit the inconsiderate *British Public Press* all meddling in every operation, we can hardly expect the promptitude and decision

[81] *Admiralty Papers* (Adm. Sec. Out-Letters, Naval Book, Pol. and Secret Branch), 2/1702, pp. 85-86.
[82] *Sebastopol Committee Report*, IX, Part II, 151.
[83] *Admiralty Papers* (Adm. Sec. Out-Letters, Naval Book, Pol. and Secret Branch), 2/1702.
[84] *Admiralty Papers* (Adm. Sec. Out-Letters, Transport Service), 2/1317, pp. 174-175. One packet marked for delivery to Malta was sent to Southampton, England! *Ibid.*, 2/1316, pp. 88-89.
[85] *Admiralty Papers* (Adm. Sec. Out-Letters, Naval Book, Pol. and Secret Branch), 2/1702, p. 361.
[86] *Admiralty Papers* (Adm. Sec. Secret Orders and Letters), 2/1697, pp. 132-133.

which are so necessary in war.'[87]   And this appalling situation continued until Dundas was replaced by Lyons on December 30th. Thereafter the situation in the Black Sea improved: Lyons swept the sea of Russian ships, rigorously enforced the blockade, and raided Odessa, Kimburn, and other cities.

At the same time, however, the situation had been equally bad at home. In June Graham wrote to the Duke of Newcastle that there were 83 sailing vessels and 22 steam vessels ready for duty but 'not being aware of the movements of the military force under Lord Raglan's Command',[88] he would like to know how many were actually needed. When the Sebastopol Committee, investigating the conduct of the war, asked Dr. Andrew Smith, Director-General of the Army and Ordnance Medical Department, who his superior was, he replied: 'The Commander-in-Chief, the Secretary-at-War, the Minister-at-War, the Master-general of the Ordnance, the Board of Ordnance, and I hardly know how many more.'[89] And Graham testified before the same committee that he himself received orders from seven different sources and that 'the Admiralty had to provide as best they could without previous notice for the supplies from those seven sources'.[90]

The cabinet, too, consisting of brilliant but independent men, and held together chiefly by affection for Aberdeen, did not work well together. Graham, for instance, had no respect for Newcastle's ability and did not completely trust Russell. 'The war of departments rages furiously,' Greville wrote to Argyll, 'Graham complained frivolously of the contradictory orders which he received. He pitched indirectly into the Commissariat and the Secretary-at-War — the latter pitched into the Cabinet and the Commander-in-Chief, who, having no friends, was hard hit.'[91] Efforts to resolve this quarrelling were unavailing[92] and Graham dolefully wrote to Aberdeen: 'Without are fightings and within are fears. The latter are the most deadly.'[93]

But the tragi-comedy staged in the Black Sea was only the pre-

---

[87] Burgoyne to Cowley, in *Secrets of Second Empire*, 49.
[88] *Admiralty Papers* (Adm. Sec. Out-Letters, Transport Service), 2/1316, p. 337.
[89] *Sebastopol Committee Report*, IX, Part I, 392.
[90] *Ibid.*, Part III, 257.
[91] Greville to Argyll, in FITZMAURICE, *Life of Granville*, I, 87.
[92] See *Ill. News*, XXV, No. 693, p. 63.
[93] Graham to Aberdeen, in BALFOUR, *op. cit.*, II, 271.

lude to a more aggravating one in the Baltic. Since the bulk of Russia's fleet, as well as her chief naval bases, was in the Baltic, and since any Russian attack on England would obviously have to come from that quarter, elaborate plans were made by Graham for naval operations in that sea. It was known that the Russian Baltic Fleet in the Gulf of Finland consisted of three divisions with nine line-of-battle ships each stationed at Reval in Esthonia, Helsingfors in Finland, and Kronstadt in Russia. Graham hoped that a successful English attack here would prevent these three groups from uniting, and at the same time fix the wavering neutrality of Sweden, Denmark, and Prussia.

To provide a fleet adequate to this task was, of course, Graham's responsibility and he discharged it with his customary zeal and efficiency. In February and March 1854 all available ships were assembled and the dockyards were emptied of their stores. The imposing fleet assembled at the Downs on March 6th, had, for real power, according to Yonge, 'never been surpassed'.[94] The public, anxious for a short, sharp and successful war, probably expected too much from 'the terrible squadrons' which the *Illustrated News* glowingly predicted would soon 'swamp the Baltic'.[95] Popular attitude was well-reflected in Charles Mackay's lines:

> Tis a foolish course you've chosen,
> Mighty Czar! Mighty Czar!

> Ere you feel the summer breezes,
> You may thank your lucky stars
> If you do not yield to Napier,
> And his gallant Jack Tars.[96]

The fleet was ready, fully equipped with supplies and with Norwegian, Swedish and Danish interpreters, harbour pilots, and seamen.[97] But was Napier ready? Was he fit to do the task assigned him? We have already seen with what misgivings Graham had recommended Napier's appointment to the command of the Baltic Fleet.[98] And Graham's low opinion of Napier was shared

---

[94] C. D. YONGE, *The History of the British Navy*, III, 290. See also the *Ill. News*, XXIV, No. 672, p. 206.
[95] *Ill. News*, XXIV, No. 672, p. 226.   [96] *Ibid.*, 207.
[97] *Admiralty Papers* (Adm. Sec. Out-Letters, Military Branch), 2/1565, pp. 137-138; *Napier Papers*, VII (Br. Mus. Add. MSS., 40024).
[98] *Supra*, 337.

by almost all who knew him. Clarendon declared that Napier was 'one of the most ill-conditioned men that ever lived', and that 'the ablest officers of his own profession' disliked him. What was even worse to the mid-Victorians, he was uncouth, ill-educated, and slovenly in appearance. His appointment was, therefore, excusable only on the grounds that no one else had been available. On the other hand, the cabinet cannot be excused for its lamentable performance at the famous Reform Club banquet held on Tuesday, March 7th, 1854.[99] Palmerston was the chairman and the party was characterized by a spirit of levity and carefree abandon. With the country on the verge of war it was hardly the time for such levity, or for a meeting which *The Times* said 'smelt of gunpowder',[100] and which Greville properly denounced as 'unwise and in bad taste'.[101] Palmerston's speech was so indiscreet that John Bright took him to task for it in the House of Commons, and Graham's equally indiscreet speech was denounced by the *Standard* as utterly disgusting.[102] Napier, lauded by Palmerston, got up and said that when he got to the Baltic he hoped he would have the opportunity of declaring war on Russia, to which Graham responded: 'I, as the First Lord of the Admiralty, give him my free consent to do so.'[103] Even if this *carte-blanche* authority was given in a spirit of fun, it was most unwise, as Graham was soon to discover.

Napier, 'hero of the knife and fork', as Greville put it, and 'banqueting on victories still to be won', congratulated Graham on having fitted out 'such a splendid fleet', and a week later departed for the Baltic. But on that very day he began to lose his vaunted nerve. To the Mayor and Council of Portsmouth, who gave him a farewell dinner, he said he hoped that England 'would not expect too much', because his fleet was a new one, the system of warfare was new and different, and great consideration was necessary 'to manage a fleet urged by steam'.[104] This from the man to whom Graham had written: 'If you are dissatisfied with the preparations which have been made, and are in process,

---

[99] Napier was one of the so-called 'advanced reformers'.
[100] *The Times*, March 16th, 1854, p. 7.
[101] GREVILLE, *Journal of the Reign of Queen Victoria, 1852-1860*, I, 145.
[102] *Standard*, September 21st, 1854, p. 2.
[103] Quoted in *The Times*, March 8th, 1854, p. 10.
[104] Cited in *Ill. News*, XXIV, No. 673, p. 243.

if you have not entire confidence in the strength of the combined forces of France and England, you had better say so to me at once, and decline to accept [the] command!'[105]

True to form Napier began to disobey orders. On March 18th he was instructed to remain at Wingo Sound until he received further orders, but he left it on the 23rd without explaining why and without the approval of the Admiralty Board.[106] When questioned about it, Napier replied that if he had stayed at Wingo Sound 'the Russians might have seized that opportunity and passed a squadron through the Sound, when I was passing the intricate passage of the Belt'.[107] And on the same day he wrote to Clarendon that it was going to be difficult to strike at Russia and that it would have been wiser to have sent all the men who were off for Turkey to the Baltic instead — about 100,000![108] On March 30th, war having been declared, Napier was ordered to advance to the Gulf of Finland to establish a close blockade there as well as in the Gulf of Bothnia; to prevent Russian ships from getting into the North Sea; and to 'undertake warlike operations'.[109] He was given 'the largest discretionary power' in carrying out this task, was urged fully to co-operate with the French Admiral, and was supplied with a large quantity of maps, charts, diagrams of the Russian fortresses, as well as a batch of papers describing naval operations in the Baltic during the Napoleonic wars.[110]

Napier carefully studied the latter. Then, on April 18th, fearful of entering the Gulf of Finland, he wrote to the Admiralty: 'I find that in 1808-1809 the fleet never entered the Gulf of Finland till the month of July. I should wish their lordships' instructions on that head.'[111] In 1808-1809, replied the Admiralty on May 2nd, 'there were no ships of war propelled by steam employed within the Gulf of Finland'. Dispatches received on May 16th, 20th, and

[105] *Napier Papers* VII, 4, (Br. Mus. Add. MSS. 40024).
[106] *Graham Papers* (Correspondence between the Admiralty and Vice-Admiral Sir Charles Napier Respecting Naval Operations in the Baltic), Dispatch No. 5, p. 3 (Hereinafter cited as Corr. with Napier).
[107] *Ibid.*, Dispatch No. 8, p. 5.
[108] See G. B. EARP, *History of the Baltic War*, 95.
[109] *Admiralty Papers* (Adm. Sec. Secret Orders and Letters), 2/1697, p. 93. See also *Napier Papers*, VII, 88, (Br. Mus. Add. MSS., 40024).
[110] *Admiralty Papers* (Adm. Sec. Secret Orders and Letters), 2/1697, pp. 102-103; 97-98; and (Adm. Sec. In-Letters), 1/5635.
[111] *Graham Papers* (Corr. with Napier), Dispatch No. 11, p. 6.

30th further served to lower Napier's reputation in the eyes of the First Lord. In the first, he said he had 'no fear of the Russian Fleet';[112] in the second, the querulous admiral said that as for steam, 'it had no effect upon fogs', and that some of his ships were 'perfectly unfit to go into action';[113] and in the third, he declared that Sweaborg and Helsingfors were 'unattackable either by sea or land'.[114] On June 12th, he wrote again that Sweaborg was unassailable by ships, and on July 1st that 'any attack upon Cronstadt . . . with our means is perfectly impossible' — but an army, he thought, could attack it by way of St. Petersburg![115]

At the same time Graham had received reports from Captain Plumridge, Rear-Admiral Chads and General Jones, each of whom had reconnoitred the region about Sweaborg, and each of whom had reported that it was assailable. But Graham, quite properly, accepted Napier's reports and on July 11th ordered him to meet the French Admiral at Faro and to proceed from there to Baro Sound where plans should be perfected for an attack on Bomarsund. If that succeeded then perhaps Napier could attack Sweaborg, which 'would be a noble prize'.[116] At the same time, he told Napier that he must closely blockade the enemy's fleet in the Gulf of Finland and that 'wherever the bulk of your fleet may be, your duty as Commander-in-Chief is to be with it, and the paramount duty of this command must not be delegated to any other officer'.[117]

But instead of meeting the French Admiral, Perceval Deschênes, at Baro Sound as directed, Napier met him at Ledsund, the outer roadstead of Bomarsund. Then he protested that Graham's directive was obviously based on certainty of success at Bomarsund whereas he himself had also to 'provide for want of success'.[118] Not only that, but he also began to quarrel with Deschênes, whom Cowley had described as 'a very conciliatory good-tempered man'.[119] Alarmed at fancied signs of bad weather, fearful of the

[112] Napier to Graham, in PARKER, op. cit., II, 232.
[113] Graham Papers (Corr. with Napier), Dispatch No. 14, p. 8.
[114] Ibid., No. 15, p. 8.   [115] Ibid., No. 24, p. 12.
[116] Napier Papers, VIII (Br. Mus. Add. MSS. 40025).
[117] Admiralty Papers (Adm. Secret Orders and Letters), 2/1697, pp. 151-154.
[118] Graham Papers (Corr. with Napier), July 24th, 1854, No. 28, p. 16; Napier Papers, VIII, 63 (Br. Mus. Add. MSS. 40025).
[119] Cowley to Clarendon, in Secrets of Second Empire, 55.

strength of the Russian fleet and the bomb-proof forts, Napier would perhaps not even have attacked Bomarsund were it not that Graham had ordered him to do so.[120] At length, on August 8th, a combined English and French land and sea assault was launched. It was entirely successful. On August 16th the Russians surrendered the fort along with 2000 men, and Napier, announcing the victory, stated that 'the loss on either side was inconsiderable'.[121]

After the capture of Bomarsund, Napier decided to send General Jones with the French Admiral to make another reconnaissance of Reval and Sweaborg. The Admiral reported that neither place could be taken 'with the forces we now have'.[122] But, to Napier's horror, General Jones not only declared that Sweaborg could be taken in seven or eight days, but actually drew up a plan of attack.[123] Jones sent a copy of this report to the Admiralty, which three days later received an additional report from Niel, the French General, confirming Jones's findings.[124] On the basis of these reports, and anxious to have Sweaborg taken before the French army went home for the winter, Graham directed Napier to consult with his French allies as to what further operations could be undertaken which would 'justify before the Public the confidence which has been placed in you',[125] and to put in writing the joint opinion of himself and Admiral Deschênes if it was decided not to attack Sweaborg.[126]

But Napier and Admiral Deschênes decided at a council of war, on August 28th, that neither Sweaborg nor Reval could be taken at that season of the year, and began to make plans for returning home. Graham, regretting the decision not to attack Sweaborg, ordered Napier to continue the blockade of the Gulf of Finland, saying that in former years an English fleet had 'remained there as late as November'.[127] and adding that if the fleet withdrew now the Russians might come out to make the whole Baltic

[120] *Napier Papers*, VIII, 134 (Br. Mus. Add. MSS. 40025).
[121] *Admiralty Papers* (Adm. Minutes), 3/265.
[122] *Admiralty Papers* (Adm. Sec. In-Letters), 1/5625.
[123] *Graham Papers* (Corr. with Napier), No. 33, pp. 19-20.
[124] *Admiralty Papers* (Adm. Sec. In-Letters), 1/5625).
[125] *Admiralty Papers* (Adm. Secret Orders and Letters), 2/1697, pp. 172-174.
[126] *Ibid.*, 178-184.
[127] *Napier Papers*, IX, 118 (Br. Mus. Add. MSS. 40026).

summer operation appear ridiculous, and 'we shall be covered with shame'.[128]

Then, right out of the blue, Napier after another reconnaissance of Sweaborg reported that an attack could be made and described in detail how it could be done.[129] Graham, completely surprised, asked 'What, then, are the obstacles to an immediate attempt?'[130] Napier, having fully expected to be told not to make the attempt at that season of the year, was now clearly on the spot. But, not having intended to attack Sweaborg, he replied that he had never said Sweaborg was assailable, that no man in his right senses would attack it at that late season, and that Jones's scheme was sheer 'madness'.[131] What was even worse, he violated the Admiralty's orders by sending the sailing ships home and ordering the screws to Kiel.

In the meantime, the Admiralty had received a report from Sir Robert Peel, one of the Lords of the Admiralty who had been at Kronstadt, in which Peel declared that if Napier had had any energy at all, even Kronstadt could have been taken. General Niel, had made the same report. General Jones also now reported to the Duke of Newcastle that Napier had refused to let him reconnoitre Kronstadt. Graham, justifiably provoked, wrote to Napier that he strongly regretted this refusal to let Jones make a reconnaissance and ordered him to explain the reasons,[132] told him about the reports of Peel and Niel, reminded him that 'war [was] not conducted without risks and dangers',[133] and acidly stated that no instructions had been given him to proceed to Kiel.

Napier's reply angered Graham and the other members of the Admiralty Board. Peel and Niel, he said, were 'a couple of old women';[134] he had not permitted Jones to make the reconnaissance of Kronstadt because he had received no orders to do so from the Admiralty; he had ordered the ships to Kiel because of 'frightful gales'.[135]

[128] *Napier Papers*, IX, 148.

[129] *Graham Papers* (Corr. with Napier), No. 46, p. 23.

[130] Graham to Napier, September 22nd, 1854, in PARKER, *op. cit.*, II, 236.

[131] *Graham Papers* (Corr. with Napier), No. 56, pp. 39-40.

[132] *Admiralty Papers* (Adm. Sec. Out-Letters, Naval Book, Pol. and Secret Branch), 2/1702, pp. 33-34.

[133] *Napier Papers*, IX, 205 (Br. Mus. Add. MSS. 40026).

[134] Napier to Graham, October 3rd, 1854, in PARKER, *op. cit.*, II, 238.

[135] *Graham Papers* (Corr. with Napier), No. 52, p. 38.

When, late in September, it was publicly known that the Baltic fleet was on its way home, a storm of protest arose. The *Illustrated News*, for instance, declared that having merely taken Bomarsund and cruised about the Baltic, the fleet should be ashamed to come home. It was like the French King:

> The Baltic fleet, with fifty thousand men,
> Sailed up the seas—and then sailed home again.[136]

'We doubt if any man will be so mortified as Sir Charles Napier',[137] wrote the *Leed's Mercury*, while *The Times* declared that Sweaborg or Kronstadt, not Spithead, ought to be the fleet's destination,[138] and *Fraser's* denounced Napier for having 'neither conquered nor attempted conquest'.[139]

Aware of the fact that the public and the Admiralty were disgusted with his summer's work, Napier became even more querulous. On September 25th, he wrote that he meant that Sweaborg was assailable if he had mortars, rockets, and Lancaster guns. Later notes complained that the Admiralty criticized some of his reports and ignored others, and that when he had said that Sweaborg was assailable he had 'never meant to infer that it could be taken by ships alone'.[140]

At last, on October 31st, Graham dispatched the following letter to Napier:

> I am very unwilling to be involved in a written controversy with you; but you have brought it on yourself in your report of the 25th of September... That report appears to me to be entirely at variance with the opinions previously expressed by you and I certainly understood you then to say, that if you had Mortars, Rockets and Lancaster guns, you considered Sweaborg assailable by Sea. In May you declared it to be unassailable by sea or land and the Admiralty did not send to you the appliances which in September you declared to be wanting because they believed they would be useless against a place which in the first instance you pronounced to be impregnable. I could not bring myself to believe that the want of Lancaster guns, or even of Mortars rendered a sea attack on your plan of the 25th of September impossible, if you had 25

[136] *Ill. News*, XXV, No. 708, p. 387.
[137] *Leeds Mercury*, September 30th, 1854, p. 4.
[138] *The Times*, September 13th, 1854, p. 6.
[139] *Fraser's*, LII, 724.
[140] *Graham Papers* (Corr. with Napier), No. 70, p. 49.

Sail-of-the-Line assembled before the place with all their means of vertical fire. . . .[141]

To this note the Admiral replied that the Admiralty continuously misinterpreted his explanations and that instead of being criticized he should be given credit 'for not trying to do something which must have led to inevitable disaster'.[142] And Graham immediately replied that the Admiralty could not permit 'any officer under their orders to suppose that they can deliberately misinterpret explanations on which they still require further explanation'.[143]

In November another incident took place which further embittered the strained relations. Two ships had crashed into each other and the Admiralty ordered an investigation and full report. But Napier, in his report, simply wrote a series of comments on the Admiralty's order. This was too much and the Admiralty directly informed him that such orders were given 'with a view to your carrying them out, and not for comments'.[144]

Completely disgusted with Napier's performance, and knowing that the Baltic was now safely frozen over, Graham, on December 1st, ordered the fleet home. On December 22nd, 'his great battle unfought, his immortal laurels unwon, and much of the work . . . remaining undone', as the *Illustrated News* aptly described it,[145] Napier anchored at Spithead, and, to his surprise and consternation, found this order awaiting him: 'You are hereby required and directed to strike your Flag and come on shore.'[146] Did this mean, asked Napier, that his command was at an end? 'The order which you have received . . . to strike your Flag and come on shore', answered Graham, 'is always the termination of a Flag officer's command.'[147]

The infuriated Admiral, on January 12th, 1855, wrote to the Admiralty Board that the fleet he had been given was 'wretchedly manned and inefficient', that his character had been meanly

---

[141] *Napier Papers*, IX, 225 (Br. Mus. Add. MSS. 40026).
[142] *Graham Papers* (Corr. with Napier), No. 72, p. 52.
[143] *Admiralty Papers* (Adm. Sec. Out-Letters, Naval Book, Pol. and Secret Branch) 2/1702, pp. 183-184.
[144] *Ibid.*, 267.   [145] *Ill. News*, XXV, No. 719, p. 642.
[146] *Napier Papers*, IX, 283 (Br. Mus. Add. MSS. 40026).
[147] *Admiralty Papers* (Adm. Sec. Out-Letters, Naval Book, Pol. and Secret Branch), 2/1702, pp. 347-348.

calumniated, and that nothing remained for him but to demand a court-martial.[148] This demand was turned down by the Board because no censure had been passed on Napier's conduct. The Admiral then wrote to Aberdeen, who replied that he had just resigned (January 30th) and could therefore do nothing. Completely frustrated, Napier then turned to the Duke of Newcastle, who merely stated that since this was a naval question it was outside his jurisdiction.[149]

Not to be silenced, Napier carried the matter to the public. In an address at the Mansion House, he denounced Graham, the Admiralty Board, and the officers and men of the Baltic Fleet. It caused such a furor that Graham was asked about it in the House of Commons. He refused to discuss it, however, because to do so would have entailed producing documents and dispatches 'interwoven with questions of naval preparations about to be resumed in the Baltic'. The Admiralty, he said, had asked Napier to specify the ships and officers that had been so ill-manned and ill-disciplined, but he had refused. Furthermore, the Admiralty had not blamed Napier for his management of the Baltic campaign, but for having used 'offensive language' to the Admiralty Board. 'I must say', concluded Graham, 'that the gallant officer . . . has proclaimed himself a hero . . . but it is not my intention to allow him to dub himself a martyr as well as a hero; and, therefore, I have no intention whatever of advising the Crown to take any further notice of the matter.'[150]

Aside from these actions in the Black and Baltic Seas, the year saw naval activity in two other quarters. On August 1st Captain Ommaney was ordered to blockade the White Sea and a British squadron destroyed a large part of Kola, the capital of Lapland, but did no damage at Onega or at Archangel.[151] At the same time,

[148] *Graham Papers* (Corr. with Napier), No. 100, p. 72.

[149] Cited in EARP, *op. cit.*, 560.

[150] *Hansard*, 3rd Ser., CXXXVI, 1469-1472. This ended the affair so far as Graham's professional relations to it are concerned. The controversy was not over, however, but continued as a personal feud and will be discussed from that angle in the next chapter.

[151] The principal reason why no damage was done at these ports was that Ommaney had been told by the Admiralty that property of various kinds which had been bought and paid for by British and French merchants was still there and that he should therefore 'endeavour to avoid the destruction of property not known to be wholly belonging to the enemy, or which can inflict losses only on private individuals'. *Admiralty Papers* (Adm. Minutes), 3/265.

Captain Price's Pacific squadron failed completely in its attacks on the Kamchatka peninsula. In fact, it was badly battered and compelled to retire to San Francisco for repairs.[152]

The year 1854, therefore, ended on a very sour note. Greville called it 'one of the most melancholy and disastrous years' he had ever lived through. 'Almost everybody is in mourning and grief and despair over-spread the land.'[153] Having expected a short, successful war, the public impatiently refused to believe that it was the military system that was to blame for the failures on the fighting fronts. The fact that by the end of the year the Black Sea, the Baltic, and the White had been successfully block-aded and Russian merchant vessels swept from the seas, did not impress a public which thought primarily in terms of expected glories unachieved and of the death and destruction in the Crimea. The indignant Press, voicing popular opinion, scathingly de-nounced the Government of Aberdeen. Most of this criticism was directed against Aberdeen[154] and Newcastle; none against Graham.

But if 1854 ended on a gloomy and sour note, the new year began on one equally so for now, with Lyons, who had replaced Dundas in the Black Sea, making a brilliant and successful assault on Kerch, and with Richard Dundas, who had replaced Napier, making an equally successful assault on Sweaborg, the troubles were not at the fighting fronts but at home. 'Do what I will, I can't help gloomy forebodings', wrote Lord Clarendon on November 9th, 1854.[155] The Duke of Newcastle, after a discussion with Russell, wrote to Graham that 'fresh signs of discontent' had been revealed by Russell, who, he suspected, was meditating 'the revival of personal projects tending to his own aggrandize-ment'.[156] The usually gloomy Graham replied that he foresaw 'a coming storm'.[157] Lord Lansdowne was more despondent over domestic troubles than over what was transpiring at Sebastopol.

Most of these melancholy forebodings were based on doubts

---

[152] See *Annual Register*, XCVI, 402-403.
[153] GREVILLE, *Journal*, I, 212.
[154] The *Standard* (September 28th, 1854, p. 2), even went so far as to say that Aberdeen did not want Napier to demolish the fortresses of 'his friend of forty years' (The Czar).
[155] Clarendon to his wife, cited in BALFOUR, *op. cit.*, II, 254.
[156] In *Ibid.*, 255.   [157] *Ibid.*

of Russell's loyalty to the Government. Early in 1854, on threat of resigning from the cabinet, he had demanded, and quite correctly too, that the Colonial Office and the War Office be separated. This was done in June; Sir George Grey took over the duties of the former and Newcastle those of the latter. By November, however, having assumed that military failures in the East were due to Raglan's uselessness and to Newcastle's lack of drive and energy,[158] Russell demanded that Aberdeen replace Newcastle with Palmerston. Aberdeen refused to do so and Russell therefore brought the matter before the cabinet on December 6th. First, Aberdeen offered to resign, but the cabinet would not hear of it; then Palmerston offered to quit, saying he had not carried a single measure through the House. His only criticism was that he thought Sebastopol should have been attacked sooner, but, he reminded them that when he had proposed that action it was Russell who had demurred. No one now supported Russell, so Palmerston agreed to stay on.

Parliament recessed for the holidays on December 23rd, but Graham, though ill most of the time, continued to prosecute his duties with his customary efficiency. He requested the Earl of Clarendon to have the consuls at Boston, Philadelphia, and New York purchase steam vessels for the fleet;[159] he ordered Admiral Lyons to institute an immediate inquiry into Admiral Boxer's inefficient transport service in the Bosporus where his helpless inactivity had kept sorely needed supplies lying idle, and if he thought fit, to order Boxer to strike his flag.[160] Boxer was not discharged, however, for Lyons discovered that much of what had gone wrong was not Boxer's fault so much as it was the complete lack of a unified command. Boxer himself explained it as follows: 'On my arrival at Constantinople I applied to the Ambassador for a site for a coal depot . . . but my request was not complied

---

[158] As a Secretary for War Newcastle left much to be desired, but it must be remembered that he held office for only a brief period; that he did not have full control over the branches of the army; that the machinery at his command was weak and outmoded; that Raglan drove him to distraction as much as Napier did Graham. 'I wish he [Raglan] would devote less time to his desk and more to his saddle,' he wrote to Clarendon, 'but long use at the Horse Guards has made his fingers stiff and his b—— tender.' In MAXWELL, op. cit., II, 55.

[159] Admiralty Papers (Adm. Sec. Out-Letters, Transport Service), 2/1317, pp. 338-339.

[160] Admiralty Papers (Adm. Sec. Secret Orders and Letters), 2/1697, pp. 251-252.

with.' He had little help in doing his job, too: 'I have been for weeks without a Ship of War in Port, with my Flag in a Transport, my only assistants were my Flag Lieutenant, and Lieutenant Kietly, agent for Transport . . . I have not even had a boat's crew . . . being dependent on the Transports for a boat.'[161]

When Lyons investigated the charge that much of the damage done in the harbour of Balaclava by the gale on November 14th was due to the inefficiency of Captain Christie, he found that the charge was correct and recommended Christie's removal.[162] Christie was therefore replaced; Captain Caldwell was sent to Marseilles to be the Transport Director in that area; and, on February 17th, a unified command was secured by an Admiralty order placing the whole of the transport arrangements in the hands of Lyons and Lord Raglan.[163]

In the meantime, the situation at home grew steadily worse. On January 23rd Parliament reassembled and the Government was at once faced with the motion made by Roebuck for an inquiry into the conduct of the war. Russell immediately resigned,[164] and the cabinet, unwilling to let Newcastle be made the scapegoat, and knowing that Russell's resignation would be fatal to the Government, since he was the leader in the House of Commons, decided to resign in a body. The Queen refused to accept this resignation, but when the motion against the Government was carried by the huge margin of 305 to 148, she had to do so. Derby, whom she asked to form a new government, was unable to get Palmerston to join unless Clarendon did and the latter would not because he detested what he regarded as Derby's lack of principle. Gladstone also refused to come in unless Aberdeen and Graham should do so, and that was obviously out of the question. When Lansdowne, too, failed in an attempt to form a government, Russell was called upon. But only Palmerston of all the members of Aberdeen's Government would serve under

[161] *Admiralty Papers* (Adm. Sec. In-Letters), 1/5650, No. 186.

[162] *Ibid.*, No. 137.

[163] *Admiralty Papers* (Adm. Sec. Out-Letters, Transport Service), 2/1317, pp. 398-399, 403.

[164] *The Times* (January 31st, 1855, p. 8), affirmed its belief that Russell had quit so that he could become the premier himself and form a government of Greys, Russells, and Howards, i.e., a purely Whig government. The *Ill. News* (XXVI, No. 726, p. 97), and the *Chronicle* (January 27th, 1855, p. 4), declared that Russell's resignation had every appearance of treachery.

him; some would not even see him; while Graham plainly told him what he thought about his treatment of Lord Aberdeen.

The Queen then turned to Palmerston, who immediately asked Graham, Gladstone, and Herbert, among others, to remain in the cabinet. Since Graham lay ill at the Admiralty, Gladstone, Aberdeen, and Herbert came to see him. Here they decided to join as a group if Aberdeen would announce in the Lords his support of the Government. Upon his agreeing to do so, and having secured pledges from Palmerston as to foreign policy and the pending Vienna negotiations, they all joined the latter's Government. But, assuming that Palmerston would resist the demand for an inquiry into the conduct of the war because they knew he had disapproved such an inquiry, they neglected to secure his pledge on the question.[165]

During these negotiations, from January 31st to February 8th, almost everyone expressed the hope that Graham would remain at the Admiralty. Prince Albert told Aberdeen that 'it would be a great relief to the Queen' if Graham should remain.[166] The *Leeds Mercury*, *Morning Chronicle*, and *The Times* all expressed the same desire, while *Blackwood's*, though it thought Graham 'an unscrupulous politician' hoped he would continue in office because he was 'the only really able administrator' of the Peelite group.[167] They were all pleased when it was announced that he had consented and the Queen wrote to Graham that it gave her 'great satisfaction' because his staying at the Admiralty was of 'the greatest importance to herself and the country'.[168]

On February 16th, Graham presented the Naval Estimates for the year calling for an increase of about £2,000,000. He explained that there were now 70,000 men in the Navy and that the entire force had been made up without resort to impressment. This had been made possible, he said, because of his rule that marines should be paid for service while afloat as well as on shore, because of the prompter payment of wages and of the higher pay for those who enlisted for not less than ten years, and because seamen could now dispose of their earnings as they saw fit, i.e., allot it to

[165] See PARKER, *op. cit.*, II, 266; ARGYLL, *op. cit.*, I, 528-529.
[166] *Letters of Queen Victoria*, III, 125.
[167] *Blackwood's*, LXXVIII, 113-114.
[168] Queen Victoria to Graham, cited in PARKER, *op. cit.*, II, 265.

anyone they wished. Since the marines had proved to be 'perfect soldiers, [and] accomplished sailors', he suggested the creation of a permanent force of 16,000 marines. He concluded by stating that the Navy had everywhere done its duty and with 'a commerce covering every sea . . . I am not aware that a single merchant ship has fallen into the hands of the enemy'.[169] The Estimates were quickly agreed to and only a few questions of minor importance were asked. Phillimore asked why Odessa had not been bombarded; Graham replied that attacks were left to the discretion of the admirals. Captain Drummond inquired why £10,000 had been appropriated for building a yacht for the Emperor of Japan; Graham answered that Captain Stirling had just been favourably received in Japan and had been given the right to use Japanese ports for refitting and victualling English naval and merchant vessels — the yacht was therefore merely a gift to the Emperor.[170]

A few days later Collier complained that it was taking too long to win the war and declared that the failure to blockade the Black, Baltic, and White Seas was the main reason. He knew such orders had been issued, but why were they not enforced? The orders had been issued in May, replied Graham, but the method of execution had naturally been left to the admirals. The latter decided to enforce it at the Bosporus, but the ambassadors at Constantinople disagreed, so it was referred to the home Governments. Three months were then lost and by that time all the forces were needed at Sebastopol. Now, however, it was in effect in the whole of the Black Sea except for Odessa, which it was useless to blockade as long as the Russian army held the left bank for forty miles above the Sulina mouth. The blockade in the White Sea had posed a different problem. The customary practice here had been to make large advances in the antecedent year for Russian produce to be exported to England and France. These advances were usually made in the autumn of the year antecedent to the last and if England had instituted the blockade as soon as the sea opened, the English and French merchants, having made these advances, Russia would have both the produce and the money. So, thinking of the merchants, the blockade was withheld until they had received the goods. This was now the case and the

[169] *Hansard*, 3rd Ser., CXXXVI, 1473 et seq.
[170] *Ibid.*, 1494.

blockade was in force. Duncan, on behalf of the merchants, thanked Graham for his solicitude for their welfare![171]

The very next day the Government collapsed. Palmerston, on February 10th, had told the cabinet that the House was determined to have an inquiry on the conduct of the war, and that if a 'fair' committee were appointed he was disposed to agree. According to Morley, Graham and Gladstone 'fought [this] with extreme tenacity'.[172] When, because of public pressure and the demand of Parliament, Palmerston at last decided to approve the inquiry, Graham, Gladstone, and Herbert promptly resigned (February 21st). These resignations were greeted with a storm of denunciation. Clarendon declared that Gladstone had acted upon a quirk, 'Herbert from sentiment, and Graham from fear'.[173] Queen Victoria, deploring the loss of 'our *three* best men', wrote to the King of Belgium that the public was 'really a little *mad*' about it.[174] *The Times* was angry and declared they had quit because of fear of the inquiry. Greville, on the other hand, says that the 'stupid Whigs' were glad that they had now got rid of the Peelites.[175]

As for Graham, the *Manchester Guardian's* conclusion was that he had resigned in order to vindicate his own conduct.[176] While many agreed with this view, others were of the opinion that he had from the first been bent on overthrowing Palmerston because the latter had not defended him in the Mazzini case. But surely it was not necessary for Graham to resign in order to vindicate himself. Everyone agreed that he was the ablest administrator in the cabinet and that the Admiralty was a model of efficiency compared to the other departments. Nor had Graham a desire to even the score with Palmerston because he could have kept the latter out of office in the first place by simply refusing to join him, for Gladstone and Herbert would have followed suit. Graham resigned because it lay in the power of six of the eleven members of the committee to decide whether the inquiry should be secret or not. If secret sessions were to be held, 'all check of public opinion,

[171] *Ibid.*, 1708-1711. [172] MORLEY, *op. cit.*, I, 538.
[173] In MAXWELL, *op. cit.*, II, 69.
[174] Queen Victoria to the King of the Belgians, in *Letters of Queen Victoria*, III, 139.
[175] GREVILLE, *op. cit.*, I, 246.
[176] *Manchester Guardian*, February 28th, 1855, p. 4.

as operating on the committee will be withdrawn, . . . persons will be inculpated without having the opportunity of defending themselves, . . . of cross-examining witnesses or of rebutting false accusations'. If it held open sessions, the evidence would be published daily and 'most adverse comments of a party character will be applied to the evidence published. The motion for an inquiry he regarded as a vote of censure on Aberdeen's Government which he could not sanction. Appointment of a committee, he said, was unnecessary, inexpedient, and unjust. Unnecessary because most of the weaknesses had already been corrected: the Colonial and War Offices had been separated, new officers had been appointed, and the war was being successfully prosecuted. It was inexpedient because an investigation would surely inculpate their ally, France. It was unjust because it deprived the officers of the armed forces of their correlative claim on the cabinet to defend them from an inquiry behind their backs. Finally, the resolution for an inquiry had actually been carried as a vote of censure and he had therefore had no choice but to bow to Parliamentary opinion.[177]

The *Morning Chronicle* lauded this explanation as a complete vindication of Graham's motives for resigning,[178] but *Fraser's Magazine* accused Graham of having double-crossed Palmerston by betraying him into the position of Premier and then deserting him. The *Quarterly Review* felt that the country ought to be glad to be rid of ministers who had been un-English[179] and the *Morning Herald* took the same position, saying that Graham and his friends were members of the war cabinet but at heart were advocates of peace.[180]

A careful analysis of this action of Graham will show him to have been in error. Making allowance for the fact that he was ill at the time, as well as for Aberdeen's request that he join Palmerston, and keeping in mind his irrevocable opposition to the proposed inquiry, he should have extracted a pledge from Palmerston that the Government would resist the committee of inquiry. Not having done so, he should have acquiesced in the inquiry, knowing that his own reputation would not suffer from it and that

---

[177] *Hansard*, 3rd Ser., CXXXVI, 1745-1755.
[178] *Chronicle*, February 24th, 1855, p. 4.
[179] *Quart. Rev.* XCVII, 389.   [180] *Herald*, November 8th, 1855, p. 4.

both Parliament and the country at large demanded it so strenuously that Palmerston undoubtedly could not successfully resist it.
His primary error, of course, lay in joining the Palmerston Government in the first place, because he had no sound reason for believing that Palmerston would refuse the inquiry.[181]

As First Lord of the Admiralty it had been Graham's duty to
prepare the fleets, to institute blockades in the Baltic, Black, and
White Seas, to clear all Russian merchant ships from these waters,
to arrange for the transport of the land forces and the supplies
they needed, to introduce necessary changes and reform in his
department, to appoint to positions of command the best available
officers, and to help plan war strategy. How had he discharged
that responsibility?

His first task, that of fitting out the fleets, was accomplished
with speed and efficiency. We have already seen how very adequately this had been done for the Baltic campaign. What of the
fleet sent to the Black Sea? On May 10th, 1855, Admiral Dundas
was questioned about this fleet before the Sebastopol Committee.

> Was your fleet adequately equipped in point of stores when you
> were in the Black Sea? — Perfectly.
> Was it well-equipped? — Yes.
> Did you consider it well-manned? — Excellently.
> . . . Had you the full complement of surgeons on board? — Yes.[182]

So far as military and naval strategy is concerned no one has
ever questioned the wisdom of striking at the Crimea which, from
the first, Graham had insisted upon as the primary objective. But
the wisdom of sending the Baltic Fleet to attack Russian fortresses
in that area has been questioned on the ground that it might have
been wiser simply to blockade the sea and to keep the Russian
fleet bottled up in its own waters.[183] Whatever may be the merits
of that contention, certainly carrying the war into the Baltic
resulted in the destruction of Russian naval stores, and prevented
the Scandinavian States from sending supplies to Russia and
perhaps even joining her. It also meant that Russian supplies had

---

[181] This was, of course, Palmerston's opinion. See Palmerston to Russell, in *Later
Correspondence of Lord John Russell*, II, 192-193.
[182] *Sebastopol Committee Report*, IX, Part III, 219. This secret committee consisted of twelve members.
[183] This was Lord Cowley's view.

to be sent to the Baltic — supplies might otherwise have gone to the Black Sea and hence prolonged the war.

If the strategy was sound and the fleets were adequate, why was more not accomplished in shorter time? Simply because of the gargantuan nature of the task, the weaknesses in naval and military command, and the presence of conflicting and confusing authority. It was no simple task to transport men and supplies from England, France, Sardinia, and Turkey to the Crimea. As a matter of fact, the *Edinburgh Review* declared that despite the complexity of the problem, it was performed in such a manner as to command admiration rather than criticism or blame.[184]

But there was criticism and blame, especially for the mismanagement in the transport service in the Black Sea, the lack of hospital ships, the inadequacy of the mail service, etc. Graham's duty with respect to the transport service was simply to see to it that there were enough ships on hand to perform the necessary tasks, and the Sebastopol Committee later reported that this had been done. 'Within a year', it stated, 'somewhere about 150,000 men, and above 7000 horses were conveyed principally by steam, a large portion of them to a point 3000 miles distant from the country; besides which, vessels had to be provided for stores to an enormous amount . . .'[185] When Captain Milne was asked by the Committee if there had always been enough ships available for this service, he replied: 'So much so that, as far back as the 5th of June I requested Sir James Graham to have a letter sent to the Duke of Newcastle, requesting authority to recall the transports to England.'[186]

The charge that there was inadequate hospital care for the sick and wounded in the Black Sea theatre is correct with respect to the Army, not the Navy. The naval hospital at Therapia was infinitely superior to the army hospital at Scutari. John C. MacDonald, who was administering the charitable fund for *The Times*, told the Sebastopol Committee that the naval hospitals were better arranged than the military hospitals, and that 'it was very quiet' at Therapia, 'very nice; everything was hospital-like; . . . there was an air about the whole place of comfort and atten-

---

184 *Edin. Rev.*, CII, 292.
185 *Sebastopol Committee Report*, IX, Part III, 10.
186 *Ibid.*, 277.

tion'.[187] But it was equally true that no arrangements had been made for conveying the sick until after the Battle of Alma, and Graham, when questioned about it, told the Committee that no one had applied for such vessels until after that battle.

Blame for the weaknesses in the hospital service, the mail service, and the transport service must, therefore, rest on the shoulders of the military and naval commanders on the spot. They should have known what was needed and, even if they received insufficient orders from home, should have handled the problem themselves. In fact, Graham told both Dundas and Lyons that final decisions were up to them; they were allowed full authority and adequate lee-way. Graham could not be expected to anticipate all the needs of the Army and Navy and it was not his fault if they did not ask for necessaries, nor provide them on the spot under their own authority.

Nor was the fact that many of the commanders were weak, incompetent, and vacillating his fault. He had appointed them to command, to be sure, but what else could he have done? It was no responsibility of his that most of them were superannuated; he had had to select his commanders on the basis of existing naval regulations and practice, and to keep them at their posts until their incompetence was proved. When this was clearly demonstrated, the guilty persons were promptly replaced. Dundas was retired; and both Napier and Captain Christie were discharged.

Furthermore, the First Lord was not responsible for the conflict of authority between Dundas and Raglan; between the military authorities and Stratford; between the English and their French allies. Finally, he cannot be held responsible for the conflict between the various civil and military departments at home. On the contrary, he supported every effort that was made to resolve these difficulties. He vigorously supported the separation of the Colonial and War Offices; obtained the appointment of a separate Transport Board, and later proposed the transfer of the Coast Guard from the Revenue Board to the Admiralty.[188]

In accordance with orders he had issued, the Navy had succeeded in blockading the Russian coasts. This was not done as

---

[187] *Ibid.*, Part I, 351. This opinion was seconded by Augustus Stafford, an M.P. who had visited the hospitals.

[188] See *Hansard*, 3rd Ser., CXLII, 1441-1442.

quickly in the Black Sea as it should have been, because of Dundas's lack of resolution, but Lyons eventually accomplished it. Furthermore, Russian ships, though not numerous, were swept from the seas, and great quantities of supplies were destroyed. More to the credit of the First Lord, however, was the fact that while he refused to give up the 'right' of impressment, he so improved the conditions of enlistment that it was not necessary to use that right. In addition, he secured the approval of Parliament for the creation of a force of 10,000 Naval Coast Volunteers, and just before leaving office proposed a permanent force of 16,000 marines. Furthermore, he insisted on making promotions in the service a reward for merit, ability, and performance and refused to make them an agency of party patronage. Regretting Graham's resignation, Lord Cowley wrote to him on February 23rd, 1855: 'I believe that our navy was never before in so efficient a state, or its patronage more fairly administered.'[189] Sir Charles Wood, his successor at the Admiralty, declared that he found everything in perfect order, and Clarendon declared that 'the utter impossibility of finding a fit successor', made him 'tremble for the consequences of your retirement'.[190] And, after a complete investigation, the Sebastopol Committee completely exonerated Graham from any blame for the military troubles and found nothing in the Admiralty's conduct to censure. He told the Sebastopol Committee:

> I accepted office on 1st of January 1853, and until I left it in March of the present year, I was not at my country residence six days during the whole of that time. During the last summer, I went on naval business to Portsmouth and to Plymouth. I was never absent from London, I believe, with one exception, upon the arrival of the mail from the East; I did go to wait on Her Majesty at Balmoral, in pursuance of an order I received, and on both these occasions I passed my own home, both going and returning, without visiting it.[191]

It is doubtful whether any other member of the Government could honestly have made such a statement.

---

[189] Cowley to Graham, in PARKER, op. cit., II, 274.
[190] Clarendon to Graham, in Ibid., 273.
[191] Sebastopol Committee Report, IX, Part III, 285.

CHAPTER XI

THE LAST PHASE

THOSE who were informed about the state of affairs mourned the resignation of Graham. 'Our army is gone!' wrote Clarendon. 'The power and prestige of England now depend on her navy, and yet, just at the moment when operations are about to commence, the Navy is deprived of its head, and of that consummate talent for administration which has effected wonders in that branch of our service.'[1] Letters praising Graham for the services he had performed and expressing regret at his resignation came to him from many quarters. At the same time, however, he was sharply criticized for having quit the Government, and for making common cause with the peace group in the House while the war was still in progress. By doing so he seemed to have damaged himself morally as well as politically.

And, though he was out of office, Graham was not out of trouble, for the redoubtable Napier was now ready to launch a full scale assault on his former chief. On February 8th, while Graham was still at the Admiralty, Napier had made a bitter attack on him at a banquet given by the Lord Mayor of London. The Baltic Fleet, he said, was a magnificent one but it was poorly manned and badly disciplined; he had been discharged for not attacking impregnable fortresses; he had been sent insulting letters by Graham.[2] The press took up the cudgels and made the question a public issue. *The Times* declared that for Napier to have taken a grand fleet to the Baltic and instead of doing anything 'had sent the Admiralty a plan for doing something, and then not do it, [was] so utterly grotesque a proceeding that it demanded explanation one way or another'.[3] Other Whig, Peelite, and Radical papers took the same view; the *Chronicle*, for instance, wrote that Napier's attack on Graham was of 'the type often heard from infuriated females who are too much in a passion to speak dis-

[1] Clarendon to Graham, February 21st, 1855, in PARKER, *Life of Graham*, II, 272-273.
[2] See *Ill. News*, XXVI, No. 727, p. 139.
[3] *The Times*, February 8th, 1855, p. 6.

tinctly'.[4] The *Standard*, though an anti-Graham paper, gener-
ously said that it was worse than injustice 'to dispute Sir James
Graham's having faithfully, zealously and efficiently discharged
the duties of his office — a merit which he alone of the Government of which he was a member can justly claim'.[5] Napier, it
concluded, should be compelled to *prove* his charges. The *London
Morning Post* demanded that Napier be summoned before a court
martial and be honourably acquitted or punished.[6]

From the press the issue was soon carried to Parliament,
where, on March 8th, Malins not only censured Graham for his
injudicious Reform Club speech, but also proposed that all the
correspondence between Napier and Graham be brought before
the House. Graham, of course, immediately arose to oppose the
motion. He deeply regretted, he said, his Reform Club speech;
he still thought Napier 'a great and gallant officer'; he had not
been fired for failure to win battles, but for having been arrogant
in his dealings with the Admiralty. Then, facing Malins, Graham
reproachfully said: 'He [Malins] is an equity lawyer. What does
he think of the justice of a proceeding which calls upon me to
defend myself with my hands tied behind my back, when, without
a breach of duty, I cannot produce this correspondence, or even
refer to it?'[7] Admiral Berkeley, Sir Charles Ward, the new First
Lord, and Palmerston all agreed with Graham that these papers
should not now be produced. Malins therefore withdrew his
motion.

A few nights later Napier, having been newly elected to Parliament for Southwark, himself brought up the subject in the House.
He reviewed the whole story of the Baltic campaign. His fleet,
he declared, had been unfit; he was ordered to 'take care' of
Kronstadt and Sweaborg and blockade the Gulf of Finland, but
to do so had been an impossibility because the former base was
as strong as Toulon or Cherbourg. When ordered to take Bomarsund, he had reconnoitred the fort and found it unassailable.
But at this point, he claimed, the public had become critical of
the failure to take Sweaborg, Kronstadt, and Sebastopol, the
Government had needed someone to blame and Graham had

[4] *Chronicle*, February 8th, 1855, p. 4.
[5] *Standard*, February 8th, 1855, p. 4.   [6] *Post*, February 7th, 1855, p. 4.
[7] *Hansard*, 3rd Ser., CXXXVII, 286-294.

therefore picked on him, and ordered him to attack Sweaborg. Since he failed to do so, the Admiralty had then 'sent him a long jesuitical letter' of censure which 'could only have been written by the right honourable Baronet himself'. On his return, he had been ordered to strike his flag. Napier concluded his speech by moving that a select committee be appointed to inquire into the operations in the Baltic.[8] For a moment no one seconded the motion. Then Admiral Walcott did so because he could not bear to see 'a brother officer adrift without throwing out a tow-rope to him'.[9]

Careful to use only those letters and orders which, being made public, would not impede the war effort, Graham made mincemeat of Napier's charges. Napier had begged for the command, said Graham, but he had hesitated to appoint him because he (Napier) had once written a book in which he had said that men over sixty years of age were unfit to command, and at the time Napier himself had passed 'the awful limit of sixty years'. But Napier had protested to Graham that he could do the job, so Graham had appointed him. Then, Napier had asked the Admiralty to sanction compulsory service, but they had refused. When he complained about unfit ships, he had refused the Admiralty's request that he name those that were unfit. On May 30th he had said Sweaborg was unassailable but on that day he had not yet come within eight miles of it. When, in August, both General Jones and General Niel had said it was assailable, Napier was ordered to attack it. This was on September 12th and the British army had not yet landed in the Crimea. He concluded by defying Napier to prove any of the assertions he was scattering about 'with so much recklessness'.[10] Napier, having reviewed the case before the House and finding no support there, withdrew his motion.

The *Manchester Guardian* was provoked with the House for even listening to Napier and wanted the Government to strike his name from the navy list for publishing confidential papers.[11] *The Times* affirmed that Napier had entered the House with a reputation for skill and courage but that he had left it 'in a condition bearing about the same relation to the conditions in which he entered it as the fishing boat of Xerxes did to his stupendous

---

[8] *Ibid.*, CXLI, 50-71.   [9] *Ibid.*, 71-72.   [10] *Ibid.*, 81-102.
[11] *Manchester Guardian*, November 14th, 1855, pp. 4, 7.

fleet'.[12] And *Fraser's* declared that the only persons who now defended Napier were those who were provoked at Graham for quitting Palmerston's Government.[13]

When, in the summer of 1855, the new admiral in the Baltic took Sweaborg and was lauded for doing so, the jealous Napier wrote to Palmerston demanding that the Government investigate his charges against Graham, but Palmerston refused to do so because Napier's 'conduct on shore' had been bad and because Graham had done an admirable job in fitting out such a fine fleet.[14] To assuage the wounded feelings of the disgruntled Admiral, the electors at Southwark gave a party for him and presented him with a hat. 'A piece of the most sublime mockery', said *Punch*, 'to present a hat to a man who has completely lost his head.'[15]

Public and Parliament were on Graham's side in this case and he came out of it with colours flying. But in the case of Captain Christie the colours drooped badly. On February 19th Layard made a bitter attack on Captain Christie's handling of the transports at Balaclava. Gladstone, speaking for Graham, declared that Christie had been dismissed because of his inefficiency and lack of resolution, that Graham had ordered him to be tried before a court martial, but that before it could be held Christie, now 70 years of age, had died. Then, before a House Committee, Graham had looked Layard in the eye and said that Christie had died of a broken heart, implying that Layard's attacks on him had been the cause of death. But the facts show that Christie had been discharged before Layard had criticized him in the House, and that Graham's statement that he had ordered Christie to the Crimea to save him from going through Layard's hands on the Sebastopol committee was patently false because that committee was not yet in existence.

Despite the fact that Graham soon admitted he had been wrong and apologized for his statements, he was lambasted in the press.[16]

---

[12] *The Times*, March 10th, 1855, p. 9. Napier wrote numerous letters to *The Times* trying to justify his conduct.

[13] *Fraser's*, LII, 724-725.

[14] See EARP, *The Baltic Campaign*, 607.   [15] *Punch*, XXXI, 222.

[16] *Blackwood's* (LXXVIII, 113), described his conduct as 'wicked and shameless', while *Fraser's* (LI, 715-722), thought it 'scandalous'. See also *The Times*, August 14th, 1855, p. 8.

Punch showed a full-page picture of Graham as a little boy who had just made a mud pie which was labelled 'Charge against Layard'. Graham had the pie on the table and was busy eating it. The caption read: 'Jamie Gr-H-M, The Unpleasant Boy, who made a Dirt-Pie and Ate it.'[17] Then it dedicated to Graham a poem called 'Dirty Jemmy' which ran as follows:

> There is a naughty dirty boy
>   Who wants the sense of shame;
> The QUEEN has had him in employ;
>   His name is JEMMY GRAHAM.

> In fear of punishments and stripes,
>   And loss of cake and toys,
> This miry varlet goes and wipes
>   Himself on other boys!

> To MASTER LAYARD, JEMMY GRAHAM
>   Attempted so to do;
> And then he basely tried the same
>   On CHARLIE NAPIER too.[18]

In the meantime official interest turned to the maturing of a peace programme. Since Graham had been one of the peace advocates in Aberdeen's cabinet, he was glad that Russell had accepted the special embassy to Vienna where the European ambassadors were to meet to consider peace plans. The English and French Ambassadors had exchanged notes with Count Buol and as a result, on August 8th, 1854, the 'Four Points' were agreed upon: (1) Russia's protectorate over the Danubian provinces and Serbia was to be replaced by a collective European protectorate; (2) there should be free navigation of the Danube; (3) the treaty of July 31st, 1841, should be revised so as to end Russia's predominant power in the Black Sea; (4) Russia should renounce her claims to the exclusive right to protect the Christian subjects of the Porte. To the surprise of many, Russia, on January 7th, 1855, accepted these Four Points as the basis of negotiations, and on March 15th the conference met at Vienna. Though it lasted two and a half months nothing was accomplished, for Prince Gorchakoff refused to agree to limit Russia's forces in the Black Sea and

---

[17] *Punch*, XXVIII, 217. [18] *Ibid.*, XIX, 136.

this point was regarded by the Allies as the most important. The war therefore continued.

Russia had suggested that she would be willing to discuss the issue with Turkey, but Russell refused to accept this compromise. This annoyed Graham who wanted the war brought to an end as soon as possible. He was disturbed, he told the House, at the inclination to raise 'the terms which are to be demanded of Russia'. It presaged a long war — maybe thirty years — and the country could not stand that. England was fighting this war 'for the independence and integrity of Turkey. That was . . . the sole object of the war'. To that extent the conflict was necessary and just. But Russia had now agreed to three of the Four Points and the Government of which he had been a member had not regarded the limitation of Russian power in the Black Sea as an ultimatum. Was it wise, therefore, to break off negotiations on this ground? Now was the time to make peace, he said, for Russia could do so without too much loss of face; Turkey was independent; France and England had gained their objectives; Russia had been taught not to be so arrogant; and England had been taught a lesson too — not to make the mistake of 1815 in too hastily reducing her military and naval establishments.[19]

Gladstone, Herbert, Disraeli and others took the same line, but since they did not then regard with favour a change in ministry, they voted against Gibson's successful motion that point three constituted 'a good basis for a just and lasting peace'. They did, however, succeed in inserting in the motion these qualifying words: 'having seen with regret that the conferences of Vienna have not led to a termination of hostilities'.[20]

The result of Graham's activities in the interest of peace was that he was publicly castigated as a friend of the Czar and the leader of a 'peace at any price' party. The *Quarterly Review* described Graham and his colleagues as 'betrayers of the true interests of the Nation'.[21] *Fraser's* described him as the head of a group who had plunged the country into war but who now wanted to agree to 'terms of peace dictated by Russia';[22] while *The Times* criticized him for wanting to make peace short of unconditional

---

[19] *Hansard*, 3rd Ser., CXXXVIII, 1451-1468.   [20] *Ibid.*, 1758.
[21] *Quart. Rev.*, XCVIII, 254.
[22] *Fraser's*, LII, 361-362.

surrender.[23] The press was simply reflecting public sentiment in these attacks on Graham, for the war was more popular now than at its inception. France and Russia may have become weary of the war; not England. *The Times* put it quite correctly when it wrote that Graham would quit the war and willingly resist 'the temptation to military glory. Why should he care about such things', it went on to say, 'when he is just as great a man whether we take Sebastopol or are pushed into the sea? The masses, however, *have little else to care for*'.[24] Palmerston was in perfect touch with this sentiment, whether he led it or followed it; Graham was not, and by his actions helped, as Morley has put it, to 'throw the game into the hands of Lord Palmerston'.[25]

On September 9th the Russian forces abandoned Sebastopol and retreated towards Kars. This fortress was then defended by General William Fenwick Williams, who had been sent to organize the Turkish forces in Armenia and who for six months had held the fortress against terrific onslaughts. On November 28th, no longer able to hold out, he surrendered to the Russians. While this victory was pleasing to the Czar, who regarded it as a compensation for the loss of Sebastopol and who was now ready to make peace, it was of course galling to England. In fact, on April 28th, Whiteside moved a vote of censure on the Government by declaring that the fall of Kars was due to 'the want of foresight and energy on the part of Her Majesty's Administration'.[26] Those who supported this motion did so on the grounds that the Government, though not satisfied with the actions of Stratford de Redcliffe, had failed to recall him, and that the Government had also failed to send aid to General Williams in the summer of 1855. Graham came to the defence of Palmerston in this debate. He admitted that Stratford could be blamed for not having answered General Williams's letters and dispatches,[27] but condoned this negligence on the grounds that each had misunderstood the other's functions and duties. Stratford, it must be admitted, said Graham, had per-

---

[23] *The Times*, June 7th, 1855, p. 6. [24] *Ibid.*, Italics mine.
[25] MORLEY, *Life of Gladstone*, I, 546.
[26] *Hansard*, 3rd Ser., CXLI, 1594.
[27] According to Granville, Williams had sent Stratford 150 dispatches before receiving an answer. See Granville to Canning in FITZMAURICE, *Life of Granville*, I, 134. *Fraser's* (LIII, 74), attributed the fall of Kars to the 'monstrous conduct of Lord Stratford de Redcliffe'.

formed great services for England; he had checked the baleful influence of Russia at Constantinople; he had acquired almost complete ascendancy over the Sultan; he had protected the Christian subjects of Turkey. Aid had not been sent to Kars because both England and France had regarded its retention 'as altogether secondary to the capture of Sebastopol'. To be sure, money and supplies could have been sent to General Williams, but Graham and his colleagues had been opposed to loans and subsidies. He could not, therefore, censure a Government that had 'conducted the war to an honourable conclusion'.[28] Russell, as well as the Peelites, supported this stand of Graham and the motion was easily defeated.

The war now over, the country settled down to innocuous desuetude. In fact, the parliamentary session of 1856 was dull, uninteresting, and relatively barren of results. 'I never remember a more barren and more annoying sitting', wrote Graham to Herbert.[29] But peace having returned, he was ready once more to pursue a policy of retrenchment and reform. Consequently he opposed Russell's resolution providing for a national system of education.[30] He opposed it for five reasons. (1) It was unnecessary because there were enough educational opportunities in England and no country had made so much progress in the preceding 25 years as had England. (2) It was too expensive since it would cost at least £6,000,000 per annum. (3) It would diminish, not extend, education, for 'children under fifteen will no longer be employed. No farmer, if he can get a woman to hoe turnips, will ever think of employing a boy under fifteen years of age, with the odious chance of having school inspectors visiting his house to know whether the boy has been sent regularly to school'. Farmers would not employ plough-boys who were to be paid and educated at their expense. (4) It was oppressive to the poor and vexatious to industry. Com-

[28] *Hansard*, 3rd Ser., CXLI, 1835-1853.

[29] Cited in STANMORE, *Memoirs of Herbert*, II, 48. In June, only thirty M.P.s were present during the discussion on the Wills and Administration Bill.

[30] It proposed to increase the number of inspectors and to give rate-payers in deficient districts (educationally) power to impose a school-rate. Committees were to be appointed to manage the schools in which religious instruction was to be given and the Scriptures read daily. Employers of children from 9 to 15 years of age were to furnish half-yearly certificates of school attendance and to pay for their instruction. See *Annual Register* (1856), pp. 155-156; F. SMITH, *A History of English Elementary Education, 1760-1902*, p. 224.

pelling employers to educate, and the employed to be educated, would 'destroy the free competition of labour'. (5) It was constitutionally dangerous. 'It is proposed that we should at once hand over to a body of inspectors ... the appointment of some 34,000 or 35,000 school-masters, and all the influence which such a patronage cannot fail to give.' Government servants would be prying into private affairs and thus end the boasted liberty of Englishmen. Those who chose the teachers would fix the rates and regulate the teaching. If the schoolmaster were an Anglican, all others would be up in arms against him; if a Dissenter, the Anglicans would complain, and not peace but discord, would result. He believed that the voluntary system was best and that Russell's proposal was 'neither hot nor cold—neither religious nor secular'.[31]

Palmerston agreed with Graham and thought his speech 'able and powerful',[32] and Ball declared that it was 'one of the best he had ever heard'.[33] But the soundest judgment was that of Lord Granville, who wrote to Canning: 'Graham in a very able speech full of clap-traps made mincemeat of Johnny and his Education resolutions.'[34] He was absolutely correct. It was an able speech; it did make mincemeat of Russell's resolutions, for the latter withdrew about two-thirds of them and his final request that the House should not go 'beyond the resolutions dealing with the increase of inspectors' was defeated by a vote of 260-158;[35] and, finally, it *was* full of 'clap-traps'. Russell naturally pointed out that Graham himself had advocated the compulsory system in 1843. But it was the cost of such a system that worried Graham. England now had to foot a huge war debt and he did not want to add to this national bill by expending a large sum on education. Economy was necessary even at the price of national ignorance. For the same reason he denounced a Government Bill to increase the salaries and pensions of civil servants as 'altogether unjustifiable'.[36]

Graham also opposed a Bill dealing with life peerages and the appellate jurisdiction of the House of Lords. The Bill proposed that the Crown should call to the Lords, as peers for life, two judges

---

[31] *Hansard*, 3rd Ser., CXLI, 830-852. [32] *Ibid.*, 866.
[33] *Ibid.*, 927. *The Times* (April 11th, 1856, p. 8), also lauded this speech for its 'argumentative force, copiousness and weight'.
[34] Granville to Canning, April 11th, 1856, in FITZMAURICE, *op. cit.*, I, 176.
[35] See SMITH, *op. cit.*, 224.
[36] *Hansard*, 3rd Ser., CXLI, 894.

who had sat on the bench for five years to assist the Chancellor in hearing appeals. They should be called deputy-speakers and have salaries equal to those of common-law judges. Finally, it provided that appeals were to be held during prorogations.[37] When this Bill came to the Commons it was rigorously opposed by Graham who divided it for purposes of discussion, into two parts: the life peerages, and the appellate jurisdiction of the House of Lords. As to the first, he asserted that this Bill 'exhibited the feebleness and obscurity inherent in all middle measures . . . He could not conceive anything more painful than the position of a peer for life, bearing a brand of dependence, a mark of inferiority, belonging to a class termed peers, but yet not *pares*, equal'. If adopted, it would be necessary to go on and 'extend the creation of peers for life to the army, the navy, and politics for poverty was not confined to the law'. He absolutely refused to swamp the House of Lords for such 'a comparatively paltry object'. The second part of the Bill was a delusion which would 'debauch both the Bench and the Bar' because the judges, including some high legal personages, were to be paid. To be sure, the appellate work of the Lords was in need of overhauling, but careful inquiry should first be made before undermining the hereditary character of the peerage.[38]

According to the *Morning Chronicle*, real interest in the debate had not started until Graham rose and delivered 'one of his most crushing speeches' against the measure. The attempt of the Lords, it went on, to continue its inefficient appellate proceedings and yet exercise it by deputy, 'met from this clear-headed statesman . . . one of the most demolishing attacks the present time has witnessed'.[39] And the *Manchester Guardian*, which had supported the proposal in the hope that it would make the Court of Appeals respectable, admitted that 'even this opinion . . . had been greatly shaken by the masterly speech of Sir James Graham'.[40] Largely as a consequence of this speech, supported by Gladstone, Russell, and others, the Bill was defeated.

But Graham did not succeed in defeating a Bill to grant pensions to the bishops of London and Durham — £6000 to the former and £4500 to the latter — in the event of their being permitted to retire.

[37] See *Annual Register* (1856), p. 104.   [38] *Ibid.*, 106-108.
[39] *Chronicle*, July 8th, 1856, p. 4.
[40] *Manchester Guardian*, July 9th, 1856, p. 3.

Both had requested retirement because of their advanced age and infirmity. To Graham, this appeared like a simoniacal proceeding, i.e., 'the purchase or the sale of the avoidance of a spiritual cure for a money consideration'. Furthermore, the bishops of York and Norwich also desired the same arrangement. So, where would it all end? It was no more than 'a grant of bishoprics in reversion', and the disposal of two bishoprics placed in the hands of the Government. Had the House forgotten that the two resigning bishops could still vote in the Lords by proxy? In addition, he could not believe that the bishops were overworked. Was there not a dean in each diocese to do part of the work? He knew what should be done with this Bill — 'quietly inurn it with the remains of those departed measures which strew the floor of this House and over which the right hon. member for Buckinghamshire, after the manner of Pericles, is about to pronounce a funeral oration on Friday next'.[41]

On the other hand, Graham took charge of, and successfully carried through the House, a Bill relating to marriages performed on the Gretna side of the Scottish border. Contracts entered into here had been irregular to say the least. If the woman who was married there had money, the man declared the marriage to be valid; if not, she was immediately abandoned. The Bill declared all such marriages invalid unless both parties had been domiciled in Scotland for at least a fortnight.[42]

Once the Crimean War, which had acted as a cement binding the Peelites, was over, the party began to fall apart. Aberdeen, Graham, and Gladstone profoundly distrusted Palmerston's foreign policy; Herbert and Cardwell would condone it in the hope of a reunion with the Liberals. Palmerston, in that case, would be little more than the head of a reconstructed Aberdeen Government. Aberdeen and Graham would not object to this arrangement provided Russell, not Palmerston, was the leader. Gladstone, on the other hand, preferred a union with Derby. Aberdeen and Graham were nearing the end of their long public careers and did not care for office, but Herbert, Cardwell, and Gladstone were young men who did not relish political isolation. When Gladstone unburdened himself along these lines to Graham,

[41] *Hansard*, 3rd Ser., CXLIII, 1298-1313.
[42] *Statutes at Large*, 19 and 20 Vict., c. XCVI.

the latter agreed that it would be good to get rid of Palmerston, but who would replace him? If Gladstone wished to join Derby that was quite all right for he was young, while he, Graham, was 'ripened to decay'. Under no circumstances could he agree to join the Derby group.[43] Peel's commercial policies, which Gladstone admired, were not safe in Derby's hands, said Graham, and if Gladstone played his cards correctly he would soon be the leader of the Liberal party himself; but, if he joined Derby's party, he 'would have neither their confidence nor their good will and they will openly break with you in less than a year'.[44]

As a matter of fact, the Peelites were not a party at all but simply a clique of friends bound to each other by ties of friendship and long association. Gladstone was entirely correct when he said that he, Graham, Cardwell, and Herbert were accustomed to 'communicate together habitually and confidentially; . . . but rather eschewed acting, as a party . . .'[45] What made the group so important was that after 1855 no administration could remain long in office if these four went into opposition on any issue. They should have joined one or the other party, but Palmerston stood in the way of a fusion with the Liberals, and Disraeli and Derby stood in the way of a fusion with the Conservatives. But they were certainly doomed as a separate party and in 1857 the group broke up entirely.

On February 19th, Locke King brought in a Bill to equalize the county and borough franchise by giving the right to vote to all occupiers of tenements of the annual value of £10. Since the Bill was similar to the one he had himself brought in in 1854, which had been postponed because of the war, Graham supported it. Gladstone and Herbert, however, voted against the Bill. Then, on the Budget Bill, all three voted with the Opposition because they desired more retrenchment, but Cardwell voted with the Government.

About a week later, Derby in the Lords and Cobden in the Commons brought in resolutions censuring the conduct of

---

[43] Graham to Gladstone, December 1st, 1856, in PARKER, *Life of Graham*, II, 292. The wound caused by the severance of personal and party ties between Derby and Graham had never been healed. In fact, Derby had even insisted on having his named removed from the list of executors of Graham's will. *Graham Papers*, June 11th, 1854.

[44] Graham to Gladstone in MORLEY, *op. cit.*, I, 556.   [45] See *Ibid.*, I, 551.

Palmerston's Government in the Lorcha *Arrow* affair.[46] In October 1856 the Chinese authorities at Canton boarded a lorcha called the *Arrow*. It was a Chinese boat owned by Fong Ah-Ming of Hong Kong, and had been registered in accordance with the provisions of the Treaty of Nanking as a British ship.[47] It was almost impossible to control small ships like the *Arrow* in Chinese waters and since it was known that they were engaged in opium smuggling, the illicit and cruel coolie traffic, and even in piracy, the British authorities ought not to have registered them. Commissioner Yeh of Canton suspected that a notorious pirate was on board the *Arrow* and ordered his arrest. Chinese officers consequently boarded the ship, hauled down the British flag, and, despite the protests of Harry S. Parkes, the acting Consul, arrested the crew. Parkes promptly demanded the return of the crew and an apology. As usual, the Chinese delayed, and though they agreed to return the crew, refused to apologize on the grounds that the Chinese Emperor regarded all persons within his dominions as under his protection. The merchants at Canton, however, argued that they were English subjects and not under the Emperor's jurisdiction. On the Chinese refusal to apologize, the British Consul, Sir John Bowring, ordered a bombardment of Canton. It was this order which resulted in China's outlawing all English subjects and which was the basis of the censureship resolutions of Derby and Cobden.

On the second night of debate on these resolutions Graham delivered a long and very caustic denunciation of British policy in this *Arrow* affair. Bowring, he said, was a man 'more remarkable for his self-confidence than for the soundness of his judgment'. As for the *Arrow*, she 'was built by a Chinese, she was sold by a Chinese, bought by a Chinese, and was manned by Chinese'. The registry granted to the *Arrow* was invalid because 'those holding under it had no right as British owners'. Furthermore, the owners were likewise not entitled to hoist the British flag. These being the facts, the Chinese officials had a right to board the vessel and to arrest the pirate who everyone knew was on board. Bowring

[46] For a good account of this case see W. C. Costin, *Great Britain and China, 1833-1860*, pp. 206-230.

[47] At the time of the trouble her registry had expired, but she was on her way to Hong Kong where the registry would have been renewed.

and Parkes both knew this to be the case for on October 11th, 1856, Bowring had written to Parkes: ' "The *Arrow* had no right to hoist the British flag; the license to do so expired on the 27th of September, from which period she has not been entitled to protection." ' Then, on November 14th, Bowring wrote to Commissioner Yeh: 'The Lorcha *Arrow* lawfully bore the British flag under a register granted by me." ' So it was as obvious as anything could be that Bowring had 'practiced a deliberate deception on the Chinese Government, and ... proceeded to exact terms which he enforced by war'. Yeh's offer of reparation had been refused simply because Bowring 'was bent on being received into that city amid admiring multitudes, surrounded with all the pomp and circumstance of a public triumph'. Furthermore, Parkes had given Admiral Seymour a scheme for naval operations against Canton and he (Graham) wanted to know at what time civilians had arrogated to themselves the presumption that they could tell naval officers what to do? The plan was followed, but was not successful, and so Parkes shelled the city 'and devastation and carnage to an extent frightful to contemplate are carried among its peaceful inhabitants'. In addition, Bowring had used language to Yeh that was as insulting as that used by Prince Menshikoff to Turkey. 'I, for one,' he concluded, 'will wash my hands of the innocent blood which, in my opinion, has been shed.'[48]

Despite the fact that in defending Bowring and Parkes, Palmerston handed out another clever *Civis Romanus Sum* speech in which he ridiculously described Yeh as a 'savage Barbarian', the coalition of 22 Peelites, 35 Liberals and 195 Conservatives carried the resolution of censure and Palmerston was forced to resign.

To Graham, the issue was principally whether or not English consular agents should be allowed, without previous consultation with the Government in London, to take action that could involve the country in war. He did not think they should. Furthermore, he was opposed to war because it was too costly. But, what else could one expect from a Palmerston Government anyhow?

But the country not only did expect this kind of action from Palmerston, it was what they liked about him. Counting on this public support, Palmerston wisely decided to appeal to the country

---

[48] *Hansard*, 3rd Ser., CXLIV, 1552-1569.

on his handling of the China business. Graham, certain that the electorate would turn against Palmerston, immediately went to Carlisle to stand for re-election. 'I voted against war with China eighteen years ago,' he told his electors, 'I voted against it yesterday, I would do so again tomorrow. I think it an unwise and unworthy war. Englishmen ought to fight their equals, not to trample on their inferiors.'[49] He also denounced Palmerston for his warlike propensities and, to prevent him from assuming the leadership of the Liberal party, Graham very directly stated that Palmerston was not a Liberal at all but a real Tory.[50]

Graham was returned at the head of the polls at Carlisle, but Palmerston too had won a notable triumph and received a new lease on power. It was not Palmerston but the Peelites who had been snowed under. Many of them lost their seats altogether while 'the stronger swimmers — Messrs. Gladstone, Herbert and Graham', as The Times put it,[51] were returned; but the election had dug deeper the cleavage between them. In the elections, Graham and Cardwell had appeared as Liberals of the Russell persuasion and had spoken up for reform, while Herbert and Gladstone had taken a more Conservative stand. The latter thought that Graham's Carlisle speech was 'gallant, outspoken, energetic, and that it . . . enthronc[d] honesty and courage'. But, he said, Graham's demand for reform had 'undoubtedly inserted a certain amount of gap between himself and me'.[52] Graham wished to turn Palmerston out in favour of Russell, with Gladstone as leader of the House; Gladstone wanted Palmerston out but preferred Derby to Russell; Herbert wished to keep Palmerston in. The Times was therefore correct in saying: 'The Peelite Party is no more because their ground is too narrow to stand on.'[53] Graham went even further and declared: 'The Peelites as a party are gone. Indeed, I have never recognized their existence in that sense since the formation of Lord Aberdeen's Government, of which the avowed bases were fusion and reform.'[54]

[49] Cited in PARKER, Life of Graham, II, 305.
[50] Fraser's (LV, 489-492), and the Quart. Rev. (CI, 544), admired this attack on Palmerston.
[51] The Times, April 6th, 1857, p. 9.
[52] Gladstone to Herbert, in STANMORE, op. cit., II, 84.
[53] The Times, April 3rd, 1857, p. 7.
[54] Graham to Herbert, April 15th, 1857, in PARKER, op. cit., II, 309-310.

Before the parliamentary session drew to its close Graham had to face a painful personal crisis. Lady Graham had been ill for a long time and on August 21st, hoping that the sea-air would prove healthful, he took her to Cowes. But it was of no avail and on October 25th she died and was buried in Whippingham church-yard. Returning to Netherby, Sir James himself fell dangerously ill. But the pleasant surroundings and the quiet serenity of the ancestral home restored him to health once more, and by late autumn he was busy writing letters to Russell and others who sought his advice on a wide variety of problems — perhaps with the object of taking his mind off of his personal sufferings.

Politically he was now an independent elder-statesman with no taste for political strife, and advancing age only served to deepen his customary gloom and pessimism. 'The prospect is by no means alluring,' he wrote to Gladstone on January 26th, 1858, 'the state of parties is odious. I have no faith in Palmerston, . . . but the Liberal Party is bought and sold to him . . . Derby and his crew cannot man the ship, and the waves are about to run high. Dis-raeli at the helm in the Commons would swamp the vessel in calm weather.'[55]

But the waves were not about to run high. In fact everything was calm and placid. It was the dead-level of the mid-Victorian period and nothing seemed to change, or to warrant change. Everything was working for the best in the best of all worlds, and, as Villiers put it, 'Life was decent, quiet and ordered'.[56] This national mood was naturally reflected in Parliament. Strangers in the House of Commons, wrote the *Illustrated News*, would give anything to see Sir James Graham and Gladstone 'intervene to give point and animation to a discussion which, without them, seemed likely to expire of simple inanition'.[57]

But all that Parliament could produce of interest was a dis-cussion of the Orsini outrage. On January 14th, while the Emperor and Empress of France were driving to the opera, a bomb was thrown into their carriage by some Italians of whom Orsini was the leader. The Royal couple escaped injury, but many others were killed. It was soon proved that the plot was hatched in Eng-

[55] *Graham Papers.*
[56] VILLIERS, *A Vanished Victorian*, 308.
[57] *Ill. News*, XXXII, No. 904, p. 179.

land; that the bombs were made there; that Orsini had gone to France with an English passport made out in an English name. The French Government therefore protested that England by giving asylum to refugees was affording sanctuary to criminals. Count Walewski, the Foreign Minister, requested the English Government to assist the French Government in apprehending and punishing those criminals who violated the privilege of asylum in England. Clarendon, while he sent no formal reply to Walewski's note, let it be known through Lord Cowley in Paris that Parliament would not pass any law for the extradition of political refugees. The Duc de Morny, half-brother of the Emperor, then made the issue a popular one by asking how it was that the British Government could not destroy 'the laboratory of assassins'. The French and British press both took up the squabble and so, too, did Parliament. On February 8th Palmerston introduced a Bill to make conspiracy to commit murder either within or without the United Kingdom a felony punishable by life imprisonment. This proposal brought on an assault against the Government, which was led by Graham and Russell. Graham told Russell that he did not like 'altering the law of England in obedience to the dictation of France . . . All Europe would laugh at our degradation'. He then mapped out this strategy; approve the first reading of the Bill, but then allow a long lapse of time before the second reading so as to allow the public adequate time to become fully aroused.[58] The strategy worked well; the first reading was carried by a vote of 299 to 90, but the second reading never came up. Graham and Russell, with the public behind them, cleverly attacked the Government, not on the Bill itself, but by introducing an amendment condemning the Government for not having answered Walewski's dispatch. Dexterously led by Graham,[59] Conservatives like Disraeli, Liberals like Russell, Radicals like Gibson and Bright, all attacked Palmerston's Bill as an unworthy concession to French threats and as a reversal of the course of British policy which for a decade and more had been directed towards reducing the number of crimes punishable by imprisonment for life. On the division the amendment was carried by a majority of nineteen, and Palmerston

[58] Graham to Russell, in PARKER, *op. cit.*, II, 336.

[59] Prince Albert concluded that 'the whole move had been planned, and most dexterously, by Sir James Graham'. See *Letters of Queen Victoria*, III, 340.

had to resign. [60] Russell had achieved another 'tit for tat' and Graham had got rid of a minister whom he regarded as a threat to peace and an opponent of reform.

The Queen sent for Lord Derby, who, unable to get the Peelite group to join him, formed a completely Conservative Government. It was generally expected that Gladstone would now join the Conservative ranks, but, according to the *Leeds Mercury*, on 'finding that Sir James Graham, Mr. Sidney Herbert, Mr. Cardwell and the Duke of Newcastle refused, he reluctantly declined'. [61] And when Parliament assembled in March, Russell sat below the gangway with the Radicals, Cardwell behind the Opposition benches, but Graham, Gladstone, and Herbert did not change places — wishing to show, says Granville, 'that they will not join Palmerston, and that they are prepared to defend Derby from factious opposition; ready when the proper moment comes to join J. Russell in forming a government'. [62]

It was indeed fortunate for Derby that Graham was ready to support him against factious opposition, for he was at once faced with a serious problem in India. The need for a change in the government of that country had been brought home to England by the Sepoy mutiny of 1857. [63] For a century or more India's political system had been crumbling and her cultural institutions appeared to many Indians to be doomed. They did not understand the English, nor the English them, and the British decision to grease cartridges with fat from pigs and cows appeared to the Hindus as an attempt to break their caste and to the Moslems as an affront to their religion. Furthermore, 'the dispossessed Princes and landowners' as Knaplund so effectively puts it, 'young and ambitious Indians to whom neither the army nor the civil service offered chances for a career, native soldiers alarmed by a general service order requiring them to serve across dark and mysterious

[60] Palmerston's decision to resign was due in part to a desire to avoid a debate on the appointment of Lord Clanricard as Lord Privy Seal. The latter had been involved in a public scandal and was so generally disrespected that *The Times* called the appointment a public scandal. *The Times*, February 23rd, 1858, p. 6.

[61] *Leeds Mercury*, February 28th, 1858, p. 3.

[62] Cited in FITZMAURICE, *op. cit.*, I, 195. Greville declares that Aberdeen was trying to get Gladstone to join with Graham, Herbert, Cardwell, and Newcastle in a union with Russell. See GREVILLE, *Memoirs*, VII, 355.

[63] See the excellent analysis of this mutiny in THOMPSON and GARRATT, *Rise and Fulfilment of British Rule in India*, 435-458.

seas', were ready to oppose their English masters. [64] On May 9th, 1857, the insubordinate Sepoys refused to use the greased cartridges and were court-martialled and sentenced to ten years imprisonment. The next day three Indian regiments shot their officers, rescued their companions from prison, and started for Delhi. No attempt appears to have been made by Canning, who succeeded Dalhousie as Governor General in 1856, to cut off their retreat, so they took Delhi and proclaimed a Mogul Empire. From Delhi they went to Cawnpore, where they killed most of the English, and only the arrival of Sir Henry Havelock's forces prevented similar violence at Lucknow. British vengeance, though slow, was very severe. Thousands were hanged and many were blown from the mouths of cannons — a punishment especially galling to Hindus, who believed that bodies could not be reassembled in the future life.

A change in the government of India was obviously needed and Derby's Government took up the task. Before doing so, however, Derby had to face an acrimonious debate on the famous Proclamation of Oudh. Immediately after the recapture of Lucknow, Canning had issued a proclamation that all the rebellious chiefs in Oudh had lost their proprietary rights, but that if they submitted promptly, their lives would be spared (if they had not been guilty of shedding English blood). Canning may have meant this as a conditional offer of clemency, but in Oudh it was interpreted as a decree of confiscation. Sir James Outram, Civil Commissioner of Oudh, Sir John Lawrence, and Lord Ellenborough regarded this proclamation as a serious error. The latter, now President of the Board of Control, sent Canning a scathing rebuke without even consulting his colleagues. In addition, he most unwisely made it public. Speaking for the Government, Disraeli stated that they disapproved of the Oudh proclamation, whereupon Ellenborough, to save his colleagues from certain defeat, resigned.

Cardwell, who was a friend of Canning, and who had gone over to Palmerston's party, proposed a vote of censure on the Derby Government for having disavowed the proclamation. Graham, unwilling to unseat the Government for one led by Palmerston, opposed this resolution. He prefaced his speech of opposition by saying that he would deal calmly with the question because his 'shattered nerves and drooping spirits' dissuaded him from taking

[64] PAUL KNAPLUND, *The British Empire, 1815-1939*, 163.

part in angry contention and by explaining that he was sitting on the ministerial side of the House by courtesy only, for he really was 'no adherent of Her Majesty's Government'. Then he went on to declare that Ellenborough's action had been most indiscreet but that he had atoned for it by his resignation. As for Canning's proclamation, it too was indiscreet and impolitic for its object was 'to convert the tenure of land in a conquered province from tenancy for life . . . at a quit rent, to tenancy at will'. Not even Aurungzebe nor Tamerlane, nor Nadir Shah had ever tried anything like that. No, nor even Hardinge nor Dalhousie. The proclamation was a penalty next to death in severity, 'without proof against a whole people' in face of the fact that everyone would admit that there 'was a flaw in England's title to that kingdom'. Canning had not been recalled, but the Government had ordered him to mitigate the severity of his proclamation and had therefore acted properly. Therefore, he concluded, 'I think the proclamation is substantially wrong; I think the dispatch is substantially right. The error of the proclamation is in its essence; the error of the dispatch is in its form and expression'. To suppose that there was no purely partisan object in the resolution of Cardwell, as had been alleged, was too much for him to swallow: 'To tell me that . . . is to draw on my small stock of innocence and credulity to an extent that exhausts it at once, and leaves me an unbeliever.'[65]

It was a very effective speech and was largely influential in enabling the Derby Government to stave off the resolution.[66] The *Illustrated News* was amused by Graham's reference to his failing health and declared that he had not made 'so powerful a speech, so complete in all its parts, . . . since 1843 . . . when . . . [he] defied Hansard . . .'[67] Derby, of course, was pleased with the support Graham had given him and told the Queen that his speech had produced 'a very great effect'.[68] In fact, he and Disraeli now tried to get Graham to join them, but the latter was not prepared to hand over the Government to 'the Jockey and the Jew'. The feeling was mutual. Derby and Disraeli did not really want Graham and were willing to give him the leadership in the House, which

---

[65] *Hansard*, 3rd Ser., CL, 986-1002.   [66] Cardwell withdrew it on May 25th.
[67] *Ill. News*, XXXII, No. 920, p. 546.
[68] Derby to Queen Victoria, in *Letters of Queen Victoria*. III, 369.

Disraeli offered to surrender, only because they hoped in this manner to obtain the services of Gladstone, whom they wanted and needed. In fact, they offered Gladstone the Presidency of the Board of Control for India or the Colonial Office. As usual, Gladstone sought Graham's advice, saying that he felt as if he was at the bottom of a well waiting for someone to throw him a ladder. 'Derby tenders this ladder', Graham shrewdly replied. 'The Board of Control is not a bad one, though Ellenborough has just tumbled from it and broken his neck.' Gladstone ought to hold out for the leadership in the Commons, for, said Graham, Disraeli was not fit for the job and would relinquish it when he could do so without loss of face. 'The transfer which he has contemplated with respect to me is proof of this feeling on his part.' Then, he correctly diagnosed the situation with respect to the rest of their friends: 'The little band is broken up. The Duke of Newcastle studiously stands aloof, awaiting the chance which may place him at the head of affairs. Cardwell must henceforth be regarded as Palmerston's retainer, Herbert ... will act with the Whigs ... Lord Aberdeen ... must be regarded ... more as a bystander than as a confederate.' As for himself: 'I desire to wean myself from worldly affairs.'[69] Gladstone took the advice and wrote to Graham that he would refuse the offer and 'remain at the bottom of the well'.[70]

The immediate effect of the Indian Mutiny was a new Government of India Bill. Introduced to the House in a series of resolutions on April 30th, it provided for the creation of a Council of State of India to consist of fifteen members, a majority of whom must have served or lived in India for at least ten years. Eight were to be nominees of the Crown; seven to be elected in the first instance by the members of the Court of Directors. Vacancies in the latter group were to be filled by co-option, and all fifteen were to hold office on good behaviour. Actual conduct of Indian affairs was to be in the hands of a Secretary of State for India who was to replace the old President of the Board of Control, and who was authorized to overrule the Council in case of urgent necessity. Otherwise all orders were to be submitted to the Council for its opinion and concurrence. Annual reports were to be made by the

[69] Graham to Gladstone, May 25th, 1858, in PARKER, op. cit., II, 346-348.
[70] Gladstone to Graham, May 26th, 1858, in Ibid., 351.

Secretary to Parliament and any declaration of war, or further extension of territory, had to have the sanction of Parliament. All of the property of the East India Company was to be transferred to the Crown. [71]

Graham entered fully into the debates on these resolutions. For one thing he argued that a number of the members of the old Court of Directors should be chosen as the new nominated councillors. This would furnish 'an admixture of the principle of election and of nomination'. Further than that he did not believe the principle of election should go. Furthermore, the new Council should be given an effective control over the new Indian minister. If not, then he would prefer a minister who was alone directly responsible to Parliament. 'I do not want to see', he said, 'a sham and inefficient Council, the members of which shall be dependent on the power of the Government of the day, and who, like young ravens, will be opening their mouths to be fed by the Minister of the Day when the time for their re-appointment comes around.' [72] But arguing against the principle of election, and at the same time proposing to vote for a resolution embodying that principle, involved a dilemma which Graham neatly resolved by proposing that the Crown should nominate for the Council persons who, in their capacity as directors, had been elected. Graham was extremely adept at this sort of manœuvring, but the House, feeling, as Palmerston put it, that it was 'rather a strain upon language', [73] did not go along with him, and neither did Russell.

On the other hand, the House did agree with him that extensive changes ought to be made in Clause Three which dealt with the powers to be given the new Secretary of State. These powers, dealing with expenditures and patronage, ought to be strictly controlled, he said, and the Government agreed to amend the clause so as to achieve this object.

On July 27th the House of Lords passed an amendment to the Bill by which all of the patronage would be given to the Secretary of State in Council, and Graham was selected as a member of a House Committee to draw up a resolution explaining why the

[71] See *Annual Register* (1858), pp. 76-77; *Hansard*, 3rd Ser., CXLIX, App. The Company protested against this Bill in an excellent petition drawn up by John Stuart Mill. See P. E. ROBERTS, *History of British India under the Company and the Crown*, 380-382.

[72] *Hansard*, 3rd Ser., CL, 2028-2034.   [73] *Ibid.*, 2067.

House could not adopt the amendment. Not to be rebuffed, the Lords retaliated by drawing up an amendment to the effect that the system of open competition for a certain number of positions should be abolished in favour of appointment. Graham strenuously resisted this amendment on the grounds that its purpose was to keep the Government of India in the hands of 'gentlemen' to the exclusion of the middle class. It was a shabby way to treat a class which had done so much for England and India.

> Who, let me ask, founded — who won our Indian Empire? Those who bought and sold. Who extended it? Those who bought and sold. Who now transfer that Empire to the Crown? Those who bought and sold — a company of merchants — merchants, forsooth! whose sons are now not thought worthy to have even inferior offices in India . . . Who . . . were the conquerors of India? From what class have they sprung? Who was Clive? The son of a yeoman. Who was Munro? The son of a Glasgow merchant.[74]

Those who knew the history of India agreed that this was sound fact and those who wanted good government agreed with him that a system of competitive examinations was superior to patronage, but the majority in the House felt that the Lords' amendment was so minor a change that it could adopt it without materially hurting the Bill, and it was approved along with the rest of the measure.

But, having supported the Derby Government on the India question, Graham chose to oppose it on the subject of reform. On February 28th, 1857, Disraeli introduced a Reform Bill which proposed to take one seat from each of fifteen boroughs whose population was less than 6000. It also lowered the county franchise to £10, and though it did not lower the borough franchise, it extended it to doctors, schoolmasters, government pensioners, and National Fund holders.[75] The Bill did not go far enough to suit Russell and Graham so the former moved the following amendment: 'That no readjustment of the franchise will satisfy the House which does not provide for a greater extension of the suffrage in cities and boroughs than is contemplated in the present measure.' Graham solidly supported this amendment and opposed the Government measure. A reform bill that he could support would

[74] Ibid., CLI, 2341-2342.
[75] Annual Register (1859), pp. 52-55. John Bright referred to the franchise given these special groups as 'fancy franchises'.

have to provide for open voting; an occupation franchise of £10; votes for all rate-paying residents of boroughs; the disfranchisement of many small boroughs; additional representation for the large towns. He also thought that the time had come when town-labourers should be given the right to vote. 'I do not hesitate to say', he declared, 'that the time has come when political power should begin to descend to the working class.'[76]

With the powerful support of Graham, Russell's amendment was carried against the Government and Derby immediately appealed to the country. Graham, consequently, had to return to Carlisle to stand for re-election. Contrary to the advice of his doctor, he attended the nomination meeting and later made an election speech that attracted nation-wide attention. The question before the country, he asserted, was 'Reform or no Reform? — A liberal policy or tame submission to Lord Derby'. He did not like the Derby Government and hoped he would be returned to Parliament so he could call Derby to account for his many political sins. What had become, he asked of the 'peace-preserving' Premier? Portugal, helping England to enforce the Slave Trade Act, had seized a French vessel engaging in this trade. France had sent a naval force to the Tagus demanding release of the vessel, and Malmesbury, the Foreign Secretary, 'knowing France to be strong', had advised Portugal to surrender the vessel. In addition, Malmesbury had surrendered England's right to search United States ships for slaves. Pakington, the First Lord of the Admiralty, had converted the Admiralty Board into 'an electioneering machine'; Robert Peel, the Secretary for War, had been guilty of similar misconduct; and Derby had spent £20,000 for the purpose of packing the House of Commons. If elected to the new House, he promised he would 'grind such ministers to powder'. To save the Derby Government and to keep Palmerston out, he had helped carry the India Bill and had even defended the Proclamation of Oudh, but he could no longer support the Government because its Reform Bill was too weak. Graham did not approve of a £10 franchise for both boroughs and counties. Nor did he think very highly of the 'fancy franchises'. They were 'like pudding before the meat, ... the garnish of the dish without the joint, ... the cabbage and the carrots without the round of beef. I am for the

[76] *Hansard*, 3rd Ser., CLIII, 981.

round of beef. I am for a large reduction of the franchise — for the free admission of the working man'. He was now an old man, he concluded, and great changes had taken place in his life-time, and he asked:

> Shall man, frail man, . . . alone stand immovable, unaltered in his opinions and feelings? If a man is to refuse to yield to the pressure of the Times — if he is not open to conviction, and, notwithstanding the altered state of affairs and the changed condition of things around him, refuses to alter his opinions, such a man may be fit for a lunatic asylum, but I say he does not possess the true recommendations for any deliberative assembly in the world.[77]

The Times was highly pleased with this 'positively refreshing' speech[78] and Gladstone thought it 'superlative'.[79] The Conservatives, on the other hand, were furious. *Blackwood's* described his speech as the ranting and raving of 'a bitter and unscrupulous old man'.[80] The *Morning Chronicle* questioned his ethics,[81] and the *Morning Herald*, not knowing whether 'to groan, to sneer, or to laugh', described Graham as 'the first man who has elevated inconsistency into a doctrine'. Sir James's fraud charge against the Government was designed, it said, to frighten Liberals into making greater contributions, in money and effort, to the campaign against Derby.[82]

Graham was easily re-elected, a fact which pleased *The Times* because there would now be at least 'one clever man' in the new House. Carlisle, it said, ought to be proud of returning a man 'who endows it with ten times its fair proportion of public significance'.[83] But, in the country at large, the Conservatives had gained some thirty seats. Nevertheless Derby's Government was short of an absolute majority by about ten votes and therefore no reform bill could be passed that did not suit both Derby and Palmerston. And, to Graham's thinking, this did not leave the country much choice, for Palmerston, he said, was a Whig who had become a Tory, while Derby had never been anything but a Tory.

---

[77] This speech was printed in the *Leeds Mercury*, April 9th, 1859, p. 8, and in *The Times*, April 30th, pp. 3-6.
[78] *Ibid.*, April 23rd, 1859, p. 6.
[79] See STANMORE, *Memoirs of Herbert*, II, 178.
[80] *Blackwood's*, LXXXVI, 364.
[81] *Chronicle*, May 12th, 1859, p. 4.   [82] *Herald*, May 11th, 1859, p. 4.
[83] *The Times*, May 2nd, 1859, p. 9; May 12th, p. 4.

Russell, who was planning to propose a vote of censure as soon as Parliament met, asked Graham if he would support such a resolution, and, if successful, if he would serve in a new government to be headed by Russell. Graham promised to join in the vote of censure, but declined to hold any more public offices.

But it was Hartington, not Russell, who proposed the censure of the Government, and Disraeli, in defending the Government, launched into an attack on Graham for the latter's Carlisle speech. 'When I read that charge upon the Ministry . . . I could not help saying, "Young men will be young men". Youth is, as we all know, somewhat reckless in assertion, and when we are juvenile and curly one takes pride in sarcasm and ridicule.' As for the fraud charge against Derby, it was an 'impudent fabrication'.[84] Two nights later, Graham replied in kind. Disraeli, of all people, knew from experience that 'one may lose one's curls and still retain one's taste for sarcasm and invective . . . Intemperate language in a position such as the right hon. gentleman occupies is always a proof to me of a falling cause, and I regard that speech and those expressions as a happy omen of the coming success of the Motion . . . I regard him as the Red Indian of debate. By the use of the tomahawk he has cut his way to power . . .' Then came the bill of indictment against the Derby-Disraeli Government: they had brought in an inadequate and inept Reform Bill; they had asked for an Indian Exchequer loan of £5,000,000, a month later for £5,000,000 additional, and now they were requesting another £5,000,000; they had bungled the reorganization of the Indian army and had shuffled the task off on a hopelessly divided committee; their attempt to settle the Jew question had been a dismal failure, and their budget was unusually bad.[85]

With this powerful support by Graham, the resolution of censure was carried by a majority of nineteen votes and Derby resigned. The Queen then suggested that Palmerston and Russell unite in a Government led by Lord Granville, a neutral Peer. But Russell demanded the leadership in the Commons, the post Palmerston insisted upon, so this plan did not materialize. Graham then

[84] *Hansard*, 3rd Ser., CLIV, 126-127. Graham had already discovered that his charge against Derby was false and had retracted it. See *The Times*, May 17th, 1859, p. 7.

[85] *Hansard*, 3rd Ser., CLIV, 262-271.

suggested that Russell join Palmerston, that the latter serve as
Prime Minister, that Russell assume the Foreign Office, Gladstone
the Exchequer, and Granville the Lord Privy Seal. This suggestion
worked out satisfactorily and Palmerston wrote to Graham thank-
ing him for his services.[86]

The succeeding parliamentary session was a very dull one. A
Reform Bill was introduced but it died of simple inanity. Walpole
described the scene very well: 'They suffered it to lie, a waterlogged
vessel, on a sleeping ocean, till, abandoned by its pilot, it sank
beneath the waves of oblivion.'[87] Graham's activity in this session
consisted of proposing a shorter day for labourers in the bleaching
and dyeing works; recommending an independent audit of Civil
Service accounts; assisting the Government in abolishing the Law
of Settlement; and, on the request of Mrs. Gladstone, aiding her
husband in carrying his Budget Bill. In addition, he was an active
member of the Ecclesiastical Commission and helped steer its Bill
through the House. He was chairman of the committee which
drew up a plan to expedite the business of the House — a plan
which was subsequently adopted. Finally, he served as a member
of a committee on Admiralty business and on the committee to
reorganize the War Department. On the other hand, he refused
Russell's request that he defend the Government's Italian policy.
He could not agree to regard Napoleon as the liberator of Italy
and when Russell wrote his dispatch on Italian affairs stating that
the Governments of the Papacy and the King of the two Sicilies
were so bad that most Italians regarded their overthrow as a
necessity, Graham declared that he could not see how such a
document 'could have passed through a British Cabinet or received
the approval of a British Sovereign'. It was, he thought, 'a great
public wrong, a grave error', from which Garibaldi and Mazzini
would come out 'with cleaner hands'.[88]

Despite this activity, Graham's public career was about over.
The years 1858 to 1861 were years of failing health, and the death of
his close friends, Aberdeen and Herbert, hastened his own end. In
July 1860 he told Gladstone that he was suffering from mental
and moral exhaustion. In September he was one of the pall-

---

[86] Palmerston to Graham, June 29th, 1859, in PARKER, *op. cit.*, II, 390-391.
[87] SPENCER WALPOLE, *History of Twenty Five Years*, I, 204-205.
[88] See MORLEY, *op. cit.*, II, 16.

bearers at the funeral of Aberdeen, who, since Peel's death, had been his closest friend. The weather was cold and wet and when he reached Netherby he was a very sick man, with no further interest in life. 'To depart would be far better', he wrote to Mrs. Herbert. Angina pectoris set in and he could scarcely speak without grievous pain. Though he recovered sufficiently to be able to attend Sidney Herbert's funeral, the exertion was too hard on his worn-out system. On October 25th he died of a heart attack. He was buried in the churchyard at Arthuret, even though his will had directed that he be buried 'in the churchyard at Kirk Andrews on the northeast side of the church under an elm tree which grows there'.[89]

[89] Memorandum to his trustees, in *Graham Papers*.

AT the close of the Napoleonic Wars the political machinery in England, while superior to any on the Continent, was both archaic and corrupt. Political power was concentrated in the hands of an oligarchy of aristocrats by means of which about seventy families controlled the politics of the realm. The right to vote was a privilege to which the property holder was entitled by virtue of his possessions. The Parliament at Westminster was, in most respects, a council of wealthy landlords, nobles, and successful business men, who ran the Government in their own interest and in their own way. Not only did the property qualifications for voting exclude the great majority from electing representatives to Parliament, but the apportionment of members took no account either of the increase in population or of its altered distribution. No new assignment of seats had been made for about two centuries with the result that some towns which had few, and in some notable cases no inhabitants, could still send two representatives while such great new industrial centres as Birmingham, Leeds, and Manchester sent none at all. Local government, too, was in the hands of Justices of the Peace or of self-perpetuating councils who regarded their functions as private affairs and of little concern to the public.

A like situation existed with respect to the Church. There was religious toleration, but no religious equality. The Established (Anglican) Church was supported by incomes from endowments and the properties it had been given; by tithes and Church rates which all citizens had to pay; and by direct State subsidies. The religious legislation of the seventeenth century had barred from public office all conscientious Nonconformists, Catholics, and Jews. And while these acts were not in the nineteenth century generally enforced against the Nonconformists, they were enforced against the Catholics, who were regarded as enemies, and against the Jews, who were contemptuously regarded as aliens.

If the Government, as has been pointed out, was both archaic and corrupt, so too, was the Church. The archbishops and bishops were direct nominees of the Crown; the lower clergy, such as the deans, canons, archdeacons, and parsons, were nominated by patrons. Parochial patronage was vested in the Colleges of Oxford and Cambridge, the schools of Eton and Winchester, the Crown, or the families of the great landowners. As a consequence the landed gentry were the masters of the ecclesiastical as well as of the civil administration, and corruption was widespread. Such evils as nepotism, pluralism, and non-residence were universal, and the clergy were lacking in scientific curiosity and/or religious fervour.

But while the Industrial Revolution of the late eighteenth century and the Napoleonic Wars of the early nineteenth had not altered the political or religious institutions of England, they had seriously affected its economic life. Taxes were heavy; the national debt huge. With the end of the continental blockade, agricultural prices dropped, and at the same time an impoverished and war-ravaged Europe could not afford to buy English manufactured goods. In addition, the return of thousands of soldiers and sailors, together with an increasing use of labour-saving machinery, heightened the competition for jobs and inevitably depressed wages. To make matters worse, Parliament, when peace came in 1815, passed a Corn Law prohibiting the importation of food except when the price of the home produce was sufficiently high to ensure security to the British farmers. Furthermore, it neglected to repeal the Navigation Laws, which excluded foreign vessels from the colonial and coasting trade. Hence the country could not take full advantage of the inventions which had come with the Industrial Revolution.

In the social field, too, all was chaos. The shocking conditions which existed in the jails and prisons, the complete absence of any programme of public health, the woefully inadequate educational institutions, the frightful working conditions in the mines and factories, were an inevitable consequence of the total lack of national policy. 'The central government', as Halévy has so well put it, 'did nothing to secure the public safety, provided no schools, made no roads, gave no relief to the poor. With the one exception of the postal service, the State performed no function of immediate benefit to the taxpayer.' Responsibilities along these lines were held to be local problems to be handled by the local gentry, a group who were at all times jealous of their independence and hostile to administrative centralization.

At neither the national nor the local level was there anything like an efficient administration. The remuneration of public officials was a public scandal. Some received salaries alone, but most were paid in salaries and fees, the amount of the latter being determined by the amount of public money that they handled. Between the time when money which Parliament had appropriated was given to an official, and the time when he paid it to his subordinates, he could use it as he pleased. As a result, he kept it in his hands as long as he could and often loaned it out at interest. Furthermore, there was a large number of sinecures, i.e., posts to which salaries, but no public duties, were attached. In every branch of government there was an extensive patronage at the disposal of its head. In no department was there anything resembling a bookkeeping system; there was no regularized auditing of accounts, no clear relationship between the number of officials and the jobs to be performed.

The same thing was true of the courts of law. Here, too, nepotism was rife; remuneration was usually by fee, not salary (and fees were not uniform as to time, place, or circumstance); delays in justice were flagrant; and sinecures glutted the profession. Bench and bar, like Church and State, suffered from incompetence, inertia, and the deadening weight of routine and red tape.

In foreign affairs, peace was the dominant note in the years following Waterloo. The country was tired of war and wished merely to live at peace with the world and to get back to the business of making a living. By means of its command of the seas, England was safe from attack, and at the same time could maintain a balance of power in Europe and act as the arbiter of its disputes.

But domestically, the England of 1815 was one whose institutions were outmoded, and in which reform was urgently needed. Unfortunately, however, the Tories, who had been in office for many years, had no economic or political remedy to propose except the severest forms of repression. They clamped down on the public agitation for reform with the utmost vigour. They used the military to disperse meetings, suspended the writ of Habeas Corpus, and by means of the Six Acts curtailed public meetings and muzzled the press. To the Tory leaders reform was synonymous with revolution and had to be suppressed.

But while the Whigs (who also represented the landed interests

and equally disliked the tone of radical propaganda) denounced
the repressive measures of the Tory party, they could suggest no
constructive remedy of their own. They were a bit more commer-
cially-minded, however, and hence were a little less unsympathetic
with the new industrial capitalism which demanded a share in the
government of the country. They realized that the demands of the
middle class for reform of Parliament would have to be answered
because that class was now not only more numerous and more
wealthy, but also more vocal. Furthermore, the Whigs had been
out of office for a long time, due to lack of effective leadership
and to cleavages within the party, and concluded that a fusion
with the middle class in espousing the cause of moderate reform
would enable them once more to enjoy the fruits of political power.

This, then, was the economic and political situation in England
when Graham first entered upon his parliamentary career. The
influences that had surrounded his early life had been Tory. He
believed, as they did, in peace abroad and law, order, and discipline at home. On the other hand, he denounced the Tory
suspension of the Habeas Corpus Act, disapproved the pains and
penalties to which Dissenters and Roman Catholics had long been
subjected, avowed his hostility to slavery, and protested against
the financial extravagance and reactionary policies of the Tory
party. For these reasons he could not possibly join that party. But
since the same general criticisms could be levelled at the Whigs,
except that they sponsored reform of Parliament, Graham did not
find himself at home with them either. Consequently it was as an
independent north-country gentleman that Graham spent his first
few years in the House of Commons.

From 1821 to 1826 Graham was out of public life. Had he been
in Parliament he undoubtedly would have supported all of the
reforms carried out by the liberal Tories, who assumed the leadership of the party in 1822. He would have championed the economic
reforms of Huskisson, for although not a free trader by any means,
he favoured a simplification of the tariff system in the interest of a
freer trade. He would also have approved the abolition of
restrictions on exports and a scaling down of the tariff on raw
materials. The modification of the criminal code proposed by Sir
Samuel Romilly, and the law reforms of Sir Robert Peel, would
also have found in Graham a determined champion.

When Graham returned to Parliament in 1826 he discovered that Toryism had been changing into mild conservatism. The Tories naturally wanted to retain their authority and privileges, but were now reconciled to changes which did not adversely affect their own position in the State. Their changing opinion was reflected in the reforms which they had carried out since 1822, and in the repeal of the Test and Corporation Acts in 1828 and the passage of the Catholic Emancipation Act of 1829, both of which measures Graham supported. But this cautious reform policy could not be carried to fruition without a reform of Parliament. At this juncture, in the summer of 1828, the independent Graham suggested the formation of a new party — a conservative party — to comprise all those who were interested in reducing the costs of government and in reforming Parliament. The Tories, however, would not agree to such an attack on their vested interests and Graham therefore joined the Whigs in opposition to the Government. In 1830, when the Duke of Wellington made his unfortunate pronouncement against reform, some of the liberal Tories, as well as some who disliked the Catholic Emancipation Act, united with the Whigs to defeat the Government's Civil List and drive Wellington from office.

Since Graham had been a particularly severe and effective critic of the Tory government, he was given the post of First Lord of the Admiralty in the newly-formed Grey ministry. He brought to his office his consummate organizing talent, his knowledge of business methods, his zeal for economy, and his meticulous attention to detail. He succeeded, for the first time in English history, in presenting to the House in a simple and intelligible form the annual Naval Estimates. He introduced the practice of submitting an annual account of all Naval expenditures audited by an independent Board of Audit. All civil departments of the Navy were placed under the responsibility of five officers supervised by the Admiralty Board — an arrangement that remained in force for over sixty years. He astonished Whigs and Tories alike by making all promotions a reward of merit and not of party loyalty. Finally, he sought to end the impressment of seamen not by abolishing it by legislative fiat, but by so improving conditions in the Naval service that resort to impressment would be unnecessary. These reforms, carefully planned and expertly administered, have earned for Sir

James a place high on the list of England's greatest First Lords. During the 1830s, however, it was his activity as a member of the committee that drafted the Reform Bill of 1832 that earned for him his reputation as a moderate reformer.

In 1834 the independent Graham left the Whig party. Against his outspoken opposition, it secured the adoption of a Bill providing for the appropriation of the surplus revenues of the Church of Ireland to secular purposes, i.e., the general education of all classes of Christians in Ireland. In addition, Graham utterly despised the Whig alliance with the 'radicals' and with O'Connell's Irish brigade; he considered the Whigs inept administrators; and he correctly saw that the party was stricken with financial paralysis. For these reasons he concluded that the Whigs had departed from their principles and that he could therefore no longer work with them.

It was relatively easy for Graham to leave the Whig party in 1834 for in that year Peel openly accepted the Reform Bill as a definite and irrevocable settlement. Furthermore, the keen minds of both Peel and Graham were moving resolutely towards a study of the financial aspects of the relief of trade, a sound fiscal policy, and the need for government to be administered as efficiently as any business enterprise. This interest in trade and commerce enabled them to understand the financial needs of the country better than most Tories and Whigs. And the Reform Bill, giving political rights to the middle class, brought to the House of Commons a group who naturally followed the leadership of Peel and Graham. The emergent Conservative party of which they were the acknowledged leaders consisted of those Tory landlords and middle class merchants who were interested primarily in practical government, and who, like good business men, desired an efficient and economically administered government. At the same time, however, many of the landlords in the party, interested primarily in defending the Corn Laws and the Established Church, did not particularly like Peel's and Graham's solicitude for the interests of the middle class.

But the Whigs were also divided amongst themselves, and failing after 1836 to produce either a programme for the relief of the acute economic and industrial distress of the country, or a statesman of the stature of the leaders of the Conservative party, they sank beneath the weight of a succession of empty budgets and abandoned Bills, and in 1841 were voted out of office.

In the ministry which Peel promptly formed, and which was undoubtedly the ablest ministry of the nineteenth century, Graham held the important post of Home Secretary. For the five years in which he held this office, he laboured mightily to reform and improve those institutions which experience had shown to be weak and inefficient. In the political field, he secured the passage of the Registration of Voters Bill of 1843 which was designed to end the personation of voters and to simplify voting procedures. In the religious field, though a staunch adherent of the Established Church, he supported all ecclesiastical legislation the object of which was to improve and strengthen that Church. He laboured to secure the augmentation of small livings and the establishment of adequate cures in destitute districts; he fought against nepotism, pluralism, and clerical indifference. He was equally active in the field of social reform. Almost alone he strove to obtain much-needed reform in the medical profession, and with others worked assiduously in advancing the cause of public health. He managed, in 1844, to secure the passage of the Factory Act limiting the employment of women and children in silk, cotton, woollen, and flax mills. He promulgated new sets of rules and regulations to be followed in the penal institutions, and exerted his powerful influence in securing a more humane attitude in the treatment of lunatics, paupers, and other unfortunate members of society. In the legal field, too, he was a most diligent reformer. It was largely owing to his efforts that new and improved laws respecting bankruptcy and insolvency were enacted; that imprisonment for debts of less than £20 was abolished; that payment of court officials by salary instead of fee was introduced. So assiduously did he labour in securing reforms in the common law courts that Lord Campbell described him as the Chief Minister of Justice and the *Westminster Review* characterized him as 'the patron saint of our law reformers'. In the economic field, the chief achievement of this ministry was the repeal of the Corn Laws, and for this Graham deserves much of the credit. A large landowner, he was, when he first entered Parliament, an advocate of protection to agriculture. But he soon discovered that the equilibrium of the English economic system had been destroyed, that exports would continue to exceed imports (as in 1812 and 1813), and that more people were engaged in industry than in agriculture. He saw clearly that commerce, navigation, and manufactures produced a progressively greater revenue than agriculture and mining. For that reason he became a free trader, and without his active assistance, Peel would have been unable to carry the Repeal Act of 1846. Gladstone, no mean authority in economic matters, declared that Graham knew more about business than all the rest of the cabinet combined.

But to administer the reforms that had been passed since 1832 required an increased number of central administrative boards and commissions, and the resulting increase in the number of appointive officials at the disposal of the Home Office occasioned a good deal of criticism and complaint. It was argued that Graham was making the Home Office the chief tyrant in the unitary type of state towards which the country was inexorably moving. But this increasing power in the hands of the Home Secretary, enabling him to assume many of the powers of a party-whip, was due to the character and ability of the Home Secretary and to the fact that each of the great reforms that had been passed provided for a central administrative or regulative board and for inspectors, supervisors, and other officials all under the control of the Home Office rather than to any conscious desire of Graham to increase his own authority and power.

After 1846 Graham held steadfastly to his principles of peace, economy, efficient public administration, free trade, and moderate reform. After Peel's death, in 1850, he became the acknowledged leader, although he did not so consider himself, of Peel's former colleagues. These men, known as the 'Peelites', were, in the years from 1850 to 1857, often referred to as the 'Grahamites'.

The years from 1846 to Graham's death in 1861 were years of political flux in which the sands of party politics shifted constantly. There were no less than six different administrations, and none could remain in office without the support of many votes from all three parties — the Whig-Liberal, the Protectionist-Tory, and the Conservative-Peelite. The relative voting strength of these parties constantly fluctuated and the latter group never exceeded a voting strength of more than 117.

But Graham, though the unquestioned leader of a group which included such talented men as Gladstone, Herbert, and Cardwell, never regarded that group as a separate party. Nor would this thorough-going independent agree to a coalition with any other party even though political differences were insignificant. He would not join the Whig-Liberal party because he distrusted Palmerston's foreign policies and his truckling to the public; he could not believe that the Whigs had forgiven him for walking out on them in 1834; he was apprehensive lest they go too far in the line of reform; and his whole being rebelled at their fiscal incompetence. At the same time, the Netherby baronet could not join a reconstructed Tory-Conservative party, even though it did accept free trade by 1852, because he could neither forgive nor forget their malicious attacks on Peel and his colleagues for the 'great surrender' in 1846. Furthermore, a coalition with 'the Jockey and the Jew' was altogether too much for him to accept. Both parties tried on several occasions to secure Graham's services but he preferred to follow his customary independent course. And while he did agree to a junction with the Whig-Liberals in 1853, it was only because his followers were to be given the key posts in the cabinet and because his very close friend, Lord Aberdeen, agreed to serve as Prime Minister. At the close of the Crimean War, in which he had not wanted the country to become embroiled, but during which he administered the Admiralty office with his customary skill and industry, the coalition broke up.

Free trade, retrenchment, gradual reform, and sound practical government remained his guiding principles. Declining to assume the leadership of a separate party, as he was often asked to do after Peel's death, he preferred to support any party which adopted any or all of his principles. His closest friends, after Peel's death, were Aberdeen, Herbert, and Gladstone. The latter constantly sought and took his advice on almost all questions and in this sense Graham was the spiritual god-father of the Liberal party which later grew to power under the leadership of Gladstone.

Always a first-class administrator, an indefatigable man of business, acquainted with history, economics, and politics, he possessed a fine talent for gettings things done. A prodigious worker, clear-headed and forceful, he made a superb cabinet minister and one to whose opinions men like Peel, Grey, Russell, and Gladstone deferred. For thirty years or more he was regarded as the man whom 'no cabinet should be without'.

In the House of Commons, too, he was a tower of strength to the Government or to the Opposition. A recognized authority on finance and business, perfectly acquainted with the practices of the House, the possessor of a silvery voice and a handsome appearance he was if not a great orator, so effective a speaker, his expositions were so earnest, so neat and orderly in their diction, his arguments were presented so clearly and logically, that he was always listened to attentively. It was generally believed that his support was worth fifty votes on any issue.

Why was it that a man who possessed these admirable traits, who thrice adorned cabinet posts with his administrative genius, whose opinion and support were sought on every major issue for more than a decade, who was a forceful speaker and superb debater, who had the confidence of the ablest men of his generation, never attained the top rung of the political ladder?

There are, in the opinion of the author, five reasons for his failure to do so: (1) He was unpopular. Snobbish, aloof, quick to find fault with others, he was disdainful of men's opinions, suspicious of their motives, and unable to control an impulse to pulverize his opponents with offensive repartee. His caustic barbs, carefully aimed and deftly cast, cut deeply. It was this deliberate sarcasm, even when his cause was just and when the facts were all on his side, that forced Graham into a series of personal feuds that damaged his reputation. On the other hand, though it was inevitable, part of his unpopularity was not deserved. Administrative efficiency, his greatest public virtue, is not a quality that wins friends among one's contemporaries. Rarely, if ever, is an able and efficient administrator popular. (2) By the middle of his career, Graham had done so many things, sponsored or opposed so many reforms, that large segments of the population disliked and distrusted him. The legal profession looked askance at his legal reforms; thousands of medical men vilified him for attempting to introduce order in their chaotic profession; landlords regarded him as a renegade for his advocacy of repeal of the Corn Laws; the Scottish Presbyterians resented his handling of the Non-Intrusion controversy in their church; Dissenters and Anglican Churchmen, in turn, were annoyed at his educational proposals. (3) He had committed the unpardonable political blunder of changing his party affiliations too often. In his aristocratic manner and temperament, in his early training and associations, in his undeviating loyalty to the Established Church, he was a Tory. But when he joined a Whig club (Brooks's), became a 'radical' reformer and advocated a modification of the Corn Laws, the Tories turned against him. Nor did the Whigs ever completely trust him. They knew him as an independent to whom party loyalty was secondary to loyalty to principles. They resented his resignation from Grey's cabinet in 1834 and came to hate him for his splenetic attacks on them after that date. The Radicals too, came to hate him. To be sure, they admired his administrative skill, his impartial use of the patronage, his insistence upon economy and business-like methods in government, but they despised his aristocratic snobbishness, his narrow theology, and his opposition to annual Parliaments, universal suffrage, the secret ballot, and the ten hours movement. (4) He was by nature and temperament unfit for a position of highest leadership. He did not have enough confidence in his own ability to lead. People respected him; they did not follow him as a natural leader. Moody, gloomy, and pessimistic, always fearful that the future would assuredly be worse than the past, he did not inspire confidence as a public leader must do. This moral timidity, this perpetually seeing a lion in the path, this lack of resolution when grave decisions had to be made, this lack of robust hardiness of mind unfitted him for the premiership. As a second in command, a first-lieutenant, he had no superiors and few equals, but the mere thought of the responsibilities of a chief seemed to paralyse the powers of his magnificent intellect. At a higher post, he certainly would have failed. His indecision under an exterior of great strength shook men's confidence in him, and while he became at last an 'elder statesman', a 'pillar of state', he was a free-lance in politics, not a powerful party leader. (5) He did not possess the 'common touch' that is so essential to leadership. He was certain, for instance, that the State could do little to relieve the sufferings of the poor, and as a consequence he was somewhat callous about them. On the Poor Law problem, as well as in the field of penal reform, he was primarily interested in the techniques of administration, the machinery of management, not the unfortunate human beings. To be sure, he felt sorry for the poor and oppressed, but his Tory respect for property and the majesty of the law always took first place in his mind.

But failure to reach the premiership, which in fact Graham never wanted, is of itself no adequate test of his political stature. It is necessary, in order to fix his rank as a statesman, to ascertain the degree to which he was responsible for the improvements that were made in English public life during the period of his active career. Applying this criterion to the fields of public finance, institutional reform, foreign affairs, and public administration, where does Graham deserve to be ranked?

When Graham began his political career, England was in the throes of a serious and prolonged economic depression which adversely affected every segment of the population. By 1861 it was more prosperous than it had ever been and the standard of living for all classes of society had greatly improved. If this decided improvement was the result, in large part, of economy in government, balanced budgets, the removal of the Navigation Laws, and the repeal of the Corn Laws, then Graham deserves much of the credit, for without his constant aid and encouragement Peel would have had great difficulty in securing the adoption of his famous budgets, and could not have carried the Repeal Act through Parliament.

Whereas in the years immediately folowing the battle of Waterloo, England still suffered from the effects of the Napoleonic Wars, and war-time prejudices and fears still agitated men's minds, by 1861 the nation was at peace with the world and scarcely a cloud existed on the international horizon. Regarding war as unnecessary, costly, and a curse to mankind, Graham not only supported the peace policies of Aberdeen, but constantly opposed Palmerston's chauvinistic meddling in European quarrels, as well as the minor wars that were fought in such places as India and China. He even carried this opposition to a point where, during the Crimean War, he was denounced as a friend of the Czar and a leader of the 'peace-at-any-price' party. Therefore, for the peace which mid-Victorian England enjoyed, Graham deserves much of the credit.

And whereas in 1815 England's political, social, religious, and legal institutions were controlled by a system of vested interests that was archaic, a patronage that was corrupt, and an inertia that was deadening, by 1861 these institutions had been reformed, glaring abuses and evils had been corrected, and a new spirit in keeping with the changing spirit of the times had been infused into all of them. And for this achievement, too, few deserve to be more highly venerated by posterity than Sir James Graham.

But despite the magnitude of his work in the field of public finance, foreign affairs, and institutional reform, it was as an efficient administrator that Graham stands pre-eminent among the statesmen of the nineteenth century. At the commencement of his career, the direction and control of almost all of the agencies of the State lay in the hands of amateurs such as merchants, bankers, and landlords, principally interested in their private work, who gave to politics and State affairs only a small part of their time. There were no efficient administrative boards or commissions; the civil service was small, limited in function to carrying out the directives of the great departments of government, and recruited entirely by patronage. At the close of Graham's career this was no longer true owing primarily to the example he set in his superb administration of the Home Office and the Admiralty. He saw more clearly than any of his contemporaries that in the efficient management of public office, the proper articulation of government agencies, the enforcement of the law, and the proper execution of public policy lies the very essence of public administration. This knowledge was clearly reflected in his emphasis upon the proper systems of reporting and record-keeping, and the increasing of the attractiveness and prestige of a responsible civil service recruited by competitive examination.

For these reasons, Sir James Graham, next to Peel, deserves to be ranked as the ablest man in English public life in the years from Waterloo until his death in 1861.

APPENDICES

APPENDIX A

	Compared with 1830 £	Compared with 1831 £	Compared with 1832 £
Wages to seamen etc.	115,000	207,000	2,300
Victuals to seamen	200,000	210,000	24,465
Wages to artificers	52,500	82,126	44,000
Timber and materials	265,000	408,846	54,733
New works	36,000	148,400	43,300
Hired packets	14,000	10,260	4,740
Civil establishment	110,000	55,865	28,310
Other heads of service	144,321	90,280	18,652

APPENDIX B

	£
12 Commissioners with salaries of	14,200
1 Paymaster of marines	1,000
61 Superior officers of yards	19,712
37 Inferior officers of yards	3,885
102 Clerks	35,276
Totals, 213	74,073

APPENDIX C

Half-pay of all Naval officers in 1829, 1830, 1831, and 1833

January 1st, 1829	1,023,248
January 1st, 1831	1,022,013
less in two years	1,235
January 1st, 1831	1,122,013
January 1st, 1833	980,370
less in two years	41,643

BIBLIOGRAPHY

DOCUMENTARY MATERIAL

Acts of the Parliaments of Scotland, 12 vols., London:
His Majesty's Stationery Office.

Admiralty Papers: 1830-1834 and 1852-1855.
Admiralty Comptroller Out-Letters.
Admiralty Minutes.
Admiralty Navy Board, Out-Letters.
Admiralty Secretary In-Letters.
Admiralty Secretary In-Letters, Admirals.
Admiralty Secretary In-Letters, Victualling Board.
Admiralty Secretary Out-Letters; Home Stations, Military Branch.
Admiralty Secretary Out-Letters, Military Branch.
Admiralty Secretary Out-Letters, Naval Book, Political and Secret
Branch.
Admiralty Secret Orders and Letters.
Admiralty Secretary Out-Letters, Transport Service.

British and Foreign State Papers, compiled by the Foreign Office,
London: 1812.
COBBETT, W., and HANSARD, T. C., *Parliamentary Debates*, first ser.,
new ser., third ser., London: 1804.

Home Office Papers: 1841-1846.
Censures on Magistrates for Truckling with the Rioters.
Commissions of Inquiry.
Commission of Inquiry, Children.
Criminal.
Distress at Paisley.
Disturbances Book.
Disturbances, Lancashire.
Disturbances, Durham.
Disturbances, London.
Disturbances, Newcastle.
Disturbances, Paisley.
Domestic.
Domestic Book.
Inspectors of Factories.
Ireland.

Law Office.
Law Officers Reports.
Old Series (various numbers).
Outrages in Ireland.
Penitentiary and Prison Book.
Police Courts.
Post Office.
Potato Failures in Ireland.
Queen's Letters, Ireland.
Registered Papers, Old Series.
Reports of Outrages.
Scotch.
Trial of O'Connell.

HOWELL, T. B., and COBBETT, W. (comps.), *State Trials*, 33 vols., London: T. C. Hansard, 1809-1826.

Journals of the House of Lords, London: 1509.

MARTENS, G. F. (ed.), *Nouveau Recueil de Traités d'Alliance, de Paix, de Trève, de Neutralitie, de Commerce, de Limites, d'Exchange etc., et de plusieurs autres actes servant à la connaissance des relations étrangèrs Des Puissance et Etats de L'Europe, Depuis 1761 jusqua present*, Leipsig: 1817.

Parliament Papers:
Children's Employment Commission, 1842.
Correspondence Explanatory of the Measures Adopted by Her Majesty's Government for the Relief of Distress Arising from the Failure of the Potato Crop in Ireland, 1846.
First Report from the Select Committee on Commercial Distress, with Minutes of Evidence, July 7th, 1848.
Letter of Sir James Graham to the Commissioners for the Government of Pentonville Prison, April, 4th, 1844.
Report from the Select Committee on Agriculture, 1833; 1836.
Report of the Select Committee on the Andover Union, 1846.
Report from the Select Committee on the Army Before Sebastopol, with Proceedings, March 1st, 1855.
Report from the Secret Committee on the Bank Acts together with the Proceedings of the Committee, Minutes of Evidence, July 1858.
Report on the Discipline and Construction of Portland Prison and

its connection with the system of Convict Discipline now in Operation, 1850.

Report of Assistant Poor Law Commissioners on Employment of Women and Children in Agriculture, 1843.

Report of the Commissioners on the Employment of Children in the Mines, 1842.

Report of the Committee on the Employment of Women and Children in Mills and Factories, 1841.

Report of Factory Inspectors, 1842; 1846.

Report of the Commissioners Appointed to Inquire into the Conditions of the Framework Knitters, 1845.

Report of the Commissioners on Hand-Loom Weavers, 1834; 1841; 1843.

Report of the Select Committee on Hand-Loom Weavers petitions, July 1st, 1835.

Report from the Select Committee on Joint Stock Banks, together with Minutes of Evidence, July 15th, 1837.

Report of the Select Committee on Outrages (Ireland), 1852.

Report from the Select Committee on Medical Education, with Minutes of Evidence, 1834.

Report of the Poor Law Commission, 1834.

Report from the Secret Committee on the Post Office, 1844.

Report of the Surveyor-General of Prisons on the Construction and Ventillation and Details of Pentonville Prison, 1844.

Second Report of the Society of Apothecaries and the National Association of General Practitioners, August 5th, 1844.

Second Report of the Surveyor-General of Prisons, 1844; 1847.

Sixth Report of the Inspector of Factories, 1841.

Sixth Report from the Select Committee on the Act for the Regulation of Mills and Factories, 1840.

Principal Acts of the General Assembly of the Church of Scotland, Edinburgh: John Waugh, 1834.

State Papers and Letters Addressed to William Carstares, confidential secretary to King William, Edinburgh: Joseph McCormick, 1774.

Statutes at Large, Danby Pickering Edition, London: 1762.

PRIVATE PAPERS

Graham Papers (at Netherby, Cumberland).
Napier Papers (British Museum).
Peel Papers (British Museum).
Ripon Papers (British Museum).

COLLECTED WORKS

ATKINSON, R. H. M., and JACKSON, G. A. (colls.), *Brougham and His Early Friends, Letters to James Lock (1789-1809)*, 3 vols., London: 1908.

BASSETT, A. T. (ed.), *Gladstone to His Wife*, London: Methuen & Co., 1936.

BENSON, A. C., and ESHER, VISCOUNT (eds.), *The Letters of Queen Victoria, A Selection from her Majesty's Correspondence Between the Years 1837 and 1861*, 3 vols., New York: Longmans, Green, & Co., 1907.

BINDOFF, S. T., et al., *British Diplomatic Representatives, 1789-1853*, 3rd Ser., London: Royal Historical Society, 1900.

BOWRING, JOHN, *The Works of Jeremy Bentham*, 11 vols., London: William Tate, 1843.

FITZPATRICK, W. J. (ed.), *The Correspondence of Daniel O'Connell*, 2 vols., London: John Murray, 1888.

GOOCH, G. P. (ed.), *The Later Correspondence of John Russell, 1840-1878*, 2 vols., London: Longmans, Green, & Co., 1925.

GREY, H. E. (ed.), *The Reform Act of 1832, the Correspondence of the Late Earl Grey with his Majesty King William IV, and with Sir Herbert Taylor*, 2 vols., London: John Murray, 1867.

LONDONDERRY, E. (ed.), *Letters from Benjamin Disraeli to Frances Anne Marchioness of Londonderry, 1837-1861*, London: Macmillan Co., 1938.

MAXWELL, HERBERT (ed.), *The Creevey Papers, A Selection from the Correspondence and Diaries of the Late Thomas Creevey*, London: John Murray, 1923.

PARKER, CHARLES S., *The Life and Letters of Sir James Graham*, 2 vols., London: John Murray, 1907.

PARKER, CHARLES S., *Sir Robert Peel from his Private Papers*, 3 vols., second ed., London: John Murray, 1899.

PARRY, E. J. (ed.), *The Correspondence of Lord Aberdeen and Princess Lieven 1832-1852*, 2 vols., Camden third ser., LXII, London: Royal Historical Society, 1939.

REID, STEWART J., *Life and Letters of the First Earl of Durham*, 2 vols., London: Longmans, Green, & Co., 1906.

WELLESLEY, F. A. (ed.), *Secrets of the Second Empire, Private Letters from the Paris Embassy, from the Papers of Henry Richard Charles Wellesley First Earl Cowley, Ambassador at Paris, 1852-1867*, New York: Harper & Bros., 1929.

ZETLAND, MARQUIS OF (ed.), *The Letters of Disraeli to Lady Chesterfield and Lady Bradford*, 2 vols., New York: D. Appleton & Co., 1929.

AUTOBIOGRAPHIES AND MEMOIRS

ARGYLL, DOWAGER DUCHESS OF (ed.), *George Douglas Eighth Duke of Argyll (1823-1900) Autobiography and Memoirs*, 2 vols., London: John Murray, 1906.

BROUGHAM, HENRY L., *The Life and Times of Lord Brougham*, 3 vols., New York: Harper & Bros., 1872.

COCKBURN, HENRY T., *Journal of Henry Cockburn*, 2 vols., Edinburgh: Edmonston & Douglas, 1874.

EDGECUMBE, RICHARD (ed.), *The Diary of Frances Lady Shelley (1818-1873)*, 2 vols., New York: Chas. Scribners, 1941.

ESHER, VISCOUNT (ed.), *The Girlhood of Queen Victoria, A Selection from Her Majesty's Diaries Between the Years 1832 and 1840*, 2 vols., London: John Murray, 1912.

FRY, Elizabeth, *Memoirs of the Life of Elizabeth Fry*, 2 vols., London: Charles Gilpin, 1847.

GATHORNE HARDY, A. E. (ed.), *Gathorne Hardy, First Earl of Cranbrook, A Memoir*, 2 vols., London: Longmans, Green, & Co., 1910.

GREVILLE, CHARLES C., *The Greville Memoirs, A Journal of the Reign of Queen Victoria from 1837 to 1852*, 3 vols., London: Longmans, Green, & Co., 1885.

HANNA, WILLIAM, *Memoirs of the Life and Writings of Thomas Chalmers*, 4 vols., Edinburgh: Thomas Constable, 1852.

HERRIES, HON. J. C., *Memoirs of the Right Honourable J. C. Herries*, 2 vols., London: John Murray, 1880.

JEFFRIES, REGINALD W., *Dyott's Diary (1781-1845)*, 2 vols., London: Archibald Constable & Co., 1907.

JENNINGS, LOUIS J. (ed.), *Croker's Correspondence and Diaries*, 3 vols., London: John Murray, 1884.

MACKAY, Charles, *Forty Years Recollections of Life, Literature and Public Affairs from 1830-1870*, 2 vols., London: Chapman & Hall, 1877.

MURRAY, JOHN (ed.), *The Autobiography of Edward Gibbon*, second ed., London: John Murray, 1897.

PALMER, ROUNDELL, EARL OF SELBORNE, *Memorials, Family and Personal, 1776-1865*, 2 vols., London: Macmillan Co., 1896.

PEEL, SIR ROBERT, *Memoirs of the Right Honourable Sir Robert Peel*, 2 vols., London: John Murray, 1857.

REEVE, HENRY (ed.), *The Greville Memoirs, A Journal of the Reigns of King George IV and King William IV*, 3 vols., second ed., London: Longmans, Green, & Co., 1874.

REID, WEMYSS, *Memoirs and Correspondence of Lyon Playfair*, New York: Harpers, 1899.

RUSSELL, JOHN E., *Recollections and Suggestions, 1813-1873*, London: Longmans, Green, & Co., 1875.

STANMORE, LORD, *Sidney Herbert, Lord Herbert of Lea, A Memoir*, 2 vols., London: John Murray, 1906.

STRACHEY, L., and FULFORD, R. (eds.), *The Greville Memoirs, 1814-1860*, 8 vols., London: Macmillan Co., 1938.

WILSON, PHILIP W., *The Greville Diary*, 2 vols., New York: Doubleday, Page, & Co., 1927.

BIOGRAPHICAL WORKS

ARCHER, THOMAS, *Gladstone and His Contemporaries: Sixty Years of Social and Political Progress ...*, 4 vols., London: Blackie & Son, n.d.

ASPINAL, ARTHUR, *Lord Brougham and the Whig Party*, Manchester: University Press, 1927.

BALFOUR, LADY FRANCES, *The Life of George, Fourth Earl of Aberdeen*, 2 vols., London: Hodder & Stoughton, 1922.

BELL, H. C. F., *Lord Palmerston*, 2 vols., London: Longmans, Green, & Co., 1936.

BREADY, J. W., *Lord Shaftesbury and Social and Industrial Progress*, London: Allen & Unwin, 1926.

CAMPBELL, LORD JOHN, *Lives of the Lord Chancellors and Keepers of the Great Seal of England ...* , London: John Murray, 1868.

CHILDERS, SPENCER, *Life and Correspondence of the Right Hon. Hugh C. E. Childers, 1827-1860*, London: John Murray, 1901.

COLE, G. D. H., *Chartist Portraits*, London: Macmillan & Co., 1941.

COOK, SIR EDWARD, *Delane of the Times*, New York: Henry Holt & Co., 1916.

DISRAELI, BENJAMIN, *Lord George Bentinck, A Political Biography*, London: Constable, 1905.

DUNCOMBE, THOMAS H., *The Life and Correspondence of Thomas Slingsby Duncombe*, 2 vols., London: Hurst & Blackett, 1868.

ELLIOT, ARTHUR D., *The Life of George Joachim Goschen, First Viscount Goschen, 1831-1907*, 2 vols., London: Longmans, Green, & Co., 1911.

EYCK, ERICH, *Gladstone* (trans. by Bernard Miall), London: G. Allen & Unwin, 1938.

FITZMAURICE, LORD EDMOND, *The Life of Granville George Leveson Gower Second Earl Granville*, 2 vols., London: Longmans, Green, & Co., 1905.

GONNER, E. C. K. (ed.), *Principles of Political Economy and Taxation*, by David Ricardo, London: G. Bell & Sons, 1895.

GORDON, ARTHUR, *The Earl of Aberdeen*, London: Sampson, Low, Marston, & Co., 1893.

GRAHAM, STEPHEN, *Tsar of Freedom, the Life and Reign of Alexander II*, New Haven: Yale University Press, 1935.

GUERARD, ALBERT L., *Napoleon III*, Cambridge: Harvard University Press, 1943.

HOBSON, JOHN A., *Richard Cobden the International Man*, New York: Henry Holt & Co., 1919.

HODDER, EDWIN, *The Life and Work of the Seventh Earl of Shaftesbury, K. G.*, 3 vols., London: Cassell & Co., 1887.

LEVER, TRESHAM, *The Life and Times of Sir Robert Peel*, London: George Allen & Unwin, 1942.

LONSDALE, HENRY, *The Worthies of Cumberland*, 6 vols., London: George Routledge & Sons, 1868.

MAXWELL, SIR HERBERT, *The Life of Wellington, The Restoration of the Martial Power of Great Britain*, 2 vols., London: Sampson, Low, Marston, & Co., 1897.

MAXWELL, SIR HERBERT, *The Life and Letters of George William Frederick, Fourth Earl of Clarendon*, 2 vols., London: Edward Arnold, 1913.

MONEYPENNY, W. F., *The Life of Benjamin Disraeli, Earl of Beaconsfield*, 6 vols., New York: Macmillan Co., 1910.

MORLEY, JOHN, *The Life of William Ewart Gladstone*, 3 vols., London: Macmillan Co., 1903.

RAMSAY, ANNA A. W., *Sir Robert Peel*, London: Constable & Co., 1928.

SAINTSBURY, GEORGE, *The Earl of Derby*, New York: Harpers, 1892.

SMITH, FRANK, *The Life and Work of Sir James Kay Shuttleworth*, London: John Murray, 1923.

STEPHEN, L., and S. LEE (eds.), *Dictionary of National Biography*, 63 vols., New York: Macmillan Co., 1885.

TORRENS, WILLIAM T. M., *The Life of Sir James Graham*, 2 vols., second ed., London: Saunders, Oatley, & Co., 1863.

TREVELYAN, GEORGE M., *The Life of John Bright*, New York: Houghton Mifflin Co., 1914.

TWISS, HORACE, *Public and Private Life of Lord Chancellor Eldon*, 2 vols., third ed., London: John Murray, 1846.

VILLIERS, GEORGE, *A Vanished Victorian, Being the Life of George Villiers, Fourth Earl of Clarendon, 1800-1870*, London: Eyre & Spottiswoode, 1938.

WALLAS, GRAHAM, *Life of Francis Place*, London: George Allen & Unwin, 1925.

WALPOLE, SPENCER, *Life of Lord John Russell*, 2 vols., second ed., London: Longmans, Green, & Co., 1889.

WOLFE, LUCIEN, *Life of the First Marquess of Ripon*, 2 vols., London: John Murray, 1921.

414 BIBLIOGRAPHY

GENERAL WORKS

ALLEN, J.; HAIG, T. W., and DODWELL, H. H., *The Cambridge Shorter History of India*, New York: Macmillan Co., 1934.

Annual Register, or a View of the History, Politics, and Literature for the Year, London: 1758.

BRIGHT, J. F., *History of England (1837-1880)*, 5 vols., new ed., London: Longmans, Green, & Co., 1907.

BRIGGS, SIR JOHN, *Naval Administrations, 1827-1892*, London: Sampson Low, Marston, & Co., 1897.

BRODERICK, G. C., and FOTHERINGHAM, J. K., *History of England from Addington's Administration to the Close of William IV's Reign*, in *Political History of England*, 12 vols., ed. by W. Hunt and R. Poole, London: Longmans, Green, & Co., 1906.

BROWN, P. H., *History of Scotland*, 4 vols., Cambridge: University Press, 1911.

BURKE, BERNARD, *Burke's Genealogical and Heraldic History of the Peerage, Baronetage and Knightage, Privy Council, and Order of Precedence*, coronation ed., London: Shaw Co., 1938.

CLAPHAM, JOHN H., *An Economic History of Modern Britain*, 3 vols., Cambridge: University Press, 1926.

CLOWES, WILLIAM L., et al., *The Royal Navy from the Earliest Times to the Present*, 7 vols., Boston: Little, Brown, & Co., 1901.

COLE, G. D. H., and RAYMOND POSTGATE, *The British Common People, 1746-1933*, New York: Alfred Knopf, 1939.

COLE, G. D. H., *A Short History of the British Working Class Movement*, 3 vols., London: Allen & Unwin, 1925.

COLE, G. D. H., and MARGARET COLE (eds.), *Rural Rides in the Southern, Western, and Eastern Counties of England . . .*, by William Cobbett, 3 vols., London: Peter Davis & Co., 1930.

DAVIS, H. W. C., *The Age of Grey and Peel*, Oxford: Clarendon Press, 1929.

FAY, CHARLES R., *Great Britain from Adam Smith to the Present Day, an Economic and Social Survey*, New York: Longmans, Green, & Co., 1928.

GEORGE, M. DOROTHY, *England in Transition, Life and Work in the Eighteenth Century*, London: George Routledge & Sons, 1931.

HALÉVY, ELIE, *A History of the English People in 1815*, trans. by E. I. Watkin and D. A. Barker, New York: Harcourt, Brace, & Co., 1924.

HETHERINGTON, WILLIAM M., *History of the Church of Scotland From the Introduction of Christianity to . . . 1843*, New York: R. Carter Bros., 1845 and 1859.

HUTCHINSON, WILLIAM T., *History of Cumberland*, 2 vols., Carlisle: F. Jollie Co., 1794.

JENNINGS, GEORGE H., *An Anecdotal History of the British Parliament*, New York: Appleton & Co., 1881.

KNAPLUND, PAUL, *The British Empire, 1815-1939*, New York: Harper & Bros., 1941.

LOW, S., and SANDERS, L. C., *The Political History of England During the Reign of Queen Victoria (1837-1901)*, in *Political History of England*, 12 vols., ed. by Hunt, W., and Poole, R. L., London: Longmans, Green, & Co., 1907.

LYSONS, REV. D., and LYSONS, S., *Magna Britannia ...*, 6 vols., London: T. Cadell and W. Davies, 1816.

MARRIOTT, JOHN A. R., *England Since Waterloo*, London: Methuen & Co., 1913.

MARTINEAU, HARRIET, *The History of England From the Commencement of the XIXth Century to the Crimean War*, 4 vols., Philadelphia: Porter & Coates, 1864.

McCARTHY, JUSTIN, *A History of Our Own Times from the Accession of Queen Victoria to 1880*, 2 vols., New York: Harper & Bros., 1881.

MOLESWORTH, WILLIAM, *The History of England from the Year 1830-1874*, 3 vols., new ed., London: Chapman & Hall, 1874.

The New International Encyclopedia, 23 vols., second ed., New York: Dodd Mead & Co., 1914-1916.

O'CONNOR, SIR JAMES, *History of Ireland*, 2 vols., London: Edward Arnold & Co., 1926.

PORTER, GEORGE R., *The Progress of the Nation in its Various Social and Economic Relations, from the Beginning of the Nineteenth Century*, new ed., London: Methuen & Co., 1912.

PORTER, GEORGE R., *The Progress of the Nation in its Various Social and Economic Relations, from the Beginning of the Nineteenth Century to the Present Day*, 2 vols., London: Charles Knight & Co., 1836.

REDFORD, ARTHUR, *An Economic History of England, 1760-1860*, London: Longmans, Green, & Co., 1931.

REDLICH, J., and HIRST, F. W., *Local Government in England*, 2 vols., London: Macmillan Co., 1903.

ROBERTS, PAUL E., *History of British India under the Company and the Crown*, Oxford: Clarendon Press, 1930.

ROBERTS, MICHAEL, *The Whig Party, 1807-1812*, London: Macmillan & Co., 1939.

ROEBUCK, JOHN A., *History of the Whig Ministry of 1830 to the Passing of the Reform Bill*, 2 vols., London: J. W. Parker & Son, 1852.

The Rolliad, in two Parts; Probationary Odes for the Laureatship; and

Political Ecologues and Miscellanies, twenty-second ed., London: printed for James Ridgway, 1812.

SCHWEINITZ, KARL DE, *England's Road to Social Security*, Philadelphia: University of Pennsylvania Press, 1943.

SETON-WATSON, R. W., *Britain in Europe, 1789-1914*, a *Survey of Foreign Policy*, Cambridge: University Press, 1937.

SLATER, GILBERT, *The Growth of Modern England*, Boston: Houghton Mifflin Co., 1932.

SMART, WILLIAM, *Economic Annals of the Nineteenth Century*, 8 vols., London: Macmillan Co., 1910.

SMELLIE, KINGSLEY B., *A Hundred Years of English Government*, New York: Macmillan Co., 1936.

SMITH, PRESERVED, *The Age of the Reformation*, New York: Henry Holt & Co., 1920.

SYDNEY, WILLIAM C., *The Early Days of the Nineteenth Century in England, 1800-1820*, 2 vols., London: George Redway, 1898.

TOOKE, THOMAS, *A History of Prices and of the State of Circulation from 1793 to 1837*, 2 vols., London: Longmans, Green, & Co., 1838.

TOOKE, THOMAS, *A History of Prices and of the State of the Circulation in 1838 and 1839, with Remarks on the Corn Laws, and on some of the Alterations Proposed in our Banking System*, London: Longmans, Orme, Brown, & Green, 1840.

TOOKE, THOMAS, *A History of Prices and of the State of the Circulation from 1839 to 1847 with a General Review of the Currency Question, and Remarks on the Operation of the Act of 7 and 8 Vict.*, 2, 32, London: Longmans, Brown, & Green, 1848.

TRAILL, H. D. (ed.), *Social England*, 6 vols., London: Cassell & Co., 1897.

TREVELYAN, GEORGE M., *English Social History, A Survey of Six Centuries from Chaucer to Queen Victoria*, London: Longmans, Green, & Co., 1942.

TREVELYAN, GEORGE M., *British History in the Nineteenth Century, 1782-1919*, London: Longmans, Green, & Co., 1937.

USHER, ABBOT P., *An Introduction to the Industrial History of England*, London: George Harrap & Co., 1921.

WALPOLE, SPENCER, *A History of England from the Conclusion of the Great War in 1815*, 6 vols., London: Longmans, Green, & Co., 1890.

WALPOLE, SIR SPENCER, *The History of Twenty Five Years*, 4 vols., London: Longmans, Green, & Co., 1904-1908.

WARD, A. W., and GOOCH, G. P., *The Cambridge History of British Foreign Policy, 1789-1819*, 3 vols., New York: Macmillan Co., 1922.

WEBB, SIDNEY, and BEATRICE WEBB, *English Local Government*, 9 vols., London: Longmans, Green, & Co., 1906.

WOODWARD, E. L., *The Age of Reform, 1815-1870*, Oxford: Clarendon Press 1938.

YONGE, CHARLES D., *The History of the British Navy from the Earliest Times to the Present Time*, second ed., 3 vols., London: R. Bentley, 1866.

TREATISES AND MONOGRAPHS

ANDREADES, ANDREAS M., *History of the Bank of England* (trans. by Christobel Meredith), London: P. S. King & Son, 1909.

BAGEHOT, WALTER, *The English Constitution and other Political Essays*, New York: D. Appleton & Co., 1897.

BARNES, DONALD G., *A History of the English Corn Laws from 1660-1846*, New York: Crofts & Co., 1930.

BEER, MAX, *A History of British Socialism*, 2 vols., London: G. Bell & Sons, 1920.

BUCHANAN, ROBERT, *The Ten Years Conflict; being the Disruption of the Church of Scotland*, 2 vols., new ed., Glasgow: Blackie & Son, 1859.

BUTLER, JAMES R. M., *The Passing of the Great Reform Bill*, London: Longmans, Green, & Co., 1914.

CARPENTER, SPENCER C., *Church and People, 1789-1889; A History of the Church of England from William Wilberforce to 'Lux Mundi'*, New York: Macmillan, 1933.

CHRISTIE, OCTAVUS F., *The Transition from Aristocracy, 1832-1867*, London: G. P. Putnam's Sons, 1928.

CLAPHAM, SIR JOHN, *The Bank of England, A History*, 2 vols., New York: Macmillan Co., 1945.

CLARK, GEORGE K., *Peel and the Conservative Party, 1832-1841*, London: G. Bell & Sons, 1929.

CLAY, WALTER L., *Our Convict Systems*, London: (printed), 1862.

COBBETT, WILLIAM, *Cottage Economy . . . to which is added The Poor Man's Friend*, New York: 1833.

COSTIN, WILLIAM C., *Great Britain and China, 1833-1860*, Oxford: Clarendon Press, 1937.

CREIGHTON, MANDELL, *Historic Towns, Carlisle*, London: Longmans, Green, & Co., 1906.

CREW, ALBERT, *London Prisons of To-day and Yesterday*, London: Ivor Nicholson & Watson, 1933.

CURTLER, WILLIAM H. R., *A Short History of English Agriculture*, Oxford: Clarendon Press, 1909.

DICEY, ALBERT V., *Law and Opinion in England During the Nineteenth Century*, London: Macmillan Co., 1914.

DUCANE, COL. SIR E., *The Punishment and Prevention of Crime*, London: Macmillan Co., 1885.

EARP, GEORGE B., *History of the Baltic War*, London: R. Bentley, 1857.

FAY, CHARLES R., *Life and Labour in the Nineteenth Century*, Cambridge: University Press, 1920.

FIGGIS, JOHN N., *The Divine Rights of Kings*, second ed., Cambridge: University Press, 1922.

FIGGIS, JOHN N., *Churches in the Modern State*, second ed., London: Longmans, Green, & Co., 1914.

GREAVES, H. R. G., *The British Constitution*, New York: Macmillan Co., 1939.

GILLESPIE, FRANCES E., *Labor and Politics in England, 1850-1867*, Durham: Duke University Press, 1927.

GRIFFITHS, MAJOR ARTHUR, *History and Romance of Crime from the Earliest Times to the Present Day*, 12 vols., London: Grolier Society, 1900.

HALL, A. D. (ed.), *English Farming Past and Present*, by Lord Ernle, London: Longmans, Green, & Co., 1936.

HAMMOND, JOHN L., and BARBARA HAMMOND, *The Age of the Chartists (1832-1854)*, London: Longmans, Green, & Co., 1930.

HAMMOND, JOHN L., and BARBARA HAMMOND, *The Village Labourer, 1760-1832, A Study in the Government of England before the Reform Bill*, London: Longmans, Green, & Co., 1920.

HANEY, LEWIS H., *History of Economic Thought*, New York: Macmillan Co., 1926.

HASBACH, DR. W., *A History of the English Agricultural Labourer*, London: P. S. King & Son, 1908.

HUTCHINS, B. L., and A. HARRISON, *A History of Factory Legislation*, third ed., London: P. S. King & Son, 1926.

IVES, GEORGE, *A History of Penal Methods*, London: Stanley Paul & Co., 1914.

JENKS, EDWARD, *A Short History of English Law from the Earliest Times to the End of the Year 1911*, Boston: Little, Brown, & Co., 1912.

KINGLAKE, ALEXANDER W., *The Invasion of the Crimea*, fourth ed., 8 vols., Edinburgh: William Blackwood & Sons, 1863.

LAMPSON, G. LOCKER, *A Consideration of the State of Ireland in the Nineteenth Century*, London: Constable & Co., 1907.

LANG, ANDREW and JOHN, *Highways and Byways in the Border*, London: Macmillan Co., 1914.

LASKI, HAROLD J., *Studies in the Problem of Sovereignty*, New Haven: Yale University Press, 1917.

LASKI, HAROLD J.; W. I. JENNINGS; and ROBSON, W. A., *A Century of Municipal Progress*, London: G. Allen & Unwin, 1936.

LIPSON, EPHRAIM, *The History of the Woollen and Worsted Industries*, London: A. & C. Black, 1921.

MACCOBY, SIMON, *English Radicalism, 1832-1852*, London: G. Allen & Unwin, 1935.

MACKAY, THOMAS, *A History of the English Poor Law*, London: P. S. King & Son, 1904.

MALLETT, CHARLES E., *A History of the University of Oxford*, 3 vols., London: Methuen & Co., 1927.

MARTIN, KINGSLEY, *The Triumph of Lord Palmerston, A Study of Public Opinion in England before the Crimean War*, New York: Dial Press, 1924.

MEDLEY, DUDLEY J., *English Constitutional History*, fifth ed., Oxford: B. H. Blackwell, 1913.

MILL, JOHN S., *Principles of Political Economy*, New York: D. Appleton & Co., 1884.

MORREL, WILLIAM P., *British Colonial Policy in the Age of Peel and Russell*, Oxford: Clarendon Press, 1930.

MOWAT, ROBERT B., *A History of European Diplomacy, 1815-1914*, London: Edward Arnold & Co., 1923.

NEFF, WANDA F., *Victorian Working Women*, London: G. Allen & Unwin, 1929.

NICHOLLS, SIR GEORGE, *A History of the English Poor Law*, 3 vols., London: P. S. King & Son, 1904.

PRENTICE, ARCHIBALD, *A History of the Anti-Corn Law-League*, 2 vols., London: W. & F. G. Cash, 1853.

REDFORD, ARTHUR, *Labour Migration in England*, London: Longmans, Green, & Co., 1926.

RUGGLES-BRISE, SIR EVELYN, *The English Prison System*, London: Macmillan Co., 1921.

SEYMOUR, CHARLES C., *Electoral Reform in England and Wales*, New Haven: Yale University Press, 1915.

SIMPSON, FREDERICK A., *Louis Napoleon and the Recovery of France, 1848-1856*, New York: Longmans, Green, & Co., 1923.

SMITH, ADAM, *An Inquiry into the Nature and Causes of the Wealth of Nations*, 2 vols., Hertford: O. D. Coole, 1804.

SMITH, FRANK, *A History of English Elementary Education, 1760-1902*, London: University of London Press, 1931.

STANLEY, ARTHUR P., *History of the Church of Scotland*, New York: Scribner Armstrong & Co., 1872.

TEMPERLEY, HAROLD, *England and the Near East: the Crimea*, London: Longmans, Green, & Co., 1936.

THOMPSON, E., and G. T. GARRATT, *Rise and Fulfilment of British Rule in India*, London: Macmillan Co., 1934.

WAKEMAN, HENRY O., *An Introduction to the History of the Church of England*, seventh ed., London: Rivingtons, 1908.

WARD, WILFRED, *William George Ward and the Oxford Movement*, London: Macmillan Co., 1889.

WEARMOUTH, ROBERT F., *Methodism and the Working Class Movements in England, 1800-1850*, London: Epworth Press, 1937.

WEBB, SIDNEY, and BEATRICE WEBB, *The State and the Doctor*, London: Longmans, Green, & Co., 1910.

WEBB, SIDNEY, and BEATRICE WEBB, *English Poor Law Policy*, London: Longmans, Green, & Co., 1910.

YOUNG, GEORGE M., *Early Victorian England, 1830-1865*, 2 vols., Oxford: University Press, 1934.

PERIODICALS AND PAMPHLET MATERIAL

Blackwood's Edinburgh Magazine, Edinburgh; London, 1817.

British and Foreign Medical Review or Quarterly Journal of Practical Medicine and Surgery, London, 1836.

Church History, Scottsdale, Penn., 1932.

CROOK, G., *The Proposed Scheme of Medical Reform in Reference to Chemists and Druggists*, London: Hasings, (1842).

Economic Journal — the Journal of the British Economic Association, London; New York, 1891.

Edinburgh Medical and Surgical Journal, Edinburgh; London, 1805-1855.

Edinburgh Review or Critical Journal, 250 vols., Edinburgh; London, 1802-1929.

English Historical Review, London, 1886.

Fraser's Magazine for Town and Country, 106 vols., London: J. Fraser (etc.), 1830.

Gentlemen's Magazine, 303 vols., London, 1731-1907.

GRAHAM, JAMES R. G., *Corn and Currency in an Address to the Landowners*, London: James Ridgway, 1828.

Journal of the Royal Agricultural Society of England, London, 1839.

Journal of the Royal Statistical Society of London, London, 1838.

Lancet: Journal of British and Foreign Medicine, London, 1823.

London and Edinburgh Monthly Journal of Medical Science, London; Edinburgh, 1841-1855.

London Medical Gazette, A Weekly Journal of Medicine and the Collateral Sciences, new ser., London, 1843-1851 (?).

The Medical Times, A Journal of English and Foreign Medicine, London, 1839-1851.

The Medico-Chirurgical Review and Journal of Practical Medicine, new ser., London, 1827-1844.

Observations on Medical Reform addressed to the Members of the North England Medical Reform Association, by R. M. G., in Miscellaneous Pamphlets, vol. 242, No. 145313, Surgeon-General's Office Library, Wash. D.C.

Observations on the Present System of Medical Education with a View to Medical Reform, London: Sherwood and Piper, 1834.

Provincial Medical and Surgical Journal, London: John Churchill, 1840-1852.

Punch (or the London Charivari), London, 1841.

QUAIN, RICHARD, *Observations on the Education and Examinations for Degrees in Medicine as affected by the New Medical Bill . . .*, London: John Murray, 1845.

The Quarterly Review, London: John Murray; (etc.), 1809.

Records of the Hull Election, London: Benjamin Tate, 1818.

The Reformed Ministry and the Reformed Parliament, anonymous pamphlet, sixth ed., London: James Ridgway, 1833.

Remarks on Medical Reform and on Sir James Graham's Medical Bill, London: Whitaker & Co., 1845. (Army Medical Library, Wash. D.C., p. vol. 895, No. 84430).

Remarks on Medical Reform, Edinburgh: Anderson and Bryce, 1841. (Surgeon-Generals Office Library, Wash. D.C., p. vol. 888, No. 84223.)

Review of Economic Statistics, Cambridge, Mass., 1919.

Saturday Review of Politics, Literature, Science, and Art, London, 1855.

Speech of the Right Honourable Sir James Graham at Glasgow, Carlisle: C. Thurman (printer), December 29th, 1838.

Speech of the Right Honourable Sir James Graham on Being Nominated as one of the Candidates for the Representation of the Eastern Division of Cumberland, London: James Ridgway, 1835.

SYME, JAMES, *Letter to the Right Honourable Sir James Graham, Bart.*, Edinburgh: Stark & Co.,1845.

Three Reports by the Joint Deputation of the Society of Apothecaries and the National Association of General Practitioners appointed to confer with the Secretary of State, London, 1846. (Surgeon-Generals Office Library, Wash. D.C., vol. 389, No. 14).

Transactions of the Cumberland and Westmoreland Antiquarian and Archeological Society, Kendal: Titus Wilson, new ser., 1901.

The Westminster Review, 181 vols., London: Baldwin, Cradock, and Joy (etc.), 1824-1914.

NEWSPAPERS

Carlisle Independent.
Cumberland Chronicle.
Leeds Mercury.
Globe.
Illustrated News.
Morning Chronicle.
Morning Herald.
Morning Post.
Standard.
The Times.
Manchester Guardian.
The Nation, Dublin.
The Pilot, Dublin.

INDEX

INDEX

555555555

555555555

55555555

Waitongi, Treaty of, 267-268
Wales, 188, 212, 243, 316
Ward, Colonel, 70, 116-117, 120
Waterloo, 30, 278 n 538, 342, 395, 404, 405
Weavers, hand-loom, 59, 148 n 84
Webster-Ashburton Treaty, 267
Wellington, Duke of, 37, 59, 65-70, 75, 81, 88, 110, 120, 127 n 238, 148, 150, 163, 178, 299, 328; in Spain and Sicily, 17-23; Prime Minister (1828), 60; repeal of Test and Corporations Acts, 74; resigns, 76-77; Conservative party, 140, 152 n 104; in Peel's ministry (1841), 156; Corn Laws, 263, 266, 289; Ireland, 274, 278 n 538
Westminster school, 4, 13, 15
Whigs, 18, 27ff, 40, 54, 59, 65-66, 69, 71, 74, 78, 86, 106, 110, 117-126, 131, 133-137, 140, 142, 150, 152, 154-158,

192, 208, 209, 225, 259 n 471, 263, 273, 279, 288ff, 293-294, 299, 303, 305, 308, 313, 316, 319, 323-325, 328-330, 356 n 164, 359, 365, 385, 389, 395, 403
Widdrington, Lady Catherine, 6, 7
Wilberforce, W., 14
William III, King of England, 5
William IV, King of England, 135
Williams, General F. W., 371-372
Wills and Administration Bill, 372 n 29
Wiseman, Cardinal, 315-316
Wood, Sir C., 73, 303-304, 364
Workhouses, 148 n 84, 179ff, 259 n 469, 295
Workingman's Association, 161 n 29

Yeomanry Corps, 163
Young England party, 285 n 561
Young, Robert, 200